THE ART OF THE SELF

The *Blue Book* of Eranos Founder Olga Fröbe-Kapteyn

Riccardo Bernardini

Foreword by Fabio Merlini

Preface by Murray Stein

Afterword by Her Royal Highness Princess Irene of The Netherlands

Zurich Lecture Series in Analytical Psychology

Volume 12

CHIRON PUBLICATIONS • ASHEVILLE, NORTH CAROLINA

www.ChironPublications.com

Interior and cover design by Danijela Mijailovic
Printed primarily in the United States of America.

ISBN 978-1-68503-615-7 paperback
ISBN 978-1-68503-616-4 hardcover
ISBN 978-1-68503-617-1 electronic
ISBN 978-1-68503-618-8 limited edition paperback
ISBN 978-1-68503-619-5 limited edition hardcover

Cover image
Olga Fröbe-Kapteyn, *The Central Spiritual Sun* (*The Physical Sun is but a golden disc before the Spiritual Sun*).
"Meditation Plates," c. 1926–1934. Mixed technique (tempera, India ink, and gold leaf) on cardboard.
Eranos Foundation Archives, Ascona-Moscia. All rights reserved.

Biographical profile photograph
Courtesy of Michela Di Savino/Eventi Letterari Monte Verità, Ascona-Monte Verità. All rights reserved.

This book is published under the auspices of the Eranos Foundation.

Library of Congress Cataloging-in-Publication Data Pending

To Eleonora

TABLE OF CONTENTS

FOREWORD

Over the last ten years, Olga Fröbe-Kapteyn's iconographic work has been the subject of such marked and convinced interest that it has taken even the Eranos Foundation by surprise. Prestigious institutions such as the Nicola Trussardi Foundation in Milan, the New Museum in New York, the Centre Pompidou in Paris, the Guggenheim Museum in Bilbao, the Kunsthalle in Mainz, the Casa Rusca Museum in Locarno, the Catharijneconvent Museum in Utrecht, and the Swiss National Museum in Zurich have approached her work with a sense of wonder and admiration, not only for a body of work that had previously been silent and reserved for a small private circle of admirers, but also for the undeniable artistic value of a work that is pioneering in many respects.

Riccardo Bernardini's book takes us on a journey through this work, reconstructing its motives and genesis, thus helping us to better understand, beyond possible interpretations, the extraordinary production of images to which the founder of Eranos devoted herself with assiduity and commitment over the years. It is therefore fortunate that, at a time when critical and public interest in this hitherto little-known side of Fröbe-Kapteyn's personality is reawakening, a book is now available that allows us to contextualize and frame its significance within the different moments of an intense life dedicated to promoting, at the highest levels, knowledge and interdisciplinary dialogue on the great questions of existence.

In these few lines, I would like to focus on two aspects of Fröbe-Kapteyn's pictorial production that I consider central if we do not want to misunderstand its meaning. The first concerns the spirit with which the artist understood her own work, while the second concerns the discontinuity that characterizes her entire output, where two groups of works belonging to different periods and distinguished by styles that are irreconcilable with each other stand face to face.

With regard to the first point, we can say this. There is no artistic intention in the pictorial gesture of composing the image, and this applies to the entire iconographic production. We are beyond or on the other side of the aesthetic dimension, so much so that we can even say that Fröbe-Kapteyn was not at all interested in making art, let alone thinking of herself as an artist. In this case, the pictorial production belongs to another order of meaning. We are rather in the archaic horizon, so to speak, of a symbolic production, in which life manifests its desire to see itself reflected in an elsewhere capable of retroacting, through the power conferred upon it, on life itself, transforming it. "Transformation" is the noun that gives the precise meaning of this iconographic operation: inscribing life in an imaginal relationship where figures and colors are assigned a therapeutic task, in the etymological sense of "art of healing." A healing that, in this case, has as its object the transformation of the soul, through the power conferred both on the figuration and on the precise and meticulous gestures that realize it.

As for the second aspect, the radical change in style that characterizes the second phase of Fröbe-Kapteyn's art—in which a comment by Jung, and their frequent contact since the 1930s, seem to have played a fundamental role—suggests that we are dealing with a different way of understanding the therapeutic power of images. The adamantine geometry of the so-called "Meditation Plates," which convey the desire to annihilate oneself in the perfection of a disembodied and historyless spirit, dissolves into the tormented world of a production of "Visions" in which, on the contrary, the vicissitudes of an interiority that recounts its own torments and aspirations are given substance, taken on board and, in their imaginal objectification, seek the path to their own redemption. What in the first phase appeared as an unmediated desire for perfection becomes here a laborious confrontation with one's inner life: a staging of variously symbolized visions, in which one recognizes one's destiny as revealed self-knowledge.

The yearning for perfection of the geometric period of the "Meditation Plates" in a certain sense skips the hard work of confronting oneself: it is meditative without being introspective. One could say: it is the contemplation of a perfection with which one wants to identify, an ascending path conveyed by the iron discipline of the executive gestures that represent it. It is a pictorial practice that is realized through anabasis, looking upward and heading toward its conquest in order to savor its peace. What is missing is the reverse movement, the downward orientation, *in interiore homine*.

It is precisely this movement that we see taking place in the paintings of the second period, that of the "Visions," where the aspiration to the sky is first and necessarily measured by the catabasis of an introspective need that directs its attention to the inner world, making its contours visible without reticence, with ruthless sincerity. In this sense, there is something absolutely complementary in the two figurative phases that distinguish the work: from their juxtaposition, we better understand the tribulations and ideals of a painting that, before being an aesthetic gesture, corresponds, as mentioned, to a profound cognitive operation.

That all this emanates an unprecedented beauty, sometimes pacifying and sometimes disturbing, is "only" an effect of the authenticity with which Fröbe-Kapteyn undertook this commitment during her life in Ascona. I am very grateful to Riccardo Bernardini for illuminating this very important chapter in the life of the founder of Eranos with his historiographical work.

Fabio Merlini
President of the Eranos Foundation
Minusio, June 2025

PREFACE

Until recently, Olga Fröbe-Kapteyn was recognized principally as the founder and organizer of the much-acclaimed Eranos Conferences that were held annually on the grounds of her home in Ascona, Switzerland, and for the original collection of images now housed in the Archive for Research in Archetypal Symbolism (ARAS). This view has widened considerably in the past several years due primarily to the dedicated efforts of Riccardo Bernardini, Scientific Secretary of the Eranos Foundation. As a result of his research, lectures, and publications, a bright light has now been cast upon her work as an artist, which predated the founding of the Eranos Conferences in 1933 and continued during the years of those famous annual gatherings. As Bernardini also shows in this present ground-breaking work, Fröbe-Kapteyn's life and artistic style changed significantly after meeting C.G. Jung and including him as a key collaborator in her enterprise of bringing world class scholars together to discuss shared themes in the religions of the East and West. Jung became a central figure at the Eranos gatherings from the time of their inception until his retirement after 1952 for health reasons. With him came his brilliant student, Erich Neumann, who also had a significant impact on Fröbe-Kapteyn's life and work.

The annual Zurich Lecture Series (ZLS), for which Bernardini prepared this book, are dedicated to the purpose of inviting significant Jungian scholars to write an original work for publication and to lecture on it at the International School of Analytical Psychology (ISAP) in Zurich. The scholars are asked to share their most recent thinking and research with the ISAP community of analysts, students, and visitors in congenial surroundings in the city that is the birthplace and home of Analytical Psychology. ZLS 2025 is the sixteenth in the Series. This contribution was conceived several years earlier with the express wish to feature Bernardini's research in the Archives of the Eranos Foundation, which house the papers and paintings of the founder. These materials have been largely unknown to scholars until now, and Bernardini's meticulous documentation of the contents has resulted in many remarkable insights into the life and works of the founder. Among the most significant findings has been the exceptional quality of her paintings. This revelation of Fröbe-Kapteyn's development as an artist constitutes the central theme of his lectures presented at ZLS 2025 and of this present book.

It is an honor to host Riccardo Bernardini at ISAP and to include his brilliant study among the ZLS volumes published by Chiron Publications.

Murray Stein
Chair of the Zurich Lecture Series (ZLS) Committee
Goldiwil, May 2025

ACKNOWLEDGEMENTS

I would like to thank the Board of the Eranos Foundation: President Fabio Merlini, Vice President Sandro Rusconi, and Members Raphaël Brunschwig, Maurizio Checchi, Paola Costantini, and Claudio Metzger, for the trust placed in this editorial project; Giovanni Merlini, legal advisor to the Foundation; and Monica Pongelli, administrative secretary of the Foundation and also as representative of the Municipality of Ronco s/Ascona, for assistance with documentary research; in addition, Gisela Binda, previous administrative secretary of the Foundation, for aid in deciphering Olga Fröbe-Kapteyn's handwritten notes and assistance with research at Eranos over the decades. Mayor Giorgio Gilardi, Deputy Mayor Michela Ris, Municipal Secretary Paola Bernasconi, and the Municipality of Ascona, with extended gratitude to former Mayor Luca Pissoglio. Her Royal Highness Princess Irene of the Netherlands, for her contribution of ideas and research in the Royal Family archives relating to the relationship between Her Majesty Queen Juliana and Olga Fröbe-Kapteyn. Luca Musini and Roberto Turganti of Fortitude Wealth Management, along with Manuela Pizzini and Arianna Turganti. Tiziana Zaninelli, as representative of the Foundation for Culture in the Locarnese Region. Benno Schubiger, as representative of the Dr. Hans Dietler/Kottmann Foundation. Mara Folini and Michela Zucconi-Poncini of the Municipal Museum of Modern Art of Ascona. Nicoletta Mongini and the staff of the Monte Verità Foundation. Murray Stein and the International School of Analytical Psychology (ISAP). Steve Buser and Jennifer Fitzgerald of Chiron Publications. Misser Berg, Pilar Amezaga, and the Officers of the International Association for Analytical Psychology (IAAP). Beatrice Trussardi, Massimiliano Gioni, and Roberta Tenconi, for their collaboration on the exhibition at the Nicola Trussardi Foundation in Milan (and curator Gioni also for the exhibition at the New

Museum in New York). Christine Macel, for her collaboration on exhibitions at the Centre Pompidou in Paris and the Guggenheim Museum in Bilbao. Federica Chiocchetti, for her collaboration on the exhibition at the Musée des Beaux-Arts in Le Locle. Yasmin Afschar, for her collaboration on the exhibition at the Kunsthalle in Mainz. Sébastien Peter and the staff of the Casa Rusca Museum, with special mention to Alessia Bottaro and Giada Muto, for their collaboration on the exhibition curated by Raphael Gygax in Locarno. Josien Paulides, Rozanne de Bruijne, Sanne Groen, and Lonneke Visser, for their collaboration on the exhibition at the Museum Catharijneconvent in Utrecht. Denise Tonella, Stefan Zweifel, and Sophie Dänzer, for their collaboration on the exhibition at the Swiss National Museum in Zurich. Francesco Piraino, Wouter Hanegraaff, Andreas Kilcher, and Marco Pasi, for their collaboration in the context of the Giorgio Cini Foundation. Thomas Fischer, Carl Christian Jung, and Bettina Kaufmann, as representatives of the Foundation of the Works of C.G. Jung. Sergio Guarino, Giuliana Caldirola, and Lucia Bassignana, as representatives of the Institute of Psychosynthesis founded by Roberto Assagioli. Heike Kühn, as representative of the Foerster House Archive—Marianne Foerster Foundation at the German Foundation for Monument Protection. Franziska Fellerer-Wistuba and Andreas Fellerer, as representative of the heirs of Margarita Marianne (Margarethe) Fellerer. Bill Sherman, Martina Mazzotta, Paul Taylor, Eckart Marchand, John Tresch, and Claudia Wedepohl, and as representatives of the Warburg Institute. Greta Biasca-Caroni and Andrea Biasca-Caroni, as representatives of the Luigi Pericle Archive. Diana Mirolo, as representative of the Epper Museum. Anne Buechi and Christine Eggenberg, as representatives of the Stiftung Szondi-Institut. Joost R. Ritman and Barbara Miller, as representatives of the Ritman Library. Vicente L. de Moura, for assistance in consulting the Picture Archive of the C.G. Jung-Institut Zürich. Annkathrin Wollert of the Paul & Peter Fritz AG, Literary Agency, for permission to use unpublished material by Carl Gustav Jung. Sabina Tenti of the Museum für Gestaltung, for obtaining new photographs of Fröbe-Kapteyn's sartorial creations kept in the Zurich museum collection and permission to publish them. Georgie Gerrish and Henry Gerrish of Gerrish Fine Art. The Fiorenzo Abbondio Museum. Carlo Martinoni and Jonathan Valcancel, as representatives of the Andreotti & Partners. Maurizio Olivero, Alessandro Defilippi, Robert Michael Mercurio, Vittorio Piccioni, Ferruccio Vigna, and the colleagues from the Association for Research in Analytical Psychology (ARPA). Maurizio Gasseau and Gian Piero Quaglino, as representatives of the Institute of Analytical Psychology and Psychotherapy (IPAP). Stefano Carta and the Editorial Staff of the *Rivista di Psicologia Analitica*. Gianfranco Bonola, Petra Branderhorst, Hans Thomas Hakl, Robert Hinshaw, Maite Karssenberg, Peter-Robert König, Jonas Sebastian Lendenmann, Wanda Luban, Catherine McGilvray, Maria Cruz Mañas Peñalver, Maria Teresa Marraffa, Shanti Pappu, Veronica Provenzale, Christa Robinson, Marco Rogantini, Shantena Augusto Sabbadini, Giovanni Sorge, Lucy Stein, Werner Weick, and Clemens Alexander Wimmer, for their scientific contribution to the research, with special remembrance for conversations with Hetty Rogantini de Beauclair (1928–2018), Pauline Catherine Ritsema-Gris (1917–2007), Rudolf Ritsema (1918–2006), Ximena de Angulo-Roelli (1918–2018), Harald Szeemann (1933–2005), Boris Luban-Plozza (1923–2022), and Annemarie Äschbach (1926–2008). Stephen Aizenstat, Joseph Cambray, Linda Carter, Maren Hansen, Nancy Furlotti, Tom Kelly, Marianne Müller, and Heyong Shen, for congressional meeting opportunities on the topic. Ugo Nespolo, Francesca Gemnetti, Adriana Pancaldi, Rolando Pancaldi, Dimitri D'Andrea, Adriano Fabris, Franco Ferrari, Amelia Valtolina, Natale Spineto, Martino Lioy, Veronica Caciolli, Adriano Aymonino, Silvia Davoli, Tobias Kämpf, Elena Boldrini, Paolo Agazzone, Raffaella Biroli, Sira von Waldner, Lara Merlini, and Manuela Antognini, for the opportunities for dialogue on the subject. Georgia Zara, as representative of the M.A. Course in Criminological and Forensic Psychology at Turin University. Giancarlo Marenco, as representative of the Order of Psychologists of Piedmont and the National Council of the Order of Psychologists. Daniela Brockmann and Floriano Martinaglia, for the restoration of Olga Fröbe-Kapteyn's artworks, along with Italia Margaroli and Raffaella Zappalà, for their safekeeping. My family, Ludovica and Eleonora, with Liliana and Umberto, Gabriella and Giorgio, who patiently accompanied this work through its various stages, from 2002 to 2025.

EDITORIAL NOTE

Chapter 1, "Olga Fröbe-Kapteyn's Interest in Art and Symbolism," and Chapter 2, "Olga Fröbe-Kapteyn's Iconographic Corpus," are a reworking of an article originally published as Riccardo Bernardini and Fabio Merlini, "Olga Fröbe-Kapteyn (1881–1962): A Woman's Individuation Process through Images at the Origins of the Eranos Conferences," *ARAS Connections: Image and Archetype*, 4 (2020), pp. 1–18. Some preparatory lectures that led to that paper—in the context of a teaching and conference activity carried out between Switzerland (Eranos Foundation and the Master of Arts in Theatre at the Accademia Dimitri, Ascona), Italy (Master Course in Symbolic Cultures for the Professions of Art, Education, and Care at the University of Milano-Bicocca), and South America (Museo de Arte Latinoamericano de Buenos Aires) covering about a decade (2014–2025)—were given at Monte Verità, "Ascona e la 'qualità femminile' del luogo: uno sguardo all'arte di Olga Fröbe-Kapteyn, fondatrice di Eranos," on November 24, 2017; at the congress "Art and Psyche: Conference IV. The Illuminated Imagination," on April 4–7, 2019 at the University of California Santa Barbara, on the topic "Olga Fröbe-Kapteyn (1881–1962): A Woman's Individuation Process Through Images at the Origins of the Eranos Conferences"; as part of a study day organized by the International School of Analytical Psychology (ISAP), "Eranos Live," on October 20, 2023 at the Foyer St. Anton in Zurich, on the topic "Eranos: A Retrospective Look at its Contribution to Analytical Psychology and a Future Perspective on the Study of Olga Fröbe-Kapteyn's Art"; as part of the national conference of the Associazione per la Ricerca in Psicologia Analitica (ARPA) marking the 150th anniversary of Jung's birth, "Human life is an experiment with an uncertain outcome," on June 14, 2025, at the Casa delle Donne in Milan, with the title "Il *Libro blu* di Olga Fröbe-Kapteyn: l'esperienza creativa di una donna e il suo rapporto con C.G. Jung—una storia del nostro tempo, un'opera per il nostro tempo"; a further lecture, titled "The *Blue Book* of Olga Fröbe-Kapteyn (1881–1962), founder of Eranos," was presented as part of the XXIII Congress of the International Association for Analytical Psychology (IAAP), "Experiences of the Unintelligible: Jungian Explorations and Contributions," at the Kongresshaus in Zurich on August 24–29, 2025; a series of five lectures on the topic "The Art of the Self. The *Blue Book* of Olga Fröbe-Kapteyn, founder of Eranos" were finally held in the context of the 2025 Zurich Lecture Series, promoted by the International School of Analytical Psychology (ISAP) and Chiron Publications on October 15–16, 2025 in Zurich: on that occasion, this book—*The Art of the Self. The* Blue Book *of Eranos Founder Olga Fröbe-Kapteyn*—was officially presented. A further version of the 2020 study was released, in Italian, as Riccardo Bernardini and Fabio Merlini, "L'arte di Olga Fröbe-Kapteyn, fondatrice di Eranos," *Rivista di Psicologia Analitica*, 108 (56, 2024), pp. 281–303 and as "L'arte di Olga Fröbe-Kapteyn, fondatrice di Eranos," in Veronica Caciolli, ed., *Atti del convegno Arte, Mistica, Comunità, Seconda edizione. MUSEC—Museo delle Culture, Lugano, 11 e 12 febbraio 2022* (Milan: Postmedia Srl, 2024), pp. 34–44. A revised Italian/English bilingual edition was then reissued as Riccardo Bernardini and Fabio Merlini, "The *Blue Book* of Olga Fröbe-Kapteyn, Founder of Eranos," in Raphael Gygax, ed., *Olga Fröbe-Kapteyn. Artista—ricercatrice. Volume pubblicato in occasione della mostra Olga Fröbe-Kapteyn: artista–ricercatrice, Museo Casa Rusca, Locarno, 8 agosto 2024–12 gennaio 2025* (Locarno/Ascona/Bellinzona: Museo Casa Rusca/Fondazione Eranos/Casagrande, in collaboration with Kunsthalle Mainz, 2024), pp. 44–51. That article was subsequently greatly expanded and published in the issue of *Religiographies*, 4 (1, 2025), pp. 7–39, edited by Wouter J. Hanegraaff, which collects the proceedings of the congress "The Eranos Experience: Spirituality and the Arts in a Comparative Perspective," organized by the Centre for Comparative Studies of Civilizations and Spiritualities, the Institute of Music, and the Intercultural Institute of Comparative Music Studies (IISMC) of the Giorgio Cini Foundation and the Centre for the History of Hermetic Philosophy and Related Currents (HHP) of the University of Amsterdam on November 17, 18, and 19, 2023 on the Island of San Giorgio Maggiore in Venice. Chapter 2 includes some expanded sections from a contribution originally published as Riccardo Bernardini, "Jung nel giardino di Eranos: il paesaggio dell'analisi," *Eranos Yearbook*, 70 (2009–2010–2011), pp. 731–38, reprinted (revised) in Ferruccio Vigna, ed., *L'Ombra del Flâneur. Scritti in onore di Augusto Romano*

(Bergamo: Moretti&Vitali, 2014), pp. 35–46; translated into English, that article also appeared as Riccardo Benardini, "Jung in the Garden of Eranos: The Landscape of Analysis," in Henry Abramovitch and Murray Stein, eds., *Eranos. A Play* (Asheville, NC: Chiron, 2025), pp. 127–40. Much of the historical information included in Chapter 3, "Artistic Itineraries from Monte Verità to Eranos," comes instead from Riccardo Bernardini, "Itineraries of the Feminine from Monte Verità to Eranos," in Nicoletta Mongini, Chiara Gatti, and Sergio Risaliti, eds., *Monte Verità. Back to Nature* (Turin: Lindau, 2022), pp. 25–43, and above all from the preparatory materials for the volume by Riccardo Bernardini, *Jung a Eranos. Il progetto della psicologia complessa*, forewords by Fabio Merlini, Gian Piero Quaglino, Maurizio Gasseau, and Hans Thomas Hakl, afterword by Her Royal Highness Princess Irene of the Netherlands (Milan: FrancoAngeli, 2011), which provides a useful historical contextualization of Olga Fröbe-Kapteyn's art in light of the history of Eranos.

INTRODUCTION

Olga Fröbe-Kapteyn (London, October 19, 1881–Ascona, April 25, 1962) is known for being the pioneering founder of the Eranos Conferences, which since the early 1930s have attracted to Ascona (Switzerland) some of the most influential scholars of the twentieth century, making an extraordinary contribution to world intellectual history.[1]

Carl Gustav Jung (1875–1961) was one of the main sources of inspiration for the Eranos project. The publication of the *Liber Novus* or *The Red Book*[2] and, more recently, *The Art of C.G. Jung*[3] and his *Black Books*[4] has further highlighted the conjunction between his personal life path, his imaginative world, and the construction of his scientific thought. In Fröbe-Kapteyn's case, on the other hand, the link between existence, imagination, and creativity was not entirely clear. Some of her allusions on the subject

[1] For a panoramic view of Eranos, see Hans Thomas Hakl, *Der verborgene Geist von Eranos. Unbekannte Begegnungen von Wissenschaft und Esoterik. Eine alternative Geistesgeschichte des 20. Jahrhunderts* (Bretten: Scientia nova-Neue Wissenschaft, 2001), later revised and expanded as *Eranos. An Alternative Intellectual History of the Twentieth Century* (Montreal & Kingston: McGill-Queen's University Press, 2013). On Jung's involvement in the Eranos project and a bibliography on the subject (updated 2011), see more specifically Riccardo Bernardini, *Jung a Eranos. Il progetto della psicologia complessa* (Milan: FrancoAngeli, 2011). For a list of the Eranos *Yearbooks*, lecturers, and contents, see instead Fabio Merlini and Riccardo Bernardini, eds., *Eranos in the Mirror: Views on a Moving Heritage. Eranos allo specchio: sguardi su una eredità in movimento* (Ascona: Aragno*Eranos Ascona, 2019) and, further updated, in *Eranos Yearbook* 76 (2022–2023–2024).

[2] Carl Gustav Jung, *The Red Book. Liber Novus*, ed. Sonu Shamdasani (New York, NY: W.W. Norton & Company, Inc., 2009).

[3] Foundation of the Works of C.G. Jung, Ulrich Hoerni, Thomas Fischer, and Bettina Kaufmann, eds., *The Art of C.G. Jung* (New York, NY: W.W. Norton & Company, Inc., 2018).

[4] Carl Gustav Jung, *The Black Books: 1913–1932, Notebooks of Transformation*, ed. Sonu Shamdasani, 7 vols. (New York, NY: W.W. Norton & Company, Inc., 2020).

were, in fact, rather difficult to understand. For example, she wrote, "You must pardon me for speaking in images! It is the way my mind works."[5] And again: "The story of Eranos can be found in an unwritten book, which I often leaf through, read, examine, and compare—I also look at the pictures, since there are many of them in this book—and search for the connections that form the whole in a meaningful and unifying way. The overall figure, the pattern that becomes visible, is so twisted and intertwined with the pattern of my life that it is indeed difficult to separate them."[6]

Only today do Fröbe-Kapteyn's words become clearer, thanks to the unpublished anthology of her works, which we might consider classifying under the name *Blue Book*. The title refers to the chromatic motif of her iconographic corpus, traceable to two distinct styles and moments: the "Meditation Plates" phase (c. 1926–1934) and the "Visions" period (1934–1938).

This volume documents, in an unfinished form, a research journey on these pictorial and graphic materials, which began more than two decades ago. The reflections presented here, beyond the author's personal findings, have benefited—in the last decade in particular—from a growing number of discoveries and insights related to two perspectives of study. On the one hand, master's, doctoral, and post-doctoral dissertation works and independent research attest to an increasing interest in the life of Fröbe-Kapteyn—a creative and visionary woman who has not yet been given a proper biography, despite being one of the most important and independent female figures in the development and dissemination of Jungian psychology.[7] On the other hand, an astonishing series of exhibitions,

---

[5] Olga Fröbe-Kapteyn, "An Attempt at Definition and Description of Eranos and of the *Eranos-Jahrbücher*" (unpublished typescript, 1953; Eranos Foundation Archives, Ascona-Moscia), p. 1.

[6] Olga Fröbe-Kapteyn, "Eranos Vortrag" (unpublished typescript, 1939; Eranos Foundation Archives, Ascona-Moscia), p. 1.

[7] The main biographical information on Fröbe-Kapteyn is contained to date in the unpublished works by Gerhard Wehr, "Eranos in seiner Geschichte" (unpublished typescript, 1995–96; Eranos Foundation Archives, Ascona-Moscia), and Catherine Ritsema-Gris, "L'Œuvre d'Eranos et Vie d'Olga Froebe-Kapteyn" (unpublished typescript, undated; Eranos Foundation Archives, Ascona-Moscia), as well as in the aforementioned works by Hakl and Bernardini. Information about her early years also comes from her correspondence with Marie Stopes (now at the British Library), which we were able to access thanks to the transcripts kindly provided by Maite Karssenberg in April 2024, based on her research for her

staged in some of the world's most important museums, have gradually introduced her pictorial works to the general public. After the first exhibition conceived by Harald Szeemann (1933–2005) in 1978, dedicated to the history of "Monte Verità. The Breasts of Truth,"[8] the most relevant event was the exhibition "La Grande Madre" ["The Great Mother"], organized by the Nicola Trussardi Foundation on the occasion of the Milan Expo 2015 and conceived by Massimiliano Gioni.[9] That exhibition was followed by others, promoted by the New Museum in New York in 2016 ("The Keeper"), the Centre Pompidou in Paris in 2021 ("Elles font l'abstraction") ["Women in Abstraction"], the Guggenheim Museum in Bilbao in 2021–2022 ("Mujeres de la abstracción") ["Women in Abstraction"], the Kunsthalle in Mainz in 2023 ("Olga Fröbe-Kapteyn. Tiefes Wissen") ["Olga Fröbe-Kapteyn: Deep Knowledge"], the Musée des Beaux-Arts Le Locle in 2024 ("La scia del Monte ou les utopistes agnétiques") ["The Trail of the Mount or the Magnetic Utopians"], the Casa Rusca Museum in Locarno in 2024–2025 ("Olga Fröbe-

---

forthcoming work on the life and work of Geertruida Kapteyn-Muysken: Maite Karssenberg, *Dubbelleven. Geertruida Kapteyn-Muysken 1855–1920* (Amsterdam: De Arbeiderspers, 2026 {in press}).

[8] According to Yasmin Afschar, "The 'drawer' that Szeemann opens with his preoccupation with Fröbe-Kapteyn is that of the 'parallel image-worlds' he had introduced a few years earlier at documenta 5. The artistic and the nonartistic revealed themselves therein as unified into an encyclopedic image-world. Fröbe-Kapteyn, considered an outsider figure at the time, had piqued Szeemann's interest, thereby setting the stage for the evolution of the critical reception of Fröbe-Kapteyn throughout the following decades: on the one hand, in relation to an expanded concept of art; on the other, in relation to the opening of the realm of art toward its margins" (Yasmin Afschar, "Olga Fröbe-Kapteyn: conoscenza profonda / Olga Fröbe-Kapteyn: Deep Knowledge," in Raphael Gygax, ed., *Olga Fröbe-Kapteyn. Artista—ricercatrice. Volume pubblicato in occasione della mostra Olga Fröbe-Kapteyn: artista–ricercatrice, Museo Casa Rusca, Locarno, 8 agosto 2024–12 gennaio 2025* (Locarno/Ascona/Bellinzona: Museo Casa Rusca/Fondazione Eranos/Casagrande, in collaboration with Kunsthalle Mainz, 2024), p. 15). Szeemann's work continues to be invaluable in contextualizing Fröbe-Kapteyn's cultural creation, Eranos, within the utopias that originated in Ascona, directly or indirectly linked to the Monte Verità experience. See Harald Szeemann, ed., *Monte Verità. Antropologia locale come contributo alla riscoperta di una topografia sacrale moderna* (Locarno/Milan: Armando Dadò/Electa, 1978); Germ. ed., *Monte Verità. Berg der Wahrheit. Lokale Anthropologie als Beitrag zur Wiederentdeckung einer neuzeitlichen Topographie* (Locarno/Milan: Armando Dadò/Electa, 1978). On Szeemann's archival fund, cf. Claudia Lafranchi and Andreas Schwab, eds., *Dalla visione al chiodo. Dal chiodo alla visione. Il Fondo Harald Szeemann dell'Archivio Fondazione Monte Verità*, "Quaderni del Bollettino Storico della Svizzera Italiana," Vol. 12 (Bellinzona: Salvioni, 2013), and spec. pp. 56–59 and 159–60 for the Eranos materials displayed in room 2l at Casa Anatta, Ascona, now permanent venue for the exhibition on the history of Monte Verità.

[9] Gioni had already curated the 55th Venice Biennale (June 1–November 24, 2013), "The Encyclopedic Palace," inspired by Jung's *Red Book*: see Massimiliano Gioni and Natalie Bell, eds., *The Encyclopedic Palace. 55th International Art Exhibition: La Biennale di Venezia*, 2 vols. (Venice: Marsilio, 2013).

Kapteyn: Artist—Researcher"), the Museum Catharijneconvent in Utrecht in 2025 ("Tussen hemel en oorlog. Kunst en religie in het interbellum") ["Between Heaven and War. Art and Religion in the Interwar Period"], and again the Nicola Trussardi Foundation in 2025 ("Fata Morgana: memorie dall'invisibile") ["Morgan le Fay: Memories from the Invisible"]. The exhibition currently on display at the Swiss National Museum, "Landscapes of the Soul: C.G. Jung and the Exploration of the Human Psyche in Switzerland," organized to mark the 150th anniversary of Jung's birth and whose catalog was presented in August 2025 on the occasion of the XXIII Congress of the International Association for Analytical Psychology (IAAP), also includes a series of works by Fröbe-Kapteyn.[10]

Biographical investigation and artistic rediscovery, in short, seem to have gone hand in hand in patching together the scattered pieces of the story of a scholar who devoted the second half of her life to her own cultural enterprise, Eranos, and whose primary concern in the last decades of her existence was that it would survive her. On the other hand, we do not know if she had imagined that her pictorial works, besides enduring, would also have elicited such widespread interest today, nearly a hundred years later, becoming for some even a therapeutic tool to heal—as she did with herself—deep, sometimes unspeakable wounds. What is certain is that, for some reason—unlike the fate of her other personal papers—she chose not to destroy these creations; in fact, it seems she used to entrust her own notes to a purifying fire from time to time, in order to be able to look to the future with greater freedom. Thus, from the second half of the 1930s, paintings and drawings were stored by her in the attic of Casa Gabriella, sometimes protected in heavy dark wooden boxes.

The works had to wait forty years before the visionary genius of Szeemann dreamed of reviving them, just as he did with the scattered and often forgotten testimonies of the many utopias conceived, lived, and suffered at Monte Verità.[11] Therefore, we should not be surprised if Fröbe-

[10] For a complete list of all exhibitions that have included works by Olga Fröbe-Kapteyn and references to their catalogs, see the Conclusion to this volume.

[11] The utopian spirit of Monte Verità, to which Szeemann also attributes the conception of Eranos, has been admirably translated into film by Werner Weick in a series of documentaries, with particular reference to his most recent work, *Monte Verità. Berg der Wahrheit* (Ascona: Fondazione Monte Verità, 2012).

Kapteyn herself, endowed with exceptional insight and an equally rare ability to anticipate the cultural currents of the time, had the idea that, sooner or later, someone would have rediscovered and studied them, and now restored and protected them. The scientific investigation is in fact today proceeding in parallel with the conservation of these materials, through the careful restoration of a substantial iconographic fund, currently awaiting a final placement by the Eranos Foundation in a dedicated museum space in Ascona.

In terms of content, we should have the courage to look at Fröbe-Kapteyn's *Blue Book* as an initiatic corpus of our time and perhaps with answers that are still relevant to our moment: an imaginal compendium, received and realized by an artist capable of objectifying through the graphic medium—thanks to a skillful and trained use of tempera, India ink, pastel, and gold leaf—an intimate mystery of feminine transformation; an illuminated manuscript, in which the golden brightness of the Self, one's transcendent and imperishable nature, often stands out against a generative blue background, that is unparalleled to other works of her time (although art historians are rightly pointing out similarities and differences with other spiritual creatives of the last century, such as medium Georgiana Houghton (1814–1884), mystic Hilma af Klint (1862–1944), naturopath Emma Kunz (1892–1963), and journalist, art critic, and scholar of Tibetan Buddhism Charmion von Wiegand (1896–1983), who were pioneers of abstraction).

Moreover, we are faced with a work that, although inextricably linked to Fröbe-Kapteyn's personal history and the conception of her cultural project, Eranos, invites us into a performativity, a movement, when we chase its meaning; a significance to be found not only in the iconographic, textual, and epistolary apparatus, but also in the places that documented its impetuous and painstaking composition, lasting altogether just over a decade: that "Bermuda Triangle of the spirit" which, in Ascona and around Lake Maggiore, with its history and utopias, exiles and architectures, nature and magnetism, still holds its innermost secret. The Ivrea Verbano area is, in fact, a very special geological structure, defined by a positive gravitational anomaly (which indicates the presence of a body with a higher density than that of the surrounding environment), to be attributed to the ultra-basaltic rock complex (diorite, gabbro, peridotite, amphibolite, etc.). The mountains between Lake Maggiore and the Centovalli were formed by a series of rock layers that originated in deep areas of the Earth's crust. During the positive bradyseism phase (the slow uplifting of the ground) and the raising of the Alpine chain, these layers crumbled and were torn away from the depths, partly pushed to the Earth's surface and extruded. It is therefore not only a place of special geological interest, as it is home to outcrops of rocks belonging to the lower crust that are normally inaccessible or invisible, but also characterized by an exceptional magnetic anomaly.[12] *(Figure 198)*

Having settled in Ascona in mid-life, Fröbe-Kapteyn documented in her *Blue Book* the forms of imagination of a creative and independent subjectivity. Because of the care she had taken to paint or draw, collect, and preserve her works, she perhaps hoped that her *Blue Book* would survive her and, also, allow future generations to rediscover and make it their own, as a special testament to that endless search for self, at once personal and universal, that Jung would theorize with the idea of the "individuation process."[13]

---

[12] See Jörg W. Hansen (Cantonal Geological Office of Bellinzona), quoted in the explanatory panel "L'anomalia magnetica nel territorio di Ascona," as part of the exhibition on the history of Monte Verità, on permanent display at Casa Anatta, Ascona. See also Claudio Andretta, *Luoghi energetici in Ticino* (Bellinzona: Casagrande, 2016), § "Ascona, il Monte Verità e Arcegno," pp. 117–24 and Paola Giovetti, *I luoghi di forza. Guida alle località che emanano energia, pace e armonia* (Rome: Mediterranee, 2002), § "Monte Verità e i convegni di Eranos (Ascona, Canton Ticino)," pp. 129–31. On the continuity between Eranos in Ascona and the industrial utopia of Ivrea, articulated in many aspects of Italian society thanks to the genius of engineer and entrepreneur Adriano Olivetti (1901–1960), see Vv.Aa., *L'Ombra. Tracce e percorsi a partire da C.G. Jung*, 9 (1, 2018), ed. Riccardo Bernardini ("Jung e Ivrea"). Olivetti served as the first publisher of Jung's works in Italy, underwent analysis with Ernst Bernhard (1896–1965), the pioneer of Analytical Psychology in Italy, and was in touch with Count Hermann von Keyserling (1880–1946), who offered him editorial advice for his publishing house, Nuove Edizioni Ivrea (NEI); Keyserling's circle in Darmstadt, the Schule der Weisheit, was attended by Fröbe-Kapteyn, Jung, and other scholars subsequently involved in Eranos as lecturers; the "School of Wisdom" even became a "model" for Fröbe-Kapteyn's nascent Eranos. See Riccardo Bernardini, "Jung nelle Nuove Edizioni Ivrea (NEI). Con la corrispondenza inedita C.G. Jung-Cesare Musatti/NEI," *L'Ombra. Tracce e percorsi a partire da C.G. Jung*, 9 (1, 2018) ("Jung e Ivrea"), pp. 167–200.

[13] The first lecture given by Jung at Eranos in August 1933 was precisely devoted to the concept of the individuation process: Carl Gustav Jung, "Zur Empirie des Individuationsprozesses (Hiezu fünf Bildtafeln)," *Eranos-Jahrbuch*, 1 (1933), pp. 201–14; Engl. Ed. "A Study in the Process of Individuation," {1934/1950}, in *The Collected Works of C.G. Jung*, Vol. 9i (Princeton, NJ: Bollingen Series XX, Princeton University Press, 1969), pp. 290–354.

CHAPTER I
Olga Fröbe-Kapteyn's Interest in Art and Symbolism

Olga Fröbe-Kapteyn was born on October 19, 1881, to Dutch parents, who lived at 7 South Villas in Bloomsbury, London. *(Figures 3 and 4)*

Her father, Albertus Philippus Kapteyn (or Kapteijn, 1848–1927), in addition to being one of London's best-known private photographers and a friend of photography pioneer George Eastman (1854–1932),[1] was a mechanical engineer. *(Figure 5)* Son of Gerrit Jacobus Kapteyn (1812–1879), boarding school owner, and Elisabeth Cornelia Koomans (1814–1896), among his fifteen brothers were theologians, engineers, scientists, and also the famous astronomer Jacobus Cornelius Kapteyn (1851–1922).[2] Albertus Kapteyn went on to become director general of the Westinghouse Brake & Signal Company in London in 1881; he moved there in March 1880 from Paris, where he had started working for the company in the summer of 1878. He was in charge of supervising the installation of Westinghouse materials for the Trans-Siberian Railway, later becoming vice-president of Westinghouse's activities for the entire European area. The American George Westinghouse (1846–1914) had invented the automatic continuous pneumatic brake for railways. Under Kapteyn's leadership, the company expanded rapidly, opening branches in numerous European and South American countries. Kapteyn continued to make improvements to

[1] Albertus Kapteyn wrote a number of articles for various trade journals such as *Lux* in 1914 and 1915 and *Focus* in 1917 (Augustus J. Veenendaal, Jr., "Kapteijn, Albertus Philippus (1848–1927)," in *Biografisch Woordenboek van Nederland*, http://resources.huygens.knaw.nl/bwn1880-2000/lemmata/bwn2/kapteijnap). Maite Karssenberg also kindly contributed to clarifying some biographical details.

[2] Ritsema-Gris, *op. cit.*, pp. 1–4.

make the brake suitable for all types of trains; it is largely thanks to him that the Westinghouse brake was adopted by railways almost everywhere in the world. In 1909, he was also appointed first chairman of the aviation department of the Royal Dutch Aviation Association.[3]

Fröbe-Kapteyn's mother, Geertruida (Truus) Agneta Kapteyn-Muysken (1855–1920), was instead involved in various movements for women's emancipation and social renewal.[4] *(Figures 3 and 5)* Daughter of Antoine

---

[3] Veenendaal, *op. cit.*

[4] *Ibid.*, pp. 4–6. Geertruida Agneta Kapteyn-Muysken suffered from psychological problems and went through a number of hospitalizations; she lived in a time before the advent of psychology and, for this reason, as Fröbe-Kapteyn recognized, she could not receive proper treatment (Olga Fröbe-Kapteyn, "Vision meiner Mutter" (unpublished typescript, February 15–27, 1957; Eranos Foundation Archives, Ascona-Moscia), p. 5). Kapteyn-Muysken died on September 5, 1920 in a psychiatric institution in Arnhem (Maite Karssenberg, "Muysken, Geertruida Agneta," in *Digitaal Vrouwenlexicon van Nederland*, https://resources.huygens.knaw.nl/vrouwenlexicon/lemmata/data/Muysken). In 1952, in some notes relating to her inner work, Fröbe-Kapteyn recalled the significance of her maternal family line in Eranos' work: "*Blood* (spiritual) is the *carrier of archetypes.* Eranos is the work of my maternal ancestors. The *archetypal mission* has always been embedded in this bloodstream. I have therefore carried it within me since birth. *My resistance* to all those of the same blood was rooted in the fact that I opposed the accumulated spiritual energies in my own blood related to that mission … I am now connected to the maternal bloodstream, the spiritual values of this blood flow into me as in a blood transfusion. I am the last link in the chain, now closed into a circle, a *Catena Sanguinea*, a cycle. Eranos is the work of all my maternal ancestors, to whom this opus was imposed prematurely. Through my awareness of this fact, *the ancestors, as well as my mother, experience* a *rebirth*. Through this recognition of the spiritual value of the ancestral hereditary units (genes), they are included in the Eranos work and have fulfilled their mission. I have paid my debt to them. My connection to the spiritual blood of my ancestors also means a connection to the *collective Dutch psyche* and *its 'mother'* [Her Majesty Queen] *Juliana*. In psychological terms: *to the Self* (Olga Fröbe-Kapteyn, "Anschluss an den Blutstrom der Ahnen. 22 Mai 1952" (unpublished typescript, May 22, 1952; Eranos Foundation Archives, Ascona-Moscia). Queen Juliana of the Netherlands (1909–2004) reigned from 1948 to 1980. Interested in the phenomenology of religions, she had invited Fröbe-Kapteyn to her residence on October 19, 1951, to hear her talk about Eranos. The meeting took place on Fröbe-Kapteyn's 70th birthday (see the Afterword to this volume, written by her daughter, Her Royal Highness Princess Irene of the Netherlands). She continued: "It is not in the physical but in the *Subtle Body* that the *Circulation* of the spiritual Blood of the ancestors has been set going. Not only does the Blood carry the archetype of Eranos as *Aufgabe* [task] but also of the Ancestors and their Pattern—the *Pattern of the Clan*. Of my mother's clan! It seems that this realisation had to come via the *direct line of my mother and her ancestors*. It looks as if, for *a woman* this should or must *or can only* happen through the maternal ancestral line. That would mean a bit *of woman's psychology*" (Olga Fröbe-Kapteyn, "28 Mai 1952" (unpublished typescript, May 28, 1952; Eranos Foundation Archives, Ascona-Moscia). These reflections on her "self-healing" linked to the restoration of a psychological relationship with the Netherlands were already present in 1951, the year in which she recognized—thanks in part to the role played at Eranos of Dutch historian of religions Gerardus van der Leeuw *(Figure 206)*, who together with Jung in August 1949 had the idea of dedicating a monument "to the unknow spirit of the place" (*genio loci ignoti*) of Eranos *(Figure 208)*—the synchronicity of having liberated her feeling function and restored her relationship with the Netherlands, whose landscapes she found even more beautiful than those of Switzerland and whose

Charles Muysken (1803–1868), notary and mayor of Hillegom, and Constantia Susanna Commelin (1810–1864), she was the youngest in a large family in Hillegom: twelve children were born before her, six of whom died in infancy. She grew up with two brothers and four sisters. Her mother died when she was nine, her father when she was thirteen.[5] She was friends with Dutch pacifist and anarchist Bartholomeus (Bart) de Ligt (1883–1938);[6] anarchist communist theorist Pyotr Alexeyevich Kropotkin (1842–1921), who, based on her writings and personality, told her: "You are a great anarchist without knowing it";[7] socialist politician and later anarchist Ferdinand Jacobus Domela Nieuwenhuis (1846–1919);[8] lawyer and anarchist feminist activist Clara Gertrud Wichmann (1885–1922);[9] and playwright and socialist George Bernard Shaw (1856–1950).[10] Through

---

rituals associated with tulips represented for her a mystery of fertility (Olga Fröbe-Kapteyn, "[The Mysteries of the Nether'Lands] 11 Mai 1951" (unpublished typescript, May 11, 1951; Eranos Foundation Archives, Ascona-Moscia). Confirmation of all this came during her conversation with H.M. Queen Juliana, in her room and in their mother tongue (Id., "The Blood Consciousness and the Feeling function" (unpublished typescript, undated [1952?]; Eranos Foundation Archives, Ascona-Moscia).

[5] Karssenberg, *op. cit.*

[6] Bart de Ligt and his wife Catharina Lydia (Ina) de Ligt-van Rossem—who signed the Eranos Guestbook in 1935—were portrayed by Margarethe Fellerer in a series of photographs, still held by the Eranos Foundation Archives.

[7] Ritsema-Gris, *op. cit.*, 5; Kropotkin spent some months in Cannobio, Ascona, and Locarno in 1908, 1909, 1911, and 1913 (cf. Hans Manfred Bock and Florian Tennstedt, "Raphael Friedeberg: medico e anarchico ad Ascona," in Szeemann, *Monte Verità…*, cit., p. 43).

[8] Tjeu van den Berk, *In de ban van Jung. Nederlanders ontdekken de analytische psychologie* (Alblasserdam: Meinema, 2014), § 6: "De grote moeder en haar held. Olga Fröbe-Kapteyn (1881–1962)."

[9] *Ibid.*

[10] George Bernard Shaw visited Ascona in the 1920s, staying with the writer Emil Ludwig (1881–1948) (cfr. Theo Kneubühler, "Gli artisti, gli scrittori e il Canton Ticino (dal 1900 ad oggi)," in Szeemann, *op. cit.*, 176), who owned a property adjacent to Fröbe-Kapteyn's land since 1906. See Karl Vester, "Tagebuecher. 16. Juni 1902 - 31. Dezember 1919" (unpublished typescript, 1902–1919; The Getty Research Institute, Los Angeles / 2011.M.30 Harald Szeemann papers, 1800–2011, bulk 1949–2005 / Topical files, 1806–2005, bulk 1967–2005 / Places, 1851–2004, undated / Switzerland, 1851–2004, undated / Ticino (Tessin), 1851–1855, 1863, 1874–1876, 1886–2005, undated / A to Z, 1855, 1900–2005, undated / Box 3399, Vacchini–Vester, 1919, 1946–1968, 1975–1998, undated / Folder 25, Vester, Carl (Carlo), 1919), Tagebuch III, pp. 4, 22, 32, 33, 36, 38, 39, 42, 44, 61, 65, 74, 76, 82, 88, and 90; and Id., "[Tagebuecher] Ascona. 1. Januar 1920 bis 31. Dezember 1922 (unpublished typescript, 1920–1922; The Getty Research Institute, Los Angeles / 2011.M.30 Harald Szeemann papers, 1800–2011, bulk 1949–2005 / Topical files, 1806–2005, bulk 1967–2005 / Places, 1851–2004, undated / Switzerland, 1851–2004, undated / Ticino (Tessin), 1851–1855, 1863, 1874–1876, 1886–2005, undated / A to Z, 1855, 1900–2005, undated / Box 3400, Vester–Werefkin, 1922–1923, 1932, 1945, 1965–1972, 1988–1996, undated / Folder 1, Vester, Carl (Carlo), 1922), pp. 24, 58, 60, 73, 78, 82 130, and 132; and Id., "[Tagebuecher]. Askona. 1.

family connections, Fröbe-Kapteyn in her younger years had the opportunity to spend time with Ellen Key (1849–1926),[11] the Swedish writer and feminist whom she deeply admired: "She is a great woman," Kapteyn wrote at the age of 20 to her friend Marie Charlotte Carmichael Stopes (1880–1958), "the greatest of our time."[12]

Fröbe-Kapteyn's parents were married in Haarlem on December 21, 1880. Olga ("Olly") Kapteyn was the eldest of three children. *(Figures 6, 7, and 8)* The second child, Marie ("May") (1883–1972), lived in Holland and—after her amicable separation from art historian Jan Kalf (1873–1954), Chief Restorer of Dutch churches—in Paris, where she was active in the resistance during World War II. She had no children.[13] The third son, Albert (1886–1964), graduated in mechanical engineering in Zurich; enamored with the United States, he moved there soon after marrying. Beyond a temporary move to The Hague (where their parents owned a house, later sold) from 1937 to December 1939 for professional reasons (he was the

Januar 1923 bis 31. Juli 1925 (unpublished typescript, 1923–1925; The Getty Research Institute, Los Angeles / 2011.M.30 Harald Szeemann papers, 1800–2011, bulk 1949–2005 / Project files, 1836-2007, bulk 1949–2005 / Monte Verità: The breasts of truth (Monte Verità/Berg der Wahrheit) (1978 July 7 to August 30) / Papers / Box 349 / Folder 3), pp. 3, 26, 49, 67, 80, 95, and 99. I would like to thank both Nicoletta Mongini and Jonas Sebastian Lendenmann for his kind assistance in locating these materials. Cf. also Yvonne Bölt and Gian Piero Milani, eds., *Ascona caleidoscopio. Storie e testimonianze del passato / Geschichten und Zeugnisse aus der Vergangenheit* (Ascona, Unicorno, 2024), § "Emil Ludwig (1881–1948) cittadino onorario di Ascona," pp. 8–13.

[11] See, e.g., Luisa Ceccarelli, "Ellen Key e la rete delle scuole nuove in Europa (1899–1914)," Ph.D. Dissertation, Dottorato di Ricerca in Scienze Pedagogiche, Alma Mater Studiorum—Università di Bologna, Bologna, 2020, p. 73.

[12] Olga Fröbe-Kapteyn, letter to Marie Stopes, July 26, 1901 (British Library, London; transcript kindly provided by Karssenberg). Stopes became a paleontologist and paleobotanist.

[13] It seems that Fröbe-Kapteyn was never on particularly good terms with her sister May, who she used to dismiss bluntly as a "communist" (Rudolf Ritsema, personal communication, September 5, 2003, Ascona-Moscia). According to Fröbe-Kapteyn, the hatred that had always existed between the two was an expression of deep jealousy, since May was always their father's favorite; he (inventor and tester of railway brakes!) had instead "put on the brakes" with Olga (Olga Fröbe-Kapteyn, "Mein Vater. Albertus Philippus Kapteyn. Vision" (unpublished typescript, February 1 and 5, 1957; Eranos Foundation Archives, Ascona-Moscia), p. 3). In his daughter's memory, he defined her as incapable of concentration, perseverance, and discipline (*ibid.*, p. 5). Since childhood, Olga had thus projected her "darkest shadow" onto May, against whom all his aggression, rejection, and defenses were directed (Olga Fröbe-Kapteyn, "Der Schatten" (unpublished typescript, May 17–August 1, 1957; Eranos Foundation Archives, Ascona-Moscia), p. 1). May also acted as a barrier between Olga and their father until his death (Olga Fröbe-Kapteyn, "Drei Zeichnungen" (unpublished typescript and drawings, March 23, 1934; Eranos Foundation Archives, Ascona-Moscia), p. 1).

European representative for United Aircraft, conducting business at Schiphol Airport, Amsterdam, mostly with KLM), Albert remained in the US permanently. He had two children, Polly Kapteyn Brown and James Kapteyn.[14]

If we wanted to pinpoint the origins of Olga Kapteyn's interest in art, we would probably have to turn our gaze far back to the very beginnings of her personal history. She herself acknowledged in fact that her predisposition for iconography and symbolism could be traced back to her childhood years, when her father Albertus was processing photographic film in the darkroom of their in their Bloomsbury home, under the curious gaze of his daughter. She recalled: "As a child, I must have walked past him hundreds of times in the darkroom while he was developing negatives. The emergence of images during the development of negatives fascinated me like nothing else. We were in that dark room, lit only by a red light, so close, and it was like a second life: a life made up of images. Now, as I see it today, that's where the unconscious manifested itself. That dark world naturally grabbed me and activated my own inner world of images. In my imagination, my father became the creator out of nothing. He created a world of images! For more than ten years, I stood next to him in that small dark room whenever he had time."[15]

---

[14] Polly Kapteyn Brown, letter to William McGuire, undated (Eranos Foundation Archives, Ascona-Moscia). A few notes on Olga Fröbe-Kapteyn are included in the book by Polly Kapteyn Brown's son, Peter Falkenberg Brown, *Waking Up Dead and Confused is a Terrible Thing—Stories of Love, Life, Death & Redemption* (Gray, ME: World Community, 2020), pp. 197 f.

[15] Fröbe-Kapteyn, "Mein Vater…," cit., p. 10; see also Ritsema-Gris, *op. cit.*, 7; William McGuire, *Bollingen—An Adventure in Collecting the Past* (Princeton, NJ: Bollingen Series, Princeton University Press, 1982), p. 21; and Hakl, *Der verborgene Geist von Eranos…*, cit., p. 34. Albertus had also built a boat which he named "Olga" in honor of his daughter (Olga means "fish" in the language of the Chaldeans—a symbol that appears in both the Kapteyn and Muysken family coats of arms) (cf. Olga Fröbe-Kapteyn, "My marriage" (unpublished typescript, undated [1945?]; Eranos Foundation Archives, Ascona-Moscia). *(Figures 1 and 2)* "Olly" lived with him for nine weeks in this private "retreat" of which he was the captain and which, decades later, she recognized as a prototype of the "Eranos *Maṇḍala*." They also received guests there; her mother, instead, never came on the boat. "Olly" learned to cook on the "Olga" from Gerrit, the boat's helmsman. When, in 1934, Fröbe-Kapteyn had the vision of the second "Eranos *Maṇḍala*," in which she saw Jung dancing with her on skates on the frozen surface of a lake *(Figures 149, 150, and 151)*, she had in mind just one of those Dutch waterways for which the flat-bottomed "Olga" had been specially built. The "clan *maṇḍala*" was thus linked to the future second "Eranos *Maṇḍala*," drawn in 1934, both in terms of the creative atmosphere of the place and at the same time in terms of "taboo": "It is the place set apart for a definite piece of work inspired by the Self … The

Every Sunday evening, moreover, Albertus used to read to his three children large, richly illustrated volumes: in particular, Jules Verne's *Twenty Thousand Leagues Under the Sea* and a voluminous edition of Miguel de Cervantes's *Don Quixote*, illustrated by Gustave Doré. Olly, May, and Albert listened spellbound as he read to them aloud and recounted the characters. This custom went on for years and years. They grew up with these two books, fascinated and "filled" by the fantastic and compelling illustrations in them: "They were our inner world of images," Fröbe-Kapteyn still vividly recalled in the last years of her life.[16]

Fröbe-Kapteyn's predisposition for symbolic art can also be traced back to her schooling and, in general, to the cultural environment in which she lived. *(Figures 9–14)* She attended the North London Collegiate, a renowned girls' school open to children from the age of four. Even at a very young age, she also had the opportunity to visit important European museums and sites with her family: for example, in Paris, in 1899, the Louvre (she was particularly impressed by the works of Rubens and Rembrandt) and Notre-Dame. A 1889 portrait by Willem Witsen (1860–1923), the famous Dutch painter and photographer associated with the Amsterdam Impressionism movement, depicts Olly at age 8 and is still on display at Eranos today. *(Figure 9)*

---

original clan *mandala* was only the *Keimzelle* [germ cell]" (Olga Fröbe-Kapteyn, "The *Mandala*" (unpublished typescript, undated [1945?]; Eranos Foundation Archives, Ascona-Moscia)). Albertus' passion for the adventures of Captain Nemo as told by Jules Verne in *Twenty Thousand Leagues Under the Sea* was passed on to his daughter. Moreover, the name of their most distant ancestor on their father's side was Cornelis ("Captain"): he lived around 1580, the age of great discoveries, and that was probably his profession—he took this title as his own name. Fröbe-Kapteyn recalled how, on one occasion, during a party organized during an Eranos Conference, Jung called her "Our Captain!" and toasted her (Fröbe-Kapteyn, "Mein Vater...," cit., p. 9).

[16] Olga Fröbe-Kapteyn, "Mein Vater...," cit., p. 8. The library of Casa Gabriella still holds the splendid edition of Jules Verne's *Vingt Mille Lieues sous les Mers*, illustrated with 111 drawings by Alphonse de Neuville and Édouard Riou (a pupil of Gustave Doré) (Paris: J. Hetzel et Cie, 1889); from the same series, i.e., the "Voyages extraordinaires par Jules Verne," are also held at Eranos *Le tour du monde en quatre-vingts jours* (Paris: J. Hetzel et Cie, undated); *Les enfants du Capitaine Grant. Voyage autour du monde* (Paris: Librairie Hachette, undated); *L'Île mystérieuse* (Paris: Librairie Hachette, undated); *Cinq Semaines en Ballon. Voyage de découverte en Afrique* (Paris: J. Hetzel et Cie, undated [1890]; and *Les Indes-Noires* (Paris: J. Hetzel et Cie, undated).

Beginning in 1901, after moving to Zurich with her family because of Albertus' work on January 18,[17] Kapteyn began working every morning in the studio of the chief draughtsman at the Kunstgewerbeschule (School of Arts and Crafts or School of Applied Arts), from 9 a.m. to noon, also taking violin lessons.[18] In addition, she devoted herself weekly to botanical drawing sessions. She was then admitted to the Gewerbeschule (Drawing School) in early May 1901 and practiced intensive training in drawing for many hours a day, from 7 a.m. (with wake-up at 5:30 a.m.) to noon and from 2 p.m. to 5 p.m.[19] Alongside her training in drawing and tailoring, she also had the opportunity to listen to some university lectures on theoretical and clinical psychology.[20] In 1904, she worked four days a week in the metalworking department of a school of applied arts in Haarlem, where she learned everything she needed to know about metalworking—chiseling, hammering, firing, design, and welding—for her field.[21] She became very skilled at sewing, embroidery, and jewelry making.

Among her many trips to Europe in those years, the journey to Florence helped imprint on her memory the magnificence of the art galleries, incomparable with anything else she had seen up to that time. During this period, she also traveled to the Swiss mountains with her father and brothers for strenuous mountaineering led by mountain guides. She was impressed by the majesty of the glaciers, with their peaks, crevasses,

---

[17] Olga Fröbe-Kapteyn, letters to Ernst Bernhard with biographical information, September 1 and September 2, 1954 (Ernst and Dora Bernhard Collection, Historical Archive of Italian Psychology (ASPI), University of Milan-Bicocca; kindly provided by Catherine McGilvray in June 2025; in that account, she actually indicates to Bernhard 1900 as the year of her move from London to Zurich, rather than 1901, probably due to a memory lapse); and Id., letter to Marie Stopes, January 24, 1901 (British Library, London; transcript kindly provided by Karssenberg, to whom I am also grateful for clarifying the correct year of Fröbe-Kapteyn's move to Zurich).

[18] Olga Fröbe-Kapteyn, letter to Marie Stopes, February 2, 1901 (British Library, London; transcript kindly provided by Karssenberg).

[19] Olga Fröbe-Kapteyn, letter to Marie Stopes, May 8, 1901 (British Library, London; transcript kindly provided by Karssenberg).

[20] Olga Fröbe-Kapteyn, letter to Marie Stopes, June 17, 1901 (British Library, London; transcript kindly provided by Karssenberg).

[21] Olga Fröbe-Kapteyn, letter to Marie Stopes, November 12, 1904 (British Library, London; transcript kindly provided by Karssenberg).

and seracs.[22] She also enjoyed the contemplative quiet of Lake Zurich, which she would experience again years later, on the shores of Lake Maggiore.

From 1906 to 1909, Kapteyn continued her education in art history at the University of Zurich. In 1908 she purportedly worked as a horsewoman in a circus[23] *(Figure 14)* and, a skilled and trained skier,[24] she may have been among the first women to climb Mont Blanc.[25] In 1908, her parents returned to the Netherlands and Scheveningen became their home.[26]

On May 13, 1909, Kapteyn married flutist and orchestra conductor Iwan Fröbe (1880–1915), an Austro-Hungarian citizen but Slovenian by

---

[22] See Olga Fröbe-Kapteyn, letter to Marie Stopes, July 22, 1901. In August 1901, during a family holiday in the Blausee area of Kandersteg in the Canton of Bern, Kapteyn went on a series of glacier excursions that made a deep impression on her. *(Figure 23)* In the following days, they also reached Zermatt via the Gemmipass (Olga Fröbe-Kapteyn, letter to Marie Stopes, August 1, 1901). On 31 March 1907, she wrote a postcard to her friend Johanna Westerdijk (1883–1961), who became a botanist and plant pathologist, from the San Gottardo Hospice (the letters were kindly provided by Karssenberg in April 2024).

[23] As a young girl, during stays in Vienna, Kapteyn had arranged with the director of a circus to come every morning at 6 a.m. to practice as a horsewoman with a teacher; all this, of course, without her father's knowledge, who would not have appreciated such fantasies (cf. Ritsema-Gris, *op. cit.*, 8; and Olga Fröbe-Kapteyn, "Erster Abend..." (unpublished typescript, undated [prob. 1957–1958 ca.]; Eranos Foundation Archives, Ascona-Moscia), p. 6).

[24] In the Eranos Foundation Archives there was a silver towel holder engraved with her name, as the winner of a ski race, a summer competition held in the Swiss canton of Grisons (cf. Ritsema-Gris, *op. cit.*, 8; see also Sybille Rosenbaum-Kroeber, "Eranos e Olga Fröbe-Kapteyn," in Szeemann, *op. cit.*, p. 121). In the winter of 1906, she skied for several weeks in Engadine (Olga Fröbe-Kapteyn, letters to Marie Stopes, January 19, January 31, and November 19, 1906). In 1907, besides skiing in St. Moritz, she also enjoyed memorable ski touring trips with Norwegian skiers, climbing and descending challenging mountains, such as Piz Lucendro (2964 m) from the San Gottardo Pass (Olga Fröbe-Kapteyn, letter to Marie Stopes, Spring 1907). *(Figure 24)* In December 1907 and January 1908, she went skiing in Lenzerheide, stopping at the Alphütte Fops; in January 1909, she skied in the Rigi area. Here, together with Iwan, she was able to admire the "*Nebelmeer*" (sea of fog), which is particularly spectacular from the Rigi, giving the impression that one can walk on the sea, with the mountain peaks rising like islands (Eranos Foundation Archives). *(Figures 19–22)* Who knows if, in the experience of the *Nebelmeer*, with the snow-capped mountain peaks disappearing and reappearing as they emerge from the fog, she found something similar to her early childhood experiences, when her father created images "out of nothing," making them appear on the photographic film in their darkroom in Bloomsbury? Moreover, the autumn and winter landscape he admired from Villa Gabriella in Ascona could have given her similar feelings: low clouds, heavy with rain, often engulf the mountains surrounding the lake, giving the impression of an ever-changing landscape, from which the sinuous shapes of the Alps emerge in ever-changing forms.

[25] McGuire, *op. cit.*, p. 21; and and Christine Derleth, *Das Fleischlich-Geistige. Meine Erinnerungen an Ludwig Derleth* (Hessen: Hinder + Deelmann, Bellnhausen über Gladenbach, 1973), p. 96.

[26] Van den Berk, *op. cit.*

birth. *(Figures, 16, 18, 21, and 26)* The couple had met in Zurich while enjoying the winter sports they both loved.[27] *(Figures 17–22)* Their wedding took place in London in a Dutch Reformed Church ceremony.[28]

After a brief stay in Munich, the Fröbe couple moved to Berlin in 1914.[29] Their acquaintance with André Jolles (1874–1946) was facilitated by their shared residence in the Berlin suburb of Wannsee. Jolles had known the Kapteyn-Muysken family for a long time. One of his best friends, Jan Kalf, would marry Fröbe-Kapteyn's sister, May.[30] Jolles was a philologist and scholar of classical literature, an art historian, and a devotee of Italian culture: between 1894 and 1900, he resided in Florence, making the acquaintance of Aby Warburg (1866–1929). Jolles had created a cultural circle in Berlin that brought together writers, painters, and musicians. In their small wooden house on Hohenzollernstrasse, Iwan Fröbe used to delight those present with excellent chamber music.[31] In 1911, Jolles also founded a sewing circle, "The Needle." Fröbe-Kapteyn participated in this circle together with her close friend Annemarie Pallat (1875–1972), who like her lived in Wannsee with her husband, the archaeologist and educationalist Ludwig Pallat (1867–1946), co-founder and director of the Berlin Center for Education and Teaching and one of the leading reformers of art education in secondary schools.[32] Jolles loved to make women's dresses inspired by the fashion of ancient Greece: cuts were kept to a

[27] Ritsema-Gris, *op. cit.*, p. 9. Even Fröbe-Kapteyn's mother, in her youth, wanted to marry a musician, but she was not allowed to (Fröbe-Kapteyn, "Vision meiner Mutter," cit., p. 4).

[28] See Olga Fröbe-Kapteyn, "My marriage," cit. Fröbe-Kapteyn's earliest ancestors were probably Catholic; her grandparents were Protestant; her parents, although Protestant, no longer belonged to the Church and turned toward an "ethical culture" that she considered "completely sterile." She distanced herself from this and was welcomed back into the Catholic Church (Olga Fröbe-Kapteyn, "Winter 1938. London. Vorläufer der jetzigen, 12 Jahre späteren Visionen in der Arbeit mit Dr. Szondi" [belonging to the "Arbeit mit Dr. Szondi"] (unpublished typescript, undated [1950]; Eranos Foundation Archives, Ascona-Moscia).

[29] In Berlin, Fröbe-Kapteyn had also the opportunity to meet and spend time with harpsichordist and pianist Wanda Aleksandra Landowska (1879–1959) (Ritsema-Gris, *op. cit.*, p. 9).

[30] Cf. Olga Fröbe-Kapteyn, letter to Marie Stopes, December 2, 2019 (British Library, London; transcript kindly provided by Karssenberg).

[31] Ritsema-Gris, *op. cit.*, p. 10.

[32] Walter Thys, ed., *André Jolles (1874–1946), „Gebildeter Vagant." Brieven en documenten* (Amsterdam/Leipzig: Amsterdam University Press/Leipziger Universität GmbH, 2000), pp. 994 ff. The Pallats, together with their daughter Marianne von Machui-Pallat (born in 1912), continued to visit Fröbe-Kapteyn after she moved to Villa Gabriella in Ascona.

minimum and their beauty came almost exclusively from the play of the fabric's natural folds. Fröbe-Kapteyn embellished her sartorial creations with refined embroidery. *(Figures 25, 33, and 34)* One of her silk blouses with colorful embroidery was exhibited in 1916 as part of a textile exhibition at the Museum of Applied Arts in Zurich.[33] *(Figure 32)*

Returning to Switzerland in April 1914, the Fröbe couple lived for about nine months in Gersau am Vierwaldstättersee, then moved to Zurich in December of that year.

With the declaration of war in July 1914, Iwan Fröbe, who had trained as a pilot, was enlisted as a military pilot in the Austro-Hungarian army. When he left home in May 1915, Fröbe-Kapteyn was convinced that she would not see him again until the end of the war. [34] He passed away on September 11, 1915, during a training flight in a military plane,[35] but not without giving his wife twin daughters, Bettina Gertrude, dark-haired with her mother's dark eyes,[36] and Jngeborg Helene, blonde with blue eyes, born in Zurich on May 3, 1915.[37] *(Figures 27 and 28)*

---

[33] See Vv.Aa., *1875–1975. 100 Jahre Kunstgewerbemuseum der Stadt Zürich*, eds. Elisabeth Grossmann, Hansjörg Budliger, and Urs Stahel, texts by O. Birkner, K. Akeret, E. Grossmann, E. Billeter, and P. Obermüller (Zurich: Zürcher Hochschule der Künste, Kunstgewerbemuseum der Stadt Zürich, 1975); the image is reproduced in Szeemann, *op. cit.*, p. 120); when she moved to Ascona, she also learned the gobelin stitch from Russian Anna ("Mama") Kessa (1880–1967): see Giorgio Vacchini, ed., *Ascona. Verdetti popolari e documenti* (Ascona: Comune di Ascona, 1996), par. 2034; Curt Riess, *Ascona, Die Geschichte des seltsamsten Dorfes der Welt* (Zurich: Buchclub Ex Libris, 1964), p. 111; and Bernardini, *Jung a Eranos...*, cit., p. 249. The sewing and embroidery work, which also included meticulously applying pearls to the dresses she created, was an occupation that kept Fröbe-Kapteyn busy during the winters at Villa Gabriella since the 1920s: see Ritsema-Gris, *op. cit.*, p. 10.

[34] Olga Fröbe-Kapteyn, letter to Marie Stopes, June 17, 1915 (British Library, London; transcripts kindly provided by Karssenberg).

[35] Iwan Fröbe entered service in September 1915, assigned to Vienna, where he was to carry out tests with aerial photography at Fischamend airport before leaving for the front. The plane crashed, killing both the pilot and him. See Olga Fröbe-Kapteyn, letters to Ernst Bernhard with biographical information, September 1 and September 2, 1954 (Ernst and Dora Bernhard Collection, Historical Archive of Italian Psychology (ASPI), University of Milan-Bicocca; kindly provided by McGilvray); and Id., letter to Marie Stopes, September 20, 1915 (British Library, London; transcripts kindly provided by Karssenberg).

[36] Bettina subsequently spent many years in the mountains, as doctors believed she had bronchial tuberculosis. She married painter Rudolf Béguin in Holland in 1939 and they had two children. See Olga Fröbe-Kapteyn, letter to Ernst Bernhard with biographical information, September 2, 1954 (Ernst and Dora Bernhard Collection, Historical Archive of Italian Psychology (ASPI), University of Milan-Bicocca; kindly provided by McGilvray).

[37] Little Jngeborg was born with severe mental and physical retardation due to medical complications during a difficult birth. As a double birth was not expected, the presence of the second baby girl was

After her husband's death, Fröbe-Kapteyn created in Zurich her own cultural circle, "La Table ronde."[38] *(Figures 29–31)* Among others, she rubbed shoulders with Baron Hanns-Henning von Voigt (1887–1969). Von Voigt, better known as Alastair, was an artist and esotericist with whom Fröbe-Kapteyn cultivated a lasting friendship.[39]

Fröbe-Kapteyn knew the Ticino area from her youth: she had already vacationed with her family in Bellagio, Como, and Pallanza by 1899.[40] On April 1, 1920, she returned to Ticino[41] and spent her vacations first in Lugano and then in Porto Ronco, on the Swiss shores of Lake Maggiore, a few kilometers from Ascona.[42] *(Figure 35)* In 1920, Fröbe-Kapteyn was

---

in fact noticed only an hour or two after Bettina's birth, and Jngeborg was extracted with forceps, which damaged her brain. Fröbe-Kapteyn consulted numerous doctors in Switzerland, Germany, and Vienna, but to no avail. In 1922, she decided to take Jngeborg to a pediatric clinic near Berlin; she could no longer afford to keep her in Switzerland, while Germany was much cheaper (Olga Fröbe-Kapteyn, letter to Ernst Bernhard with biographical information, September 2, 1954 (Ernst and Dora Bernhard Collection, Historical Archive of Italian Psychology (ASPI), University of Milan-Bicocca; kindly provided by McGilvray); and Id., letters to Marie Stopes, March 23, 1922 and October 4, 1923 (British Library, London; transcripts kindly provided by Karssenberg)). She thus finally decided to have her admitted to a Berlin institution, where she tried to ensure she received the best care available and visited her regularly (but without taking Bettina with her, fearing she would be too shocked). After being moved from a nursing home near Bremen (where Fröbe-Kapteyn had last seen her) to Gunzburg, in south Germany, Jngeborg died in 1941, probably as a result of the Nazi euthanasia program, according to Fröbe-Kapteyn; she had received a letter from the Heil und Pflegeanstalt des Bezirksverbandes Schwaben im Gürzburg, signed by Toni Schmidt-Kraepelin, simply informing her that Jngeborg had died of flu. Jngeborg's story represented "the most tragic and darkest chapter of [her] whole life," which also led to a series of psychosomatic symptoms related to breathing, such as vasomotor rhinitis and bronchial asthma (linked to the painful fantasy that, along with the other children, Jngeborg herself had been killed by asphyxiation in the Nazi gas chambers) (Olga Fröbe-Kapteyn, "History of a Symptom. Rhinitis vasomotoris" (unpublished typescript, 1949; Eranos Foundation Archives, Ascona-Moscia); Id., "7 November 1950" [belonging to the "Arbeit mit Dr. Szondi"] (unpublished typescript, November 7, 1950; Eranos Foundation Archives, Ascona-Moscia); and Id., "The Lapis Exilis and the Grail MSS" (unpublished typescript, February 20, 1952; Eranos Foundation Archives, Ascona-Moscia); see also Ritsema-Gris, *op. cit.*, pp. 11 f.; Wehr, *op. cit.*, p. 20; Hakl, *Eranos…*, cit., p. 14; and Bernardini, *op. cit.*, p. 249).

[38] Cf. Robert Faesi, *Erlebnisse, Ergebnisse, Erinnerungen* (Zurich: Atlantis, 1963), 224 ff., and van der Berk, *op. cit.*

[39] Cf. Hakl, *Der verborgene Geist von Eranos…*, cit., pp. 36 f.

[40] Olga Fröbe-Kapteyn, letters to Marie Stopes, April 2 and 15, 1899 (British Library, London; transcripts kindly provided by Karssenberg).

[41] Olga Fröbe-Kapteyn, letters to Ernst Bernhard with biographical information, September 1 and September 2, 1954 (Ernst and Dora Bernhard Collection, Historical Archive of Italian Psychology (ASPI), University of Milan-Bicocca; kindly provided by McGilvray).

[42] Cf. Rosenbaum-Kroeber, *op. cit.*, pp. 119 ff.

treated—perhaps with her father—at the Sanatorium Monte Verità with natural remedies for her gastritis, probably caused by poor nutrition during World War I, as the food available was not always of the best quality.[43]

In 1920 Fröbe-Kapteyn lived for a time at Casa Monte Tabor in Porto Ronco. *(Figure 36)* She described to Stopes its garden full of mimosas, eucalyptus trees, camellias, and other tropical plants.[44] Although it had a large atelier of about sixty-five square meters, probably used by the previous tenants as a music room, Casa Tabor did not satisfy the new tenant, who soon set out to find a new home.[45]

In December 1921, Fröbe-Kapteyn moved to Villa Gabriella, in the hamlet of Moscia, near Ascona, with her daughter Bettina.[46] The old farm building had been purchased on October 12, 1920 by her father (at the time retired and residing in Scheveningen, The Hague) from the German ophthalmologist Ugo von Hoffmann (son of Ermano from Lippedetmold or Lippe-Detmold),[47] with whom he shared a passion for chess.[48] Hoffmann had probably lived in Ascona without practicing since about 1905. He had in turn bought Villa Gabriella from one of Monte Verità's first settlers, Karl Vester (1879–1963), *(Figure 37)* who had purchased Villa Gabriella in 1904

---

[43] Vacchini, *Ascona*, cit., par. 2034.

[44] Olga Fröbe-Kapteyn, letter to Marie Stopes, April 21, 1920, written from Monte Verità, Ascona (British Library, London; transcript kindly provided by Karssenberg).

[45] In 1931, Casa Monte Tabor became the property of Erich Maria Remarque (1898–1970) and, upon his passing, that of his wife Paulette Remarque Goddard (1910–1990), actress and former first wife of Charlie Chaplin (1889–1977) (see Ritsema-Gris, *op. cit.*, p. 14). Swiss painter Eduard Rüdisühli (1875–1938) was relatively certainly the previous owner of Casa Monte Tabor before Remarque, from 1905 to 1931, and used the villa as a summer residence from 1905 to 1915.

[46] Olga Fröbe-Kapteyn, letters to Ernst Bernhard with biographical information, September 1 and September 2, 1954 (Ernst and Dora Bernhard Collection, Historical Archive of Italian Psychology (ASPI), University of Milan-Bicocca; kindly provided by McGilvray). Although older, Casa Gabriella appears on the 1861 cadastral map of the Ascona area, drawn up by engineer Giuseppe Roncajoli. The letters sent to Stopes on December 25, 1920, and November 16, 1921 are still sent from "Porto Ronco." The first letter sent to Stopes from "Villa Gabriella" is dated March 23, 1922 (British Library, London; transcripts kindly provided by Karssenberg).

[47] Extract from the census records of the Municipality of Ronco/A, "Purchase and sale between Ugo von Hoffmann and Alberto Kapteyn deed drawn up by Notary Vittorio Pedrotta on October 12, 1920. We would like to thank the Land Registry Office in Locarno for the kind cooperation. A certain Hoffmann from Ascona signed the Guestbook of the International Centre for Spiritual Research from 1930 to 1932.

[48] Ritsema-Gris, *op. cit.*, p. 15.

from lawyer Carlo Abbondio (1859–1920) and lived there with his wife Hedwig Rohde until 1909, before moving in 1919 to a farm on Monte Verità.[49] The French writer André Germain (1882–1971), a former guest of Fröbe-Kapteyn's Zurich literary salon, for several years her "closest and most precious friend,"[50] and a friend of the Baron Eduard von der Heydt (1882–1964, owner of Monte Verità since 1926), had also lived there in the 1920s.[51]

---

[49] Vacchini, *op. cit.*, par. 2631. As can be seen in *Figure 37*, from the years when Villa Gabriella was inhabited by the Vesters until Fröbe-Kapteyn's arrival, the building underwent two major extensions—one towards the hill, with the addition of a wing that still houses part of the library, and one towards the lake, with the addition of the large terrace of the "Copte" room, the windowed room of the apartment below, and the current dining room on the ground floor. The original building was therefore narrower and more slender, but probably already had a dock at lake level (a note in the concrete of one of the pillars of the house refers to an exceptional rise in the lake level on October 18, 1907). The purchase of Villa Gabriella by Carlo Abbondio is mentioned in Vester's private diaries: cf. Karl Vester, "[Tagebuecher]. Ascona. 1. Januar 1920 bis 31. Dezember 1922 (unpublished typescript, 1920–1922; The Getty Research Institute, Los Angeles / 2011.M.30 Harald Szeemann papers, 1800–2011, bulk 1949–2005 / Topical files, 1806–2005, bulk 1967–2005 / Places, 1851–2004, undated / Switzerland, 1851–2004, undated / Ticino (Tessin), 1851–1855, 1863, 1874–1876, 1886–2005, undated / A to Z, 1855, 1900–2005, undated / Box 3400, Vester–Werefkin, 1922–1923, 1932, 1945, 1965–1972, 1988–1996, undated / Folder 1, Vester, Carl (Carlo), 1922), p. 38; I would like to thank both Nicoletta Mongini and Jonas Sebastian Lendenmann for his kind assistance in locating these materials. The sale of Villa Gabriella by Abbondio to Vester is also mentioned in Vacchini, *Ascona. Verdetti popolari e documenti*, cit., par. 645. Carlo Abbondio was the brother of notary and member of the Grand Council Giovanni Abbondio (1870–1922) and the father of poet Valerio Abbondio (1981–1958), a French teacher at the High School di Lugano, sculptor Fiorenzo Abbondio (1892–1980), creator of several religious statues in churches and of patriotic and funerary monuments in Ticino, and Angelo Abbondio (1889–1973), fisherman. Among the families from Como who took refuge in Ticino to escape Spanish tyranny in the 15th century were the Abondio or Abbondio (Vacchini, *op. cit.*, pars. 647 ff.; see also the fictional character Don Abbondio in *I promessi sposi* [*The Betrothed*], set by Alessandro Manzoni on Lake Como, mainly between 1628 and 1630, in Lombardy under Spanish rule, a period marked by famine, war, and plague). The noble Abbondio family, whose presence is documented in Ascona since the fifteenth century, had its residence and land holdings specifically in the hamlet of Moscia, where Villa Gabriella was built at some point; in the first half of the seventeenth century, a branch of the family settled in Locarno. Among its members were several clergymen, including canons of the collegiate church of Locarno and parish priests of Ascona, as well as sculptors: among them, in particular, Antonio Abondio, known as "l'Ascona" (died in 1578); his son Antonio Abondio "il Giovane" (1538–1591), medallist and ceramist; that activity was then continued by his sons, Giovanni Antonio Abondio, sculptor, and Alessandro Abondio (1580–1653), also a medallist, ceramist, and engraver (cf. Vacchini, *op. cit.*, pars. 647 ff.; Angelo Nessi, *Scrittori ticinesi*, eds. Renato Martinoni and Clara Cavezzano Tanzi (Locarno: Armando Dadò, 1997), § "Valerio Abbondio," pp. 215–18; Alessandra Maffioli, "Abbondio," in *Dizionario Storico della Svizzera DSS*, version of May 7, 2020; and Bölt and Milani, eds., *Ascona caleidoscopio...*, cit., § "Casate asconesi. Gli Abbondio (fino al 19. Sec.: Abondio)," pp. 120–23, and § "Giovanni Antonio Abondio (1524–1592) l'Asconio," pp. 128–31).

[50] Olga Fröbe-Kapteyn, letter to Marie Stopes, October 4, 1918; see also the letters of February 18, 1919, December 25, 1920, and 1922 (British Library, London; transcripts kindly provided by Karssenberg).

[51] On October 8, 1920 from Ronco, Albertus Kapteyn wrote to Germain (who was staying at that time at the Grand Hotel in Brissago) who was about to meet Hoffmann: the latter was already close to

"To live in Casa Gabriella, yes; to live there with you, no," was Fröbe-Kapteyn's reply to her father when he asked her if she wished to share her new residence with him. She loved him very much, but with two strong personalities like theirs, it was also easy for them to clash frequently.[52]

The property of Villa Gabriella purchased by Albertus Kapteyn and Olga Fröbe-Kapteyn in 1920 (Olga's mother had died in September of that year) was immense: it covered about four and a half hectares of mainly wooded land, which stretched towards the hills, in the direction of Arcegno and Monte Verità on the right and Ronco sopra Ascona on the left. The estate stretched out on both sides of the current cantonal road, with grounds in the areas of Moscia and Rive Belle (in the municipality of Ascona) and of Curafora and Gruppaldo (in the municipality of Ronco). The four-story Villa Gabriella stood directly on the lake, with a well-kept garden that still extends over three terraces sloping down from the road to the water. Olga and Bettina lived on the lower floor of the house, which had a large kitchen and veranda, and on the first floor, which had bedrooms and a study, which is still the center of the building. The second and third floors, with bedrooms and mansard rooms, were reserved for their guests.[53] *(Figures 38–48)*

Fröbe-Kapteyn obtained a residence permit in the municipality of Ronco sopra Ascona, issued by the Central Police Directorate in Bellinzona, on November 5, 1920.[54] She and her daughter Bettina became citizens of the Republic and Canton of Ticino, in the municipality of Ascona, fourteen

finalizing the sale with another buyer, but he would wait to meet Albertus Kapteyn before deciding to whom to sell the property; Albertus Kapteyn saw Casa Gabriella for the first time, together with the then owner, on October 9, 1920, at 3 p.m. (Albertus Kapteyn, letter to André Germain, October 8, 1920 (Eranos Foundation Archives, Ascona-Moscia); more in general, see André Germain, *Florence et Ascona* (Paris: Sun, 1952)).

[52] Ritsema-Gris, *op. cit.*, p. 15. In Fröbe-Kapteyn's memory, her father did not like that mountainous landscape; he was Dutch and had always wanted to look beyond those mountains and was only happy in the plains, in the landscapes of his childhood. He could never have lived here. When he suggested that they share Villa Gabriella, she responded with that refusal, convinced that living together would never work between them (Fröbe-Kapteyn, "Mein Vater...," cit., p. 2). Yet, she would recall in her later years, "Gabriella was the building block of Eranos. This house determined where Eranos was to take shape. His donation of the house came at the 'right moment.' It was 'the moment'" (*ibid.*, p. 4).

[53] *Ibid.*, p. 16.

[54] No. 38561/2438.

years later, on January 10, 1934. She swore allegiance to her new homeland on January 30, 1934.[55]

At Casa Gabriella, Fröbe-Kapteyn spent a long period of "concentration discipline" lasting seven years (*siebenjährige Konzentrationsdiszipline*)[56], during which she devoted herself—with only the company of Bettina and a servant woman—to studying the *Vedānta* and other classics of Eastern thought, meditation practices, and Eastern and Western paths of spiritual realization.[57] Since the second half of the 1920s, she also began her geometrical painting practice, probably strongly influenced by the spiritualist and esoteric readings to which she had so intensely devoted herself in those years.[58]

During this phase, Fröbe-Kapteyn's contact with the outside world was sporadic. Only in 1926 did Fröbe-Kapteyn begin writing again to her friends to come and visit her in Moscia.[59] Starting in the second half of the 1920s, with the money she inherited from her father, she was also able to invite a relatively small number of people to Casa Gabriella. These included those few Dutch, English, and French artists, those few men of letters, musicians, and spiritualists with whom—despite her skepticism toward

---

[55] Bernardini, *op. cit.*, p. 252.

[56] Olga Fröbe-Kapteyn, "Die Geschichte von Eranos" (unpublished typescript, 1952–58; Eranos Foundation Archives, Ascona-Moscia), and specifically "Eranos. Fortsetzung" (unpublished typescript, 1952; Eranos Foundation Archives, Ascona-Moscia), p. 1; and Id., "Shadow of my Dedication to Eranos" (unpublished typescript, February 11, 1954; Eranos Foundation Archives, Ascona-Moscia), where she wrote about "the concentration training of 8 years. That kept me on the singleminded track of Eranos."

[57] The "concentration training," from 1926 to 1933, enabled her to understand how to open the door to the visionary world when she wanted to and also how to close it again. This was very important, because otherwise she would have remained "submerged" in the world of images. When she told Jung about this in 1934, he said, "Since you didn't slip away, this ability is a tool in your hands!" And so it was. Without that ability, she recognized, she would never have been able to work psychologically on her own. Both her father, with the development of photographic films in their darkroom in London and reading to her illustrated books, and her training in concentration stimulated her intuition—without which she would never have been able to lead Eranos (Fröbe-Kapteyn, "Mein Vater...," cit. ("Kommentar," February 10, 1957), p. 2). The exercise in concentration was a "Yahwistic activity" for her: she followed her method scrupulously without missing a single day. Such dedication explains the exceptional pictorial output documented in the "Meditation Plates" (Fröbe-Kapteyn, "Der Schatten," cit., August 1, 1957, "Kommentar," p. 5).

[58] Ritsema-Gris, *op. cit.*, pp. 17 f.

[59] *Ibid.*, p. 16.

the Ascona bohemianism of the 1920s and 1930s—she felt a spiritual affinity.

In 1927, while she was visiting the *Semaine Européenne* organized in Lausanne by Germain, Fröbe-Kapteyn made the acquaintance also of the Dutch poet Adriaan Roland Holst (1888–1976). She felt particularly in tune with him, probably because of their common interest in myth and dreams. Holst visited her in 1929, staying at Casa Gabriella until the following year and working with her on the English translation of the autobiographical work *De Afspraak*.[60]

The famous perennial breeder and garden philosopher Karl Foerster (1874–1970) and his wife Eva also stayed at Casa Gabriella in the late 1920s. *(Figure 65)* In Potsdam-Bornim, in 1912, Foerster had begun creating a display and experimental area for perennials in his garden. He aimed to demonstrate the diversity of perennials and shrubs, treating each plant as an individual entity. He was contacted by Fröbe-Kapteyn, who visited him in Bornim in 1929,[61] and helped his hostess to lay out, at least in part, her wonderful grounds overlooking the shores of the lake.[62]

Gardening was indeed Fröbe-Kapteyn's great passion. *(Figure 44)* She planted at Casa Gabriella the most beautiful and rare flowers and shrubs of all kinds. She was also proud to offer her guests delicacies from her lush vegetable garden.[63] On the top terrace close to the house stood a magnificent large cedar tree (now accompanied by an equally majestic cypress tree), under which one could enjoy the view of the lake from the upper terrace in front of the guest room. For her friends, Casa Gabriella was the most beautiful place to relax every year. *(Figures 50–55)* *"Wenn wieder ich geboren werde, So sei's in Olga's Blumenerde!"* ["When I am reborn,

[60] Cf. Jan van der Vegt, *A. Roland Holst. Biografie* (Baarn: de Prom, 2000), pp. 282 ff. Holst revisited Fröbe-Kapteyn in later years (cf. Hakl, *Eranos…*, cit, p. 17).

[61] See Clemens Alexander Wimmer, *Gärtner der Nation. Die vier Leben des Karl Foerster* (Weimar: Verlag und Datenbank für Geisteswissenschaften, 2024), p. 176.

[62] Annemarie Pallat, "Olga Fröbe" (unpublished typescript, April 29, 1962; Eranos Foundation Archives, Ascona-Moscia).

[63] Ritsema-Gris, *op. cit.*, p. 12.

let it be in Olga's flower soil!"] her friend Ludwig Pallat wrote in her guest book.[64] *(Figure 52)*

Annemarie Pallat recalled that, besides gardening, at that time Fröbe-Kapteyn's "favorite pastime was painting, and she used a very unique technique to create fantastic images out of colors and line ornaments, all of which had deep symbolic meanings. She had become a theosophist.[65] To us as laymen, they appeared as pure, wonderfully beautiful symphonies of color, which she sometimes also executed as embroidery with bright silk threads on a black background."[66] *(Figures 66–76)*

Fröbe-Kapteyn was also in contact with Rudolf Maria Holzapfel (1874–1930), psychologist, philosopher, and "prophet of Pan."[67] A photograph of Fröbe-Kapteyn with Anton (Rudolf) Mauve Jr. (1876–1962), a Dutch naturalist painter, was probably taken in Moscia in the late 1920s. *(Figure 49)*

The scholar Ludwig Derleth (1870–1948), although not directly involved in the Eranos adventure, would significantly influence its birth. He provided stimulus for Fröbe-Kapteyn's journey into the symbolic realm.[68] A poet and mystic, in his youth Derleth was close to the Kosmiker ("Cosmic" circle) of Munich, the group led by Alfred Schuler (1865–1923) that sought salvation from the corruption of contemporary civilization

---

[64] Ludwig Pallat, "An Olga Fröbe-Kapteyn" (unpublished typescript, October 11, 1927; Eranos Foundation Archives, Ascona-Moscia). The custom of placing fresh flowers in the rooms of guests and lecturers at Eranos was typical of Fröbe-Kapteyn, so much so that Mircea Eliade, arriving in Ascona for the umpteenth time in July 1959 and finding her in poor health, regretted not finding in her room "for the first time since 1952, the flowers that Olga used to put there a few hours before the train arrived" (Mircea Eliade, *Fragments d'un journal I–III, 1945–1985* (Paris: Gallimard, 1973-91); It. Ed. *Giornale* (Turin: Boringhieri, 1976), p. 211).

[65] As Karssenberg pointed out, Geertruida Kapteyn-Muysken accompanied psychiatrist Frederik Willem van Eeden (1860–1932) in London to see Helena Blavatsky, who was living with Annie Besant in their theosophical headquarters, in October 1890, when Olga was nine years old (from the Kapteyn-Muysken diaries); therefore, she had probably heard about Blavatsky already at that age. Also, in her correspondence with Marie Stopes, she refers to Blavatsky's readings and William Crookes's (1832–1919) spiritualism (Olga Fröbe-Kapteyn, letter to Marie Stopes, April 4, 1901 (British Library, London; transcripts kindly provided by Karssenberg)).

[66] Pallat, *op. cit.*

[67] Hakl, *Der verborgene Geist von Eranos…*, cit., pp. 54 f.

[68] Ritsema-Gris, *op. cit.*, 17 f.; Wehr, *op. cit.*, pp. 30 ff.

through the revival of a pagan-style religiosity.[69] Derleth was also an advocate of a militant and archaic Christianity and was in some ways close to Jung in noting how the individual soul had impersonal forces capable of being awakened under certain historical circumstances and at particular moments of cultural crisis.[70] Countess Franziska zu Reventlow (1871–1918), the queen of the Munich bohème who had settled in Ascona in 1909,[71] was an admirer of Derleth: she made a portrait of him and the "Cosmic" group in her novel *Herrn Dames Aufzeichnungen*.[72] Derleth, whom Fröbe-Kapteyn had known since the early 1910s,[73] had a considerable influence on her, not only by shaping her interest in symbolism but also by helping to initiate the Eranos project.[74]

Lothar Helbing (Wolfgang Frommel, 1902–1986), a student of the poet Stefan George (1868–1933), recalled: "Once, [Derleth] confirmed to

---

[69] On the Munich Cosmic circle, see Richard Faber, "Der Schwabinger Imperatorenstreit, (k)ein Sturm im Wasserglas. Über die Münchener Bohème im allgemeinen und die ‚Kosmiker Runde' insbesondere," in Richard Faber and Christine Holste, eds., *Kreise, Gruppen, Bünde. Zur Soziologie moderner Intellektuellenassoziation* (Würzburg: Könighausen + Neumann, 2000), pp. 37–64; on the connection between the Kosmiker circle and Eranos, see Barbara von Reibnitz, "Der Eranos-Kreis. Religionswissenschaft und Weltanschauung oder der Gelehrte als Laien-Priester," in Renate Schleiser and Roberto Sanchiño Martinez, eds., *Neuhumanismus und Anthropologie des griechischen Mythos. Karl Kerényi im europäischen Kontext des 20. Jahrhunderts* (Locarno: Rezzonico, 2006), p. 427; Hakl, *op. cit.*, pp. 38–51; and Georg Dörr, "Archetipo e storia ovvero Monaco-Ascona: prossimità tipologica e umana (con lettere di Olga Fröbe a Ludwig Derleth)," in Elisabetta Barone, Adriano Fabris, and Flavia Monceri, eds., *Eranos. Monte Verità. Ascona* (Pisa: ETS, 2003), pp. 105–21.

[70] *Ibid.*, pp. 114 f.

[71] See Franziska zu Reventlow, *Der Geldkomplex* (Munich: Albert Langen, 1916).

[72] Franziska zu Reventlow, *Herrn Dames Aufzeichnungen- oder Begebenheiten aus einem merkwürdigen Stadtteil* (Munich: Albert Langen, 1913); see also Richard Faber, *Männerrunde mit Gräfin. Die „Kosmiker" Derleth, George, Klages, Schuler, Wolfskehl und Franziska zu Reventlow* (Frankfurt am Main: Peter Lang, 1994), and Alexandra Tischel, "Tra i profeti. I romanzi di Franziska zu Reventlow e le 'tensioni' di fine secolo," in Barone, Fabris, and Monceri, *op. cit.*, pp. 253–67.

[73] See Dominik Jost, *Ludwig Derleth. Gestalt und Leistung* (Stuttgart: W. Kohlhammer GmbH, 1965), p. 74. In some notes prepared for her analysis with Léopold Szondi, she wrote that she had met Derleth in September 1920. Both aware that they belonged to a circle of kindred spirits, in the 1920s Fröbe-Kapteyn not only invited Derleth, her "Cher Illuminé" and "Maître fabuleux," to Ascona several times, but also offered him a permanent home, with a room always ready for him. Their correspondence continued until the 1940s. She had initially refused to collaborate on Jost's book, but then, after consulting the *I Ching*, she changed her mind (Stiftung Szondi-Institut Archive, Zurich).

[74] Ludwig Derleth, *Gedenkbuch*, texts by Lothar Helbing, Stefan George, Dominik Jost, Christine Derleth, and Anna Maria Derleth (Amsterdam: Castrum Peregrini, 1958), p. 70; Jost, *op. cit.*, pp. 99 ff.; and Hakl, *op. cit.*, p. 40.

me what I had already learned from Mrs. Olga Fröbe, namely that a hidden thread led from the 'Cosmics' in Munich to the founding of Eranos in Ascona, and that it was Derleth himself who brought the first news about Creuzer, Bachofen, and various mysteries involving Baalbeck, Eleusis, and Samothrace to the then still silent house on Lake Maggiore."[75] There could be "secret threads"[76] that linked the "Cosmic" group to the "prehistory"[77] of Eranos and its birth;[78] Fröbe-Kapteyn would probably have wanted Derleth to take part in the founding of Eranos—something that never happened.[79] Derleth, for whom Fröbe-Kapteyn had a long-standing affection,[80] visited her and her daughter Bettina at Casa Tabor, but never at Casa Gabriella.[81] In October 1922, Fröbe-Kapteyn and Derleth went together to Rome,[82] a city to which she would return on several occasions during the 1930s and 1940s for her iconographic research.

On August 23, 1921, Fröbe-Kapteyn wrote to Derleth, "You have brought me into relation, for the first time, with antiquity, and for this I am deeply grateful. It is strange how vivid and familiar these things are to me. I learn quickly and am far richer than in the Spring. Symbols are something that have become near and obvious to me. Now I look for them, and find them, in all things. In the Romanesque church of Sant'Ambrogio in Milan, [André] Jolles suddenly said, 'Here you find magic in its highest form.' I am sending you today a photograph of a bas-relief of Dionysus in London, which I have carried with me for many years. Jolles was telling the beautiful story of Ariadne and the Labyrinth yesterday."[83] Philosopher of religions Alfons Rosenberg (1902–1985)

---

[75] Derleth, *op. cit.*, p. 70.

[76] Jost, *op. cit.*, pp. 99 ff.

[77] *Ibid.*

[78] Derleth, *op. cit.*, p. 70.

[79] Hakl, *op. cit.*, p. 40.

[80] *Ibid.*, pp. 42 ff.

[81] Derleth, *op. cit.*, pp. 96 f.

[82] Jost, *op. cit.*, p. 103; James Webb, *Il sistema occulto. La fuga dalla ragione nella politica e nella società del XX secolo* (Milan: SugarCo, 1989 {1976}), p. 277; Hakl, *op. cit.*, p. 46; and Dörr, *op. cit.*, p. 106, fn. 3.

[83] Quoted in Hakl, *op. cit.*, pp. 43 f., and Dörr, *op. cit.*, pp. 119 f. When he was back from his Italian travels, André Jolles used to stop for a few days at Casa Gabriella to catch up with his great friend, often in the

recalled the episode in which Derleth invited Fröbe-Kapteyn to Munich: meeting at midnight sharp at Marienplatz, they walked together until dawn. Derleth described to her the symbolism of Munich, transfigured the city into a "carpet woven with symbols."[84] Christine Derleth, who used to address Fröbe-Kapteyn amicably with the expression "*Liebe Symbolistin!*" ["Dear Symbolist!"], wrote: "Olga, with sparkling eyes, sat on the Marienplatz opposite Ludwig, and absorbed the jumble of mythological images that formed the theme of the conversation. They expanded her inner life and transformed her into what she was to become in a decade: the founder of Eranos."[85]

From 1926 to 1935, Paul Zillmann, founder of the Metaphysische Hauptquartier and editor of the *Neue Metaphysische Rundschau* created in 1896, also played a decisive role in Fröbe-Kapteyn's life; she described him as "present in the spirit at the laying of the foundation stone of Eranos" and felt him to be Jung's "forerunner" in influencing her. He gave her a copy of *The Secret of the Golden Flower* (1929)[86] and the journal *Yoga*.[87] In 1926, at a time when she "was feeling about for something to undertake, and did not yet know what," he told her, "[t]he work will be found" (*das Werk wird sich schon finden*). Zillmann, whom Fröbe-Kapteyn considered an alchemist (he used homeopathic remedies, based on the studies of Paracelsus), gave her "distant treatment" (*Fernbehandlung*) for seven years. For her, he was nothing more than a voice throughout this period; they spoke by phone once a week and met once or twice a year

---

company of his second wife, Margarethe Grittli Boecklen (1895–1967) a drawing teacher with whom Fröbe-Kapteyn delighted in building puppets and other handicrafts (Hakl, *op. cit.*, p. 44, fn. 60). She reached him in Venice in August 1937 and they returned together to Casa Gabriella in September of the same year (Olga Fröbe-Kapteyn, letter to Marie Stopes, October 4, 2023 (British Library, London; transcript kindly provided by Karssenberg).

[84] Quoted in Hakl, *Eranos…*, cit., p. 22. A testimony by Rosenberg regarding the importance of Fröbe-Kapteyn's iconographic research can be found in Alfons Rosenberg, "Eranos oder Der Geist am Wasser," *Flugblätter für Freunde* 80 (1977), pp. 7–8.

[85] Derleth, *Gedenkbuch*, cit., p. 96; also quoted in Dörr, *op. cit.*, p. 106.

[86] *Das Geheimnis der Goldenen Blüte. Ein Chinesisches Lebensbuch*, ed. Richard Wilhelm (Munich: Dornverlag, 1929).

[87] As Vittorino Vezzani recalls, Fröbe-Kapteyn had the inspiration to invite contributors to the magazine *Yoga* published by Helmut Palmié in 1931 (and appeared in a single issue) to speak at the 1933 Eranos Conference (Vittorino Vezzani, "Eranos (simposio)," *Luce e Ombra*, 52 (5, 1952), pp. 301–04).

for a few hours. He was her "directing Voice from beyond, or from within."[88]

In September 1927 (her father had died in January of that year), Fröbe-Kapteyn had the "sudden idea" (*Einfall*) of building a Lecture Hall and organizing conferences on topics she had been interested in for years.[89] The idea came to her when she was intent on making a "geometric drawing," belonging to the "Meditation Plates" which she had begun painting in the mid-1920s. In that geometric drawing—inspired by the daily view from the windows of Casa Gabriella on the Brissago Islands, which played a significant role in her imagination *(Figure 56)*—she recognized the "first manifestation of the Temple plan" (*Erstes Aufkommen des Templergrundrisses*)[90] from which the plan of Casa Eranos took shape. *(Figure 57)* According to her, the highly geometrized style of the basic structure of the building harkened back to the "mathematical Animus" she inherited through the long line of mathematical geniuses in her father's family.[91] Jung wrote: "Anticipatory dreams, telepathic phenomena, and all

---

[88] Olga Fröbe-Kapteyn, "Paul Zillmann. 1926–1935" (unpublished typescript, undated [1944?]; Eranos Foundation Archives, Ascona-Moscia). Zillmann "possessed my deep affection, which Jung has never done," Fröbe-Kapteyn recalled (*ibid.*). In a series of reflections on her inner visions, Fröbe-Kapteyn associated Zillmann with a "white magician" and Derleth with a "black magician" (Fröbe-Kapteyn, "Drei Zeichnungen," cit., p. 2). Zillmann is also mentioned by Alice Bailey in a letter sent on February 5, 1931 to Fröbe-Kapteyn, concerning the second meeting of the International Centre for Spiritual Research (Eranos Foundation Archives, Ascona-Moscia). Fröbe-Kapteyn even noted: "Zillmann impersonated all occult knowledge (even more than A.[lice Ann] Bailey), alchemy, healing power, plus great scientific knowledge, plus *humility*. So my occult komplex was divided, half in Europe [with Zillmann], and half in America [with Bailey]. I have not lost him, because he is so evidently the reflection of the occultist and alchemist within myself. The only negative thing about him was his suppression of all his problems, their projection onto his wife [Lene], who as a result had all kinds of illness. That is Zillmann was deeply unconscious of his own problems" (Fröbe-Kapteyn, "Paul Zillmann. 1926–1935," cit.; Jung's inner image eventually helped her to free herself both from Zillmann, the German person to whom she was most attached, and with him also symbolically from Germany (see Id., "Vision. 5 August 1946" (unpublished typescript, August 5, 1946; Eranos Foundation Archives, Ascona-Moscia)).

[89] Olga Fröbe-Kapteyn, "Eranos Institute for Research into Religious Symbolism (Archetypal Images)" (unpublished typescript, 1947; Eranos Foundation Archives, Ascona-Moscia), p. 4; and Id., "Eranos Institut für Symbolforschung" (unpublished typescript, September 28, 1947; Eranos Foundation Archives, Ascona-Moscia), p. 2.

[90] Olga Fröbe-Kapteyn, "Die Eranos *Mandala*" (unpublished typescript, 1927–49; Eranos Foundation Archives, Ascona-Moscia).

[91] Fröbe-Kapteyn, "Eranos Vortrag," cit., p. 1; cf. also Id., "Die Geschichte…," cit., and specifically "Notes for the Story of Eranos" (unpublished typescript, undated [1957?]; Eranos Foundation Archives, Ascona-Moscia), p. 1.

that kind of thing are intuitions ... It is always something that is unconscious until the moment it appears ... The Germans call it *Einfall*, which means a thing which falls into your head from nowhere."[92] Casa Eranos was thus built in the Bauhaus style in 1928.[93] *(Figure 58–60)* The third house on her property, together with Casa Gabriella and Casa Eranos, was probably built between 1928 and 1929 and named Casa Shanti (Sanskrit for "peace") in 1932;[94] *(Figures 77 and 78)* the ceremony was presided over by a young Telugu-speaking Brahmin, Venkatesa (Venkatesh) Narayana Sharma (1897–1986), who had come to Europe from India through the Theosophical movement.[95]

Before the creation of the actual Eranos project in 1933, Fröbe-Kapteyn made a first attempt at a congressional experience, with a more markedly esoteric imprint. Around 1928, while visiting her brother Albert in Long Island, United States, she got to know the works of the theosophist Alice Ann Bailey (1880–1949) and her Arcane School, which arose in 1923 from a split of the Theosophical Society of Helena Petrovna Blavatsky

[92] Carl Gustav Jung, "The Tavistock Lectures. On the Theory and Practice of Analytical Psychology" {1935}, in *The Collected Works of C.G. Jung*, Vol. 18 (Princeton, NJ: Bollingen Series XX, Princeton University Press, 1976), par. 26.

[93] The first documented cadastral change (no. 86) relating to the construction of Casa Eranos is dated December 29, 1928. Construction work began in fact in December of that year: see Olga Fröbe-Kapteyn, letters to Ernst Bernhard with biographical information, September 1 and September 2, 1954 (Ernst and Dora Bernhard Collection, Historical Archive of Italian Psychology (ASPI), University of Milan-Bicocca; kindly provided by McGilvray). The identity of the building's designer is unknown, but it could reasonably be an architect belonging to the school of Carl Weidemeyer (1882–1976) and the "Rationalists of Ascona": see Bruno Mauer, "Carl Weidemeyer und ‚die Rationalisten von Ascona'," in Letizia Tedeschi, ed., *Carl Weidemeyer 1882–1976. Künstler und Anarchist zwischen Worpswede und Ascona* (Mendrisio/Ascona/Milano: Accademia di architettura, Università della Svizzera italiana/Museo comunale d'arte moderna/Skira, 2001), p. 142, fig. 1, showing Casa Eranos in a photograph taken by Sigfried Giedion in 1930 (ETH Library Zurich).

[94] Cf. Ritsema-Gris, *op. cit.*, p. 19. The first documented cadastral change (no. 736) relating to the construction of Casa Shanti is dated July 27, 1932. Casa Shanti was sold by Fröbe-Kapteyn in 1937 to Emma Hélène von Pelet-Narbonne, who was joined in the same year by Alwina (Alwine) von Keller (cadastral mutation no. 1253 of August 14, 1937).

[95] McGuire, *op. cit.*, p. 152; Id., "The Arcane Summer School," *Spring* (1980), p. 152; and Ritsema-Gris, *op. cit.*, p. 81. Sharma was also among the audience at the 1933 symposium (see Riccardo Bernardini, Gian Piero Quaglino, and Augusto Romano, "Appendix II. Alwine von Keller (1878–1965). A Biographical Memoir," in Carl Gustav Jung, *The Solar Myths and Opicinus de Canistris. Notes of the Seminar Given at Eranos in 1943*, eds. Riccardo Bernardini, Gian Piero Quaglino, and Augusto Romano (Einsiedeln: Daimon, 2015), p. 130, fn. 20; and Riccardo Bernardini, "In analisi con Jung. I diari di Emma von Pelet," *Rivista di Psicologia Analitica*, 91 (39, 2015), pp. 219–36).

(1831–1891).[96] Fröbe-Kapteyn spent a few days at Bailey's estate in Stamford, Connecticut (made available to the Baileys by millionaire James Graham Phelp-Stokes, 1872–1960), and proposed to her to collaborate in the creation, in Ascona, of a "nondenominational spiritual center open to all scholars of esotericism of any geographical origin and religious faith," offering hospitality to Alice and her husband Foster Bailey (1888–1977) and Bailey's three young daughters, Dorothy Margaret Matilda Evans, Mildred Evans, and Ellison Anne Sybil Evans.[97] *(Figure 79)*

---

[96] Alice Ann Bailey, born in Manchester to an Anglican family, had a mystical experience at the age of fifteen that was particularly significant for her: one Sunday morning in Scotland, she was visited by a man dressed in elegant clothes, wearing a turban, who introduced himself as "the Master" and announced that she had been predestined for a mission. Twenty-three years later, having become a member of the Theosophical Society and editor of its magazine, *The Messenger*, and working as manager of the vegetarian café in Krotona, among the paintings on display in the temple of the "Esoteric Section" of the Theosophical Society, she recognized in the figure of Master Koot Hoomi, who had already appeared to other leaders of the society, such as Blavatsky herself and Jiddu Krishnamurti (1895–1986), the mysterious individual who had visited her in Scotland. Divorced in 1919 from her first husband, Reverend Walter Jenkin Evans (1856–1927), rector of a church near Fresno, with whom she had three daughters, she married the then National Secretary of the Theosophical Society, Foster Bailey. She left meanwhile the Theosophical Society to found her own Arcane School in 1923: a school that was "non-doctrinal, non-sectarian, and based on the eternal wisdom that has been handed down to us since the dawn of time." The dispute behind the split saw Annie Besant, then president of the Theosophical Society, as a co-protagonist. In addition to the aforementioned Koot Hoomi, another "visitor" had an equally important destiny for Bailey. He appeared in November 1919 and was identified by her as "the Tibetan," Djwhal Khul, who entrusted her with the task of writing and publishing several books. In May 1929, in New York, Fröbe-Kapteyn was initiated into the Arcane School at the rank of "Disciple." She was active in the school for about two years; she belonged to the highest rank of the Arcane School—a rank created specifically for the study of her "Meditation Plates"; she also drew the large figure used by the Arcane School and displayed at its headquarters in New York; she would disaffiliate from this group four years later, in June 1933. Cf. Olga Fröbe-Kapteyn, "19 Mai 44" (unpublished typescript, May 19, 1944; Eranos Foundation Archives, Ascona-Moscia), p. 2.

[97] See Alice Ann Bailey, *The Unfinished Autobiography of Alice A. Bailey* (New York, NY: Lucis Publishing Co., 1951), pp. 217 ff.; Ritsema-Gris, *op. cit.*, 17 f.; and Wehr, *op. cit.*, pp. 35 ff. Referring to their meeting in the United States, Bailey's autobiography mentions the year 1930; McGuire suggests however that the author made a mistake and dates the meeting between the two women to two years before the start of the Ascona "Summer School" sessions, i.e., 1928 (cf. McGuire, *op. cit.*, p. 147). The Baileys stayed at Casa Gabriella for their first year, then moved to Casa Shanti in 1931. The rest of the participants stayed at the Hotel Monte Verità or the Hotel Collinetta (*ibid.*, p. 154). In Ascona, a friendship developed between the Bailey family and Baron Eduard von der Heydt, owner of Monte Verità since 1926 (Alice Ann Bailey, letter to Olga Fröbe-Kapteyn, November 12, 1930 (Eranos Foundation Archives, Ascona-Moscia); see also the "Gästebuch Monte Verità," ed. Alexandra Barbian, in Eberhard Illner, ed., *Eduard von der Heydt. Kunstsammler, Bankier, Mäzen*, (Munich/London/New York, NY: Prestel, 2013), p. 239; Fröbe-Kapteyn's signature appears in the "Gästebuch" on August 18, 1930 – *ibid.*). However, the girls were involved in alleged erotic adventures that caused quite a scandal in Ascona: there is even mention of a little "getaway" to France, accompanied by Fröbe-Kapteyn's driver, Mario Nigra: an episode that

In 1929, Fröbe-Kapteyn devoted herself to preparing the first symposium,[98] and on August 3, 1930, at 5 p.m., courses began at the International Centre for Spiritual Research.[99] *(Figure 80)* There were eighty chairs in the conference room and fifteen nationalities were represented: the register of the congress collected the signatures of ninety-four participants. The sessions lasted for three weeks, from Monday to Saturday, with three lectures per day, while a fourth week was made available for private meetings with the speakers. In Fröbe-Kapteyn's inaugural speech, which opened the courses, the idea of "creating a meeting place between East and West" already appeared, which was later taken up in the subsequent Eranos project, where the spiritual peculiarities of both realities could be discussed and brought back to a common "synthesis."

In this "prehistory" of Eranos, in addition to Fröbe-Kapteyn and the Baileys, the following lecturers were involved between 1930 and 1932: philosopher Frederick Kettner (1886–1957), founder of Biosophy (the doctrine of intelligent living based on character qualities); Shri Vishwanath Keskar, author, together with James Graham Phelps-Stokes, of *Pillars of Life* in 1931; mystical freemason Grand Duke Alexander Mikhailovich of Russia (1866–1933); spiritualist Violet Tweedale (1862–1936), disciple of Blavatsky and member of the Hermetic Order of the Golden Dawn; Irish writer and poet James H. Cousins (1873–1956), founder with his wife Margaret of the Irish Vegetarian Society in 1905 and whose first lecture was accompanied by an exhibition of modern art; Dutch artist Agnes Johanna Elisabeth van Stolk (1898–1980); Stephen Annett, scholar of the Grail tradition and alchemy; art historian, painter, and museum director Count Kuno von Hardenberg (1871–1938), formerly active in Count Hermann Keyserling's "School of Wisdom"; astronomer Robert Henseling (1883–1964); J.L. Schmitt; Paul S. Bendix; Hebraist Leo Baeck; Mírzá Aḥmad Sohráb (1890–1958), founder of the New History Society and the Caravan of East and

she did not appreciate at all (Olga Fröbe-Kapteyn, letter to Alice Ann Bailey, March 22, 1933 (Eranos Foundation Archives, Ascona-Moscia)).

[98] Fröbe-Kapteyn, "Eranos Vortrag," cit., p. 1.

[99] The original name, "Summer School," was replaced that same year with "International Centre for Spiritual Research."

West: of Bahá'í faith, he had served as secretary of 'Abdu'l-Bahá's (the eldest son of Bahá'u'lláh, founder of the Bahá'í faith) and was excommunicated in 1939 by Shoghi Effendi; Gerald Reynolds, director of the American Conservatory in Fontainebleau; J.C. Demarquette, who authored *Vers l'Australie. Notes d'un naturiste européen* in 1930; Prince Hubertus zu Löwenstein-Wertheim-Freudenberg (1906–1984), later decorated by Pope John XXIII for his work in reconciling the Catholic Church and the Greek Orthodox Church; Nikolaj Konstantinovič (Nicholas) Roerich (1874–1947), painter, theosophist, and expert on Tibet who contributed to fueling the Blavatskian myth of Shambhala in the collective imagination of the West; psychologist Jean Émile Marcault (1878–1968), who authored *Psychology of Intuition* (1927) and *The Evolution of Man. Being an Outline of the Development of Human Consciousness as Illustrated by the Pre-Aryan and Arian Races* (1931) and translated the *Bhagavadgītā* commented by Sarvepalli Radhakrishnan (he was awarded the Subba Row Medal in 1936 for his contribution to theosophical literature); novelist Raja Rao (1909–2006), among the fathers of Anglo-Indian literature; Eugen Georg, author of *The Adventure of Mankind* (1931); Dutch scholar of Celtic religions F.C.J. Los; Pāli scholar and Buddhist Helmut Palmié (1896–1954), first publisher of the journal *Yoga*; Orientalist Erwin Rousselle; psychologist Roberto Assagioli (1888–1974), founder of Psychosynthesis;[100] and finally Vittorino Vezzani (1885–1955), appointed in 1938 to the position of Professor of General Animal Husbandry at the Faculty of Agricultural Sciences of the

[100] Present at the sessions of 1930, 1931, and 1932, Roberto Assagioli had met Jung in 1907, while he was at Burghölzli preparing his thesis on the subject of psychoanalysis. Fröbe-Kapteyn had already mentioned Assagioli to Derleth in a postcard sent from Italy on May 23, 1928 (Eranos Foundation Archives, Ascona-Moscia). During the symposiums of the International Centre for Spiritual Research, Assagioli stayed at the Hotel Monte Verità. When Fröbe-Kapteyn visited Assagioli in Rome in 1940, she saw a series of her "Meditation Plates" displayed in his room (Fröbe-Kapteyn, "19 Mai 44," cit., p. 2). *(Figure 81)* In a letter dated July 31, 1963, Assagioli informed Rudolf Ritsema that he would be unable to speak at that year's Eranos Conference because he was busy with the International Meeting for the Education of the Supergifted (Capolona and Arezzo, August 3–6, 1963); nevertheless, he expressed his interest in the work of Eranos and sent his best wishes for the success of the conferences. On Assagioli's participation in the activities of the International Centre for Spiritual Research, see Roberto Assagioli, *Educare l'uomo domani. Appunti e note di lavoro* (Florence: Istituto di Psicosintesi, 1988), pp. 29 ff.; McGuire, *op. cit.*, p. 151 ff.; Alessandro Berti, *Roberto Assagioli 1888–1988* (Florence: Centro Studi di Psicosintesi "R. Assagioli," 1988), p. 33; and Paola Giovetti, *Roberto Assagioli. La vita e l'opera del fondatore della Psicosintesi* (Rome: Mediterranee, 1995), p. 45.

University of Turin, director of the Institute of Animal Husbandry and Dairy Science for Piedmont, vice president of the Italian Society of Metapsychics since 1955, and a distinguished researcher in the field of philosophical and religious studies,[101] who continued to nurture an interest in Eranos in the years that followed.[102] According to William McGuire, Bailey would probably have liked to involve Jung in their project, but Fröbe-Kapteyn thought that the time was not right.[103] For the symposium being prepared for the following summer, Olga Fröbe also invited Albert Einstein (1879–

---

[101] See Vittorino Vezzani, *Il misticismo cristiano e indiano* (Milan: Fratelli Bocca, 1951); Id., *Il fine dell'Uomo e altri saggi spirituali* (Milan: Fratelli Bocca, 1952); and Id., *Le mysticisme dans le monde* (Paris: Payot, 1955).

[102] In 1930, Vittorino Vezzani gave a series of lectures in English at the International Centre for Spiritual Research on "Yoga & the Education of the Soul," "Our Individual Place in Life & our Mission," "The Fundamental Psychological Laws, relating to the Education of the Soul," and "The Practical Application of These Laws." In 1931, in French, he spoke on "What is Mysticism," "Mysticism in Relation to Psychology, Philosophy, Art, and Science," "The Characteristics of Modern Mysticism," and, in English, on the "Common Sense and Spiritual Life" and "Profile of a Modern Mysticism"; in 1932, he dealt with topics such as "The Goal of Man" and "The Path of Attainment." Some of these essays later appeared in English in the *Hibbert Journal* and in *The Beacon* (Alice Ann Bailey, "August 1930" (unpublished typescript; Eranos Foundation Archive, Ascona-Moscia), p. 10), where also Fröbe-Kapteyn published an article (Olga Fröbe-Kapteyn, "Know Thy Self," *The Beacon. A Periodical devoted to Occultism*, 8 (May 2, 1929), pp. 31–35). Vezzani, who was also among the listeners at the Eranos Conferences in 1934, 1938, 1952, and 1953, published two contributions on Eranos in the parapsychology magazine *Luce e ombra* (see Gian Piero Quaglino, Augusto Romano, and Riccardo Bernardini, eds., *Carl Gustav Jung a Eranos 1933–1952* (Turin: Antigone, 2007), p. 15). The magazine, founded in 1901 and suppressed in 1939 by the fascist regime, was edited in those years by Gastone de Boni (1908–1986), founder of the Archivio di Documentazione Storica della Ricerca Psichica (Archive of Historical Documentation of Psychic Research) in Bologna, who had a personal interest in Jung's work (Gastone de Boni, "Una visita a Carl Gustav Jung," *Luce e Ombra*, 49 (4, 1949), pp. 212–19). The correspondence between Fröbe-Kapteyn and the Vezzani couple, Letizia and Vittorino, testifies to a sincere and deep bond. Contact was temporarily interrupted due to the war, but resumed in 1945 (Vittorino Vezzani, letters to Olga Fröbe-Kapteyn, November 5, 1945 and December 31, 1945, both from Rialmosso di Balma Biellese (Eranos Foundation Archives, Ascona-Moscia)). In 1938, his signature in the conference register was followed by that of Pietro Ubaldi (1886–1972), a teacher, philosopher, and scholar of metaphysics who lived in Gubbio.

[103] McGuire, *Bollingen...*, cit., p. 22. In a letter written by Fröbe-Kapteyn to Jung on January 30, 1931, she invited him to give a lecture on "The Secret of the Golden Flower" (which he had received from Richard Wilhelm in 1928) during the second session of the International Centre for Spiritual Research. The letterhead, of course, did not yet bear the name "Eranos" (the Conferences would begin in 1933), but rather "Casa Gabriella." In a letter dated June 15, 1932, Jung replied to her: "If I should ever be in your area, I would like to visit you. I would prefer not to talk about the 'Secret of the Golden Flower,' as this would require psychological preparation that would be too demanding" (University Archives, ETH-Bibliothek, Zurich / Eranos Foundation Archives, Ascona-Moscia; © 2007 Foundation of the Works of C.G. Jung, Zurich). Jung did not participate in the three sessions of the International Centre, but he began attending the Eranos Conferences from their very first edition in August 1933.

1955), who was in Berlin at the time but about to leave for Princeton. The physicist thanked her but declined the invitation due to his busy schedule.[104]

The International Centre for Spiritual Research remained operational for three years, from 1930 to 1932, a period generally referred to as the "Shadow" (*Schatten*) of Eranos, its "roots" (*Wurzeln*), or rather—as Jung used to call it—its "dark spirit" (*dunkler Geist*).[105] When this enterprise came to an end after the third session, in 1932, due to both Fröbe-Kapteyn's intellectual maturation and certain personal differences with Bailey that had become irreconcilable,[106] the Eranos project was finally ready to start.[107]

The name "Eranos" (from Greek "banquet") was suggested to Fröbe-Kapteyn by historian of religions Rudolf Otto (1869–1937), who led the Marburg ecumenical group and wrote *The Holy* (1917), the ground-breaking essay on phenomenological analysis of religious experience.[108]

---

[104] Albert Einstein, letter to Olga Fröbe-Kapteyn, November 12, 1932 (Eranos Foundation Archives, Ascona-Moscia). Einstein's colleague at Princeton University, Max Knoll, would go on to speak at Eranos on four occasions between 1951 and 1965.

[105] Olga Fröbe-Kapteyn, "Arcane School. Positive Values. Negative Values" (unpublished typescript, undated [second half of the 1940s?]; Eranos Foundation Archives, Ascona-Moscia), p. 2; and Id., "The 4th Function and the Tibetan" (unpublished typescript, 1944; Eranos Foundation Archives, Ascona-Moscia), pp. 5 and 9.

[106] In Fröbe-Kapteyn's memory, Bailey directed everything in the early meetings of the International Centre. As head of the Arcane School, she wrote her books under the dictation of a Tibetan lama—a bit like Blavatsky with *The Secret Doctrine* (1888). She had an air of superiority and was a brilliant speaker, always surrounded by the mysterious aura of her Tibetan master, who was inaccessible to anyone else (he lived in Tibet, remained anonymous, and dictated telepathically). Fröbe-Kapteyn had read Blavatsky's *The Secret Doctrine* in 1908, and, although she did not understand it, she considered it the most important book on theosophy (Olga Fröbe-Kapteyn, letter to Marie Stopes, July 28, 1908 (British Library, London; transcript kindly provided by Karssenberg)). In the third year of the Centre's activity, Bailey's leadership and power became unbearable to Fröbe-Kapteyn, who realized that Eranos's work would end up in a dead end if it continued in that way. She fell seriously ill just before the third symposium with neuropathic pains in her back and head and a fever of 40°C. In the end, she opened the conference with enormous effort and in the fall she severed her working relationship with Bailey (Fröbe-Kapteyn, "Drei Zeichnungen," cit., p. 2; see also Id., letter to Alice Ann Bailey, March 22, 1933 (Eranos Foundation Archives, Ascona-Moscia).

[107] On the project of the International Centre for Spiritual Research, see McGuire, "The Arcane Summer School," cit., and Bernardini, *Jung a Eranos...*, cit., pp. 259–64.

[108] Rudolf Otto, *Das Heilige. Über das Irrationale in der Idee zum Göttlichen und sein Verhältnis zum Rationalen* (Breslau: Trewendt & Granier, 1922).

Another of Otto's works, *Mysticism East and West: A Comparative Analysis of the Nature of Mysticism* (1926)—a comparative study of Śankara and Meister Eckhart—inspired Fröbe-Kapteyn in her choice of subtitle for her project: *Begegnungsstätte für Ost und West* ("Meeting Place for East and West").[109] Fröbe-Kapteyn had approached Otto in 1931. The Marburg ecumenical group, which emerged from liberal evangelical theology, took its name from the German university where its most prominent representatives taught. Among them were the historians of religion Friedrich Heiler and Ernst Benz, who were later involved in Eranos as lecturers. This circle allowed Fröbe-Kapteyn to encounter for the first time a conception of religiosity that went beyond the study of religions as codified systems: this approach shifted the focus of the religious phenomenon towards a religiosity understood as a universal happening of the human soul, namely the individual experience of the "numinous" (*numinosum*).

Fröbe-Kapteyn recalled her meeting with Otto as follows: "When, on that memorable evening in November 1932, I rang the doorbell of the great religious scholar Rudolf Otto, a creative moment began for me and, as if on a stage, the curtain rose. Otto himself came to open the door and everything about him welcomed me, Eranos, and the moment itself. It was both an inner and outer encounter, and he himself realized the significance of the situation."[110] Otto welcomed Fröbe-Kapteyn's proposal with particular enthusiasm, exclaiming, "I'm leaving for Locarno the day after tomorrow!" He thus visited her in Ascona the following December.[111] It was on that occasion, at Fröbe-Kapteyn's request to suggest a name for her project, that Otto proposed the Greek lemma "*Eranos*" ("banquet.")[112] He

---

[109] Rudolf Otto, *West-Östliche Mystik. Vergleich und Unterscheidung zur Wesensdeutung* (Gotha: Leopold Klotz, 1926).

[110] Quoted in Aniela Jaffé, "Carlo Gustav Jung e i convegni di Eranos" {1975}, in Id., *Saggi sulla psicologia di Carl Gustav Jung* (Rome: Paoline, 1984), p. 113.

[111] Fröbe-Kapteyn, "Die Geschichte...," cit., "Eranos. Fortsetzung," cit., p. 1.

[112] *Ibid.*, 2. In 1933, Otto also said he would call her "*Erana*" (Olga Fröbe-Kapteyn, "Mary and Eranos" (unpublished typescript, November 23, 1942; Eranos Foundation Archives, Ascona-Moscia). On the Greek meaning of the word and its use throughout history, up to Fröbe-Kapteyn's Eranos, see Bernardini, *op. cit.*, § 1.1: "La parola *eranos*," pp. 29–39.

also gave her a long list of names of scholars who might be of interest to her program, thus "sponsoring" an initiative that he had not been able to realize until then with his Religiöser Menschheitsbund ("Interreligious League of Mankind"), founded in 1921. Although he was too ill to take part in this new venture, Otto was considered by Fröbe-Kapteyn to be the "godfather" (*Pate*) of Eranos.[113] *(Figures 95 and 97)*

Sinologist Richard Wilhelm (1873–1930), who presented his translation of the ancient oracular Chinese text, the *I Ching*, in 1923,[114] was another important influence on Fröbe-Kapteyn. His work marked a turning point in the academic interpretation of the religious testimonies of extra-European cultures: they were no longer merely ethnological material, but expressions of subjectivity endowed with their own existential and spiritual reality.[115]

At the Schule der Weisheit ("School of Wisdom"), led in Darmstadt by Count Hermann von Keyserling (1880–1946), Fröbe-Kapteyn found a group of researchers devoted to the search for the "common roots of all religions" and encountered for the first time Wilhelm's edition of the *I Ching*. Jung himself gave some lectures within this circle.[116] Among the

---

[113] On the influence of Rudolf Otto on the work of Eranos, see Josef Höfer and Karl Rahner, eds., *Lexikon für Theologie und Kirche* (Freiburg im Breisgau: Herder, 1959), Vol. III, pp. 954 ff.; Hakl, *Der verborgene Geist von Eranos…*, cit., pp. 92–99; Id., *Eranos…*, cit., pp. 39–43; Henry Corbin, "De l'Iran à Eranos," *Du. Schweizerische Monatsschrift*, 15 (4, 1955), p. 29; Gerard Wiegers, "Henry Corbin and the *Gospel of Barnabas*," in: Mohammad Ali Amir-Moezzi, Christian Jambet, and Pierre Lory, eds., *Henry Corbin. Philosophies et sagesses des Religions du Livre. Actes du Colloque « Henry Corbin ». Sorbonne, November 6–8, 2003. Colloquium organized by the École Pratique des Hautes Études and the Centre d'Études des Religions du Livre* (Turnhout: Brepols, 2005), p. 189; and more recently Marianna Ferrara, "Olga Fröbe-Kapteyn's *Ashram*: The Great Mother and the Personal History of Eastern Religions," *ASDIWAL. Revue genevoise d'anthropologie et d'histoire des religions*, 16 (2021), pp. 79–94.

[114] *I Ging. Das Buch der Wandlungen*, ed. Richard Wilhelm (Jena: Eugen Diederichs, 1924).

[115] See Wehr, *op. cit.*, pp. 47 f., and Rudolf Ritsema, "Encompassing Versatility: Keystone of the Eranos Project / Allumfassende Wendigkeit: Schlußstein des Eranos-Projekts / Versatilité englobante: Clef de voûte du projet Eranos," *Eranos-Jahrbuch*, 57 (1988), pp. VII–LVII. On the significance of the *I Ching* throughout the history of Eranos, see also the recent works by Matteo Sgorbati, *L'I Ching a Eranos. Wilhelm, Jung e la ricezione del classico dei mutamenti* (Naples, Orientexpress, 2021); MariaCruz Mañas Peñalver, "El Oráculo del *I Ching*: Un Capitulo de la Historia de la Psicología Profunda," Ph.D. Dissertation, Escuela Internacional de Doctorado, Universidad Nacional de Educación a Distancia (UNED), Madrid, 2021; Id., "El *I Ching* en Eranos," in *I Ching. El Libro de los Cambios. El proyecto del I Ching de Eranos*, eds. Rudolf Ritsema, Shantena Augusto Sabbadini, and María Cruz Mañas Peñalver (Córdoba: Editorial Cántico, 2022), pp. 93–118; and Shantena Augusto Sabbadini, "Rudolf Ritsema," in *I Ching. El Libro de los Cambios…*, cit., pp. 119–33.

[116] Fröbe-Kapteyn and Jung are believed to have met in Darmstadt in 1930, on the occasion of the last conference organized at the "School of Wisdom" (see Fröbe-Kapteyn, "Erster Abend…," cit., p. 15;

intellectuals close to the "School of Wisdom," brought together by their interest in promoting Eastern spiritual thought,[117] were psychiatrist and psychoanalyst Alfred Adler (1870–1937); ethnologist and Africanist Leo Frobenius (1873–1938); Thomas Mann (1875–1955), winner of the Nobel Prize for Literature in 1929; philosopher Max Scheler (1874–1928); Rabindranath Tagore (1861–1941), winner of the Nobel Prize for Literature in 1913; theologian Ernst Troeltsch (1865–1923); philosopher of history Leopold Ziegler (1881–1958), and Count Kuno von Hardenberg.[118] Some of them, such as psychotherapist and astrology scholar Sigrid Strauß-Kloebe (1896–1987), historian of religions Gerardus van der Leeuw, and Leo Baeck, would later reappear at Eranos as lecturers.[119]

In August 1933, Fröbe-Kapteyn started the Eranos Conferences (*Eranos Tagungen*), which would attract over the following decades some of the most influential scholars of the twentieth century. *(Figures 117–120)* In addition to Jung, among them were psychologists Gustav-Richard Heyer (1890–1967), Joseph Bernhard Lang (1881–1945), Erich Neumann (1905–1960), Louis Beirnaert (1906–1985), Marie-Louise von Franz (1915–1998), Ira Progoff (1921–1998), James Hillman (1926–2011), Hayao Kawai (1928–2007), and Wolfgang Giegerich (1942); historians of religions Raffaele Pettazzoni (1883–1959), Gerardus van der Leeuw (1890–1950), Friedrich Heiler (1892–1967), Joseph Campbell (1904–1987), Mircea Eliade (1907–1986), and Ernst Benz (1907–1978); historians of Christianity Ernesto Buonaiuti (1881–1946) and Jean Guénolé Marie Daniélou (1905–1974); scholars of classical world religions Walter Friedrich Gustav Hermann Otto (1874–1958) and Károly Kerényi (1897–1973); orientalists Caroline Augusta Foley Rhys Davids (1857–

Ritsema-Gris, *op. cit.*, p. 20; Jaffé, *op. cit.*, p. 113; McGuire, *Bollingen...*, cit., p. 24; Rosenbaum-Kroeber, *op. cit.*, pp. 119 f.; Nadia Neri, *Oltre l'Ombra. Donne intorno a Jung* (Rome: Borla, 1995), p. 187; Hakl, *Eranos...*, cit., p. 26; and von Reibnitz, *op. cit.*, p. 110; in a private document, Fröbe-Kapteyn recalls instead that her first meeting with Jung took place in May 1933: cf. Olga Fröbe-Kapteyn, "Thinking Function" (unpublished typescript, undated [1944?]; Eranos Foundation Archives, Ascona-Moscia)).

[117] Sonu Shamdasani, "Il viaggio di Jung verso l'Oriente," in Carl Gustav Jung, *La psicologia del Kundalini-Yoga. Seminario tenuto nel 1932* (Turin: Bollati Boringhieri, 2004), pp. 25 ff.

[118] Kuno von Hardenberg participated in the second symposium of the International Centre for Spiritual Research (1931).

[119] On the relationship between the "School of Wisdom" and Fröbe-Kapteyn's Eranos, see Webb, *op. cit.*, pp. 278 ff.; Ritsema-Gris, *op. cit.*, pp. 20 f.; Wehr, *op. cit.*, pp. 45 ff.; Hakl, *Der verborgene Geist von Eranos...*, cit., pp. 63 ff.; and von Reibnitz, *op. cit.*, pp. 110 ff.

1942), Jakob Wilhelm Hauer (1881–1962), Paul Masson-Oursel (1882–1961), Heinrich Zimmer (1890–1943), Erwin Rousselle (1890–1949), and Giuseppe Tucci (1894–1984); scholars of Judaism Leo Baeck (1873–1956), Martin Buber (1878–1965), Erwin R. Goodenough (1893–1965), and Gershom Scholem (1897–1982); theologians Paul Tillich (1886–1965), Martin Cyril D'Arcy (1888–1976), Hugo Rahner (1900–1968), Pierre-Jean de Menasce (1902–1973), Victor White (1902-1960), Heinz Westman (1902-1986), and David L. Miller (1936); scholars of Islam Louis Massignon (1883–1962), Henry Corbin (1903–1978), and Toshihiko Izutsu (1914–1993); Egyptologists Georges Hermann Nagel (1899–1956), Charles Robert Cecil Augustine Allberry (1911–1943), and Erik Hornung (1933–2022); sinologists Paul Pelliot (1878–1945) and Hellmut Wilhelm (1905–1990); scholars of Gnosis Henri-Charles Puech (1902–1986) and Gilles Quispel (1916–2006); Zen Buddhism scholar Daisetsu Teitarō Suzuki (1870–1966); anthropologists Paul Radin (1883–1959), Edwin Oliver James (1888–1972), John Layard (1891–1974), Laurens van der Post (1906–1996), and Gilbert Durand (1921–2012); ethnologists Theodor-Wilhelm Danzel (1886–1954), Wilhelm Koppers (1886–1961), Richard Thurnwald (1896–1954), and Jean Servier (1918–2000); archaeologists Charles Virolleaud (1879–1969), Vera Christina Chute Collum (1883–1956), and Charles Picard (1883–1965); philosophers Helmuth Plessner (1892–1985), Karl Löwith (1897–1973), Jean Brun (1919–1994) and Pierre Hadot (1922–2010); art historians Rudolf Bernoulli (1880–1948), Julius Baum (1882–1959), and Carl Moritz von Cammerloher (1882–1945); literary critic Herbert Edward Read (1893–1968);[120] physicists Erwin Schrödinger (1887–1961), Friedrich Dessauer (1881–1963), Hans Leisegang (1890–1951), and Shmuel

[120] On August 6, 1964, British museologist Hans Hess (1907–1975) suggested that artist Luigi Pericle (1916–2001) meet Sir Herbert Read (1893–1968) during the art critic's upcoming participation as a lecturer at the Eranos *Tagung* (Read attended the Eranos meetings regularly from 1952 to 1964). Read visited Pericle's studio in Ascona and was impressed by his work. With the support of the Arts Council, of which Read was a commissioner, Hess thus organized a traveling solo exhibition of Pericle's work in 1965, which he curated together with Read, in several British museums, including York, Newcastle, Hull, Bristol, Cardiff, and Leicester. After this successful period, Pericle chose to abandon the art world to devote himself to his own personal pictorial and mystical research, immersed in the tranquility of his home in Ascona, not far from Monte Verità and Eranos. See Andrea Biasca-Caroni, *Luigi Pericle: il maestro ritrovato* (Turin: Nino Aragno, 2022), and also Martina Mazzotta, "Heterography: Luigi Pericle and Herbert Read: Encounters in Ascona through the Eranos Circle," *Religiographies* 4 (1, 2025), pp. 131–39. I am grateful to Greta and Andrea Biasca-Caroni for the information kindly provided and their ongoing scientific collaboration.

Sambursky (1900–1990); electronic engineer Max Knoll (1897–1969); mathematicians Andreas Speiser (1885–1970) and Hermann Klaus Hugo Weyl (1885–1955); historians of esotericism Antoine Faivre (1934–2021) and Wouter J. Hanegraaff (1961); musicologists Victor Zuckerkandl (1896–1965) and Hildemarie Streich (1921–2012); Chinese medicine scholar Manfred Porkert (1933–2015); and many others.

In the following years, Fröbe-Kapteyn focused on further enriching the annual symposia, which were becoming a "ritual," a "dance," which started anew each year, but always with different "dancers." For a long time, Eranos was the sole venue for gathering together experts and lay people who were inspired by different cultural and spiritual interests and unfettered by their fields of specialization. As the only European conference center to remain active during World War II, Eranos has made an extraordinary contribution to European intellectual history.

Right in the early years of her congressional project, Fröbe-Kapteyn received further decisive impetus in her research into the world of symbols from Jung himself. *(Figure 123 and 124)* He, beyond being a guiding spirit in the first twenty years of symposia, around 1934 also commissioned her to search for iconographic material for his studies on alchemy and the concept of archetypes.[121] She recalled a conversation they had in Zurich, in which Jung said to her: "I have a job here. So far, no one has wanted to do it. Perhaps you are the only one who can. I am looking for images [*Ich suche Bilder*]." Jung took an old illuminated parchment from his bookcase and showed her some woodcuts. They were symbolic representations of alchemy, completely unknown to her. Jung reiterated: "Images of this kind. There must be many images of this kind in the world, only I don't know where. Someone has to look for them." Fröbe-Kapteyn replied without hesitation: "I am willing to do this work." Although she knew nothing about alchemy at the time, she threw herself into this adventure without a moment's hesitation.[122] *(Figure 152)*

Fröbe-Kapteyn thus began collecting a series of images illustrating the various archetypes "as a complement to Jung's theoretical treatises on

---

[121] Ritsema-Gris, *op. cit.*, p. 27.

[122] Fröbe-Kapteyn, "Erster Abend...," cit., p. 14.

alchemy."[123] *(Figure 168)* Between 1935 and 1938, she carried out this iconographic research exclusively for Jung.[124] She later recalled that this iconographic research was very hard work for her. Not only did Jung never pay her a proper fee, he also gave her very little money, which was often not even enough to cover her accommodation expenses during her research trips or the cost of the images that had to be photographed. However, she never rebelled. This task gradually became increasingly important to her; for at least ten years, this work, together with organizing conferences, became her main occupation.[125] The photographs she obtained from the various archives were gradually placed in Casa Gabriella. *(Figure 174)* However, "living" with all this "archetypal" material caused Fröbe-Kapteyn serious insomnia. At a certain point, Jung suggested that she take a vacation "anywhere," in order to get a clear break from her work: *"Archetypen schlafen nie, denn sie sind identisch mit dem Strom des Lebens, der in uns fliesst, auch wenn wir schlafen"* ["Archetypes never sleep, because they are identical to the river of life that flows within us, even when we are asleep."][126]

The Eranos Archive, as envisioned by Fröbe-Kapteyn herself,[127] over the years and especially starting in 1941, became extremely important for the research of many scholars.[128] She constantly emphasized the link between the Eranos Archive and Jung's work: "The recurrence of these archetypal images through the centuries and their frequently simultaneous appearance in widely countries show how their derivation from a common source or reservoir in the unconscious of mankind. C.G. Jung's conception of archetypes is hereby fully confirmed."[129] Jung, for his

[123] *Ibid.*, p. 7.

[124] *Ibid.*, p. 14; see also Id., letter to Marie Stopes, December 1, 1937 (British Library, London; transcript kindly provided by Karssenberg).

[125] Fröbe-Kapteyn, "Erster Abend...," cit., p. 15.

[126] Carl Gustav Jung, letter to Olga Fröbe-Kapteyn, September 20, 1937 (University Archives, ETH-Bibliothek, Zurich / Eranos Foundation Archives, Ascona-Moscia; © 2007 Foundation of the Works of C.G. Jung, Zurich).

[127] Olga Fröbe-Kapteyn, "The Eranos Archive" (unpublished typescript, undated [1947?]; Eranos Foundation Archives, Ascona-Moscia), p. 1.

[128] Olga Fröbe-Kapteyn, "Eranos Archive for Research in Symbolism" (unpublished typescript, undated [1947?]; Eranos Foundation Archives, Ascona-Moscia), p. 1.

[129] *Ibid.*, p. 1.

part, recognized its scientific value on several occasions.[130] Many illustrations featured in his works, particularly those depicting alchemy, came from the Eranos Archive or from iconographic research carried out on his behalf by Fröbe-Kapteyn.[131]

The iconographical research that Fröbe-Kapteyn did between 1938 and 1941 was funded by Mary Elizabeth Conover Mellon (1904–1946) and Paul Mellon (1907–1999), who for more than twenty years (1947–1967) were the main sponsors of Eranos, personally and later through the Bollingen Foundation.[132] *(Figures 195 and 196)* In the spring of 1943, Fröbe-Kapteyn transformed Eranos into a legally recognized Foundation, which could qualify for public and private funding. Thanks to Jung's intervention, the new foundation obtained the support of the Swiss Federal Institute of Technology (ETH) in Zurich, from 1936 to 1956, and of the Pro Helvetia Foundation, which contributed funds from 1943. Once again, thanks to Jung, the Bollingen Foundation placed Eranos within its Program of Contributions to Institutions (General Humanities) beginning in 1947.[133] In 1949, the Bollingen

---

[130] *Ibid.*, p. 8.

[131] Olga Fröbe-Kapteyn, letter to Carl Gustav Jung, August 9, 1939 (University Archives, ETH-Bibliothek, Zurich / Eranos Foundation Archives, Ascona-Moscia).

[132] On the links between the Bollingen Foundation and Eranos, see Bernardini, *op. cit.*, pp. 247–353, and Id., "Neumann at Eranos," in Murray Stein and Erel Shalit, eds., *Turbulent Times, Creative Minds: Erich Neumann and C. G. Jung in Relationship* (Wilmette, IL: Chiron, 2016), pp. 199–236.

[133] The Board of the "first" Eranos Foundation, which remained active until 1955, was composed of Adolf Portmann (1897–1982; Professor of Biology and Zoology at the University of Basel and later Rector Magnificus of the same University); Tadeus Reichstein (1897–1996; Professor at the Institute of Organic Chemistry, University of Basel and the 1950 co-winner of the Nobel Prize in Physiology or Medicine, with Edward Calvin Kendall (1886–1972) and Philip Showalter Hench (1896–1965), for the discovery of cortisone); renowned Zurich psychiatrist Hans Conrad Bänziger (1895–1956); and Zurich lawyer Walter Keller-Staub. A "second" Eranos Foundation was established in August 1961. As stipulated in Fröbe-Kapteyn's will, Portmann was nominated as its first president. When Fröbe-Kapteyn passed away in 1962, the role of guiding Eranos was inherited by Portmann, who was assisted by Rudolf Ritsema, the scholar of the *I Ching*. The Alwine von Keller Foundation was established in von Keller's memory by Emma Hélène von Pelet-Narbonne shortly before her death. Von Keller was a student of Jung's who lived at Eranos from 1937 to the early 1960s. In March 1980, the Eranos Foundation and the Alwine von Keller Foundation merged, becoming the Eranos and Alwine von Keller Foundation. After Ritsema stepped down, there were several successive presidents: Christa Robinson (1994 to 2001; analytical psychologist), Wanda Luban (2001 to 2002; psychotherapist), Maria Danioth (2002 to 2005; analytical psychologist), and John van Praag (2005 to 2009; classicist and businessman). In January 2008, the Foundation reverted to its original name, Eranos Foundation. The Board of the Eranos Foundation, headed since 2009 by Fabio Merlini, now includes representatives of the Government of the Canton of Ticino and of the Municipality of Ascona.

Foundation acquired a duplicate of the Eranos Archive. A further copy of the approximately 6500 images was subsequently sent by Fröbe-Kapteyn to Jung, who, shortly before his death, transferred this material to the C.G. Jung-Institut in Zurich. The Bollingen Foundation also supported the project of cataloguing and expanding the Eranos Archive, beginning in 1959. The original Eranos collection was donated to the Warburg Institute (University of London) in 1954. The New York archive was renamed in 1960 to Archive for Research in Archetypal Symbolism (ARAS): from then on, the history of the two holdings continued along independent paths.[134] *(Figure 210)*

Fröbe-Kapteyn devoted her entire life to cultivating her cultural enterprise, Eranos, and personally edited the first thirty *Eranos-Jahrbücher* (1933–1961).[135] She passed away in Casa Gabriella, at the age of 80, on April 25, 1962.[136] *(Figure 215)*

---

[134] On the history of the Eranos Archive for Research in Symbolism, see Bernardini, *Jung a Eranos...*, cit., § 3: "Tracce. Jung e l'Archivio di Eranos," pp. 247–353. A recent contribution on the subject is that of Frederika Tevebring, "Images from the Collective Unconscious. Olga Fröbe-Kapteyn and the Eranos Archive," *The Public Domain Review* (February 22, 2023).

[135] The *Eranos Yearbooks* were published by Rhein-Verlag (volumes I/1933–XXXVIII/1969), E.J. Brill (XXXIX/1969–XLV/1976), Insel Verlag (XLVI/1977–LVII/1988), Eranos Foundation (LVIII/1989–LX/1991), and Spring Journal, Inc. (LXI/1992 and LXV/1996–LXVIII/1999); currently the proceedings are published by Daimon Verlag (LXIX/2006–2007–2008–LXXVI/2022–2023–2024). Moreover, the Swiss National Sound Archives keep 216 magnetic audiotapes, donated by the Eranos Foundation in 2009. The audiotapes record about 200 hours of lectures held at the Eranos Conferences organized between 1968 and 1998. The recordings (in German, French, and English) are now available on digital media for listening at the Swiss National Sound Archives. In some cases, the Eranos talks published in the *Yearbooks* were republished in special series: in English, edited by Joseph Campbell, the *Papers from the Eranos Yearbooks* (Princeton, NJ: Princeton University Press, 1954–1868, 6 vols.), besides the *Eranos Lectures* (Dallas, TX: Spring Publications, Inc., 1984–1989, 9 vols.); in Italian, edited by Claudio Risé, the *Quaderni di Eranos* (Como: Red, 1989–1999, 9 vols.) and, edited by Fabio Merlini, the *Saggi di Eranos* (Turin: Rosenberg & Sellier, 2013–2022, 6 vols.); in Japanese, edited by Rudolf Ritsema and Toshihiko Izutsu, the *Eranos Series* (Ascona/Tokyo: Eranos Foundation/Heibonsha Ltd., 1990–1995, 11 vols.); in Spanish, edited by Andrés Ortiz-Osés, the *Círculo Eranos (Cuadernos de Eranos)* (Barcelona: Anthropos, 1994–2004, 3 vols.).

[136] Upon Fröbe-Kapteyn's death, violinist Szandor (Sándor) Végh came specially from Basel to play Bach's *Chaconne* for her (Ritsema-Gris, *op. cit.*, p. 22).

CHAPTER II
Olga Fröbe-Kapteyn's Iconographic Corpus

The first phase of Olga Fröbe-Kapteyn's artistic production, with a strongly geometric imprint, is recorded in a series a series of about 128 "Meditation Plates,"[1] painted between c. 1926 and 1934.[2] These images, some of which were originally displayed in the Lecture Hall of Casa Eranos, express a rigor eschewing any naturalism of form and a choice of predominantly cold colors. There is a basic chromatic contrast between black (nocturnal, unconscious, and destructive energy; deathly and disintegrative vibration;

[1] The number 128 refers to the "Plates" preserved at Eranos or found to date in external funds. It has not been ruled out that the total number of works is greater; this may even be likely. A series of fourteen "Meditation Plates" was sent by Fröbe-Kapteyn in the 1930s to Turin, Italy, to Industrie Grafiche Vincenzo Bona (still in existence), probably through Vittorino Vezzani (Foster Bailey, letters to Olga Fröbe-Kapteyn, February 25, 1931 and January 12, 1932 (Eranos Foundation Archives, Ascona-Moscia)). High-quality reproductions were to be made, but the printing press was partly destroyed by bombing. On the night between June 11 and 12, 1940, the first Allied raid struck Turin: bombs fell on the city until April 5, 1945, hitting factories, homes, public buildings, monuments, and streets, and causing hundreds of deaths among the civilian population. Of the fourteen original paintings shipped to Turin, traces of ten were lost. Of the set of fourteen, however, several reproductions were saved; they are still preserved at the Art Institute of Chicago or for sale in European and American art galleries. We thank the Bona family and Pierdomenico Chiarabaglio, previously General Manager of Bona Industrie Grafiche, for their availability in searching for these works. In 2025, Gerrish Fine Art (London) organized the first exhibition in the United Kingdom dedicated to that series of "Plates," as well as to other rare reproductions acquired by them over the years: see Gerrish Fine Art, *The "Meditation Plates"—Olga Fröbe-Kapteyn. 17/07/2025–17/10/2025, Gerrish Fine Art, London* (London: Gerrish Fine Art, 2025).

[2] An early, still very embryonic study of the "Meditation Plates" is contained in Riccardo Bernardini, "Da Monte Verità a Eranos. Elementi di una rete culturale per lo studio della psiche e della complessità umana," M.A. Dissertation, Facoltà di Psicologia, Università degli Studi di Torino, Turin, 2003, § 2: "Eranos: una retrodatazione? Le Tavole di meditazione della Arcane School, New York/Ascona," 119–87, and "Appendice alla Parte Seconda, § 2: Tavole di meditazione dipinte da Olga Fröbe-Kapteyn spedite a Dion Fortune, con una lettera inedita di Olga Fröbe-Kapteyn del 19 marzo 1934. Su gentile concessione di Maria Babwahsingh/S.R.I.Am., Bayonne, NJ, ottobre 2023."

Yin principle in Taoism and *I Ching*) and gold (diurnal, conscious, and constructive energy; vital and integrative vibration; *Yang* principle)[3] with the constant presence of red, almost always on a blue background. Fröbe-Kapteyn recalled that the idea of Eranos gripped her when she was drawing a "Plate" for accompanying these words: "Down from the Gates of gold, down to the Pit of darkness, rides the secret Avatar, bearing the Sword that pierceth." These paintings, created using mixed media on paper or cardboard and employing tempera, India ink, and gold leaf, document an obvious recurrence of certain stylized symbols: the sun, the cross, the chalice, the tao, the crystal, the lotus, the rays, the portal, the sword, the ladder, and "mandalic" shapes.[4] The overall result is an abstract figure, in which a spirituality purified of all corporality is staged.[5]

Alice Ann Bailey made use of the "Meditation Plates" during the congress activities of the International Centre for Spiritual Research in Ascona. In its first session, on August 20, 1930, Fröbe-Kapteyn and Bailey gave a "Talk on Symbolism, and demonstration of a series of Occult

---

[3] Olga Fröbe-Kapteyn, "The Hut and the Sacred Word" (unpublished typescript, Easter Monday 1945; Eranos Foundation Archives, Ascona-Moscia). In her visions, the color gold often appears as a symbol of the Self (cf., e.g., Olga Fröbe-Kapteyn, "Vision. 3 Juli 1947" (unpublished typescript, July 3, 1947; Eranos Foundation Archives, Ascona-Moscia)). Fröbe-Kapteyn had been using gold in her "Plates" for at least three or four years before meeting Jung; the latter spoke about that color in his very first lecture at Eranos, pointing out that gold expresses "sunlight, value, divinity itself" (Carl Gustav Jung, "Zur Empirie des Individuationsprozesses…," cit., quoted in Medea Hoch, "La concezione junghiana del colore nel contesto dell'arte moderna," in Foundation of the Works of C.G. Jung, Ulrich Hoerni, Thomas Fischer, and Bettina Kaufmann, eds., *L'arte di C.G. Jung* (Turin: Bollati Boringhieri, 2019 {2018}), p. 45).

[4] The phrase that inspired her is mentioned in Fröbe-Kapteyn, "19 Mai 44," cit., p. 2. The "unifying" psychological function of the *Maṇḍala*, which we find widely present in both of Fröbe-Kapteyn's artistic periods through the iconographic motif of the "Eranos *Maṇḍala*" (series that was reconstructed and commented for the first time in Riccardo Bernardini, "Carl Gustav Jung a Eranos. Il contributo junghiano al Circolo di Eranos: ideazione, contributi e iniziative dal 1933 al 1952," Ph.D. Dissertation, Dottorato di Ricerca in Studi religiosi: Scienze sociali e studi storici delle religioni, Alma Mater Studiorum—Università di Bologna, Bologna, 2009, § 4.2: "Il 'mandala' di Eranos," pp. 330–51; and Id., *Jung a Eranos…*, cit., § 1.5, pp. 83–111 and 165 f.), is well documented in the seminar given at Eranos in 1943 by Jung, *The Solar Myths and Opicinus de Canistris…*, cit.

[5] See Fabio Merlini and Riccardo Bernardini, "Olga Fröbe-Kapteyn. 1881, Londres (Royaume-Uni)–1962, Ascona (Suisse)," in Christine Macel and Laure Chauvelot, eds., *Elles font l'abstraction. Exhibition Album* (Paris: Centre Pompidou, 2021), p. 54; the biography sheet was later republished in *AWARE: Archives of Women Artists, Research and Exhibitions a pour objet la création, l'indexation et la diffusion de l'information sur les artistes femmes du XIX*e *et XX*e *siècle*, https://awarewomenartists.com/en/artiste/olga-frobe-kapteyn/.

Symbols,"[6] using eighty images from the "Meditation Plates." Fröbe-Kapteyn exhibited some of the paintings and gave a short lecture on them. Bailey, on the other hand, offered an interpretation of a series of eighteen of these figures, which had been selected by Fröbe-Kapteyn, Bailey herself, and her husband Foster Bailey, and were scheduled to be published shortly thereafter in New York; Bailey wrote some commentaries about each "Plate."[7] The complete series, in her interpretation, "represents the path of evolution from the dawn of the great creative process to the consummation of the age, including the path of discipleship and the path of initiation, as trodden by the human being."[8] Also in the second session of the "School," in August 1931, several "Lectures on Symbology" were given and some "Teachings through Symbols" were imparted. They delved into the use of "Geometric Symbols" in the context of "occult training" and meditation.[9]

Between the late 1920s and early 1930s, Fröbe-Kapteyn composed a series of writings for her daughter Bettina[10] and her friends. In these works, she sought to empathize with the existential questions and difficulties of others, recognizing that these themes were, in essence, her own. In the preface to one of these writings, *Gleichnisse* ("Parables"), she acknow-

[6] Olga Fröbe-Kapteyn, "Lecture Program. August. 1930" (unpublished typescript, 1930; Eranos Foundation Archives, Ascona-Moscia), p. 1.

[7] See Foster Bailey, letter to Olga Fröbe-Kapteyn, November 12, 1930 (Eranos Foundation Archives, Ascona-Moscia).

[8] Alice Ann Bailey and Olga Fröbe-Kapteyn, "International Centre for Spiritual Research. First Session. August 1930" (unpublished typescript, 1930; Eranos Foundation Archives, Ascona-Moscia), p. 6; Bailey's interpretation of these images were sometimes accompanied by a verse or paragraph "from the old commentaries contributed by the Tibetan" (cf. Alice Ann Bailey, "August 1930" (unpublished typescript, 1930; Eranos Foundation Archives, Ascona-Moscia), pp. 9 f.), the disembodied entity their group communicated with in those years and whom Fröbe-Kapteyn recognized in Master Koot Hoomi (see Fröbe-Kapteyn, "The 4th Function and the Tibetan," cit., p. 3), using the techniques of *channeling* or ultraphany (see Bernardini, "Da Monte Verità a Eranos...," cit., pp. 128 f.).

[9] Alice Ann Bailey and Olga Fröbe-Kapteyn, "International Centre for Spiritual Research. Program of Lectures. Second session. August 2nd to 22nd, 1931" (unpublished typescript, 1931; Eranos Foundation Archives, Ascona-Moscia), p. 2.

[10] Olga Fröbe-Kapteyn, "Im Anfang war das Wort. Geschrieben für Bettina. Ostern. 1928" (unpublished typescript; 1928; Eranos Foundation Archives, Ascona-Moscia); Id., "Zwei Erzählungen. Der Ewige Gefährte. Der Turm. Geschrieben für Bettina. Zu Weihnachten. 1929" (unpublished typescript; 1929; Eranos Foundation Archives, Ascona-Moscia); and Id., "Erzählungen. Geschrieben für Bettina. Ostern. 1931" (unpublished typescript; 1931; Eranos Foundation Archives, Ascona-Moscia).

ledged that "the deepest things in human life ... can only be expressed in images."[11] She used to give a copy of "Parables" to a very small circle of friends and correspondents, including reproductions of her "Meditation Plates." Among those recipients was the painter Sophie Della Valle di Casanova Browne (1866–1960), who, together with her husband, Marquis Silvio Della Valle di Casanova—a musicologist, scholar of German literature, and poet with a taste for symbolism—hosted numerous artistic personalities at Villa San Remigio in Pallanza, including Gabriele D'Annunzio (1863–1938), Umberto Boccioni (1882–1916), and Ferruccio Busoni (1866–1924).

Today, we know the names of other recipients of Fröbe-Kapteyn's geometric works and, in some cases, their reactions and comments. The "Meditation Plates," some of which in those years were displayed on the walls of the Lecture Hall, often revolved around the Grail theme, as in the case of the painting donated to psychologist Roberto Assagioli (1888–1974), who was among the scholars involved in this "prehistory" of Eranos.[12] *(Figure 81)* Philosopher of religions Alfons Rosenberg, who had worked for weeks in Fröbe-Kapteyn's private graphic archive, recalled the "Plates" as "severe, mysterious, and solemn. But they exuded an atmosphere of frightening coldness. They were painted with the intellect and not with the heart; they were effective, but unsympathetic."[13] Magda Kerényi believes that Fröbe-Kapteyn brought some "Meditation Plates" with her to show Ludwig Derleth during their meetings.[14] Rudolf Otto had some

[11] Olga Fröbe-Kapteyn, "Gleichnisse" (unpublished typescript, October 1933; Eranos Foundation Archives, Ascona-Moscia), p. 1. The "parables" were composed by Fröbe-Kapteyn "for individual people, often in response to a question, but sometimes also in an attempt to capture the essence of an individual in a symbolic form that corresponded to him. The deepest things in human life can only be expressed or indicated in the form of images. Only in this way is it possible to hint at what is essential and alive in a visible and tangible way. These stories are an attempt to penetrate the depths of the human soul and gently point to the gateways to reality. In some cases, a parable proved so compelling to the person for whom it was written that it seemed justified to make the collection accessible to a wider audience" (*ibid.*).

[12] The use of the "Meditation Plates" within the International Centre for Spiritual Research is also documented by McGuire, "The Arcane Summer School," cit.

[13] Quoted by Wehr, *op. cit.*, 42, and Hakl, *op. cit.*, p. 62.

[14] Hakl, *op. cit.*, p. 47, fn. 73.

examples of these on display in his home.[15] *(Figures 95 and 96)* Fröbe-Kapteyn even dedicated a "Plate" painted in 1933 to him. *(Figure 97)* Friedrich Heiler appreciated their symbolic meaning and color rendering.[16] *(Figures 66–76, 81–98, 105–116)*

The first letters exchanged between Jung and Fröbe-Kapteyn concerned precisely these images. In June 1932, for example, Jung wrote to her: "Dear Madam, receive my best thanks for kindly sending me your images. According to your description, you draw your images in exactly the same way as my patients draw theirs. These images originate from conscious perception, they arise in the unconscious, i.e., in the unknown. This unknown seems to have a collective character and not an individual one. The way in which these images are represented, however, is very different, but the underlying thoughts are of a general nature, and therefore such expressions can be subjected to psychological criticism. They have the value of *yantras*, which are intended to support a certain path of self-development as an instrument, and should therefore be examined for their psychological significance."[17] In May 1933, Jung noted the extreme technical perfection of these geometric images and asked Fröbe-Kapteyn how she could bring the content of these figures back to a broader spiritual structure and how she interpreted them from an intellectual point of view.[18]

Despite Jung's initial appreciation of the "Meditation Plates," Fröbe-Kapteyn also told Rosenberg how Jung had helped lessen the influence that theosophy had on her, just as Zillmann had done regarding the Arcane School as early as 1931 by giving her the journal *Yoga*.[19] She admitted that she had been very shaken when Jung, on his first visit to Eranos in August

---

[15] *Ibid.*, p. 62 and fn. 115.

[16] *Ibid.*

[17] Carl Gustav Jung, letter to Olga Fröbe-Kapteyn, June 15, 1932 (University Archives, ETH-Bibliothek, Zurich / Eranos Foundation Archives, Ascona-Moscia; © 2007 Foundation of the Works of C.G. Jung, Zurich).

[18] Carl Gustav Jung, letter to Olga Fröbe-Kapteyn, May 20, 1933 (University Archives, ETH-Bibliothek, Zurich / Eranos Foundation Archives, Ascona-Moscia; © 2007 Foundation of the Works of C.G. Jung, Zurich).

[19] Fröbe-Kapteyn, "The 4th Function and the Tibetan," cit., p. 10.

1933, harshly criticized the "Meditation Plates," when he saw them arranged on the walls of the Lecture Hall. *(Figures 65 and 80)* This led to a breakthrough in her research. The problem was not primarily the geometric aspect of the images. The members of Jung's Zurich circle who were with him were in fact particularly shocked to have seen (whether consciously or not), among the eighty images, the symbol of the "Curse." Pointing to that depiction of the "black *Om* [ॐ]," Jung even exclaimed, "*Das ist der Teufel!*" ["This is the devil!"] Curiously, the artist herself would later note that, among the many "Meditation Plates," it was precisely this painting with which she had always most identified.[20] *(Figure 98)*

The *Om*, the most sacred and representative *mantra* in various Far Eastern traditions, from Hinduism to Buddhism, from Jainism to Sikhism, is a sacred sound, a vibration, and an invocation. It refers to the Absolute, to consciousness, to Ātman, and to Brahman. *(Figure 64)* In Fröbe-Kapteyn's "Meditation Plates," the "Golden *Om*" or "Sacred Word," corresponding to the "golden swastika" (right-handed) and a "symbol of solar energy and power," is contrasted with the "Black *Om*" or "Cursed, Damned Word," corresponding to the "black or left-handed swastika, as it is [used] in Germany [i.e., as] a symbol of dark power [and] destruction.... Both of these black symbols [the "black *Om*" and the "black swastika"] of highest but destructive power mean possession by the Devil. Just as Germany is possessed by him, the dark aspect of the Self. Or by Kālī the Destroyer."[21] In 1942, regarding the role of Eranos in the context of the war catastrophe, Fröbe-Kapteyn explained: "The commencement of Eranos in the year 1933, at the same time that Hitler came into power, is a fact that must not be overlooked. It is clear to me, and perhaps to a few others, that Eranos belongs to the *army of constructive forces*, as over against the destructive ones which seem to be ruling the world, and that it is one of the first visible signs that the former are beginning to stir."[22]

---

[20] Olga Fröbe-Kapteyn, "The Curse" (unpublished typescript, undated [1944?]; Eranos Foundation Archives, Ascona-Moscia). See also Bernardini, *op. cit.*, § 2: "Eranos: una retrodatazione? Le Tavole di meditazione...," and Id., *Jung a Eranos...*, cit., 2 p. 63.

[21] Fröbe-Kapteyn, "The Hut and the Sacred Word," cit.

[22] Olga Fröbe-Kapteyn, "Eranos—A Survey of its history since 1933, of the facts connected with it, a. the *Tagungen*, b. the Eranos Archive. The conclusions I have arrived at, my psychological realisations

Such a "dark aspect of the Self," which in all later "Meditation Plates" manifests itself as "black radiation," *(Figures 105–115)* identified for Fröbe-Kapteyn not only her own personal Shadow, that "black occultism" that lived in her (over twelve years, Jung helped her with the difficult task of disidentification from it) but also the "dark spirit of Eranos." That dark spirit was connected with the "complex of the Arcane School, sunk in the unconscious," which led to the reversal to the negative of the figure of the Tibetan, who, as spiritual master for Bailey (Koot Hoomi, believed to live at Shi-ga-tse in Tibet),[23] the followers of the Arcane School, and a small

---

concerning it, its differences from other congress centres, and its chief problem" (unpublished typescript, 1942; Eranos Foundation Archives, Ascona-Moscia), p. 15.

[23] Olga Fröbe-Kapteyn, "12 Mai 44" (unpublished typescript, May 12, 1944; Eranos Foundation Archives, Ascona-Moscia), p. 1. Between 1919 and 1949, Bailey composed nineteen books on esoteric philosophy, known as the "Blue Books," which were supposedly dictated to her telepathically by "the Tibetan" (Master Djwhal Khul); she also wrote five additional volumes independently. Djwhal Khul was considered by her to be one of the "Masters of Ancient Wisdom" and spiritual guides of humanity, who lived in Tibet (according to Fröbe-Kapteyn, "Bailey once spoke of an 'underground route' from here to the Himalayas ... meaning on the physical plane!!!" (Fröbe-Kapteyn, "Arcane School. Positive Values. Negative Values," cit., p. 1). His intention, according to Bailey, was to reveal esoteric truth in a way suitable for our times, described by the Master as an important moment for humanity, as it marks the transition from the Age of Pisces to the Age of Aquarius—a topic on which Bailey gave the opening lecture at the International Centre for Spiritual Research on August 4, 1930, at 9:30 a.m. ("The New Age") and which was also present both in Fröbe-Kapteyn's view of Eranos itself (see, e.g., Olga Fröbe-Kapteyn, "The Totem-Lingam. Vision and drawing Pfingsten 1942" (unpublished typescript, Pentecost 1942). Eranos Foundation Archives, Ascona-Moscia) and *Figure 197*) and in Jung's reflections (cf. Jung, *The Black Books...*, cit., Vol. V, January 16, 1916, p. 163; Id., *The Red Book...*, cit., "Liber Primus," p. 229, and "Scrutinies," p. 356; and above all Id., *Aion: Researches into the Phenomenology of the Self* (1951), in *The Collected Works of C.G. Jung*, Vol. 10ii (Princeton, NJ: Bollingen Series XX, Princeton University Press, 1969); see also Peter Kingsley, *Catafalque: Carl Jung and the End of Humanity*, 2 vols. (London: Catafalque, 2018), pp. 714 f., 351, 440, 633, 692, 745–748, 776, and 798, and Riccardo Bernardini, *Simboli di rinascita nella Basilica di San Miniato al Monte a Firenze. Da Gioacchino da Fiore a C.G. Jung / Rebirth Symbols in the Basilica of San Miniato al Monte in Florence. From Joachim of Fiore to C.G. Jung*, preface by Abbot Bernardo Francesco Gianni, O.S.B., photographs by Mariangela Montanari (Bergamo: Moretti & Vitali, 2022), pp. 60–68). Often identified by the initials "D.K.," he was considered a Master in the line of Koot Hoomi (Kuthumi, K.H.), who, in the theosophical perspective, was Djwhal Khul's direct teacher. His name appears for the first time in the work of Blavatsky, whose *The Secret Doctrine* (1888) was said to have been written by Koot Hoomi and Morya (Maurya), the "disincarnated" Masters who allegedly inspired the founding of the Theosophical Society in 1875. In January 1932, Bailey wrote to Fröbe-Kapteyn about the need to give some disciples of the school more specific training, which would be provided by the Tibetan himself; Fröbe's name did not appear in the selected group, but among others were the school's main financial backer, Alice Dupont Ortis (1863–1937), and Assagioli (Eranos Fundation Archives, Ascona-Moscia). Moreover, Fröbe-Kapteyn told Mircea Eliade about some paranormal experiences that some of his distinguished guests had had in Ascona, including Bailey herself: Bailey used to see the ghost of a monk entering through the right-hand window of Casa Gabriella, the "Copte" room. To get rid of the unwanted presence, Bailey would summon her "Tibetan

group of scholars involved in the International Centre for Spiritual Research (including Fröbe-Kapteyn herself, who belonged to the highest rank of the Arcane School), became at a certain point for Fröbe-Kapteyn the "black, the Super-Dugpa [black magician or sorcerer, in theosophical literature], the Devil,"[24] or "his dark form."[25] This reversal had occurred, according to Fröbe-Kapteyn, following her departure from the Arcane School and the "replacement" of her discipleship with the Tibetan with her apprenticeship under Jung: it was a real "betrayal" which, in other times and places, could have been punished with death for abandoning one's spiritual order. Anyway, it was always the Self that had pushed Fröbe-Kapteyn first into the Arcane School, "with the farsighted aim of getting Eranos started by the occultists," and then out of the Arcane School, "when it was in the interests of Eranos to branch off in another direction," again "rooted, through Jung, in the very heart of esotericism." Such "betrayal" would ensure that the "complex" of the Arcane School and of the Tibetan would continue to live on into her and stir both in her unconscious and in the shadows of Eranos itself. This situation of "intense conflict and tension caused by the suppressed okkult conflict" was now made clear by the shocking depiction of the black *Om*. More specifically, Fröbe-Kapteyn had covered the golden figure with a black gable (*Giebel*), consisting of the dark *Om*. In the background stood the golden temple,

---

protector" and, with the help of a ritual, managed to drive the monk away. The latter would later reappear in the next room, the "Piano" room, where a young Dutch Quaker was staying at the time: at the sight of the monk, who arrived around two in the morning, the boy would jump to his feet and begin reading the Bible aloud: at which point, according to Fröbe-Kapteyn, who was sleeping in the apartment below, the monk disappeared as if by magic (Eliade, *Giornale*, cit., pp. 132 and 158. Incidentally, Eliade had the opportunity to meet Bailey in person in London in 1940, later describing her in his diary as a "surprising and skilled" woman, but also cataloguing her books as "unreadable and worthless" (*ibid.*, p. 132)).

[24] Fröbe-Kapteyn, "Arcane School. Positive Values. Negative Values," cit., pp. 2 ff.; and Id., "The 4th Function and the Tibetan," cit., pp. 1–8.

[25] Olga Fröbe-Kapteyn, "11 June 44" (unpublished typescript, June 11, 1944; Eranos Foundation Archives, Ascona-Moscia), p. 2. Cf. also Id., letter to Hans Conrad Bänziger, May 23, 1944 (Eranos Foundation Archives, Ascona-Moscia). Fröbe-Kapteyn recognized that "in the beginning the authority back of the Eranos group was the Tibetan. Then, when the change came, one might say, the Self took over the authority. For Jung never claimed any authority, nor did I. I just followed the directions which came from within, as well as possible. So the Self of the group was really running Eranos. And that makes teamwork, groupfeeling and solidarity so important. That is why recognition of this group unity is necessary by the group" (Fröbe-Kapteyn, "11 June 44," cit.).

even if separated from the viewer by the black pattern formed by the *Om* symbol. Jung, who had harsh words for that composition, claimed that Fröbe-Kapteyn had placed the devil between herself and the sanctuary, symbol of the divine. And that she had sided with the devil. This analysis deeply disturbed Fröbe-Kapteyn to such an extent that she could no longer look at the painting.[26]

A year earlier, in 1932, Fröbe-Kapteyn had built a small, basic hut on the steep hill above Villa Gabriella as a "refuge" for herself. *(Figures 99–104)* But then she had realized that the "Hut" was rather a refuge for the "terrible

[26] Wehr, *op. cit.*, 43. See Fröbe-Kapteyn, "Arcane School. Positive Values. Negative Values," cit., p. 3; Id., "Feeling Function" (unpublished typescript, undated [1944?]; Eranos Foundation Archives, Ascona-Moscia); and Id., "Thinking Function," cit.; in this writing, in particular, Fröbe-Kapteyn speaks of Jung as "the great esoteric teacher" and about "the Tibetan in America and [Paul] Zillmann in Germany [as] the forerunners of Jung" for Eranos (*ibid.*; see also Id., "Tibet" (unpublished typescript, undated [1944?]; Eranos Foundation Archives, Ascona-Moscia)). She then noted with regard to "*The Tibetan and Jung*: I identified with both, through huge projections, and so when Jung became the centre of Eranos, his shadow was, I think, the Tibetan. I must have projected the Tibetan onto him, all the more because he had written the introduction of the [*Tibetan*] *Book of the Dead* [Carl Gustav Jung, "Psychological Commentary on the *Tibetan Book of the Dead*" (1935/1953), in *The Collected Works of C.G. Jung*, Vol. 11 (Princeton, NJ: Bollingen Series XX, Princeton University Press, 1970), pp. 509–26]. That was Jung's link with the Tibet, plus the *Tantric psychology of the Chakras* [Carl Gustav Jung, *The Psychology of Kundalini Yoga—Notes on the Seminar given in 1932*, ed. Sonu Shamdasani (Princeton, NJ: Princeton University Press, 1996)], which had also been taught to us by the Tibetan. Was my link with Jung from the beginning *through Tibet*? That is quite a revelation! If it is true. My contact with Jung was therefore possibly *through the back door of Tibet*" (Olga Fröbe-Kapteyn, "The new situation of Eranos, caused by Jung's absence" (unpublished typescript, undated [1944?]; Eranos Foundation Archives, Ascona-Moscia)). She further explained that "The East teaches *rising* through the Chackras. Jung teaches *going down* through the Chackras. Back of that quite positive Chakra teaching, there is surely a reverse side, most poisonous (I think of the mysterious illness of which Sir John Woodroffe dies, of his daughter, of the man who had been the controller of the temples on the Tibetan border, of the death of Richard Wilhelm, of the warning I have to [Giuseppe] Tucci about all this, but which also applies to myself, etc. etc.) As if the Eastern teaching, gone back by suppression, or even 'black' for us in some way, could *so poison Westerners* that they died of mysterious illness which no Wester doctor could name" (Fröbe-Kapteyn, "12 Mai 44," cit.). It is significant that Fröbe-Kapteyn and Bailey attempted (in vain) to invite the American anthropologist Walter Yeeling Evans-Wentz (1878–1965), translator of the *Tibetan Book of the Dead* and editor of the collection of translations by various scholars that he brought together in the *Tibetan Book of Great Liberation* (works for which Jung would write two "psychological commentaries," in 1935 and 1939, respectively). A rich correspondence maintained over the years with Evans-Wentz testifies to Fröbe-Kapteyn's sincere desire to have this scholar among his lecturers: the request to give a talk was renewed with admirable regularity every year from 1930 to 1938. Evans-Wentz, in his letters to Fröbe-Kapteyn, while declining these invitations with extreme courtesy due to his other commitments, constantly expressed great admiration both for the activities of the "Center for Spiritual Research" (October 28, 1930) and for the "great work for the correct understanding between East and West" in which she was engaged (May 1, 1956). The editor of the Italian version of the *Tibetan Book of the Dead*, orientalist Giuseppe Tucci, instead lectured at Eranos in 1949.

secret" she kept there, namely that gable (*Giebel*) she had designed as a black *Om*. She realized that she had projected the symbol of the curse onto the "Hut" on the hill in two ways: the *Om* symbol painted on the front of the shelter and the sign with the word "Private," which she had affixed to it so that no one would set foot there. Yet, despite this apotropaic attempt to ward off and confine the curse, it was only later that she realized that the symbol was also there in Eranos, in the large *Om* drawing hanging in the Lecture Room. The fact that Jung, in August 1933, had referred to it as "the devil" made her aware that the devil was *everywhere*. "The psychologists were all horrified," she wrote, "more so than they knew, not really because they were geometrical drawings, but because this symbol of the curse was there! It is the drawing with which I was most identified!" That symbol had made the entire hill a "cursed" place. No wonder, she thought, that people were afraid of that place, and she herself rarely went there. No wonder, too, that people didn't want to buy that land. The symbol dominated the entire place, warning everyone, threatening terrible misfortune—a real curse.[27]

After Jung's harsh reaction, anyway, that *Om* symbol became conscious and transformed into a healing symbol, with the "cursed child" turning into the "Redeemer."[28] The hill returned to being a normal hill: it could now be seen, looked at, the veil of invisibility having been lifted.[29] The hill was finally "free," and with it, Fröbe-Kapteyn herself.[30] That was "the great transformation" for her, which she felt happening deeply both within herself (healing a shadow that had been buried in her family history, in her

[27] Fröbe-Kapteyn, "The Hut and the Sacred Word," cit. Fröbe-Kapteyn was deeply emotional involved with the hill: she *was* the Hill itself. At some point, the hill had become "invisible" because it was completely *esoteric*, and therefore *hidden*, on another plane. It had become "the Secret Place." The "Hut" and the *Om* symbol had added a further quality to all this: the "Hut" was in fact a place of worship. For all these reasons, it could have been called the "Sacred Hill" or "sacred land" (Olga Fröbe-Kapteyn, "The White Elephant" (unpublished typescript, 1940; Eranos Foundation Archive, Ascona-Moscia).

[28] Fröbe-Kapteyn originally had designed that symbol as a "Healing Symbol" for Lene Zillmann, whom she associated with her own shadow. But *au fond*, it was created for herself (Fröbe-Kapteyn, "The Hut and the Sacred Word," cit.).

[29] Fröbe-Kapteyn, "The White Elephant," cit.

[30] Olga Fröbe-Kapteyn, "The veil of ectoplasm" [belonging to a series of visions beginning on April 9, 1943] (unpublished manuscript, April 9, 1943; Eranos Foundation Archive, Ascona-Moscia).

ancestors) and around her (the physical place). It was a realization that shocked her, gripped her, and shook her more than any other discovery. Nothing Jung could have said would have had a similar effect. The birth of a symbolic thought of a new consciousness would finally bring her peace, which she felt reverberating in the corresponding hexagram of the *I Ching*, "The Peace."[31]

As a result of Jung's criticism—which was therefore a powerfully transformative occasion for Fröbe-Kapteyn's existence—she removed all the geometrical paintings from the Eranos Lecture Hall and showed them only rarely and to only a few people, while continuing to work on them, almost in secret, for a few more years.

Fröbe-Kapteyn sent some reproductions of the new figures that she began to create in March 1934 to occultist Dion Fortune (Violet Mary Firth, 1890–1946). *(Figures 125–146)* She explained to her in this way the inner and artistic change that was taking place within her, partly as a result of Jung's decisive and harsh comments the previous Summer: "Since I last wrote, I have been working hard at the correspondences between Psychoanalysis, the Kabbalah, and ancient cults. Something seems to be happening to my subconscious regions, for suddenly after drawing geometrical symbols for about 8 years, and being quite incapable of drawing realistically—suddenly mythical pictures have begun to appear, when I am meditating. Perhaps one should not call this meditation, but rather a condition of waking trance. The pictures are perceived inwardly, and I am sending you photos of this first series, which seem to me to be a definite set, all on the same background, all connected with the Cult of the Great Mother. It is like a mystery play, and also like some initiation through an ancient rite. The symbols seem to rise from what Jung calls the Collective Sub-consciousness. They might be connected with a Mithras Ritual or Cybele cult. Some of the symbols are not familiar to me, for ex. the horned and winged male figure in the cave, *(Figure 129)* and also the

[31] Lines of the 11th Hexagram: 979888 (*ibid.*). Such a "breakthrough" involved consciously reclaiming a great deal of psychic energy that had been stuck in her unconscious for many years, and also a positive psychosomatic effect on her physical health (see Olga Fröbe-Kapteyn, "Der Durchbruch" (unpublished typescript, undated [1944?]; Eranos Foundation Archives, Ascona-Moscia).

second horned figure, in which snakes curl round the horns. *(Figure 131)* This last picture as well as two others seem to be connected with the process of Kuṇḍalinī. *(Figure 133 and 136)* At any rate it may interest you to see them. Probably many other others will follow, now the channel for symbols of this level is free."[32]

On the subject of the realism of spontaneously experienced images, which Fröbe-Kapteyn began to experiment with in this new form similar to an active imagination from the spring of 1934,[33] Jung had already written in *Psychological Types* (1921), with reference to our mind's ability to cyclically return to functioning in a creatively archaic way: "Among primitives ... the imago, the psychic reverberation of the sense-perception, is so strong and so sensuously coloured that when it is reproduced as a

[32] Olga Fröbe-Kapteyn, letter to Dion Fortune, March 19, 1934 (Eranos Foundation Archives, Ascona-Moscia). In addition to her esoteric interests (she was initiated into the Golden Dawn and joined the Christian Mystic Lodge within the Theosophical Society, which later became the Society of the Inner Light), Dion Fortune cultivated her passion for psychoanalysis, becoming one of the highest-paid analysts in London (cf. Massimo Introvigne, *Il cappello del mago. I nuovi movimenti magici, dallo spiritismo al satanismo* (Milan: SugarCo, 1990), pp. 293–98). She recognized in Jungian theory a psychology correlated with esoteric psychology (Dion Fortune, *The Magical Battle of Britain* (Cheltenham: Skylight, 2012 {1939}), pp. 158 ff., and Id., "Lettera mensile n° 18, per il maggio 1944 – 'Introduzione alla Psicologia Esoterica,'" in Id., *La battaglia magica d'Inghilterra* (Rome: Tre Editori, 2000), pp. 185–89) and maintained a correspondence with Fröbe-Kapteyn for some years (Gareth Knight, *Dion Fortune and the Inner Light* (Loughborough: Toth, 2000), p. 217; mentioned in Hakl, *Eranos...*, cit., p. 333, fn. 12). Beyond the common sensitivity to the "initiatic" value of psychological science, Fröbe-Kapteyn also applied some of the magical practices described by Fortune on a few occasions. Upon learning of the death of her former lecturer Max Pulver on June 13, 1952, Fröbe-Kapteyn was unable to sleep that night. The next morning, she slipped on a concrete flower bed shaped like a coffin, which reminded her of what had happened to her the previous year, on the death of Gerardus van der Leeuw on November 18, 1950, when she fell face down and had time to realize that she had been "grabbed by the heels." As she had done for van der Leeuw, she also performed a water-based separation ritual for Pulver, taken from Dion Fortune's book *Psychic Self-Defense* (London: Rider & Co., 1930), although, Fröbe-Kapteyn specifies, it was more difficult with him because she disliked him (Eliade, *op. cit.*, p. 135). A portion of the "ritual scenes" had a curious fate, connected with Dion Fortune. Copies of them were preserved in the archives of an American Rosicrucian order, the Societas Rosicruciana in America (S.R.I.Am.) of George Winslow Plummer (1876–1944), which was formed in 1907 by Sylvester C. Gould from a schism of the American Societas Rosicruciana in Civitatibus Foederatis of Charles E. Meyer (1839–1908) and later led by Maria Babwahsingh. The latter, about 45 years ago, acquired a "Dion Fortune Collection," in which a series of reproductions of Fröbe-Kapteyn's works were included (Maria Babwahsingh, personal communication, August 30, 2003; and Hans Thomas Hakl, personal communications, July 2 and 4, 2003; see also Hakl, *op. cit.*, p. 182, fn. 9, and Bernardini, *Jung a Eranos...*, cit., p. 264, fn. 94.)

[33] Fröbe-Kapteyn, "Drei Zeichnungen," cit.; and Id., "Visionen. Juni–Juli. 1934" (unpublished typescript; Eranos Foundation Archives, Ascona-Moscia).

spontaneous memory-image it sometimes even has the quality of an hallucination ... We only 'think' of the dead, but the primitive actually perceives them because of the extraordinary sensuousness of his mental images ... When the primitive 'thinks,' he literally has visions, whose reality is so great that he constantly mistakes the psychic for the real. How easily the primitive reality of the psychic image reappears is shown by the dreams of normal people and the hallucinations that accompany mental derangement. The mystics even endeavour to recapture the primitive reality of the imago by means of an artificial introversion, in order to counterbalance extraversion."[34]

In April 1934, when he also received copies of nine "ritual scenes" *(Figures 125–131, 133, and 134)*—which belongs to drawings contained in the first album of the "Visions"—Jung wrote to Fröbe-Kapteyn that he had the impression that the figures were reminiscent of a sort of initiation into the kingdom of the "Great Mother," leading him to wonder of what, in general, an entrance into the cult of the Goddess consisted. It was a cult that actually existed, he specified, in parallel to that of Mithra: in the latter, however, women were not allowed and thus came to the cult of the Goddess.[35]

Some "Meditation Plates" and perhaps the same early "Visions" were sent to esotericist Arthur Edward Waite (1857–1942), who in 1935 wrote to Fröbe-Kapteyn that he was interested in her symbolic images, some reproductions of which she had sent him a long time ago; he noted how they had now shifted from a geometric stage to one of "ritual scenes," acknowledging that her interpretation of them was also most suggestive

---

[34] Carl Gustav Jung, *Psychological Types* {1921}, in *The Collected Works of C.G. Jung*, Vol. 6 (Princeton, NJ: Bollingen Series XX, Princeton University Press, 1971), paras. 46 f.

[35] Carl Gustav Jung, letter to Olga Fröbe-Kapteyn, April 16, 1934 (University Archives, ETH-Bibliothek, Zurich / Eranos Foundation Archives, Ascona-Moscia; © 2007 Foundation of the Works of C.G. Jung, Zurich). The Picture Archive of the C.G. Jung-Institut in Zurich actually holds black and white copies of nine drawings from "ritual scenes" belonging to the first album of "Visions," with handwritten notes by the author. Fröbe-Kapteyn's drawings were not included in the exhibition held in 2018 on the occasion of the seventieth anniversary of the founding of the C.G. Jung-Institut (1948) at the Museum im Lagerhaus - Stiftung für schweizerische Naive Kunst und Art Brut in St. Gallen: see Ruth Ammann, Verena Kast, and Ingrid Riedel, eds., *Das Buch der Bilder. Schätze aus dem Archiv des C.G. Jung-Instituts Zürich*, (Ostfildern: Patmos, 2018).

to him.[36] In 1936, Waite wrote to her that he was particularly interested in the "flowering of the Grail"—one of the most recurring themes in both the "Plates" and the "Visions"—in her representations.[37] *(Figures 81, 82, 87, 89, 93, 114, and 160–165; see also the Grail symbol in Paul Speck's Eranos monument, "Genio loci ignoto," Figure 208)*

As a result of delving more deeply into Analytical Psychology and the maturation of her intellectual relationship with Jung, Fröbe-Kapteyn's production thus increasingly turned toward a figurative style that recalled the active imagination, i.e., the psychological practice of dialoguing with the unconscious that Jung learned through his self-experimentation described in the *Liber Novus* or *Red Book* and that became a "working model" his patients were invited to use.[38] The collection of 315 "Visions," arranged in twelve blue-bound albums, drawn between 1934 and 1938, can be traced at least in part to that technique.[39] These are the crucial years of the beginning of Fröbe-Kapteyn's cultural enterprise, Eranos, of her enduring intellectual relationship with Jung, who was among the main sources of inspiration for the Eranos Conferences, and of her search for iconographic material, for which Jung provided the impetus, which led to the creation of the Eranos Archive for Research on Symbolism.

In her artistic-therapeutic productions, Fröbe-Kapteyn abandoned the geometries and symmetries of the "Meditation Plates" and, over the course of about five years, passing through some representations that

---

[36] Arthur Edward Waite, letter to Olga Fröbe-Kapteyn, April 16, 1935 (Eranos Foundation Archives, Ascona-Moscia).

[37] White believed it might be useful for her to join his group—probably the Fellowship of the Rosy Cross founded in 1915—but this would involve a long initiatory path in their London temple (see Arthur Edward Waite, letter to Olga Fröbe-Kapteyn, April 19, 1936 (Eranos Foundation Archives, Ascona-Moscia)).

[38] See, e.g., Jill Mellick, *The Red Book Hours. Discovering C.G. Jung's Art Mediums and Creative Process* (Zurich: Scheidegger and Spiess, 2018), § "Teaching patients," pp. 415 ff.; and Riccardo Bernardini, "L'ultimo Jung nella stanza di analisi," *Elephant & Castle*, 18 (2018) ("Postludi. Lo stile tardo"), pp. 4–34.

[39] A work on the "Visions" that was still propaedeutic is documented in Riccardo Bernardini, "Jung nel giardino di Eranos: il paesaggio dell'analisi," *Eranos Yearbook*, 70 (2009–2010–2011), pp. 731–38, later reissued as Id., "Jung nel giardino di Eranos: il paesaggio dell'analisi," in Ferruccio Vigna, ed., *L'Ombra del Flâneur. Scritti in onore di Augusto Romano* (Bergamo: Moretti&Vitali, 2014), pp. 35–46, and as Id., "Jung in the Garden of Eranos: The Landscape of Analysis," in Henry Abramovitch and Murray Stein, ed., *Eranos. A Play* (Asheville, NC: Chiron, 2025), pp. 127–40.

seem to contain stylistic elements from both periods, *(Figure 116)* created numerous small-format figurative drawings using oil pastels or wax crayons. As Rosenberg notes, she kept these images carefully hidden from the eyes of the public, in contrast to the "Plates." This means that these drawings, although laden with symbolism like the geometric paintings, had a completely different function: the "Visions" were not intended to have a suggestive effect on viewers, but rather to articulate the painter's inner life in the sense of an artistic-therapeutic activity.[40] Among the "negative values" of the Arcane School, Fröbe-Kapteyn had in fact recognized in retrospect the "suppression of all dark things, including the *shadow*," and the "direction of all work 'upwards'! never into the depths";[41] where she had the impression she was instead being led by the new images, which she began to make spontaneously in March 1934.

The "Visions" show a visionary reinterpretation of the nature, landscape, and architecture of the place where the author lived: they include real details—Lake Maggiore, the Alps, the Brissago Islands, and the Bauhaus style Lecture Hall of Casa Eranos—"transfigured" into symbolic and imaginative elements, in which reality and fantasy, outer environment and inner world, intertwine, permeate, and mingle in a stunning way. *(Figures 153–158, 177 and 178, 181 and 182, 185, and 186)* Some "initiatory" motifs also appear in the "Visions": the somatic experience (breathing, lactating, bleeding) and physical transformation (into plant, animal, or divine being) of the female body.[42] There are also the identification with a deity, the cosmic journey, and the complementary union of opposites.[43]

---

[40] Cf. Rosenberg, *op. cit.*, 2 f.; see also, for more details on his meetings with Eranos, Alfons Rosenberg, *Die Welt im Feuer. Wandlungen meines Lebens* (Freiburg im Breisgau/Basel/Wien: Herder 1983), *passim*; and Wehr, *op. cit.*, p. 43.

[41] Fröbe-Kapteyn, "Arcane School. Positive Values. Negative Values," cit., p. 1.

[42] In Fröbe-Kapteyn's personal library, which forms the original fund of the present Eranos library, we encounter numerous books from which she evidently drew reflections and suggestions that reverberated in her artistic practice. Among the many containing her notes and annotations, for example, is the work of Ella Adelia Fletcher, *The Law of the Rhythmic Breath. Teaching the Generation, Conservation, and Control of Vital Force* (London: William Rider & Sons, Limited, 1908).

[43] On female initiations, see the fundamental study by Bruce Lincoln, *Emerging from the Chrysalis. Studies in Rituals of Women's Initiation* (Cambridge, MA/London: Harvard University Press, 1981); for an initial interpretive reading of Fröbe-Kapteyn's "Visions" in this perspective, see Riccardo Bernardini, "Donne terrene, divine e demoniache. Le iniziazioni femminili: materiali antropologici per la psicologia

(Figures 125–146 and 159–167) Fröbe-Kapteyn recalled: "Jung once told me that all orders, such as that of St. John, the Templars, Freemasonry, and all others, are merely an outer expression of the *One Order of Brotherhood* in the unconscious (the White Lodge in Theosophy comes near to that). He also told me that any real initiation is only in the unconscious, for ex. the rites I used to draw of such visions, in which I was initiated. He also said: *Sie brauchen nicht mehr getauft zu werden, Sie sind schon mit allen Wässern getauft!* [You no longer need to be baptized, you have already been baptized with all waters!] meaning these visions. Therefore, any ritual or initiation or degree on the outer plane puts us in touch with the *Inner Rite*. And *that* is the irrevocable thing. A brother who deserts his order, or a priest who leaves the church cannot *have his power taken from him*. He can only be excommunicated."[44]

The relationship with Jung represented a particularly fortunate experience for Fröbe-Kapteyn for at least two reasons: firstly, his circle of acquaintances that stretched all over the world, and especially in the United States—as in the case of Paul and Mary Mellon—proved to be crucial for the financial survival of Eranos;[45] secondly, Jungian psychology represented the "container" within which it was possible for her to deal with her own insights and questions of an inner nature.[46] It is Ximena de Angulo-Roelli (1918–2018), since the 1950s Fröbe-Kapteyn's personal assistant, who points to Jung's importance for Eranos precisely in having helped the latter to better understand her personal psychology and to give a broader meaning to what was happening to her inwardly.[47]

---

del profondo," in Marina Barioglio, ed., *La danza delle streghe. Energie femminili per una pedagogia spregiudicata* (Milan: FrancoAngeli, 2018), pp. 176–90.

[44] Fröbe-Kapteyn, "19 Mai 44," cit., p. 3. The theme of Baptism is addressed by her in a series of reflections, e.g., "The White Elephant," cit.—a vision that, in her opinion, could have been entitled "The Book of Transformation"—and "The Circle and the Point" (unpublished typescript, 1949; Eranos Foundation Archives, Ascona-Moscia).

[45] See, e.g., McGuire, *Bollingen…*, cit., and William S. Hoffman, *Paul Mellon—Portrait of an Oil Baron* (Chicago, IL: Follett, 1974), *passim*; and more specifically Bernardini, *Jung a Eranos…*, cit., § 3.4: "La 'prima' Bollingen Foundation e l'Archivio di *Eranos*"; § 3.6: "I sospetti di spionaggio"; and § 3.6: "La 'seconda' Bollingen Foundation e l'Archivio di *Eranos*."

[46] *Ibid.*, pp. 170 ff.

[47] Ximena de Angulo-Roelli, personal communication, August 17, 2010, Cavigliano, and March 31, 2012, Ascona.

While Fröbe-Kapteyn attributed Jung with having a fundamental influence on her life, Jung, for his part, recognized her uncommon spiritual strength.[48] Although many criticized Fröbe-Kapteyn for her "inflated" attitude (Jung often feared that she was on the verge of "falling into the collective unconscious"[49]) and her inability to accept other people's ideas and an overly authoritarian attitude[50] (from the outset it was impossible for her to work with committees or even with other people), Jung always defended her remarkable organizational skills.[51] Mary Bancroft (1903–1997), American journalist and spy who spent World War II in Switzerland,[52] remembered Fröbe-Kapteyn walking along the road to Ascona—talking, talking, talking—and Jung walking beside her, smoking his pipe and listening. She was dressed as usual: a large hat, a loose-fitting dress that was too long to be fashionable, and around her neck, chains or pearls of "things" with esoteric meanings. Bancroft had the impression that she was in possession of some mysterious talisman—and Jung, in a way, was. It always seemed so strange to her that she could do everything, organize everything at Eranos. She struck her as one of those people who floated through life an inch or two above the ground.[53] De Angulo-Roelli also recalled that Fröbe-Kapteyn "always seemed to be in the business of 'Higher Things.'"[54] *(Figure 118)*

Between Jung and Fröbe-Kapteyn there was never a real analytic relationship.[55] At least initially, perhaps, she would have wished it, but it did not happen. In October 1934, after having already had some talks with Jung in Zurich, Fröbe-Kapteyn experienced a vision in which she saw herself drawing the same floor plan of the temple that had appeared to

[48] Deirdre Bair, *Jung—A Biography* (New York, NY: Little, Brown and Company, 2003), p. 413.

[49] Ximena de Angulo-Roelli, personal communication, July 2, 2007, Cavigliano.

[50] Jane Cabot Reid, ed., *Jung, My Mother and I—The Analytic Diaries of Catharine Rush Cabot* (Einsiedeln: Daimon, 2000), p. 371.

[51] Bair, *op. cit.*, p. 470.

[52] See Mary Bancroft, *Autobiography of a Spy* (New York, NY: William Morrow, 1983), p. 173.

[53] Quoted in McGuire, *op. cit.*, pp. 27 f. and Bair, *op. cit.*, p. 413.

[54] *Ibid.*

[55] Rudolf Ritsema, personal communication, August 20, 2003, Ascona-Moscia; see also McGuire, *op. cit.*, p. 26, and Neri, *op. cit.*, pp. 189 ff.

her seven years earlier, in 1927, from which Casa Eranos had taken shape. *(Figure 57)* In this case, she saw herself skating with Jung on the frozen surface of a lake. *(Figures 149–151)* Holding hands, they made evolutions together, drawing figures on the ice. They then walked around the perimeter of an immense rose, which began to grow three-dimensionally from the surface of the ice water. While she and Jung were at the center of this ice flower, the petals vanished and only the track at the base remained. This, too, at a certain point, rose and formed a small temple, also made of ice, whose roof was an inverted rose with many petals. She and Jung, in the middle of the temple, held hands. As Fröbe-Kapteyn related, Jung was extremely impressed by her story and by the fact that the two of them were together in a *maṇḍala*. From that moment on, however, it seems that he did not want to work analytically with her anymore.[56]

Despite the absence of a proper analytical relationship, from 1934 until Jung died in 1961, Fröbe-Kapteyn continued to turn to him, not only to discuss issues concerning her cultural project, but also to ask him for advice on personal issues,[57] as she did later with other analysts, such as Erich Neumann in 1948[58] *(Figures 207–208)* and Léopold Szondi (1893–

[56] Fifteen "Visions" referring to her analytical work with Jung in October 1934 have unfortunately been lost—or, in any case, not found to date. With regard to ice skating, a sport she had actually practiced in her youth, some photographs show Olga Kapteyn at age 27 with Iwan Fröbe skating on the ice in the Rigi area in January 1909 (the couple would marry on May 13 of that same year). *(Figures 17 and 18)*

[57] Maggy Anthony, *The Valkyries—The Women Around Jung* (Shaftesbury, Dorset: Element Books Limited, 1990), pp. 70 ff.

[58] Fröbe-Kapteyn kept track of her psychological work with Neumann (Eranos Foundation Archive, Ascona-Moscia). Julie Blumenfeld Neumann, Erich Neumann's wife, was an analytical psychologist and practiced palm reading; she possessed a large collection of palm prints for purposes of comparison (Hakl, *Eranos…*, cit., 2013, p. 149) and did a palm reading of Fröbe-Kapteyn too. During her lifetime, Fröbe-Kapteyn also consulted a number of astrologers for personal advice, including Ernst Bernhard (see the Fröbe-Kapteyn—Bernhard correspondence, kept at the Ernst and Dora Bernhard Collection, Historical Archive of Italian Psychology (ASPI), University of Milan-Bicocca; kindly provided by McGilvray). She was also in contact with Dagmar Bendix, an astrologer who lived in Ascona, who participated as a listener in both the activities of the International Centre for Spiritual Research and the Eranos Conferences (he was portrayed in conversation with Jung in several photographs taken by Margarethe Fellerer). Fröbe-Kapteyn also wondered about the astrological implications of the birth of the International Centre, which she traced back to August 3, 1930, at 5:00 p.m.: see Riccardo Bernardini, "Nota introduttiva a: Ernst Bernhard e Alwine von Keller (?): Tema natale di Emma von Pelet e sinastria Emma von Pelet–C.G. Jung," *L'Ombra. Tracce e percorsi a partire da C.G. Jung*, 9 (1, 2018) ("Jung e Ivrea"), p. 324, fn. 28. Some astrological reflections have recently been proposed by Paolo Crimaldi, "Il grande

1986) in Zurich from 1950 until 1957, the father of "fate analysis" (*Schicksalsanalyse*).[59] Jung suggested that she write down her dreams and try to interpret them, making himself available to meet her in person when she no longer knew how to deal with material from her unconscious.[60] As he instructed, she should devote herself every day for four hours to reflecting on her dreams and therapeutic work related to her inner development.[61]

Jung provided Fröbe-Kapteyn with particular assistance when she was conducting research for the Eranos Archive for Research in Symbolism, during which she often had intense psychic experiences. Fröbe-Kapteyn's iconographic missions in fact corresponded to inner happenings, reflected in her "Visions." *(Figure 174)* In 1937, for example, she wrote to Jung about her intention to collect images of the "Great Mother" archetype for the Eranos Archive. *(Figure 187)* At the British Museum in London, she had found "surprising things," i.e., amazing representations from Crete, Cyprus, Asia Minor, and other places. In January 1938, while researching images of the "Great Mother," Fröbe-Kapteyn went through a profound soul ordeal, which she described as a "descent into Hell." Those "visions" had revealed to her the "maternal aspect of Hell," in the form of a cave covered by black breasts from which milk flowed. Later, between September and November 1938, she conducted research in Athens and Crete, and then in Rome. Before moving to Berlin, she wrote to Mary Mellon from Rome: "I feel as if

---

Insegnamento Spirituale ed Archetipico della Fondazione Eranos: un'Analisi Astrologica," *Linguaggio Astrale Plus. Trimestrale di cultura astrologica del Centro Italiano di Astrologia*, 51 (204/4, 2021), pp. 127–44, in which the author also offers an interpretation of the natal charts of Fröbe-Kapteyn and Eranos and their synastry, and Id., *Iniziazione all'Astrologia dei cicli di vita* (Rome: Mediterranee, 2023), § 5: "Due esistenze profondamente individuate: analisi psico-astrologica di Olga Fröbe-Kapteyn e di Hermann Hesse," pp. 131–48. A testimony of Erich Neumann's self-analysis work through active imagination and image drawing can be found in Nancy Swift Furlotti, *Eternal Echoes—Erich Neumann's Timeless Relevance to Consciousness, Creativity, and Evil* (Asheville, NC: Zurich Lecture Series X, Chiron, 2023), § "Erich Neumann's Watercolor Paintings," pp. 8–24; further documentation relating to his work with images of his inner world is kept in the archives of the Eranos Foundation.

[59] Fröbe-Kapteyn also kept documentation relating to her psychological work with Szondi (Eranos Foundation Archive, Ascona-Moscia), in which she also had the opportunity to work on her relationship with Jung, realizing at a certain point that her feeling towards him had changed and evolved (for a more detailed description of the transformation of their relationship, see Bernardini, *Jung a Eranos…*, cit., § 1.5: "Il rapporto tra Jung e Olga Fröbe-Kapteyn," pp. 83–112).

[60] Hakl, *op. cit.*, p. 52, fn. 87.

[61] Cf. Bernardini, *op. cit.*, p. 86.

I were going into the unknown, because this cruise into the territory of the Magna Mater [Great Mother], where all her cults were alive, is a different thing from getting her images from the northern museums. I am going to collect every archetypal representation I can find."[62] She reported to Mary Mellon that in Crete she had "the greatest experience" of her life.[63] She also wrote to Cary Baynes about this, explaining that some of her psychosomatic symptoms during her trip were connected with her identification with the "Great Mother." When looking for archeological traces of that mythologem, she was completely "inflated" by it. In Knossos Palace, where a Serpent-god was worshipped, she saw herself as an "island of ancient traditions." *(Figure 188)* She thus realized the reason for the importance in her imagination, since 1934, of the Brissago Islands, on which a temple dedicated to Aphrodite was said to have stood in antiquity. Her vision of the 1927 Eranos *Maṇḍala* reflects this influence.[64] Her trip into the "Great Mother" realm was definitively so intense and destabilizing that she had to look to Jung for help—as she often did in those years.[65]

---

[62] Quoted in McGuire, *op. cit.*, pp. 29 f. In the vision of January 1938, which she called "The infernal vision" (or the "vision of Mother Earth" or "vision of the milk of the earth"), the conclusion was incomplete, neither "seen" nor experienced, because she was still "in Mother Earth and, therefore, in a state of unawareness and "blindness." Throughout this series, which began in 1938, three other "seminal" visions followed, which she listed as follows: in 1950, the vision of Jacob–Yahweh–Jung and the detachment from transference and the experience of "letting go"; in 1953, the transformation of the "dark child" into the "shining child" through tears: "Unless a grain of wheat falls into the earth and dies..." (*John* 12:24); again in 1953, during the Eranos Conference dedicated to the theme *Mensch und Erde* ("Human Being and Earth"), held from August 19 to 27, her definitive birth from Mother Earth (Olga Fröbe-Kapteyn, "Die sich überlagernde Visionen" (unpublished typescript, undated [1953?]; Eranos Foundation Archives, Ascona-Moscia).

[63] McGuire, *op. cit.*, p. 30.

[64] See Doris Hasenfratz, "Il destino delle Isole di Brissago: dal tempio di Venere all'albero di eucalipto / Das Schicksal der Brissago-Inseln. Vom Venustempel zum Eukalyptusbaum," *Ferien-Journal. Ascona* (1994), and more in general, on the history of Brissago Islands, Giuseppe Mondada, *Le isole di Brissago nel passato e oggi* (Isole di Brissago/Locarno: Amministrazione delle Isole di Brissago/Tipografia Stazione S.A., 1975). Formed by the Isola Grande (Island of St. Pancrazio) and the Isola Piccola (Island of St. Apollinare or Rabbit Island), the Brissago Islands played a significant role in Fröbe-Kapteyn's imagination at both stages of her creative life, from the "Meditation Plates" to the "Visions."

[65] For a more complete reconstruction of Fröbe-Kapteyn's iconographic research journeys for the Eranos Archive and the reverberations of this pioneering undertaking on her imaginal world, see Bernardini, *op. cit.*, § 3: "Tracce. Jung e l'Archivio di Eranos," 247–353; a contribution more specifically devoted to the theme of the "Great Mother" in the context of Olga Froebe-Kapteyn's iconographic research is represented by Bernardini, "Neumann at Eranos," cit.

Beyond their personal relationship, the "therapeutic" significance that Fröbe-Kapteyn attributed to her collaboration with Jung can therefore be found in the very meaning of the Eranos project itself. Fröbe-Kapteyn used to say that the originality of Eranos lay in its ability to proceed without a specific program drawn up in advance: she admitted that her methods were partly irrational and that, in part, there was no real "method." Yet it worked, because Eranos, rather than a simple series of scientific conferences, represented her individuation process. She wrote to de Angulo-Roelli: "Eranos is my individuation [*Eranos ist meine Individuation*]. It has been so since its inception, throughout its entire development, and so it is today in its greatest intensity. It seems to be my destiny to complete my journey toward individuation in this way [*Es scheint mein Schicksal zu sein, meinen Weg zur Individuation auf diese Weise zu vollziehen*]. And I had to do this alone. Everyone is alone on their inner journey. There is no alternative. This is why I never worked with anyone, because I did everything connected with Eranos alone ... I know I must continue on my path to the end, alone. There will be no delegation. Eranos and I cannot be separated as long as I live."[66] Thus, in a letter to Henry Corbin: "I would like to talk to you about the subject you briefly mentioned in your last letter, namely the responsibility of preserving spirituality in the East. It seems to me that this is your mission and your *Opus*, in a psychological sense. This means a solitary quest, full of unknown difficulties, hard and often without any promise of satisfaction. There is only 'visionary certainty' and *pistis*, that is, loyalty to inner experience. Only this, but it is enough for a human path. And I believe that you have reached the point where you have touched your individual secret. Just as Eranos is for me the reflection of the inner *pistis*, your search for spirituality in the manuscripts of the East is for you. We are both possessed by an archetypal idea, and you have, it seems to me, formulated your idea for the first time in your letter. As for me, throughout my work for Eranos, I sank into terrible isolation. No one realized that I had no choice. Even Jung, who knew, often worked *against* Eranos. And that was hard. You are

[66] Olga Fröbe-Kapteyn, letter to Ximena de Angulo-Roelli, September 7, 1951, quoted in McGuire, *op. cit.*, p. 145 and Hakl, *op. cit.*, p. 285; see also Bair, *op. cit.*, p. 414.

the first person I have spoken to about this."[67] She reiterated her conviction to Joseph Campbell: "The Way of Becoming of Eranos … is closely linked to my individual way. Eranos is, as Jung would say, my *Opus*."[68] She reaffirmed this to herself in the last years of her life: "When I look back today on the entire journey that Eranos has taken, on how it winds its way through a landscape that is very familiar to us, then everywhere along this way I feel at home. The way of Eranos is my homeland."[69] *(Figure 182)*

Fröbe-Kapteyn felt constantly torn between her duties as a "spiritual mother" to Eranos—a recurring theme in the "Visions" seems to be the generative dimension of her femininity in relation to her work—and her duties as a "natural mother" to her daughter Bettina. In a series of reflections in the late 1950s, she noted: "In the shadow of Eranos there has been, from the very beginning, an aspect that has caused me a great deal of pain, namely my relationship with my daughter Bettina and her relationship with me. It was inevitable that many problems would arise in this area, because all my feelings, which should rightly have been devoted to Bettina, were instead directed toward Eranos. However, I had no choice. Such a work requires all one's strength without exception, and because of this, my relationship with Bettina obviously suffered. She simply did not have a mother, and this is a heavy burden for a child. I could not split myself in two, and I felt compelled from within to carry on with Eranos. This resulted in Bettina feeling so lonely that she suffered greatly. Friends and acquaintances all condemned me because they never understood my inner compulsion. Something like this can only be understood if you experience something similar yourself. My daughter hated Eranos, which was understandable, but it was also the reason why I never let her attend the conferences. During the conferences, I was surrounded by so many difficulties, so overwhelmed by technical problems and everything else that if I had also introduced the endless problems of my relationship with Bettina, I would not have been able to cope. My situation between my

[67] Olga Fröbe-Kapteyn, letter to Henry Corbin, November 30, 1951, quoted in Ritsema-Gris, *op. cit.*, p. 91.

[68] Fröbe-Kapteyn, "An Attempt at Definition and Description of Eranos…," cit., p. 1.

[69] Olga Fröbe-Kapteyn, "Der unbekannte Genius" (unpublished typescript, 1957; Eranos Foundation Archives, Ascona-Moscia).

family and Eranos was always so complicated that it was almost unbearable. People can tell me over and over again that this was my destiny. But that wouldn't be true, because I had no choice. The inner compulsion was a hundred times greater than any external solution. We are dealing here with an Idea, an Idea that completely absorbed me and inexorably forbade and precluded everything else. One might think that it is not so difficult to live with an idea. However, I have thirty years of experience behind me, and it is a unique experience."[70]

Convinced that anyone who follows the path to wholeness cannot escape the characteristic suspension represented by crucifixion, on August 20, 1945, from the quiet solitude of Bollingen, Jung wrote one of his most significant letters on this subject to Fröbe-Kapteyn. We reproduce it here in its entirety.

"Dear Frau Fröbe,

The opus consists of three parts: insight, endurance, and action. Psychology is needed only in the first part, but in the second and third parts moral strength plays the predominant role. Your present situation is the result of pressure of circumstances which are unavoidable. It is *conflicts of duty* that make endurance and action so difficult. Your life's work for Eranos was unavoidable and right. Nevertheless it conflicts with maternal duties which are equally unavoidable and right. The one must exist, and so must the other. There can be no resolution, only patient endurance of the opposites which ultimately spring from your own nature. You yourself are a conflict that rages in itself and against itself, in order to melt its incompatible substances, the male and the female, in the fire of suffering, and thus create that fixed and unalterable form which is the goal of life. Everyone goes through this mill, consciously or unconsciously, voluntarily or forcibly. We are crucified between the opposites and delivered up to the torture until the 'reconciling third' takes shape. Do not doubt the rightness of the two sides within you, and let whatever may happen, happen. Admit that your daughter is right in saying you are a bad mother, and defend your duty as a mother towards Eranos. But never forget that Eranos is also the

[70] Olga Fröbe-Kapteyn, "Im Schatten von Eranos…" (unpublished typescript, undated [prob. 1958]; Eranos Foundation Archives, Ascona-Moscia).

right thing and was latent within you from the beginning. The apparently unendurable conflict is proof of the rightness of your life. A life without inner contradiction is either only half a life or else a life in the Beyond, which is destined only for angels. But God loves human beings more than the angels. With kindest regards,

Yours sincerely, C.G. Jung."[71]

Although the correspondence between Jung and Fröbe-Kapteyn does not record any significant disagreements, recalls Aniela Jaffé (1903–1991), it can be assumed that it was nonetheless not easy for two personalities as strong, independent, and creative as theirs to collaborate without coming into conflict or, at least, without finding themselves on divergent positions on certain issues. *(Figure 190)* Although, on rare occasions, Jung even openly and severely expressed his disagreement, it was always for reasons of little consequence. And, in any case, never in the terms to which Fröbe-Kapteyn resorted when speaking of their relationship[72] as a "battle."[73] Fröbe-Kapteyn identified in a pictorial theme, the "Eranos *Maṇḍala*," the deepest essence not only of her congressional project, but also of her relationship with Jung. It is a series in its own right, overlapping with the two phases of her artistic practice and documenting their thematic continuity despite the stylistic change. There are eight versions of the "Eranos *Maṇḍala*," made between 1927 and 1949, accompanied by preparatory sketches or supporting commentaries. *(Figures 57, 151, and 199–204)* In them, the figure of Jung seems to stand as a perpetual dialectical pole in relation to Fröbe-Kapteyn: at times, the very energy of the *Maṇḍala* seems to arise from their relationship; at other times, the *Maṇḍala* seems to show the inextricability of their bond, its being "imprisoned" in an impersonal configuration. Fröbe-Kapteyn

[71] Carl Gustav Jung, letter to Olga Fröbe-Kapteyn, August 20, 1945, in Id., *Letters: 1906–1961*, ed. Aniela Jaffé and Gerhard Adler, 2 vols. (Princeton, NJ: Bollingen Series XCV/1-2, Princeton University Press, 1973–75), Vol. I, p. 375.

[72] See Jaffé, *op. cit.*, pp. 115 ff.

[73] Olga Fröbe-Kapteyn, "Erster Abend…" (unpublished typescript, undated [prob. around 1957–58]; Eranos Foundation Archives, Ascona-Moscia), p. 1.

regarded the Round Table as an image of the "Eranos *Maṇḍala*" or, more precisely, its "concretization" [*Konkretisierung*].[74] *(Figure 205)*

The complexity of their relationship, which is also expressed in the "Visions" (Jung is the only recognizable figure in Fröbe-Kapteyn's drawings), is also evidenced by one of the most emblematic episodes involving them, which occurred during the 1935 Conference. Fröbe-Kapteyn recalls: "At the 1935 conference, Jung, [Erwin] Rousselle, and I had been invited by Mrs. Jay.[75] Dinner was served on a veranda overlooking the garden ... Jung sat to my right and Rousselle to my left. A musician was the fourth guest. The others, Mrs. Jay, Mrs. Jung, and perhaps someone else, came in to play music. Jung drank heavily and was already quite tipsy. In the center of the table is a small silver bowl with the head of a deity engraved on the bottom. Jung now asks for four glasses and more wine. Sparkling wine, aged Kirsch, and other wine are brought in. At this point, he fills the silver bowl with red wine, then fills our glasses, but only halfway. Then Jung begins to perform a ritual on the table, with himself as the priest [*Priester*] and me as the initiate [*Initiant*]. He takes the bowl and pours a little wine from it into all our glasses. Then he says, 'Drink.' He then refills the glasses with more wine, but again only halfway, and now begins a theatrical performance [*Spiel*] of pouring and decanting the wine from one

[74] Olga Fröbe-Kapteyn, [untitled] (unpublished typescript, June 29, 1953; Eranos Foundation Archives, Ascona-Moscia). See also, more extensively, Bernardini, *Jung a Eranos...*, cit., § 1.5: "Il rapporto tra Jung e Olga Fröbe-Kapteyn," pp. 83–112; the eight "Eranos *Maṇḍalas*" are reproduced on pages 165 f.

[75] This was probably Baroness Hertha Jay-von Seldeneck, who lived in Ascona at Villa Sogno, where Jung was a frequent guest during the Conference period. *(Figure 172)* On August 10, 1937, he wrote in Hertha Jay's guestbook: "This time sober" (Hakl, *op. cit.*, p. 320, fn. 39). Is this perhaps a reference to the "ritual" of two years earlier? Magda Kerényi also recalls how, in April 1943, she moved with her husband and two daughters to a house chosen by Fröbe-Kapteyn on the hill of Ascona called Villa Sogno (the same as Hertha Jay's?), which represented for her "the fulfillment of a dream, in which, in a certain way," she wrote, "Jung played a part. During the 1941 or 1942 conference, Professor Jung invited my husband [Károly Kerényi] to accompany him to his son's in-laws, the Merker family, on the hill [of Ascona]. The walk began in Moscia, where both Professor Jung, in Casa Eranos, and my husband, in Casa Gabriella, lived, and passed in front of a stone wall. As luck would have it, the heavy wooden gate was open, revealing a splendor of plants and flowers such as my husband had never seen before. The inscription on the large open gate, bearing the name of the villa, was not visible to passers-by. When, in 1943, we found ourselves once again in front of the villa, which had been rented out, my husband recognized 'the dream house' he had admired once during his walk with Jung and whose name was now visible: 'Villa Sogno'..." (Magda Kerényi, "Psicologia e mitologia. I rapporti tra C.G. Jung e Karl Kerényi," *L'immaginale. Rassegna di psicologia immaginale*, 4, (6, 1986), pp. 55 ff.).

glass to another, while occasionally refilling the bowl. During this time, only Jung speaks. His sentences are incoherent. He speaks mostly to me or to himself. It seems as if a storm is brewing, and every now and then there is thunder. Each time [there is thunder], he says, 'This [the thunder] is also part of it.' He addresses me as if I were a novice, giving me no explanation. He speaks solemnly. I understand little. I think: if we drink so much, what will become of me, since I can't handle wine and I have to be clear-headed for the conference the next morning. However, I understand that what is happening is so important that I cannot ruin the performance. Consequently, I drink red wine, Kirsch, sparkling wine, Burgundy, all mixed together, without feeling the slightest effects. My head is very clear and I think only: just don't let me forget anything. I look at Jung. He has become completely transparent. He has even become beautiful, and the same is true of Rousselle. Jung always wears a large ring with a Gnostic seal.[76] He puts it in the bowl filled with wine, then takes it out and puts it on the ring finger of my left hand. And they start pouring and drinking wine again, while Jung continues to talk to himself and to me. At one point he asks me, 'What color are you?' I said, 'Red.' Rousselle says, 'Green.' Jung says, 'I only know that I am yellow.' Blue is probably the unknown musician, who is the fourth in the circle [*Kreise*] and acts almost as an extra. Overall, the ritual lasts about an hour and a half, then Jung takes my hand, slips off the ring, and puts it back on his finger, saying, 'Now I take this ring back from

---

[76] Jung described the meaning of his ring to Miguel Serrano as follows: "It is Egyptian. It has a snake engraved on it, symbolizing Christ. Above the snake is the face of a woman; below, the number eight, a symbol of infinity, the labyrinth, and the path to the unconscious. I had a couple of things changed to make it a Christian symbol" (cf. Carl Gustav Jung, *C.G. Jung Speaking—Interviews and Encounters*, eds. William McGuire and Richard Francis Carrington Hull (Princeton, NJ: Bollingen Series XCVII, Princeton University Press, 1977); It. Ed. *Jung parla. Interviste e incontri* (Milan: Adelphi, 1995), p. 573). Jung had carved the ring from an ancient Gnostic gem dedicated to Abraxas, the Gnostic god of the *Seven Sermons to the Dead* (Carl Gustav Jung, *Septem Sermones ad Mortuos. Die sieben Belehrungen der Toten. Geschrieben von Basilides in Alexandria, der Stadt, wo der Osten den Westen berührt* ([without publishing information] 1916); It. Ed. "I sette sermoni ai morti. Scritti da Basilide in Alessandria, la città in cui l'Oriente tocca l'Occidente," in Id., *Ricordi, sogni, riflessioni*, ed. Aniela Jaffé (Milan: Biblioteca Universale Rizzoli, 1992), pp. 449–63), the enigmatic work written by Jung between 1916 and 1917 and subsequently circulated only privately (a copy of the original edition is still kept in the library of Casa Gabriella). Jung decided to publish this work as an appendix to *Memories, Dreams, Reflections* only after much hesitation and solely "for the sake of honesty," without ever revealing the anagram with which the writing ends. He gave a copy to Hermann Hesse in 1919 (Carl Gustav Jung, letter to Hermann Hesse, December 3, 1919, in Id., *Letters...*, cit., Vol. I, pp. 573 f.).

you, warmed by you.' Shortly thereafter, the performance comes to an end. From time to time during the performance, the musicians or others come and watch what we are doing, they don't understand anything and then they leave again."[77] The day after the "ritual," when everyone was awake and the Zurich group arrived at Eranos, Fröbe-Kapteyn said to Jung: "You, as a psychologist, have done something very serious. You have bound me to yourself!" And Jung replied: "It wasn't me, it was the Self..." (*'Das war nicht ich, sondern das Selbst...'*)[78] *(Figures 159–167)*

Fröbe-Kapteyn attributed great importance to this unusual moment: "I always clung to the Ring ritual," she wrote twelve years later, "but now even that has had its day. It was perhaps the main attachment I had to free myself from, along with my attachment to Mary [Mellon]. These two bonds were the strongest I have ever had."[79] *(Figure 196)* And again: "In the realization of the 1935 ritual, the external and the internal are simultaneously present. The timeless is simultaneously represented as within time, visible, audible, perceptible by all the senses. An event on an inner level and, at the same time, in external reality. This experience was decisive for my own psychology and for the development of Eranos. My round table (on which the larger round table top is placed),[80] is the point in my life where the conscious and the unconscious meet, and also where my individual activity coincides with the work of Eranos. This determines my place at the round table."[81] *(Figure 191)*

Only in the last years of her life, through the practice of active imagination, Fröbe-Kapteyn had the opportunity to process their enduring but conflicted relationship. The visions that were the outcome of that practice hint at a long and laborious confrontation with her own shadow:[82] "I am lying in bed," she wrote documenting that experience, "and I reflect

---

[77] Fröbe-Kapteyn, "Erster Abend...," cit., pp. 8 ff.

[78] Eliade, *Giornale*, cit., pp. 133 and 136; However, Eliade erroneously traces the "ritual" back to 1936.

[79] Fröbe-Kapteyn, "Vision. 3 Juli 1947," cit., p. 2.

[80] It is still customary for the large green wooden round table to be placed on top of a smaller round table made of Ticino granite; next to it is a second granite table of the same size as the first.

[81] Fröbe-Kapteyn, "Die Eranos *Mandala*," cit.

[82] Olga Fröbe-Kapteyn, "Der Schatten," cit., pp. 1 ff.

on Jung and me, or rather, I see the *Eranos-landscape* of today and of before and the events that can still be seen quite clearly in this landscape. At this point the curtain opens and Jung enters ... He is as I met him in the year 1935, so more than twenty years younger. He says, 'I am able to help you, especially since a clarification of our twenty-six-year relationship seems to me necessary. You might call it more a 'battle' [*Kampf*] than a relationship, but you have now made it possible for me to take part in this mutual understanding [*Verständigung*], in that you were ready to have visions. It is the only way, this, because it leads through the *land of the sympathy of all things*. There everything is possible. Barriers are no longer present.'"[83]

Fröbe-Kapteyn was able to recognize how the conflictual nature of their relationship was determined, in large part, by her projections. That is, the significance of their difficulties could be traced back to the intense negative transference toward Jung, onto whom, from 1934 to 1950, she had projected the image of a powerful and dark "Jahweh," as conveyed by the *Book of Job*.[84] It was this irrational and wrathful "Jahweh," for example, that Fröbe-Kapteyn had encountered in the summer of 1948, when, upon her refusal to send the newly founded C.G. Jung-Institut the Eranos address list, Jung was seized by a sudden and severe attack of anger, in the face of which she was deeply disturbed and shaken.[85] Indeed, Fröbe-Kapteyn continued, "Jung's appearance seems to change. Sometimes it is his face and benevolent expression. Sometimes his figure is huge, and then again he returns to his normal size. For an instant he appears demonic as in 1948, but immediately his features are human again, indeed more human than I have ever seen them. I see, as it were, the *Jahweh-projection* hovering over him, now entirely loosened, no longer firmly attached to him ... The mighty image, demonic, unjust, greedy, full of power, indeed lethal, that I had built for myself of Jung and that extended the taboo-Jahweh's law, precisely on Eranos, has now become defenseless. The old law has

[83] Fröbe-Kapteyn, "Erster Abend...," cit., pp. 1 ff.

[84] *Ibid.*, p. 23.

[85] *Ibid.*, p. 19.

dissolved, and I find myself under a new law. So from Jung detaches, and falls, much unreal guilt."[86]

After more than fifteen years of "battle," the Jahwistic image projected onto Jung finally crumbled, giving way to the image of Jung as an individual. Fröbe-Kapteyn recognized how behind this projection lay her own negative Animus,[87] namely, her aggressive masculine side. This projection, although destructive, had nevertheless helped her to confront her own masculine side, namely that Animus which, in its positive aspect, had enabled her to give birth to Eranos. Fröbe-Kapteyn reflected again, "If I had not projected 'Jahweh' I would not have come to grips with this archetype, I would not even have attempted it, because I would not have arrived at the problem. I would never have understood to the end that it was in myself … Jung, now, has become 'human,' since I no longer deify him through projection-Jahweh. His human stimuli are no longer altered through the speaker of Jahweh, oversized and crammed with archetypal energy and violence. Perhaps, now, the real confrontation can take place. As my resentments and condemnations have disappeared, something has been transformed in me, and certainly in Jung, and this transformation embraces the concept of freedom for both of us, for neither obsession nor projection is freedom, but always constraint and contraction."[88] The acceptance and integration of this hitherto split and projected part of the self meant that, from the point of view of their relationship, what had hitherto been a "battle" gradually changed into a "tender and reconciling feeling without affection: a kind of compassion."[89]

Fröbe-Kapteyn recalled one of their last meetings, which probably took place in August 1951 (he would attend Eranos for the last time in 1952, only as a listener), when Jung gave his last, seminal lecture at Eranos, "On Synchronicity." During that August Conference, Szandor (Sándor) Végh

---

[86] *Ibid.*, pp. 1 f.

[87] On the idea of negative Animus, see, in particular, Carl Gustav Jung, *Visions. Notes from the Seminar Given in 1930–1934*, ed. Claire Douglas (London/New York, NY: Routledge, 1998), Vol. I, pp. 560, 614, and 622.

[88] Fröbe-Kapteyn, *op. cit.*, pp. 2 ff.

[89] *Ibid.*, p. 3.

(1905–1997), the Hungarian composer and violinist (later naturalized French), professor at the Budapest Academy from 1941 to 1946 and, from 1953, at the Basel Conservatory, played with Sándor Zöldy (violin), Georges Panzer (viola), and Paul Szabo (cello) works by Beethoven, Schubert, and Schumann. Invited as a speaker to Eranos in 1960, he gave a lecture on the theme "Musik als Erlebnis" ("Music as Experience"). Fröbe-Kapteyn recounts: "We see the terrace [of Casa Gabriella] with the large Round Table. We sit there and look out toward the lake. It is around five in the afternoon, the most beautiful time of day in this landscape. The Végh Quartet is sitting at the edge of the terrace, playing softly. They are playing music I don't know, a wonderful melody that completely envelops us. I say, 'This is Szandor's [Végh] music, it is his very soul that he pours out like this: it is immortal music.' 'Yes,' says Jung, 'he is truly someone who has been 'seized' [*Ergriffener*], I told you that years ago.' We are completely carried away by the sounds. In fact, they play just for us. Jung is not very sensitive to music, but this music touches him too in the deepest way. I have never heard music flow like this from a human heart and seem to embrace everything that is alive. We experience the unity of nature and man through the power of sound. Jung and I no longer speak. They play for a long time. Then Jung stands up and says, 'That was hermetic music, a mystery, we will never forget it. You surely remember the alchemical saying, 'The door to peace is extraordinarily narrow': we two have now found it.' Then he goes into the garden and we don't see him anymore."[90]

At the conclusion of the visionary experience, Fröbe-Kapteyn received this message from Jung who appeared in her vision: "It is time. I think we have done it. And now, you write the story of Eranos, because for the first time you see it without taboos, and you are free. Maybe we will see each other again, maybe not, but peace is in us."[91]

---

[90] *Ibid.*, p. 21 In the context of her analytical work with Erich Neumann, commenting a vision she experienced, Fröbe-Kapteyn wrote: "The current of music is the secret current that flows from the Self, and has always carried us along—but also drives us forward, like a train rushing through a tunnel. Jung said to me 20 years ago: 'Do not forget that you are the tunnel—not the train!'" (Olga Fröbe-Kapteyn, "Vision. Lebendige Bilder & Wandlungen" [belonging to "Neumann und ich"] (unpublished typescript, January 3–20, 1957; Eranos Foundation Archives, Ascona-Moscia), "Kommentar," p. 1).

[91] Fröbe-Kapteyn, "Erster Abend…," cit., pp. 21 ff. The work referred to by Fröbe-Kapteyn is probably "Die Geschichte von Eranos," cit., a recount of reflections dated between 1952 and 1958 which, in the

The epistolary exchange between Jung and Fröbe-Kapteyn, which began in the early 1930s and is still only minimally included in the *corpus* of Jung's letters, continued until his passing. The missives of the last ten years, in particular, are the visible sign of an intimate bond, never broken, and the expression of Jung's sincere gratitude to Fröbe-Kapteyn and her creation, Eranos, on the one hand, and to Fröbe-Kapteyn toward Jung, on the other hand, for the support given to her not only on the organizational level for Eranos, but perhaps even more so on the personal level, in her continuous confrontation with her own interiority: a confrontation that, from the second half of the 1920s to the mid-1930s also found expression in pictorial form, in the compendium we now refer to as her *Blue Book*.

In August 1951, for example, on the occasion of Fröbe-Kapteyn's seventieth birthday, Jung wrote this message: "Eranos, thanks to Mrs. Fröbe's resourcefulness and devotion, has become an institution to which one can wish a long future, which represents in Europe the only occasion where, beyond all specialist limitations, experts and laymen animated by spiritual interests can come together to exchange their views. Eranos anticipated by twenty years today's efforts toward the reunification [*Zusammenfassung*] of all the sciences and thus made a contribution in its own unique way to European intellectual history. This success would not have been possible, however, had it not found in Dr. [Daniel] Brody [1883–1969] a publisher as sensitive as he was devoted to the cause, who was not afraid to take on the risk of the voluminous annals [the *Eranos-Jahrbücher*]. What made Eranos so valuable to me personally was the fact that Mrs. Fröbe's hospitable home offered from time to time the opportunity for informal discussions around the Round Table. I remember with pleasure and gratitude the countless evenings that were so rich in stimulation and teaching and that provided me with just what I needed so much, namely personal empathic contact [*Fühlungnahme*] with other fields of knowledge. For this I owe Mrs. Fröbe the deepest thanks."[92] *(Figure 207)*

author's plan, would have been intended to lead to the writing of a "history of Eranos" from the point of view of its inner life: see Bernardini, *op. cit.*, pp. 19 and 110, fn. 429.

[92] Carl Gustav Jung, "Dank an Frau Froebe" (unpublished typescript, August 1951; Eranos Foundation Archives, Ascona-Moscia), merged in Lucy Heyer-Grote, ed., "Gratulationen zum 70. Geburtstag Olga

In a letter dated June 2, 1956, he wrote to her:

"Dear Mrs. Fröbe,

I thank you wholeheartedly for sending me, and so amicably dedicating to me, the XXIV volume of the *Eranos-Jahrbücher* on the subject 'Man and the Sympathy of All Things,' and likewise for your note. Even a first glance promised an interesting read; I only regret that I must postpone it until my summer vacation period; overwork deprives me at the moment of the necessary quiet.

The Eranos Conferences have always offered me an abundance of remarkable intellectual stimulation, and the exchange of thoughts with people of similar interests as well as the resonance of a prepared audience have been a beautiful and important experience for me. Unfortunately, age now prevents me from attending symposia: my strengths would not quite be able to stand up to the inevitable onslaught of all those people. Now more than ever, I need peace of mind and must carefully avoid all meetings with lots of people. Even more so, therefore, the *Jahrbücher* are now something precious to me, since they communicate to me the spiritual essence of the meetings, although I must call to mind, alone, the sunlight, the lake, and old friends. For this year's conference I wish you a good and fruitful outcome, and I would be grateful if you could convey this wish to the individual speakers.

Yours sincerely, C.G. Jung."[93]

On March 30, 1957, in a note prepared for a publication celebrating the first twenty-five years of the life of Eranos, Jung wished, "May the light of the European spirit, which in this time of darkness has come out of Eranos for so many years, still have as a gift a long life, so that it may fulfill its role as a beacon of a European union."[94]

Froebe-Kapteyn am 19 Oktober 1951" (unpublished manuscripts and typescripts, 1951; Eranos Foundation Archives, Ascona-Moscia), and quoted (in part) in Jaffé, *op. cit.*, p. 106 and (in full) in Bernardini, *op. cit.*, pp. 77 ff. English translation by the author.

[93] Carl Gustav Jung, letter to Olga Fröbe-Kapteyn, June 2, 1956 (University Archives, ETH-Bibliothek, Zurich / Eranos Foundation Archives, Ascona-Moscia; © 2007 Foundation of the Works of C.G. Jung, Zurich), quoted in Bernardini, *op. cit.*, pp. 110 f.; English translation by the author.

[94] Quoted in Olga Fröbe-Kapteyn, ed., *25 Jahre Eranos. 1933–1957* (Zurich: Rhein-Verlag, 1957), page not numbered [p. 5]; English translation by the author.

In his old age, recalls Jaffé, epistolary advice and explanations greatly wearied Jung, who therefore generally refused to give any. For Fröbe-Kapteyn, however, he did not hesitate to make an exception. Especially late in life, what weighed heavily on Fröbe-Kapteyn was the loneliness into which she was abruptly catapulted as guests left Eranos after the lively symposium period; she was therefore very grateful to those few who could extend their stay in Ascona-Moscia by a few days.[95] During the long winters, epistolary exchanges were probably therefore particularly important to her.

In 1960, following a serious operation on her eyes, she was forced to wear a black bandage for eight days. As Mircea Eliade recounts in his diary, Fröbe-Kapteyn was distressed by the constant darkness and could not remain alone for a moment without finding comfort in the nurse's hand. However, her temporary blindness stimulated a series of visions which, dictated to her secretary, she had delivered to Jung on June 24, 1960. In the first vision there was a ruined cathedral, at night. She saw herself on scaffolding, very high up, near the dome and, at a certain moment, realized that the cathedral was herself. So she knelt down, waiting to be pierced in the heart by a spear.[96] Jung wrote her back a few days later, saying that the surgical operation had a psychic parallel: just as the threat of cataracts, and thus blindness, was an equivalent of the danger of sinking into the unconscious, of spiritual death, so her operation was equivalent to a new birth, and the recovery of the visual faculties to the salvation of conscious life from the engulfment of the unconscious.[97] This was the last letter Jung wrote to her.[98]

---

[95] Ritsema-Gris, *op. cit.*, p. 32; English translation by the author.

[96] Olga Fröbe-Kapteyn, letter to Carl Gustav Jung, June 24, 1960 (University Archives, ETH-Bibliothek, Zurich; / Eranos Foundation Archives, Ascona-Moscia), quoted in Bernardini, *op. cit.*, p. 111; and Id., "Visionen Olga F.-K. Mai–Juni 1960. Kilnik Bellinzona nach der Staroperation aus einem Brief vom 24.6.60 an C.G. Jung" (unpublished typescript, June 24, 1960; Eranos Foundation Archives, Ascona-Moscia); see also Eliade, *Giornale…*, cit., p. 255.

[97] Carl Gustav Jung, letter to Olga Fröbe-Kapteyn, June 28, 1960 (University Archives, ETH-Bibliothek, Zurich / Eranos Foundation Archives, Ascona-Moscia; © 2007 Foundation of the Works of C.G. Jung, Zurich), quoted in Bernardini, *op. cit.*, p. 111. English translation by the author.

[98] A subsequent missive to Fröbe-Kapteyn from Jung was written by Aniela Jaffé on September 15, 1960 (Eranos Foundation Archives, Ascona-Moscia); see Bernardini, *op. cit.*, p. 111.

The words with which Fröbe-Kapteyn concluded one of her last missives to Jung, sent to him on his 85th birthday, turn out to be understandable: "During the experiences of the last weeks [of hospitalization], I always held on to some expression of yours or a sentence from the *I Ching*, and thus I was able to realize what a blessing your cooperation was for Eranos and for me personally. Despite many personal difficulties, I always stuck to what you said. And now, after twenty-seven years, more than ever. I am deeply happy to have the opportunity to tell you."[99]

[99] Olga Fröbe-Kapteyn, letter to Carl Gustav Jung, June 24, 1960, cit.; also quoted in Jaffé, *op. cit.*, p. 117, and Bernardini, *op. cit.*, pp. 11 f. Their correspondence continued until February 10, 1961, the date of the last letter sent by Frobe-Kapteyn to Jung (he died on June 6, she on April 25 of the following year), in which she again shared with him her reflections on a dream she had had. She also reminded him of what he had said to her on a previous occasion: "You are too much alone" (*"Sie sind zu viel allein"*).

CHAPTER III
Artistic Itineraries from Monte Verità to Eranos

The Europe of the early twentieth century saw the birth of numerous *Lebensreform* movements that often looked to the East. In the winds of such attempts at "life reform",[1] the utopias conceived and lived in Ascona and Ticino were among the most striking and successful examples. They were often inspired by distant cultures and alternative spiritualities, which in those decades sparked the curiosity and imagination of the Europeans.[2]

Mikhail Bakunin (1814–1876) had settled in the Locarno area between 1869 and 1874, living in various places between Muralto and Locarno. From August 1873 to July 1874, he lived in the "Baronata" villa in Mappo, between Minusio and Tenero. The estate had been purchased by Carlo Cafiero (1846–1892), a revolutionary and representative of the International in Italy, both to offer Bakunin a place to spend the last years of his life and to create a base for Italian revolutionaries.[3] While Ticino was

---

[1] See, among others, Janos Frecot, "Die Lebensreform bewegung," in Klaus Vondung, ed., *Das wilhelminische Bildungsbürgertum. Zur Sozialgeschichte seiner Ideen* (Göttingen: Vandenhoeck & Ruprecht, 1976), pp. 138–52; Id., "Corona agreste sull'Europa: Monte Verità quale campo centrale di esperimenti per modi di vita alternativi fra l'inizio del secolo e la prima Guerra Mondiale," in Szeemann, *op. cit.*, pp. 54–64; and Yme Kuiper, "On Monte Verità: Myth and Modernity in the *Lebensreform* Movement," in Jitse Dijkstra, Justin Kroesen, and Yme Kuiper, eds., *Myths, Martyrs, and Modernity: Studies in the History of Religions in Honour of Jan N. Bremmer* (Leiden/Boston, MA: Numen Book Series 127, Brill, 2010), pp. 629–50.

[2] See Webb, *Il sistema occulto...*, cit.; Introvigne, *Il cappello del mago…*, cit., 270 ff.; and Id., *Il ritorno dello gnosticismo* (Carnago: SugarCo, 1993), *passim*.

[3] See Romano Broggini, "Anarchia e libertarismo nel locarnese dal 1870," in Szeemann, *op. cit.*, pp. 15–25; Vv.Aa., *Baj/Bakunin. Atti del Convegno. Monte Verità, Ascona, 5 ottobre 1996* (Lugano: La Baronata, 1996); Sam Whimster, "Conversazioni con gli anarchici. Max Weber ad Ascona," in Andreas Schwab e Claudia Lafranchi, eds., *Senso della vita e bagni di sole. Esperimenti di vita e arte al Monte Verità* (Ascona:

becoming a significant center for anarchist and libertarian ideas during those years, the nearby Brissago Islands were also a place of intense activity for supporters of Giuseppe Garibaldi (1807–1882) and Giuseppe Mazzini (1805–1872).[4]

In this context, Alfredo Pioda (1848–1909) from Locarno also played a significant role.[5] Philosopher, historian, politician (he was involved in the revolution of September 11, 1890 and was a liberal national Councilor), as well as president of the Milanese section of the Theosophical Society, in 1889 Pioda had designed a "theosophical lay convent" called Fraternitas ("Brotherhood") on the Monescia hill in Ascona.[6] Alongside Pioda, in the Fraternitas project were involved physician Franz Hartmann (1838–1912), member of the Theosophical Society and Freemason, R. Thurmann (?–1889), philosopher and university professor linked to William Crookes' spiritualism, and the Swedish Countess Constance Wachtmeister, president of the group

Fondazione Monte Verità, 2001), pp. 42–58; and Giulio Schiavoni, "Figure della bohème in Ascona. Hugo Ball e Erich Mühsam lettori di Bakunin," *Studi germanici*, 15/16 (2019), pp. 31–44. It is interesting to note that part of a certain anarchist-socialist background in Locarno had also nurtured an interest in the activities carried out at Eranos. In addition to painter and anarchist Ernst Frick, who appears among the audience at the Eranos Conferences from 1934 to 1941 (at that time he had already distanced himself from anarchist militancy), we find in the Eranos Guestbook, in 1932 and 1938, the signature of the former secretary of the Swiss trade unions who later converted to anarchism, Margarethe Faas-Brunner-Hardegger (1882–1963), director of the *Sozialist*. Hardegger, together with Hans Brunner (1887–1960), had founded the "Villino Graziella" in Minusio in 1919, an anarchist-communist agricultural community, which failed in 1964 due to the material difficulties it faced. She then supported the "Fontana Martina" agricultural community, founded in Ronco in 1924 by Fritz Jordi (1886–1938) and Heinrich Vogeler (1872–1942). See Regina Bochsler, "Esodo dall'Egitto—Margarethe Hardegger e i coloni pionieri del *Sozialistischer Bund* nel Canton Ticino," in Schwab and Lafranchi, *op. cit.*, pp. 170–87; and Ina Boesch, *Gegenleben. Die Sozialistin Margarethe Hardegger und ihre politischen Bühnen* (Zurich: Chronos, 2003).

[4] In 1885, the Brissago Islands were purchased by Baroness Antonietta von Saint-Léger (1865–1948), a Russian noblewoman of German origin, who began work on the Botanical Park the following year, which still exists today. In 1919, she received a visit from James Joyce (1882–1941). In 1928, the islands were purchased by Max Emden (1874–1940), owner of the department stores of the same name in Hamburg, who also began the construction of a palace and the expansion of the park. Upon his death, they became state property, thanks in part to the financial contribution of Baron Eduard von der Heydt. See Hasenfratz, *op. cit.*, and Mondada, *op. cit.*

[5] Virgilio Gilardoni, "Un terreno predisposto," in Szeemann, *op. cit.*, pp. 10–11.

[6] Alfredo Pioda, *Statuti, Norme e Schema del Convento Laico da fondarsi sulle rive del Lago nella Svizzera* (Bellinzona: Stamperia Colombi, 1889). In the same year, the bulletin *Lux* of the International Academy for Spiritual and Magnetic Studies in Rome announced the creation of a joint-stock company called "Fraternitas," whose aims included the foundation of the aforementioned monastery.

and, from 1884, advisor to Blavatsky. Hartmann had written in a novel about "an imaginary theosophical monastery, supposedly located in the Alps."[7] He also contributed to the magazine *Neue Metaphysische Rundschau* founded in 1896 by Paul Zillmann—who, as we have seen, played a decisive role both in the life of Olga Fröbe-Kapteyn and in the future Eranos project—with a fantasy story, in which he recounted his discovery of a secret Rosicrucian monastery in the Bavarian Alps,[8] filling readers' minds with romantic notions about adepts in the heart of modern Europe.[9] The main inspiration behind Fraternitas convent may therefore have been Hartmann himself, whose work *Die weisse und schwarze Magie* (*Magic, White and Black*) was translated by Pioda in 1906–1907.[10] Although the convent was never built, its design ensured that the future settlers of Monte Verità had found the place "most interesting."[11] Pioda's home, a symbolic crossroads between theosophical ideas and the distinctly anti-clerical Masonic tradition of Ticino, remained a must-see destination for many scholars of esotericism and related subjects during those years.[12]

Monte Verità was originally the idea of Ida Hofmann (1864–1926), a piano teacher from Montenegro, and Henry Oedenkoven (1875–1935), the wealthy son of Belgian industrialists, who founded a cooperative colony on Monescia Hill in Ascona in 1900. They bought the three and a half hectares of land from Pioda, many of whose spiritual interests would

---

[7] Franz Hartmann, *An Adventure among the Rosicrucians* (Boston, MA: Occult Publishing, 1887). See René Guénon, *Le Théosophisme. Histoire d'une Pseudo-Religion* (Paris: Ed. Traditionelles, 1975), pp. 40 f.; and Walter Schönenberger, "Monte Verità e le idee teosofiche," in Szeemann, *op. cit.*, p. 66.

[8] Franz Hartmann, "Ein Abenteuer unter den Rosenkreuzern," *Neue Metaphysische Rundschau*, 1 (1898), pp. 156–67, 232–43, 333–41, 386–89, 429–34, and 2 (1899), pp. 18–22, 46–51, 93–105, 241–54, 273–81, 305–14, 337–46.

[9] Nicholas Goodrick-Clark, *Le radici occulte del nazismo* (Carnago: SugarCo, 1993 {1985}), p. 46.

[10] Franz Hartmann, *Die weiße und schwarze Magie oder Das Gesetz des Geistes in der Natur* (Leipzig: Lotus, undated; Collection Karl Vester, Ascona). After leaving the Theosophical Society (his outbursts with Blavatsky were apparently memorable, both characters being apparently anything but peaceful), Hartmann claimed to have met an ancient Rosicrucian brotherhood in Germany that had tasked him with reviving an "Esoteric Order of the Rose Cross" (Introvigne, *Il cappello del mago…*, cit., p. 196).

[11] Schönenberger, *op. cit.*

[12] Virgilio Gilardoni, "Lettere di Alfredo Pioda a Emilia Franzoni. Appunti per la storia di un grande pittore lombardo: Filippo Franzoni," *Archivio Storico Ticinese*, 3 (5, 1960–61).

continue to live on and proliferate in the new colony project.[13] Both educated and from good families, disappointed by civilization, which they saw as having no way out except through a return to a life in harmony with nature, Hofmann and Oedenkoven despite their age difference agreed to found a settlement that would become a school of life for its members and an example for the outer world. The pioneers strived to make Monte Verità an example of an alternative lifestyle, aimed at a radical reform in nutrition ("vegetabilism," a form of vegetarianism that rejects everything that comes from animals, such as milk, cheese, eggs, wool, and leather)[14], in marital life (practicing "conscious marriage"), in writing (for example, by abolishing capital letters), in architecture (the "air-light" huts, with windows on all

[13] The library of Casa Gabriella at Eranos still houses a copy of the *Bhagavadgītā* translated by Hartmann (*Die Bhagavad Gita. Das Lied von der Gottheit oder die Lehre vom Göttlichen Sein* (Leipzig: Max Altmann, 1929), as well as three copies of the *Bhagavadgītā* edited by Annie Besant (*The Bhagavadgītā or the Lord's Song* (London: The Theosophical Publishing House Limited, 1904)), who, on October 16, 1922, signed the founding act of the Locarno section of the Theosophical Society together with the Franzoni, Bernasconi, Balli, and Balestra families. Not only did the Monte Verità settlers go on a pilgrimage to Milan in 1902 to listen to a series of her lectures, but it is also possible that both Annie Besant and Jiddu Krishnamurti (1895–1986) gave a number of lectures at Monte Verità in the mid-1920s. We also note the presence among the audience at the 1934 Eranos Conference of Marquise Carla Vitelleschi, perhaps Krishnamurti's closest friend (cf. Michele Beraldo, "Krishnamurti nell'occhio della polizia politica," in Gianfranco De Turris, ed., *Esoterismo e fascismo* (Rome: Mediterranee, 2006), p. 70, fn. 12). For further information on the theosophical background of Ascona, see Fausto Pedrotta, *Alfredo Pioda nella vita e nelle opere* (Bellinzona: [without publishing information], undated [1935]) and Vittorio Gilardoni, *Filippo Franzoni 1857–1911* (Bellinzona: La Vesconta, 1968). Locarno painter Franzoni stayed at Monte Verità for a period of treatment and developed his own theory of colors, in light of which Fröbe-Kapteyn's "Meditation Plates" could also be considered in the future; Id., "Un terreno predisposto," cit.; Schönenberger, *op. cit.*, 65–79; and Florian Illerhaus, *Gegenseitige Beeinflussungen von Theosophie und Monte Verità* (Munich: Grin, 2009). On the Ariosophic and Mazdaznan currents that touched Monte Verità, see instead Roman Kurzmeyer, *Viereck und Kosmos. Künstler, Lebensreformer, Okkultisten, Spiritisten in Amden 1901–1912. Max Nopper, Josua Klein, Fidus, Otto Meyer-Amden* (Wien: Voldemeer, 1999); Hermann Müller, ed., *Meister Diefenbachs Alpenwanderung. Ein Künstler und Kulturrebell im Karwendel* (Recklinghausen: Umbruch, 2003); and Id., ed., *Der Himmelhof. Künstlerfamilie und Landkommune* (Recklinghausen: Umbruch, 2003).

[14] See Ida Hofmann-Oedenkoven, *Vegetabilismus! Vegetarismus! Blätter zur Verbreitung vegetarischer Lebensweise* (Monte Verità/Ascona: Selbstverlag von Ida Hofmann-Oedenkoven, 1905); and Id., *Monte Verità. Verità senza poesia*, foreword by Edgardo Franzosini, afterword by Nicoletta Mongini (Bellinzona: Casagrande, 2023); see also Adolf Grohmann, *Die Vegetarier-Ansiedlung in Ascona und die sogenannten Naturmenschen im Tessin* (Halle a.S.: Verlag von Carl Marhold, 1904; rpt. Ascona: Edizioni della Rondine, 1997); and Hans-Caspar Bodmer, Paul Lioba, and Ottmar Holdenrieder, "Shaping the Mountain of Truth: An Introduction to the Monte Verità," in Frank A. Klötzli and Gian-Reto Walther, eds., *Conference on Recent Shifts in Vegetation Boundaries of Deciduous Forests, Especially Due to the General Global Warming* (Basel: Birkhäuser, 1999), pp. 1–13.

sides), in clothing (naturism, "reform" clothing, and long hair), and the female condition (adopting feminism as one of the community's precepts.)[15]

Nevertheless, disagreements within the group were not long in coming: Hofmann and Oedenkoven chose to create a nursing home, which provided them with a living, while the other members of the group—Karl Gräser (1875–1915), his brother Gustav Arthur "Gusto" Gräser (1879–1958), Lotte Hattemer (1876–1906), Ida's sister Jenny Hofmann, and Ferdinand Brune[16]—wanted to remain faithful to the project of a community based on barter. Oedenkoven thus took over Monte Verità together with Ida Hofmann, paying the others a settlement and starting the activities of the vegetarian health center. Karl Gräser bought a house on the edge of Oedenkoven's property, where he lived with Jenny Hofmann. After spending several months in prison in Hungary for refusing to fulfill his military obligations, Gusto Gräser retired in 1902 to a cave in the rock of the mountain next to Monte Verità, before resuming his pilgrimages across Europe. Hattemer is said to have lived in the ruins of a house, lighting a fire outside every evening with which she wanted to symbolically purify the world.[17]

---

[15] Cf. Ida Hofmann-Oedenkoven, *Wie gelangen wir Frauen zu harmonischen und gesunden Daseinbedingungen? – Offener Brief an die Verfasserin von "Eine Mutter für Viele"* (Ascona: Selbstverlag, Carlo Vester, 1902); and Id., *Beiträge zur Frauenfrage* (Winnenden/Württemberg: Zentralstelle zur Werbreitung guter deutscher Literatur, 1915). See also Anatole Lucet, "Natures féminines et radicalités féministes : l'émancipation des femmes sur le Monte Verità," *Cahiers d'histoire culturelle*, 29 (2018) ("Monte Verità : communautés d'expériences du corps et de retours à la nature"), pp. 53–66, and more recently Patrick Graur, "(Er-)Schöpfungstendenzen um 1900. Ida Hofmann und der Monte Verità im feministischen Kontext," in Denise Dumschat-Rehfeldt, Julia Ingold, Simone Ketterl, Jonas Meurer, Magdalena Sperber, and Anna Lena Westphal, eds., *Literatur am Ende. Putting *Schöpfung* in *Erschöpfung** (Marburg: Büchner, 2024), pp. 131–42.

[16] Brune, a theosophist, although part of the original group, did not take part in the founding of the colony, appearing sporadically at Monte Verità as a visitor only later.

[17] On the experience and period of the Sanatorium, in addition to the texts mentioned above, see also Heinrich Kropp, *Monte Verità: Schauspiel in 3 Akten aus dem Naturleben zu Ascona* (Ascona: [without publishing information], 1914); by Erich Mühsam, the following publications: *Ascona: Eine Broschüre* (Locarno/Berlin: Birger Carlson/Klaus Guhl, 1905); *Ascona: Vereinigte texte. Aus den jahren 1905, 1930 und 1931* (Zurich: Sanssouci, 1979); *Ascona, Monte Verità e Schegge* (Salorino: L'Affranchi, 1989); by Martin Green, *Mountain of Truth: The Counterculture begins. Ascona 1900–1920* (Hanover, NH/London, University Press of New England, 1986); *Prophets of a New Age: The Politics of Hope from the Eighteenth through the Twenty-first Centuries* (New York, NY: Charles Scribner's Sons, 1992); and "Una Nuova Era. New Age e nuovi 'Centri di vita' dal 1890 al 1920," in Schwab and Lafranchi, *op. cit.*, pp. 207–22. By Harald

Szeemann, "Monte Verità. La montagna della verità," in Id., *Monte Verità...*, cit., pp. 5–9; Id., "Monte Verità, Ascona. Eine Chronologie [Mit Beiträgen von Theo Kneubühler und Willy Rotzler]," in *Du. Europäische Kunstzeitschrift*, 10 (1978), pp. 32–78; and Id., ed., *Visionäre Schweiz. Zur Ausstellung im Kunsthaus Zürich, 1. November bis 26. Januar 1992, und im Städtische Kunsthalle und Kunstverein für die Rheinlande und Westfalen, Düsseldorf, 26. Juni bis 30. August 1992* (Aarau/Frankfurt am Main/Salzburg: Sauerländer, 1991). By Giorgio Vacchini, "Febbricità storica," in Szeemann, *Monte Verità...*, cit., pp. 12–13; "Monte Verità," in *ibid.*, pp. 80–84; and, edited by the same, *Ascona. Verdetti popolari e documenti*, cit. And also Nicoletta and Othmar Birkner, "L'arte come espressione di una nuova vita," in Szeemann, *op. cit.*, pp. 123–27; Giò Rezzonico, ed., *Antologia di cronaca del Monte Verità* (Locarno: I quaderni dell'Eco di Locarno, 1992). Also, Ute Druvins, "Alternative Projekte um 1900. Utopie und Realität auf dem ‚Monte Verità' und in der ‚Neuen Gemeinschaft,'" in Hiltrud Gnüg, ed., *Literarische Utopie-Entwürfe* (Frankfurt am Main: Suhrkamp, 1982), pp. 236–49; Vv.Aa., *Turicum. Schweizer Kultur und Wirtschaft*, 23 (June–July 1993) ("Ascona-Monte Verità"); Philippe Baillet, "Monte Verità (1900–1920) ou la complexité du 'romanticisme anticapitaliste.' Une première approche historique et bio-bibliographique," *Politica Hermetica*, 14 (2000), pp. 199–218; and Id., "Monte Verità: Une 'communité alternative' entre mouvance völkisch et avant-garde artistique," *Nouvelle Ecole*, 52 (2001), pp. 109–35; Andreas Schwab, *Sinnsuche und Sonnenbad. Experimente in Kunst und Leben auf dem Monte Verità* (Zurich: Limmat, 2001); Id. and Claudia Lafranchi, "Cento anni di verità?," in Id. and Lafranchi, *Senso della vita e bagni di sole...*, cit., pp. 9–21; Id., "'Frattanto gridava in me la nostalgia...' – Vedute d'esterno del Monte Verità," in *ibid.*, pp. 105–18; Id., *Monte Verità—Sanatorium der Sehnsucht* (Zurich: Orell Füssli, 2003); and Id., *Zeit der Aussteiger. Eine Reise zu den Künstlerkolonien von Barbizon bis Monte Verità* (Munich: C.H.Beck, 2021); Fabio Minazzi, "Vivere secondo natura? L'esperienza del Monte Verità nel contesto del dibattito filosofico," in Schwab and Lafranchi, *op. cit.*, pp. 59–73; Albert Wirz, "Sanitarium, non sanatorio! Spazi per la salute," in *ibid.*, pp. 119–38; Alberto Nessi, "La via delle comete," in *ibid.*, pp. 263–275; Ulrich Linse, "Il Monte Verità e la valle di Hunza. Alla riscoperta di una moderna 'topografia sacrale' in Ticino e in Pakistan," in Szeemann, *op. cit.*, pp. 238–59; Hans-Caspar Bodmer, Ottmar Holdenrieder, and Klaus Seeland, eds., *Monte Verità: Landschaft Kunst Geschichte* (Frauenfeld/Stuttgart/Wien: Huber, 2000); Irene Bignardi, *Le piccole utopie* (Milan: Feltrinelli, 2003), pp. 55–76; Samir Girgis, *Jakob und der Berg der Wahrheit: Historischer Roman über die Geschichte Asconas und des Monte Verità* (Oldenburg: Schardt, 2005); Eberhard Mros, *Phänomen Monte Verità*, 8 vols. (Ascona: Selbstverlag des Verfassers, 2007–2008); Ulrike Voswinckel, *Freie Liebe und Anarchie: Schwabing-Monte Verità. Entwürfe gegen das etablierte Leben* (Munich: Allitera, 2009); Enno van der Eerden, *Ascona: Bezield paradijs* (Amsterdam: Uitgeverij bas Lubberhuizen, 2011); Kaj Noschis, *Monte Verità e il genio del luogo*, Bellinzona: Casagrande, 2013 {2011}); Vv.Aa., *L'Elisarion e le sue origini* (Tenero: Edizioni del Comune di Minusio, 2011); Martino Giovanettina and Niccolò Giovanettina, *Ascona. Un reportage* (Foroglio: Agenzia Kay, 2012); Bianca Tosatti and Friedrich Reinhard Brüdelin, *Armand Schulthess. Il giardino della conoscenza* (Bellinzona: Sottoscala, 2013); Vv.Aa., *Initiales*, 4 (2014) ("MV"); Vv.Aa., *Le labyrinthe poétique de Armand Schulthess* (Bellinzona: Sottoscala, 2014); Edgardo Franzosini, *Sul Monte Verità. Romanzo* (Milan: Il Saggiatore, 2014); Oliver Prange, *Das Sonnenfest* (Berlin: Edition D, 2016); Stefan Bollmann, *Monte Verità: 1900. Il primo sogno di una vita alternativa* (Turin: EDT, 2019 {2017}); Micaela Mander, "Monte Verità, Ascona: il lascito di un esperimento comunitario," in Bertrando Bonfantini, ed., *Attivare risorse latenti. Metodi sperimentali per l'analisi, la mappatura e la gestione informativa integrata delle trasformazioni di territori e manufatti del patrimonio culturale diffuso* (Planum, 2017), pp. 249–63; Peter Michalzik, *1900. Vegetarier, Künstler und Visionäre suchen nach dem neuen Paradies* (Köln: Dumont, 2018); Olivier Sirost, "The recosmologisation of the world. From Monte Verità to naturism," in Bernard Andrieu, Jim Parry, Alessandro Porrovecchio, and Olivier Sirost, eds., *Body Ecology and Emersive Leisure* (London/New York, NY: Routledge, 2018), pp. 150–63; Gabriele Guerra, ed., *Tra ribellione e conservazione. Monte verità e la cultura tedesca* (Rome: Istituto Italiano di Studi Germanici, 2019); Ingeborg Luscher, *Dokumentation über Armand Schulthess. „Der grösste Vogel kann nicht fliegen,"* 2 vols. (Luzern/Poschiavo, 2021); and Nicoletta Mongini, Chiara Gatti, and Sergio Risaliti, eds., *Monte Verità. Back to Nature* (Turin: Lindau, 2022).

Between 1901 and 1902, the first buildings were constructed. These were the "air-light" huts, built by hand by the founders of the colony with an almost religious spirit: Casa Aida, Casa Andrea, Casa Elena, Casa dei russi—refuge of some Russian students after the 1905 revolution—and Casa del tè (Tea House).[18] Generally consisting of a single room (a single curtain separated the living room from the bedroom), they had windows on all sides, a feature that allowed residents to benefit from heliotherapy all year round. The largest building dates to 1904: the Casa Centrale (Central House), a building intended for the care of guests and community meetings, including a restaurant, a library with an adjoining reading room, a music room, and a large panoramic terrace accessed by two symmetrical staircases, designed by Berlin architect Walter Hoffmann (1871–1904) in Art Nouveau style. Then there was Casa Anatta (in the theosophical sense, "soul"), built probably in 1908–1909 and used as the home of the Hofmann-Oedenkoven couple, which, with its characteristic flat roof (it has been suggested that this feature was inspired by the shape of the Central House of the Theosophical Society in Adyar, India, or rather by the interior of a boat or ship, according to the most recent hypotheses),[19] was described in the *Swiss Journal of Master Carpenters* (1934) as the most original wooden house in Switzerland. Casa Semiramis was designed by the Turin architect Anselmo Secondo in 1909, commissioned by Maria Adler, who obtained the land from Oedenkoven in exchange for a night of love. The structure was later modernized, first by Baron Eduard von der Heydt, who would have bought Monte Verità in 1926, and then, in 1971, by Ascona architect Livio Vacchini. Casa Selma dates to 1911 and was inaugurated in 1983 as the second museum on the history of Monte Verità, after Casa Anatta.[20]

1904 marked the arrival in Monte Verità of Raphael Friedeberg (1863–1940), a doctor and former militant in the German Social Democratic Party

[18] Casa Aida no longer exists. Casa Elena and Tea House have both been demolished. The current Tea House was called Loreley House, built between 1952 and 1955 and renovated in 2006 (information available in the Monte Verità Foundation's information materials).

[19] Nicoletta Mongini, personal communication, October 12, 2024, Ascona-Monte Verità.

[20] See Mara Folini, "Percorso architettonico. Dalle capanne 'aria-luce' all'albergo del Monte Verità," in Schwab and Lafranchi, *op. cit.*, pp. 77–89; and Id., *Il Monte Verità di Ascona: Guide di monumenti svizzeri SSAS* (Bern: Società di Storia dell'Arte in Svizzera SSAS, 1998).

who, after being expelled, joined the German Anarchist Federation. Recognized as an expert in the fight against tuberculosis, the "disease of the proletariat," Friedeberg was also a staunch supporter of natural medicine (vegetarianism, heliotherapy, nudism, and hydrotherapy); it is possible that Fröbe-Kapteyn and his father Albertus also benefited from these natural treatments when they were guests at the Sanatorium in 1920. Friedeberg served as the community's official doctor. His presence attracted many other anarchists to Ascona, including Prince Pyotr Alexeyevich Kropotkin, Zurich workers' doctor Fritz Brupbacher (1874–1945), Swiss painter, former trade unionist, and anarchist activist Ernst Frick (1881–1956),[21] the "Herodotus of anarchy" and biographer of Bakunin, Max Nettlau (1865–1944), Karl Kautsky (1854–1938), August Bebel (1840–1913), and Otto Braun (1872–1952). He also met the patron and collector Bernhard Mayer (1866–1946) in Ascona, who would help finance many anarchists, including Kropotkin himself and Enrico Malatesta (1853–1932), as well as Otto Gross's (1877–1920) family.[22]

At Monte Verità, between 1905 and 1911, the psychoanalyst and revolutionary Otto Gross had designed a "university for the emancipation of man," which was aimed at changing the Western world. For him, Ascona embodied an ideal matriarchal society, as opposed to the violent and authoritarian society of the patriarchy. In Ascona, he wanted to revive the cult of Astarte, through liberation from morality in the sexual sphere and scientific teaching. Gross had an almost "messianic" feeling for his psychoanalytical work, which was aimed at ripping the patriarchal culture

---

[21] Cf. Esther Bertschinger-Joos and Richard Butz, *Ernst Frick 1881–1956. Anarchist in Zürich, Künstler und Forscher in Ascona, Monte Verità* (Zurich: Limmat, 2014).

[22] Cf. Bock and Tennstedt, "Raphael Friedeberg: medico e anarchico ad Ascona," cit. Friedeberg knew Rudolf Steiner (1861–1925), with whom he had taught at the Berlin Workers' School from 1900 to 1905. On September 19, 1911, Steiner gave a lecture at the Lotos Pension in Locarno-Monti on the theme "The Christ Impulse in the History of the World"; the 23 lectures given between 1911 and 1912 were published as Rudolf Steiner, *Die esoterische Christentum und die geistige Führung der Menschheit* (Dornach: Verlag der Rudolf Steiner-Nachlassverwaltung, 1962). There are no reliable sources confirming that Steiner actually visited Monte Verità, although it is plausible to assume that he did. The inhabitants of the colony were, however, mentioned in his lecture in Locarno: "... and returning to the surprising fact that strikes above all those who have gathered here today to visit their friends of the Mount [Verità], I say that it is the very fact that many of these friends have perhaps retired not into solitude but into the quiet, the gentleness of the mountains" (*ibid.*, quoted in Antje von Graevenitz, "Capanna e tempio: verso l'autocoscienza," in Szeemann, *op. cit.*, p. 91).

from its foundations. In his 1919 writing, *The Fundamental Communist Idea of the Symbolism of Paradise*, Gross claimed to have identified the origin of sin—and therefore, symbolically, the cause of human being's expulsion from paradise—in the move away from an original state of matriarchy: a consequence of this would have been the appearance, on the social plane, of authoritarian power structures and, in psychological life, of shame surrounding sex.[23] In his analytical practice, his desire to overcome the traditional hierarchical relationship between analyst and patient, also a legacy of the patriarchal culture in his opinion, led to a new conception of the clinical relationship. This opened the way to an awareness of the interdependence between therapist and patient and the modern paradigm of intersubjectivity. An idea that Jung—who for certain period had the impression of seeing in Gross the brilliant and unsettling patient sent by Sigmund Freud (1856–1939), his own "twin brother"—would have arrived at regardless of his studies in alchemy.[24]

In 1907, Hermann Hesse (1877–1962), who was interested in the writings of theosophists at the time, was also treated at the Sanatorium to detoxify himself from alcohol.[25] In reality, according to Hermann Müller, it

---

[23] Otto Gross, *Senza freni* (Florence: Gratis, [undated]), pp. 58–71.

[24] On Otto Gross's experience at Monte Verità, see, by Martin Green, *The von Richthofen Sisters: The Triumphant and the Tragic Mode of Love. Else and Frieda von Richthofen, Otto Gross, Max Weber, and D.H. Lawrence, in the Years 1870–1970* (New York, NY: Basic Books, 1974); *Mountain of Truth…*, cit., pp. 17–50; *Prophets of a New Age…*, cit., pp. 35 ff; and *Otto Gross, Freudian Psychoanalyst, 1877–1920: Literature and Ideas* (Lewiston, NY: The Edwin Mellen Press, 1999). By Emanuel Hurwitz, see "Otto Gross. Dalla psicanalisi al Paradiso," in Szeemann, *op. cit.*, pp. 109–18; *Otto Gross, "Paradies"-Sucher zwischen Freud und Jung. Leben und Werk* (Zurich: Suhrkamp, 1979); and "Conflitto e verità. La dimensione politica della psicanalisi per Otto Gross," in Schwab and Lafranchi, *op. cit.*, pp. 143–55. Also, see Jennifer E. Michaels, *Anarchy and Eros: Otto Gross' Impact on German Expressionist Writers. Leonhard Frank, Franz Jung, Johannes R. Becher, Karl Otten, Curt Corrinth, Walter Hasenclever, Oskar Maria Graf, Franz Kafka, Franz Werfel, Max Brod, Raoul Hausmann and Berlin Dada* (New York, NY: Peter Lang, 1983); and, by the same author, "Otto Gross und das Konzept des Matriarchats," in Gottfried Heuer, ed., *2. Internationaler Otto Gross Kongress. Burghölzli, Zürich 2000* (Marburg an der Lahn: LiteraturWissenschaft.de, 2002), pp. 105–15; Sam Whimster and Gottfried Heuer, "Otto Gross and Else Jaffé and Max Weber," *Theory, Culture & Society*, 15 (3–4, 1998), pp. 129–60; Whimster, "Conversazioni con gli anarchici…," cit.; Gottfried Heuer, "Otto Gross between Freud and Jung: The Secret Story of Jung's Twin Brother," in Mary Ann Mattoon, ed., *Cambridge 2001: Proceedings of the Fifteenth International Congress for Analytical Psychology* (Daimon: Einsiedeln, 2003), pp. 118–29; and, more recently, Michelantonio Lo Russo, *Otto Gross. Psiche, Eros, Utopia* (Rome: Editori Riuniti, 2011).

[25] See Kneubühler, "Gli artisti, gli scrittori e il Canton Ticino (dal 1900 ad oggi)," cit., pp. 147 f; Alois Prinz, *Vita di Hermann Hesse* (Rome: Donzelli, 2003 {2001}), pp. 88 f.; and Werner Weick, *La lunga estate di Hermann Hesse* [VHS] (Montagnola: RTSI/Fondazione Hermann Hesse, 1987).

would have been a "cover" to spend time with the guru and prophet of hermitage Gusto Gräser, who lived in those years in a cave not far from Monte Verità and would become his "guru" for a certain period.[26] Hesse lived in fact with him in a cave in the woods of Arcegno, studying the *Upaniṣad*, experimenting with fasting, meditation, and the difficulties of a life "according to nature." Although he knew Jung, Hesse was never physically present at Eranos, probably due to his health.[27] Joseph Bernhard Lang, with whom Hesse was in analysis, was instead a speaker at Eranos in 1935 and 1942 and was among the audience at the 1943 Conference.[28]

---

[26] Hermann Müller in Alfio de Paoli and Teo Buvoli, [DVD] *Il monte di Hetty. L'ultima guardiana del Monte Verità* (Lugano: Ethiva Video/PGV communications/RSI, 2009; on his relationship with Gräser, also see Hermann Hesse, *In den Felsen. Notizen eines Naturmenschen* (1908), It. Ed. "Tra le rocce," in Id., *Racconti* (Milan: Adelphi, 1987), and Id., *Monte Verità* (Carnago: SugarCo, 1988 {1911}); Hermann Müller, *Der Dichter und Sein Guru. Hermann Hesse-Gusto Gräser, eine Freundschaft* (Wetzlar: Neuland, 1977); Id., ed., *Gusto Gräser. Aus Leben und Werk. Bruchstücke einer Biographie* (Knittlingen: Wilfried Melchior, 1987); Id., "Monte Gioia. Il Monte Verità di Gusto Gräser," in Schwab and Lafranchi, *op. cit.*, pp. 188–203; Ulrich Linse, "Il ribelle e la 'Madre terra': il monte sacro di Ascona nell'interpretazione dell'anarchico bohémien Erich Mühsam," in Szeemann, *op. cit.*, p. 30); and Martin Radermacher, "Hermann Hesse—Monte Verità. Wahrheitssuche abseits des Mainstreams zu Beginn des 20. Jahrhunderts," *Zeitschrift für junge Religionswissenschaft*, 6 (2011), pp. 1–20. In 1916, Hesse was also in analysis with Johannes Nohl (1882–1963), who had arrived in Ascona with his friend and lover Erich Mühsam (1878–1934) in 1904 (Szeemann, *op. cit.*, p. 29).

[27] His first wife and mother of his children, Mia Hesse-Bernoulli, was instead interested in the Conferences (Rudolf Ritsema, personal communication, July 15, 2002, Ascona-Moscia): her signature appears in the Eranos Guestbook in 1932, the year of the third conference of Fröbe-Kapteyn and Bailey's "Summer School," and again in 1935. Hesse's third wife, Ninon Hesse (married to Hermann from 1931 until his death in 1962), also took an interest in Eranos (Regina Bucher, personal communication, September 7, 2003; see also Ninon Hesse, letter to Olga Fröbe-Kapteyn, May 10, 1958 (Eranos Foundation Archives, Ascona-Moscia)): her signature appears in the sessions of 1942 and 1943, then in two seminars conducted by Károly Kerényi at Casa Eranos, respectively from January 3 to 5, 1944, and in the spring of 1947. Cf. also Carlo Zanda, *Un bel posticino. La Spoon River di Hermann Hesse* (Milan: Marcos y Marcos, 2012), § 40: "Daniel Brody," pp. 225–32.

[28] His wife, Gertrud Lang, also showed a keen interest in Eranos, as her signature appears in the sections relating to the years 1935, 1938, 1941, 1942, 1946, 1950, 1951, 1952, and 1953 (the year in which the Guestbook ends). Joseph Bernhard Lang, a psychotherapist from Lugano, was a student of Jung and, for some years, Hesse's analyst. He treated Hesse in 1916 at the Sanatorium Sonnmatt in Lucerne; the analysis with Lang, which later blossomed into a friendship between the two, lasted from May 1916 to November 1917 (see Green, *Mountain of Truth...*, cit., p. 67; Henri F. Ellenberger, *La scoperta dell'inconscio. Storia della psichiatria dinamica*, 2 vols. (Turin: Bollati Boringhieri, 1976 {1970}, p. 1024, fn. 331; and more extensively Thomas Feitknecht, eds., *„Die dunkle und wilde Seite der Seele". Briefwechsel von Hermann Hesse mit seinem Psychoanalytiker Josef Bernhard Lang. 1916–1944* (Frankfurt am Main: Suhrkamp, 2006)). In a letter to Emanuel Maier dated March 24, 1950 (in Jung, *Letters...*, cit., Vol. I, pp. 551 f.), Jung stated that he had met Hesse in person in 1916; he also sketched a profile of Lang (who would later distance himself from Jung), describing him as an extremely cultured and curious person, with a deep knowledge of Hebrew, Arabic, and Syrian, and a keen interest in Gnosticism, which he had

evidently picked up from Jung himself and passed on to Hesse. In 1917, Hesse wrote *Demian* off the cuff, a work in which the character of Pistorius seems to be inspired by Lang and which Jung attributed to Hesse's conversations with Lang and their shared interest in Gnosticism. The "secret" origins of *Siddhartha* and *Der Steppenwolf* were also indirectly traced by Jung to some therapeutic conversations he had with Hesse (who had several sessions of analysis with Jung from February to April 1921). In Montagnola, in the same Casa Camuzzi that had hosted Hesse, the Chilean diplomat Miguel Serrano (1917–2009) lived for ten years. He was the author of *C.G. Jung and Hermann Hesse: A Record of Two Friendships* (New York, NY: Schocken Books, 1966). Fritz René Allemann (1884–1968) also spent the last years of his life in Montagnola in the mid-1960s. A banker and financier, known as "the great initiate," Allemann lived since 1927 in Küsnacht and was a member and financial supporter of the Zurich Psychology Club from 1930 (Paul Bishop, "The Members of Jung's Seminar on Zarathustra," *Spring* (1994), p. 101); he co-founded the Hermetische Gesellschaft ("Hermetic Society") in Zurich in the late 1940s, together with Rudolf Bernoulli, professor of Art History at the Swiss Federal Institute of Technology in Zurich and a frequent speaker at Eranos, co-editor of the *Zeitschrift für Parapsychologie*, and the medium Oskar Rudolf Schlag (1907–1990). The Hermetische Gesellschaft apparently played an important "occult" role in supporting Eranos (Hakl, *Der verborgene Geist...*, cit., p. 147, fn. 85). The graphologist Max Pulver (1889–1952), the journalist Hans Reinhart "Johannes" (1880–1963)—one of the financiers of the Steiner's Goetheanum in Dornach—and, more externally, Jung himself were also close to this circle. Pulver frequented Monte Verità during the period of the "triumvirate" (see Robert Landmann, *Ascona—Monte Verità. Auf der Suche nach dem Paradies* (Frauenfeld/Stuttgart/Wien: Huber, 2000), pp. 219 ff.; Kueubühler, *op. cit.*, p. 154). In addition to graphology training with Pulver, Schlag said he had undergone educational analysis in "all three" schools of psychotherapy (Peter Mulacz, personal communication, September 17, 2002): classical psychoanalysis—through Oskar Pfister (1873–1956),—Jungian analytical psychology, and Léopold Szondi's fate analysis, which had left a deep impression on him (Peter-Robert König, personal communication, January, 3 2003). Visiting professor of graphology at the University of Zurich and co-founder of the Swiss Parapsychological Society, Schlag acted as a medium in a series of parapsychological experiments between 1930 and 1932, in which Jung also participated (see Rudolf Bernoulli and E.K. Müller, "Experimentelles. Eine neue Untersuchung der Eigenschaften des Teleplasma," *Zeitschrift für Parapsychologie*, 6 (1931), pp. 313–21; Fanny Moser, *Der Okkultismus. Täuschungen und Tatsachen*, 2 vols. (Zurich: Orell Füssli, 1935), Vol. II, pp. 892 ff.; Nandor Fodor, *Freud, Jung and Occultism* (New York, NY: University Books, 1971), p. 123; Aniela Jaffé, *From the Life and Work of C.G. Jung* (Einsiedeln: Daimon, 1989), p. 10; F.X. Charet, *Spiritualism and the Foundations of C. G. Jung's Psychology* (Albany, NY: State University of New York, 1993), pp. 282 f.; Massimo Biondi, "Orizzonti spiritici di Jung," *Luce e Ombra*, 103 (1, 2003), pp. 33–42; and Bair, *op. cit.*, p. 329). In particular, on November 14, 1930, in the company of his wife Emma Jung-Rauschenbach, the future Eranos lecturer Rudolf Bernoulli "Ananda" and his wife Katharina Bernoulli-Fähndrich "Akashini" (1885–1948), Fritz René Allemann "Parikamma," Hans Reinhart, H. Stephanie (Burghölzli director Eugen Bleuler and his wife, physician specializing in human energy emissions and director of the "Salus" Institute E.K. Müller, Max Pulver and his wife, and the Strohhfer couple also participated in other sessions), Jung communicate with an entity that identified itself as "Atma," during a mediumistic experiment conducted by Schlag (see the transcript of some passages from Jung's "mediumistic" conversation in Oskar Rudolf Schlag, *Von alten und neuen Mysterien. Die Lehren des A.* (Stäfa: Rothenhäusler, 1995), pp. 40–51 and 553–62). Jung's association with Schlag and his experiments in mediumistic connection with a "Tibetan" are also documented by W.G. Fährte, "Die Brötchen Vom Nachbartisch. Ein Brief zu O.R. Schlag von W.G. Fährte," in Peter-Robert König, ed., *Das OTO-Phänomen. 100 Jahre Magische Geheimbünde und ihre Protagonisten von 1895–1994* (Munich: Arbeitsgemeinschaft für Religions- und Weltanschauungsfragen, 1994), pp. 220–22. "W.G. Fährte" is actually a pseudonym: he is referred to as "Hermann Joseph Metzger's right-hand man" and "a very close 'friend' of Herr Schlag. He is rather known in the occult and academic society and fears damage to his reputation when revealing his true identity" (Peter-Robert König, personal communication, May 3, 2002). Schlag also claimed to have lent Jung many books from his extensive library of esoteric works (Hans Jakob Haag, "Sammlung Oskar R. Schlag

In 1920, as we have seen, Fröbe-Kapteyn was probably cured, perhaps together with her father, at the Monte Verità Sanatorium. She stayed at Casa Semiramis and boarded at Casa Anatta.[29] When staying at Casa Monte Tabor in Porto Ronco, she wrote to her friend Marie Stopes: "It is not as lonely as one would think, for Ascona is full of artists—poets, painters, philosophers—many of whom I know."[30] She moved to Villa Gabriella with her daughter Bettina in December 1921. The house, purchased on October 12, 1920 by her father Albertus Kapteyn from Ugo von Hoffmann, had previously belonged since 1904 to Karl Vester, who moved to a farm on Monte Verità in 1919.[31]

---

der Zentralbibliothek Zürich," in Schlag, *op. cit.*, p. 563; see also Vv.Aa., *Wissende, Eingeweihte und Verschwiegene. Esoterik im Abendland. Katalog der Ausstellung vom 23. Sept. bis 22. Nov. in der Zentralbibliothek Zürich* (Zurich: Zentralbibliothek Zürich, 1986)), during the period when the latter was involved in alchemy and Paracelsus (Peter Mulacz, "Oscar R. Schlag," *Journal of the Society for Psychical Research*, 60 (1995), pp. 263 ff.). Schlag, who was already in touch with Kerényi (Hans Thomas Hakl, personal communication, August 21, 2003, Ascona), also had a bookshop in Ascona for a while (Hanspeter Manz, "Vom Buchhandel im Locarnese. Fremdenverkehr und Lesevergnügen," *Ferien-Journal. Ascona*, 326 (1996), pp. 5–7; and Id., "Der Mann im Bild: zu einem Foto von O.R. Schlag," in *ibid.*, p. 49). From the Eranos Guestbook, we note that the Bernoulli couple were present as listeners at the Eranos Conference in 1933, then in the following two years, with Rudolf Bernoulli as a lecturer; from 1939 to 1941 and, finally, in 1943. The Pulvers attended all sessions from 1934 to 1939, then from 1941 to 1946 (from 1941 to 1945 with Pulver as a lecturer) and finally in 1950. Allemann is listed among the listeners in 1933, 1935, 1936, 1938, 1939, and 1953. Schlag's signature appears in 1939 and 1941.

[29] Vacchini, *Ascona…*, cit., par. 2034.

[30] Olga Fröbe-Kapteyn, letter to Marie Stopes, April 21, 1920, written from Monte Verità, Ascona (British Library, London; transcript kindly provided by Karssenberg). See, more in general, Renato Martinoni, *La cultura nel Locarnese fra Otto e Novecento* (Bellinzona: Salvioni, 2014); and Vv.Aa., *Quarto. Zeitschrift des Schweizerischen Literaturarchivs*, 45 (2018) ("Lago Maggiore. Literarische Topografie eines Sees / Lago Maggiore. Topografia letteraria di un lago"), eds. Corinna Jäger-Trees and Christa Baumberger.

[31] Vester had arrived at Monte Verità in 1902, before leaving for Samoa and returning to Ascona in 1904. Although he shared in the project, he always maintained a certain distance and independence from the Monte Verità colony. A baker in the community, he inherited the Ascona property of Oedenkoven when the latter left Ascona in 1920 (Vacchini, *op. cit.*, par. 2631; see also the television report entitled "L'ultimo naturista del Monte Verità," broadcast on October 4, 1963, as part of the program "Il Regionale" of Radiotelevisione della Svizzera Italiana (RSI)). Vester was also among the audience at the last symposium of the International Centre for Spiritual Research, promoted by Fröbe-Kapteyn and Bailey in 1932. Vester was in contact with baker and former communist Hermann Joseph Metzger (1919–1990) from Ticino; the latter, alias "Paragranus," was initiated in 1943 into Theodor Reuss's (1855–1923) Lodge "Verità Mistica" of the Ordo Templi Orientis (O.T.O.) in Ascona, thanks to Genja Jantzen and Alice Sprengel (Metzger claimed to be a descendant of Margarethe Hardegger and that his position was legitimized by Linke-Hofmann's certificate). Upon his death on September 24, 1963, Metzger remembered Vester in a short obituary (cf. König, *Das OTO-Phänomen…*, cit., p. 49; Bernardini, *Jung a Eranos…*, cit., pp. 251 f.). Members of the O.T.O. Lodge "Verità Mistica" included Henry Oedenkoven, alias "Frater Pythagoras," Ida Hofmann, alias "Soror Peregrina" (who gave an inaugural

speech on "The Importance of True Theosophy" at the National Cooperative Congress of the Hermetic Illuminati Brotherhood organized by Reuss at Monte Verità from August 15 to 25, 1917); Clara Linke (1875–1923), director of the Sanatorium for several years and lover of Hans Rudolf Hilfiker-Dunn alias "Nothung" (1882–1955), also initiated into the Ascona O.T.O.; trade unionist Margarethe Faas-Brunner-Hardegger alias "Soror Hyzinthe"; Alice Sprengel (1897–1947), former collaborator of Rudolf Steiner and participant as a listener at the symposia of Fröbe-Kapteyn and Bailey's International Centre for Spiritual Research in August 1930, 1931, and 1932 (listing Casa Follini, Via Saleggi, Ascona, as her residence); the free dance theorist Rudolf von Laban (1879–1958), who would later obtain from Reuss the rank of Grand Master of the O.T.O. Lodge "Libertas et Fraternitas," founded in Zurich in 1917; Mary Wigman (Karoline Sophie Marie Wiegmann, 1886–1973), patron of expressionist dance; dancer Suzanne Perrottet (1889–1983), who also belonged to the Mazdaznan movement, which had a center at Monte Verità since 1908; and the rest of the dance troupe of Laban's Schule für Lebenskunst, consisting of Katja Wulff (who arrived in Monte Verità in 1914), Maja Lederer, Olga Feldt, and Totimo. The Eranos Library still holds a rare copy of the first edition of the *Confessions* of Aleister Crowley (1875–1947), whose poems would be recited at Monte Verità during the Masonic congress organized in 1917 by Reuss (introduced by Hofmann in 1916 to the Monte Verità community, which he would leave in 1918). Moreover, as Peter-Robert König notes, near Ascona, in Villa Verbanella, there lived a certain Frau Appia-Usteri, together with Eugen Grosche's (1888–1964) lover and secretary Hanne Wildt (who signed the Eranos Guestbook in 1950 and 1951 and spent spent time in the company of Hardegger). Grosche, founder of the Fraternitas Saturni, spent his exile in sunny Ticino and visited the local O.T.O. lodge in 1937 (at the time when Schlag was also in Ascona, whom Grosche wanted as head of his Fraternitas Saturni). Appia-Usteri was among the listeners at Fröbe-Kapteyn's activities in 1931, 1932, 1934, 1935, and 1936. Also Schlag maintained constant relations with the O.T.O., coming into contact with it in 1927 through the Lodge "Libertas et Fraternitas" of Hilfiker and Laban and thanks to Baron Ernst Theodor Herbert von Bomsdorff-Bergen (1876–1951); although Schlag was never initiated into the O.T.O., Metzger considered him "the highest initiate on earth" (Peter-Robert König, "Thelema and suppressed homosexuality," *Abraxas* (1990)). On the O.T.O. experience at Monte Verità, see Helmut Möller and Ellic Howe, "Theodor Reuss—Irregular Freemasonry in Germany, 1900–23," *Ars Quatuor Coronatorum*, 91 (1978), pp. 28–47; Id., *Jahrhundertfeier. Vom Untergrund des Abendlandes* (Göttingen: Buchdruckerel R. Walter, 1975); Id., *Merlin Peregrinus. Vom Untergrund des Abendlandes* (Würzburg: Könighausen + Neumann, 1986), pp. 206–23; von Graevenitz, *op. cit.*, p. 91; Harald Szeemann, ed., *Dalla danza libera, all'arte pura. Catalogo della mostra, 15 aprile–10 giugno 1990* (Ascona: Museo Comunale di Arte Moderna di Ascona, 1990), p. 14; Peter-Rober König, ed., *Der Kleine Theodor-Reuss-Reader* (Munich: Arbeitsgemeinschaft für Religions- und Weltanschauungsfragen, 1993), pp. 30–34 and *passim*; Id., ed., *Materialien zum OTO* (Munich: Arbeitsgemeinschaft für Religions- und Weltanschauungsfragen, 1994), p. 59; Id., ed., *Der Grosse Theodor-Reuss-Reader* (Munich: Arbeitsgemeinschaft für Religions- und Weltanschauungsfragen, 1997), pp. 243–50; Id., "Veritas Mistica Maxima," in Id., ed., *Das OTO-Phänomen...*, cit., pp. 35–50, revised and enlarged in Id., *Der O.T.O. Phänomen Remix* (Munich: Arbeitsgemeinschaft für Religions- und Weltanschauungsfragen, 2001), pp. 68-85; Id., ed., *Ecclesia Gnostica Catholica* (Munich: Arbeitsgemeinschaft für Religions- und Weltanschauungsfragen, 1998); Id., ed., *Noch Mehr Materialien zum OTO* (Munich: Arbeitsgemeinschaft für Religions- und Weltanschauungsfragen, 2000), pp. 4–48. On Metzger's O.T.O. "Abtei Thelema" in Stein (Appenzell), see also *Oriflamme*, 95 (September 23, 1969) ("Abtei Thelema"), and and Richard Butz, "Die Okkultisten von Stein AR. Mächtig geheim: Iris Blums Buch über die Psychosophische Gesellschaft und ihre ,Collectio Magica et Occulta'," *Saiten* (November 3, 2016). When Hakl's *Der verborgene Geist von Eranos* was published, it was brought to my attention by Annemarie Äschbach (1926–2008), when I met her for the first time in Stein in 2002 (cf. Riccardo Bernardini, "The Secret of Eranos," *Spring: A Journal of Archetype and Culture*, 88 (2012), pp. 331–39). In a letter dated September 1, 1935, Fröbe-Kaptyen mentioned to Jung the existence in Ascona of an esoteric "fraud" connected to the "Eastern Templars" (University Archives, ETH-Bibliothek, Zurich / Eranos Foundation Archives, Ascona-Moscia).

The Sanatorium ran until 1920, the very year Fröbe-Kapteyn arrived and the Oedenkoven spouses departed for Spain and then Brazil.[32] Monte Verità therefore went through a number of life stages.[33]

From 1923 to 1926, during the so-called "triumvirate," Monte Verità was run by Werner Ackermann (Robert Landmann),[34] Max Bethke, and Hugo Wilkens, later joined by William Werner. After the Oedenkovens left, life on Monte Verità changed radically: the homes of the first vegetarians, which had fallen into disrepair, were restored and the hill was reborn in a completely new guise. The center was no longer governed by strict vegetarian rules; instead, it promised all modern comforts and cuisine that was "exquisite enough to satisfy even the most spoiled city dwellers."[35] Carnival, like the "Under the Blue Sun" festival organized in 1924, became the celebration par excellence, in the name of lively and dynamic artistic expression. On the occasion of the summer festival "The African Night" in 1924, organized by zoologist Karl Soffel (1877–1947), painter Ernst Frick, and painter, graphic artist, and woodcutter Walter Helbig (1878–1968) built a six-meter-high idol. Hans Peter Wilhelm (Jean) Arp (1887–1966) and his wife Sophie Henriette Gertrude Taeuber-Arp (1889–1943) also took part in the last great carnival festival, "The Furious Carousel," in 1925 (the year in

[32] There, between 1921 and 1923, using the model of the Monte Verità experience, they started their Monte Sol enterprise, near Joinville, in the state of Santa Caterina. See Guilherme Zacharias Christol, *Um lugar ao sol: ensaio sobre as idéias naturistas da experiência de Monte-Veritá, Suíça, e seu desdobramento brasileiro na década de 1920*, M.A. Dissertation, Universidade Estadual de Campinas, Instituto De Filosofia E Ciências Humana, Campinas, 2015.

[33] See, in addition to the texts cited so far, Emil Szittya, *Das Kuriositäten-Kabinett* (Konstanz: See, 1923); Jakob Flach, *Ascona: Gestern und Heute* (Zurich/Stuttgart: Wernen Classen, 1960); Friedrich Glauser, *DADA, Ascona e altri ricordi* (Palermo: Sellerio, 1991 {1976}); Luigi Menapace, *Sole d'Ascona* (Lugano: Edizioni del Cantonetto, 1970 {1957}); Wolfgang Oppenheimer, *Das Refugium: Erinnerungen an Ascona* (Munich: Universitas, 1998); Boris Luban-Plozza, "Lernen am Monte Verità," *Forum. Galenus Mannheim*, 17 (1988), pp. 1–4; Id., "Creatività e Monte Verità: verso il centenario," *Schweizerisch Ärztezeitung/Bollettino dei medici svizzeri*, 53 (20, 1999), p. 1253; and Id., "Creatività al Monte Verità," in Bodmer, Holdenrieder, and Seeland, *Monte Verita...*, cit., pp. 21–22; see also Ernst R. Petzold, "Balint-Arbeit und Monte Verità-Gruppen als Teil das Ascona-Modells," *Klinikarzt*, 11 (22, 1993), pp. 485–89; Id. and Walter Pöldinger, eds., *Beziehungsmedizin auf dem Monte Verità. 30 Jahre Psychosomatik in Ascona* (Wien: Springer, 1998); and Walter Pöldinger, "Monte Verità-Gruppen," in Ernst Petzold and Volker Beck, eds., *Der alternde Mensch und sein Umfeld* (Jena: Universitätsverlag, 1993).

[34] See Landmann, *op. cit.*

[35] Folini, *Il Monte Verità di Ascona...*, cit., p. 32.

which the Locarno Treaties were sealed, drawn up during the Peace Conference held in Locarno from October 5 to 16 and signed in London on December 1), which officially ended the Expressionist period at Monte Verità.[36] During this phase, in 1924, philosopher and Hebraist Martin Buber held a free course on Lao-Tzu and Chuang-Tzu at Monte Verità, probably based on two of his earlier works;[37] a series of meetings on *Tao-tê-ching* was also attended by Fröbe-Kapteyn, who, unlike the other listeners, had a chair brought to her in the middle of the lawn so she could listen to the lecture with her torso firmly erect.[38]

A collector of contemporary, Oriental, and primitive art (especially Chinese and Indian, as a pioneer in those studies), banker to the former Emperor Wilhelm II, Baron Eduard von der Heydt purchased Monte Verità

---

[36] Sophie Taeuber-Arp and her sister Erika Schlegel Taeuber (who was in analysis with Jung and the first librarian of the Zurich Psychology Club) created the Hopi costumes for the dance at the Kunsthaus in Zurich, which were based in every detail on two small colored ritual dolls of kachinas (spirit beings in the religious beliefs of the Pueblo people) that Jung had brought back with him from New Mexico in 1925 from a study trip to the Pueblo Indians. Through Schlegel, Jung maintained close relations with Taeuber Arp and her husband Hans Arp, and through them with the group around Hugo Ball (1886–1927) and Tristan Tzara (1896–1963) (see Thomas Fischer and Bettina Kaufmann, "C.G. Jung e l'arte moderna," in Foundation of the Works of C.G. Jung, Hoerni, Fischer, and Kaufmann, *L'arte di C.G. Jung*, cit., pp. 23 f.). During the Dadaist period, Taeuber Arp also painted passe-partouts and frames in gold and silver (Hoch, *op. cit.*, p. 47)—a custom in the use of gold that we also find in many of Fröbe-Kapteyn's "Meditation Plates." See also, more in general, Stephan Kunz, Lars Müller, and Beat Wismer, eds., *Sophie Taeuber-Arp, zum 100. Geburtstag* (Aarau: Aargauer Kunsthaus, 1989).

[37] See Ron Margolin, "Tre approcci allo studio della religione a Eranos," in Barone, Fabris, and Monceri, *op. cit.*, p. 190. Buber had learned about Monte Verità from two friends, Gustav Landauer (1870–1919) and German writer and anarchist Erich Mühsam. The latter had arrived in Ascona in 1904, after the failure of the suburban commune Die neue Gemeinschaft ("The New Community") in Schlachtensee, near Berlin, founded in 1899 by the brothers Julius and Heinrich Hart. Buber himself had placed great hopes in that project (Linse, *op. cit.*, p. 31; and Green, *Mountain of Truth…*, cit., p. 126), and had joined it in the year of its foundation; it was in this context that he had met Landauer (Margolin, *op. cit.*, p. 189, fn. 1). A revolutionary and anti-Marxist anarchist, Landauer was in close contact with various anarchists who gravitated around Monte Verità; he had a profound influence on Buber's life and the formation of his political thought—Buber edited the posthumous publication of his *Die Revolution* in 1923—as well as on that of Gershom Scholem (Michael Lowy, *Redemption and Utopia: Jewish Libertarian Thought in Central Europe—A Study in Elective Affinity* (Stanford, NJ: Stanford University Press, 1992), pp. 203 ff.). Buber spoke at Eranos in 1934 and came back as a listener in August 1947 (Bernardini, *Jung a Eranos…*, cit., p. 226).

[38] Rosenbaum-Kroeber, *op. cit.*, p. 119; see also Kneubühler, *op. cit.*, p. 176; and McGuire, *op. cit.*, p. 21. During the days of the course, Buber resided at Casa Semiramis (Hetty Rogantini-de Beauclair, personal communication, August 22, 2003, Ascona; cf. Bernardini, *op. cit.*, p. 252), where architect and painter Paul Camenisch (1893–1970) would open his studio in those years, devoting himself entirely to expressionist art from 1925 onwards. Buber was also in contact with Gross, whom he deeply admired.

in 1926,[39] at the proposal of the then owner Werner, and lured by painter Marianne von Werefkin (1860–1938) and Fröbe-Kapteyn herself.[40] *(Figure 121 and 122)* From then on, the bohemian lifestyle spread throughout the village of Ascona and the Locarno valleys. Taking advantage of the very favourable climate in the area, he turned the grounds of Monte Verità into a botanical garden with a wealth of exotic plants, Chinese aviaries, and sculptures inspired by Eastern art and the corporeal nature of the "Great Mother."[41] True to his thesis that a work of art, even if owned by an individual, is in reality always a common good, von der Heydt worked tirelessly to publish art catalogs and lend pieces from his collection to public exhibitions, as well as promoting the foundation of museums and institutes, including the Chinese Institute created at Monte Verità, the Yi Yuan Museum in Amsterdam, the Society for East Asian Art in Berlin, and the Sino-International Library in Geneva.[42] At Monte Verità, von der Heydt decided to replace the Central House, originally designed as a building for community meetings and the care of Sanatorium guests, with a construction inspired by Bauhaus architecture. He commissioned the architect Emil Fahrenkamp (1885–1966) to carry out the work in 1928.[43] The rest of the building, which has since become the most important

---

[39] See Eduard von der Heydt and Werner von Rheinbaben, *Auf dem Monte Verità. Erinnerungen und Gedanken über Menschen, Kunst und Politik* (Zurich: Atlantis, 1958) and Id., *et al.*, *Ascona und sein Berg Monte Verità* (Zurich: Arche, 1979).

[40] Hetty Rogantini-de Beauclair, *Dal Monte Verità di Ascona… a Berzona in Onsernone. Hetty De Beauclair racconta il meraviglioso mondo della sua infanzia*, eds. Yvonne Bölt and Gian Pietro Milani (Losone: Serodine, 2004), p. 21, fn. 23; and Hetty Rogantini-de Beauclair, personal communication, October 1, 2010, Ascona-Monte Verità.

[41] Mara Folini and Lidia Zaza Sciolli, "La collezione del Barone Eduard von der Heydt al Monte Verità," in Manuela Khan-Rossi, ed., *Dal Seicento olandese alle avanguardie del primo Novecento. La collezione Eduard von der Heydt al Monte Verità. Sguardi sulla Collezione dello Stato del Cantone Ticino. Museo Cantonale d'Arte, 30 marzo–5 maggio 1996* (Lugano/Zurich: Museo Cantonale d'Arte/Pro Litteris, 1996), pp. 9 ff; Willy Rotzler, "Il barone a Monte Verità. Breve profilo biografico di Eduard von der Heydt," in Szeemann, *Monte Verità…*, cit., pp. 101 ff; and Id., "Der Baron auf dem Monte Verità. Kleines Lebensbild von Eduard von der Heydt," in Harald Szeemann, ed., *Von Marées bis Picasso. Meisterwerke aus dem Von der Heydt-Museum Wuppertal. Ascona, 7. Juni bis 17. August 1986–Bern, 4. September bis 2. November 1986. Albergo Monte Verità, Museo Comunale di Arte Moderna, Centro Culturale Beato Pietro Berno, Ascona, Kunstmuseum Bern, Bern* (Ascona: Museo Von der Heydt–Monte Verità S.A., 1986), pp. 21–32; and Francesco Welti, *Der Baron, die Kunst und das Nazigold* (Frauenfeld/Stuttgart/Wien: Huber, 2008).

[42] Folini, *Il Monte Verità…*, cit., p. 35.

[43] *Ibid.*

Bauhaus building in the canton of Ticino, was further transformed in 1935 by architect H. Schneider. The large terrace of the old central building was retained and is still accessible via two wide symmetrical staircases that open up to visitors like arms. Von der Heydt also ensured that his rich collection of art objects was integrated as naturally as possible into the various rooms of the hotel, just as he had done more than ten years earlier in his villa in Zandvoort near Amsterdam, which was also frequented by the family of Wilhelm II and the Thyssen industrialists: at that time, the banker was married to the psychotherapist Vera von der Heydt-Schwabach, who, even after her separation from her husband in 1927, continued to be a regular visitor to the hill of Ascona.[44] Once the first "romantic" phase of Monte Verità had come to an end and the brief "expressionist interlude" had run its course, the enchanted hill entered a new phase of life.[45] Von der Heydt, already a friend of Eranos lecturer Heinrich Zimmer,[46] had regularly attended the initiatives promoted in Moscia by Fröbe-Kapteyn since 1930,[47] despite their relationship becoming particularly conflictual at one point.[48] A statue of Viṣṇu donated by the

[44] See, e.g., Vera von der Heydt-Schwabach, "Jung and Religion," *Journal of Analytical Psychology*, 22 (2, 1977), pp. 175–83.

[45] Rotzler, *op. cit.*, p. 104.

[46] Henrich Zimmer, *The Art of Indian Asia—Its Mythology and Transformations* (New York, NY: Bollingen Series XXXIV, Pantheon Books, 1955), p. vii.

[47] Von der Heydt signed the Eranos Guestbook in 1930, 1931, 1933, 1934, 1937, 1938, 1951, 1952, and 1953 (the year in which the register ends). In a letter dated July 19, 1937 (Eranos Foundation Archives, Ascona-Moscia), the baron thanked Fröbe-Kapteyn for the invitation to the *Tagung*, also confirming the participation of Li Yu Ying, a former Chinese minister who had expressed great interest in the theme of the symposium.

[48] The relationship between Fröbe-Kapteyn and von der Heydt was particularly problematic. According to Fröbe-Kapteyn, he wanted to take over Eranos. In 1944, Fröbe-Kapteyn attempted to reconstruct, based on the few facts she knew, the circumstances that may have appeared suspicious to the FBI, which had opened a 30-page file (Bureau file no. 100-210662) on her during her international travels for iconographic research. The relationship between Eranos and von der Heydt was based on the fact that the latter owned two hotels in Ascona and was keen to welcome well-known and famous scholars, as well as a select audience, to his establishments. He therefore invited the most renowned Eranos speakers, most of whom were foreigners, to stay as his personal guests at Monte Verità during the week of the Conference. This financial relief, which took place between 1933 and 1939, was welcome, as she had to cover all other expenses herself. The speakers' travel expenses were already high, and their accommodation during the *Tagung* would have been entirely at her expense. There was never any relationship with the Baron other than that determined by the Conferences. From the fall of 1942,

---

Fröbe-Kapteyn's relations with him ceased entirely. He had allowed or arranged for an article about him to appear in the *Neue Zürcher Zeitung*, in which it was stated that he had laid the foundations for Eranos, which forced Fröbe-Kapteyn to publish a correction in the same newspaper that probably aroused his resentment towards her. On the one hand, therefore, von der Heydt had supported Eranos by inviting the lecturers to his home, but on the other hand, he had probably reported Eranos, or Fröbe-Kapteyn in particular, as "pro-Germany." According to Fröbe-Kapteyn, he wanted to be considered the founder and inspiration behind Eranos. For several years, he had been in fact in close contact with the British and American consuls in Zurich, and it was probably at these offices that, according to her, he had denounced her as a collaborator (Olga Fröbe-Kapteyn, "Erklärung über Eranos für die Amerikanischen Gesandtschaft, Bern" (unpublished typescript, 1944; Eranos Foundation Archives, Ascona-Moscia)). Despite offering hospitality at Monte Verità to Jewish artists and writers fleeing the Reich, Eduard von der Heydt made no secret of his support for National Socialism and the monarchy. At the end of the war, this cost him his German citizenship and also caused problems with the United States, from which he never obtained the return of a series of works of art that he had lent to the Buffalo Museum of Science and wanted to exhibit at the Rietberg Museum in Zurich. In any case, Fröbe-Kapteyn was unable to produce any evidence against von der Heydt. She believed that Alice Bailey herself could have been one of the possible informants, as she wrote that Fröbe-Kapteyn had set up a "German center"; when their relationship ended, Bailey may have sought revenge in this way (Fröbe-Kapteyn, "19 Mai 44," cit., p. 3). Fröbe-Kapteyn also explained that, as a result of her departure from Bailey's Arcane School and her association with Jung, "being totally suppressed, the *Tibetan* [master of Bailey] turned quite 'black' and began to poison me and everything around me. Being suppressed he *possessed me*—he had me by the neck! And become more or less the Devil, and his effects = the Devil's Paw. He was the Super-Dugpa, activating several minor Dugpas in my sourrondings who had some knowledge of the Tibet. [Gérard] Heym and [Oskar] Schlag. The Tibetan is the force that has worked magic of all kinds for the last 10 years. He took his revenge, if one may put it that way, through the denunciations of G.H.[eym] and Schl.[ag] both linked up with the Tibet, with Tantric magic, etc." (Fröbe-Kapteyn, "Thinking Function," cit.). So, "all the political suspicions against me and Eranos were the reaction against the 'black occultism' in me. It belonged to the *dark* aspect of the Self, and was the Devil's Paw in many situations" (Fröbe-Kapteyn, "Arcane School. Positive Values. Negative Values," cit., p. 4). Historian of alchemy Gérard Heym (1888–1972) helped her during the winters of 1934–35, when, on Jung's behalf, she carried out iconographic research in London, particularly at the British Museum (Olga Fröbe-Kapteyn, letter to Carl Gustav Jung, October 24, 1935; University Archives, ETH-Bibliothek, Zurich / Eranos Foundation Archives, Ascona-Moscia). Active in several esoteric societies linked to alchemy, such as Les Amants de la Licorne and F.A.R.+C.—the latter believed to be the only group in Europe practicing Chinese alchemy—Heym claimed to be a practicing alchemist himself (Hakl, *op. cit.*, pp. 215 ff. and n. 61). In the winter of 1935, in London, Heym reminded her of the unpleasant episode involving Orientalist Jakob Wilhelm Hauer (1881–1962)—who, during the 1934 Eranos Conference, which he also attended as a listener, had given an apologetic speech on Nazism, then mitigated thanks to the providential intervention of Buber—and warned her: "Now remember, don't you have any more damned Germans!" (Olga Fröbe-Kapteyn, letter to Carl Gustav Jung, January 13, 1944; University Archives, ETH-Bibliothek, Zurich / Eranos Foundation Archives, Ascona-Moscia), quoted in Hakl, *op. cit.*, p. 216). According to Fröbe-Kapteyn, Heym was somehow connected to Scotland Yard and probably denounced Eranos as a "German center" (Fröbe-Kapteyn, "Erklärung über Eranos für die Amerikanische Gesandtschaft...," cit.; cf. also Bernardini, *op. cit.*, pp. 272 ff. and 316 f.). Despite all this, the accusations and suspicions against her were dropped; Allen Welsh Dulles (1893–1969), head of the Office of Strategic Services (precursor to the CIA) in Bern, was convinced of her innocence, and the case was officially closed (see, more extensively, Bernardini, *op. cit.*, § 3.5: "I sospetti di spionaggio," pp. 306–17).

Baron to Fröbe-Kapteyn still stands in the garden of Eranos. *(Figure 122)* It was at his Hotel Monte Verità that several lecturers and listeners in the Eranos *Tagungen* used to stay. From 1933 to 1939, during the period of the conferences, the Jung couple also stayed at Monte Verità, in the elegant Bauhaus-style hotel from which it was possible to admire a splendid view of Lake Maggiore and the surrounding mountains.[49] There, "vegetarianism, champagne breakfasts, nudism, and Buddhist meditation" would be practiced.[50] In any case, lodging in the hotel was a source of suffering for Jung. As Barbara Hannah (1891–1986) recalls, being an excellent cook himself, he hated seeing good ingredients, always of the highest quality, cooked in such a "sloppy" manner.[51] In addition to Jung, other speakers from Eranos also resided at the Hotel Monte Verità, often hosted free of charge by von der Heydt himself,[52] as well as students from the "Psychology Club,"[53] who reached Eranos every morning by walking in a sort of small procession lasting about twenty minutes led by Jung along the road that connects Monte Verità to the hamlet of Moscia,[54] or via a small bus provided by the hotel.[55] Von der Heydt was also involved in the only party ever held at Eranos: the peaceful proceedings of the 1937 conference were interrupted by a nighttime party held at Casa Eranos and on the terrace, still remembered today as the "night boat trip" (*Nachtmeerfahrt*). The Baron contributed by providing the wine. There was no music, but shouts and laughter echoed across the lake. Neighbors, both near and far, complained to Fröbe-Kapteyn about the noise, but to no avail. Jung, who was tipsy like many others in the group, encouraged those who seemed too reserved to

[49] Barbara Hannah, *Vita e opere di C.G. Jung* (Milan: Rusconi, 1980 {1976}), p. 305; on the history of the Hotel Monte Verità, see Folini, *Il Monte Verità…*, cit,, and Id., "Percorso architettonico…," cit., pp. 77 ff.

[50] Rotzler, "Il barone a Monte Verità," cit., p. 22.

[51] Hannah, *op. cit.*, p. 306.

[52] Landmann, *op. cit.*, p. 290; and Ellen Thayer, *Eranos and Ascona* (unpublished typescript, 1938; Kristine Mann Library, New York, NY), p. 5.

[53] Cabot Reid, *op. cit.*, p. 207, and Thayer, *op. cit.*, p. 2.

[54] Rudolf Ritsema, personal communication, October 25, 2002, Ascona-Moscia.

[55] Thayer, *op. cit.*, p. 7.

pay due tribute to Dionysus. He appeared here and there, exuding good humor and inebriation.[56]

In the last years of his life, von der Heydt also thought about how to transform his property into a space that would house a sort of "free academy."[57] For this purpose, designs by painter Johannes Itten (1888–1967) for a Swiss academy of fine arts in line with the Bauhaus principles were considered, as were those by Walter Robert Corti (1910–1990), one of the speakers at the Eranos Conferences in 1957 and 1959, who had been in contact with the Ascona conferences since at least 1934.[58] Corti was involved with Fröbe-Kapteyn herself in the project to make Eranos an academy in line with the theories of her "Platonic Academy":[59] an idea that Fröbe described as "the biggest mistake of my life."[60] In 1956, von der Heydt

[56] Jaffé, "Carlo Gustav Jung e i convegni di Eranos," cit., p. 108.

[57] Rotzler, "Il barone a Monte Verità – Breve profilo biografico di Eduard von der Heydt," cit., p. 105.

[58] See Walter Robert Corti, "Die Eranos – Begegnungsstätte für Ost und West in Moscia-Ascona," *Schweizer Annalen*, 1 (1935), pp. 52–59; and Id., "Zwanzig Jahre Eranostagungen in Moscia-Ascona (Schweiz)," *Psyche*, 4 (1952–53), pp. 155–60.

[59] See Walter Robert Corti, "Die Platonische Akademie im Wandel der Geschichte und als Aufgabe unserer Zeit," *Eranos Jahrbuch*, 36 (1957), pp. 387–413; and Id., "Nachrichten vom Plan der Akademie," *Du. Schweizerische Monatsschrift*, 15 (4, 1955), pp. 66–74.

[60] The hilly area above Eranos, originally belonging to the property of Villa Gabriella, was sold by Fröbe-Kapteyn in 1959, as a result of her withdrawal from the contract with Corti's Bauhütte der Akademie (cadastral mutation no. 5460 of February 11, 1959). In a 1961 letter to her daughter, Fröbe-Kapteyn summed up her serious mistake as follows: "Dear Bettina, last summer I promised you to give you a clear account of our struggle with the Academy of Corti. It is not easy to look back to the beginning of that whole problem, which has now been solved. The beginning of it all was my unpardonable mistake in thinking that Eranos should join its work with that of the Academy, which was not yet a fact but only an idea. The plan for the Academy, which for some years had been in Corti's mind, seemed to me to present many possibilities for the further work of Eranos. That was a trap into which I fell without reserve. During the *Tagung* 1959 an agreement was drawn up between myself and the direction of the Academy (*Verein Bauhütte der Akademie*). Within a few months after the *Tagung* I realised my mistake. The moment that it became involved with other forms of work the clarity and straightness of the Eranos work was overshadowed. It was a dreadful situation and I could never have worked it alone. Our chief speaker, Prof. Portmann of the University of Basel, stepped in and offered to take the entire weight of this crisis on his own shoulders. *He is most certainly the force which has saved Eranos*. At the same time he suggested the union of our *seven central speakers into a closer group*, which could act as the center of Eranos. Through this formation of a central group he himself took his place as leader, together with me, of the entire Eranos. For the future that is of a great value because it is a guarantee for the continuation of the work when I am no longer capable of the duties and power of that leadership. Now the crisis has been solved, the Eranos houses and property have been freed, and there is no more contact between Eranos and the Academy. The 'Bauhütte der Akademie' claimed a compensation if they were to release their hold on Eranos. I had to present them with the lower part of the hill above the road, which in fact is unessential to Eranos. The passage through these various

bequeathed his works, which together constituted one of the most important private collections in Germany, and his property on Monte Verità to the Canton, on condition that its tradition as an artistic center be preserved.

Despite the fact that Monte Verità and Eranos had independent histories and destinies, various artists and writers, attracted to Ascona by the Monte Verità experience, participated as listeners in the Eranos Conferences over the years.

In 1924, Werefkin founded the group Der Grosse Bar ("The Great Bear") together with artists Walter Helbig, Ernst Frick, Gordon McCouch (1885–1962), Otto Niemeyer (1883–1971), Otto van Rees (1883–1957), and Albert Kohler (1899–1969). They were in contact with Werefkin's circle Louise Frederike Susanna "Li" Hutchinson-Wolf (1883–1968), author of the busts currently kept at Eranos, including that of Jung, which has always been on display in the Lecture Hall. Her signature began to appear in the Eranos Guestbook in 1935, but more regularly from 1945 onwards, and her husband William Doge "Bill" Hutchinson was always present alongside his wife. Li's artistic master, Marino Marini (1901–1980), whose search for archaic forms seems to have been reworked by Hutchinson herself in the works she created for Eranos, lived in Locarno during those years. Bill Hutchinson, who was born in Vevey, Switzerland, and died in 1966 in East Bergholt, had three children, Agley, Karin, and Iva, from his first marriage to Else Hutchinson-von Thieme (1886–1971), before marrying Li Wolf. The latter was first married to a Prussian officer (Benecke?), with whom she had a daughter (who died of typhoid at the age of four), then to psychiatrist Walter Carl Henry Osborne (in analysis with Georg Groddeck, 1866–1934), and finally, around 1930, to Bill Hutchinson, with whom she ran two famous photographic studios in Baden and Munich. Around 1945, at their home "Ronco dei Fiori" in Solduno, they cultivated a friendship with Dadaist Hans Arp (the latter bought that house in 1959 with Marguerite Arp-Hagenbach, whom he married later that

stages has been a very painful one. But on the whole we are satisfied with the result of two years of struggle ..." (Olga Fröbe-Kapteyn, letter to Bettina Fröbe, October 18, 1961 (Eranos Foundation Archives, Ascona-Moscia); cf. also Id., letter to Peter Reinhart, October 10, 1960 (Eranos Foundation Archives, Ascona-Moscia); on the topic, see Hakl, *Der verborgene Geist...*, cit., pp. 304–16; Id., *Eranos...*, cit., pp. 210–08; and Bernardini, *op. cit.*, p. 48).

year). Although they usually summered in Monte Brè, above Locarno, in their home built between 1942 and 1943 by the architect Paolo Mariotta (1905–1972), they spent the last twenty years of their lives in East Bergholt, Colchester, England. Their house on Monte Brè was donated to the Eranos Foundation in 1968, to be resold in the following decades.[61]

Paul Speck (1896–1966), professor at the Badische Landeskunstschule in Karlsruhe and creator of James Joyce's death mask, was also in contact with Werefkin's group. In 1949, inspired by Jung and van der Leeuw, he created a stone monument dedicated "to the unknown guadian deity of the place," to honor the spirit who had protected Eranos even in the darkest years of the war, allowing scientific work to continue uninterrupted.[62] Created by Speck, the sculpture *genio loci ignoto* was placed on the terrace of Casa Gabriella. *(Figure 208)* Speck's signature appears in the sessions of 1943, 1944, 1945, 1949, 1951, 1952, and 1953, on many occasions accompanied by that of his wife Else Speck.

Leo Kok (1893–1992), a Dutch pianist and bookseller, was one of those visitors to Casa Gabriella. Already a collaborator with the Ascona Puppet Theater, founded in 1937 by Jacob Flach (1894–1982), Dutch sculptor Mischa Epper Quarles van Ufford (1901–1978), Fritz Pauli (1891–1968), and Werner Jakob Müller (1899–1986), Kok composed the music for several poems written in the 1920s by Fröbe-Kapteyn, who in 1927 designed the cover of his *Petite chanson pour les enfants qui n'ont pas de Noël* (1926), graphically inspired by the geometric paintings she had recently begun to make as a form of meditative practice.[63] *(Figures 61 and 62)*

Mischa Epper signed the Eranos Guestbook in 1937, 1952, and 1953; her husband Ignaz Epper (1892–1969), an exponent of Swiss expressionism, in 1949 and 1953. The Eppers also had a personal relationship with Jung (which included analysis work), characterized by the psychologist's numerous

[61] Ritsema-Gris, *op. cit.*, p. 45.

[62] *Ibid.*, pp. 23 and 88; and Rudolf Ritsema, "The Origins and Opus of Eranos: Reflections at the 55th Conference – Eranos: Ursprünge und Werk. Eine Betrachtung anläßlich der 55th Tagung – L'œuvre d'Eranos et ses origines: Réflexions à l'occasion de la 55me session," *Eranos-Jahrbuch*, 56 (1987), p. VIII.

[63] Leo Kok, *Petit Chanson pour les enfants qui n'ont pas de Noël (Dessin de la couverture de Olga Froebe-Kapteyn). Violon & piano* (Sèvres: Allard, 1927); see Ritsema-Gris, *op. cit.*, p. 17.

visits to the Epper house when he was passing through Ticino;[64] the two artists reworked his theories in their own works. Mischa also executed a series of portraits of Jung, preserved at the Epper Museum in Ascona.[65]

Among the artists and writers connected to Monte Verità or living in the Ascona area who had an interest in Eranos's activities were also Ernst Frick, who signed the Eranos Guestbook in 1933, 1934, 1936, 1937, 1938, 1939, and 1941; painter Albert Kohler (1899–1969), in 1933, 1938, and 1944; Nettie Katzenstein-Sutro (1889–1967)—an exiled writer who translated Ignazio Silone's (1900–1978) *Fontamara* into German in 1932/1933—in 1933, 1935, 1936, 1937, 1938, 1939, 1942, 1943, 1945, 1949, 1950, 1951, 1952, and 1953 *(Figure 51)*; writer, pianist, and psychoanalyst Aline Valangin (1889–1986), in 1933, 1934, 1942, 1945, 1946, 1951, 1952, and 1953 (Jung's pupil since the mid-1920s, Valangin later moved to Ascona and married the lawyer Vladimir (Wladimir) Rosenbaum (1894-1984));[66] drawer Oskar Zaborsky-von Wahlstatten (1898–1959), in 1933; dancer Charlotte Bara (1901–1986), in 1934 (arrived in Ascona in 1919 and settled at the Castello San Materno in Ascona);[67] writer Efraim Frisch (1873–1942), in 1934; Kathe Grimm—former dancer at Rudolf von Laban's Schule für Lebenskunst ("School for the Life Arts"), who became part of the Monte Verità Individualistic Cooperative in 1913[68]—in 1934; Walter Helbig, in 1934, 1939, and 1940; writer David Luschnat (1895–1984), in 1934; writer Frances

[64] Diana Mirolo, personal communication, June 2006, Ascona; see also Vicente de Moura, *Two Cases from Jung's Clinical Practice. The Story of Two Sisters and the Evolution of Jungian Analysis* (London/New York, NY: Routledge, 2019), pp. 105–20.

[65] See Diana Mirolo, ed. *Maggy Reichstein e Mischa Epper. Ricami in seta e disegni dell'inconscio. Catalogo della mostra* (Ascona: Epper Museum, 2009).

[66] Peter Kamber, *Storia di due vite. Wladimir Rosenbaum e Aline Valangin* (Armando Dadò, Locarno, 2010 {1990}); Claudia Virz, "Aline Valangin (1889–1986). Fidèle à la liberté," in Tibère Adler, Verena Parzer Epp, and Claudia Wirz, eds., *Pionnières de la Suisse moderne : des femmes qui ont vécu la liberté* (Geneve: Slatkine, 2014), pp. 205–08; and Carlo Piccardi, "Wladimir Vogel e l'accoglienza dei musicisti nella Svizzera Italiana tra le due guerre," *Schweizer Jahrbuch für Musikwissenschaft*, 39 (2022), pp. 85–95.

[67] See Edmund Stadler, "Teatro e danza ad Ascona," in Szeemann, *Monte Verità...*, cit., pp. 128–37; and Letizia Tedeschi, "Un teatro per la danza. L'incontro tra Charlotte Bara e Carl Weidemeyer," in Schwab and Lafranchi, *op. cit.*, pp. 156–69.

[68] See Rudolf von Laban, *Ein Leben für den Tanz* (Dresden: Carl Reissner, 1935); Claude Perrottet, "Rudolf Laban. Il rinnovatore della danza nel nostro secolo," in Szeemann, *Dalla danza libera, all'arte pura...*, cit.; Valerie Preston-Dunlop, *Rudolf Laban: An Extraordinary Life* (Alton: Dance Books, 2008); and also Karine Montabord, "Zurich et le Monte Verità, un binôme favorable aux échanges entre Dada et la danse," *Transversales*, 18 (2021) ("Corps, Lieux et Appartenances").

Külpe (1862–1936), in 1935; composer Hermann Hans Wetzler (1870–1943), in 1936; painter Hugh Sartorius Whitaker (1885–1971), in 1936; essayist Erich Kahler (1885–1970), in 1938; artist Hedy Alma Wyss (1906–2009), in 1941, 1942, 1943, 1944, 1945, 1946, 1950, 1951, 1952, and 1953; Countess Carmen Hertz-Finckenstein (1889–1971), in 1945, 1950, 1951, and 1952; writer Hans Sterneder (1889–1981), in 1949; writer Ernst Wilhelm Eschmann (1904–1987), in 1950, 1951, and 1952; sculptor Régine Heim-Freudenreich (1907–2004), in 1951 and 1953; painter, graphic artist, and avant-garde film producer Hans Richter (1888–1976), in 1951 and 1952; and novelist Erich Maria Remarque (1898–1970), in 1953.

The photographs taken by Margarita Marianne (Margarethe) Fellerer (1886–1961), who was the official photographer of the Eranos Conferences from the early 1930s until the end of the 1950s, allow us to retrace the passage of these and other artists and writers through Eranos. Fellerer arrived in Ascona around 1909–1910 and married Ernst Frick, with whom she lived from 1920. Frick had lived in Ascona since 1911 (and later also in Bosco Gurin, where some photographs show him in the late 1930s together with the priest and historian of Christianity Ernesto Buonaiuti, a lecturer at Eranos)[69] together with Frieda Gross-Schloffer (1879–1956), the former wife of Otto Gross.[70] In 1928, Frick discovered a Celtic settlement on the Balladrüm mountain above Ascona and undertook a meticulous and interesting research project. Ximena de Angulo-Roelli, editorial assistant at the Bollingen Foundation and, since the 1950s, personal assistant to Fröbe-Kapteyn, recalls Fellerer's typical Viennese charm: she used to chat with the Eranos speakers with ease, holding her camera against her chest.[71] In this way, she photographed her subjects without them noticing, obtaining extremely "lively" and natural shots.[72]

---

[69] See Fabio Merlini and Riccardo Bernardini, "Preface / Prefazione," in Ernesto Buonaiuti, *Palingenesis, Resurrection, and Immortality in Primitive Christianity / Palingenesi, resurrezione e immortalità nel Cristianesimo primitivo*, ed. Adriano Fabris (Ascona: Eranos Classics 2, Aragno * Eranos Ascona, 2020), pp. VII–LII.

[70] See Green, *The von Richthofen Sisters...*, cit.

[71] It was probably a medium format Hasselblad (Paul Kugler, "Eranos and Jungian Psychology: A History in Images," in Lyn Cowan, ed., *Barcelona 2004—Edges of Experience: Memory and Emergence—Proceedings of the Sixteenth International Congress for Analytical Psychology* (Einsiedeln: Daimon, 2006), p. 99, fn. 1).

[72] Ximena de Angulo-Roelli, personal communication, July 5, 2007, Cavigliano. In 1935, the Eranos

In 1946, at Pentecost, Fröbe-Kapteyn organized three days of chamber music in the Lecture Hall of Casa Eranos with the Andreae Trio from Zurich, which she enjoyed very much. From 1947 onwards, in fact, Fröbe-Kapteyn made it a habit to organize chamber music evenings at Eranos during the summer symposia: it was the first year that music made its official debut at Eranos and, at the same time, returned to Fröbe-Kapteyn's life after the death of her husband, flautist Iwan Fröbe.[73] On August 18, 1947, the Winterthur String Quartet played in the cloister of the Collegio Papio in Ascona; on August 22, Peter Rybar (violin), Oskar Kromer (viola), and Alessandro Chasen (piano) performed Mozart at the Hotel Tamaro; on August 24, the Winterthur String Trio played in the Lecture Hall of Casa Eranos. Ascona, she wrote to her friend Ada Hondius-Crone in February 1946, was becoming an important musical center, and numerous artists were coming to give concerts there during the summer months.[74] Among them was pianist Chasen, who had come to Ascona to escape Nazi persecution and gave numerous chamber music concerts not only at Eranos but also at various other venues in Ascona. On one occasion, Chasen played for Bara at the Teatro San Materno. Together with his wife, writer and translator Ilse Kraemer (1902–1979), Chasen stayed at Casa Gabriella during the war years as a guest of Fröbe-Kapteyn, before moving to Ronco and finally to Zurich. It was he, together with Ascona lawyer

---

photographer sent Jung one of her first works, namely an image from the photographic series "The Praying Mantis" (Carl Gustav Jung, letter to Margarethe Fellerer, January10, 1936, quoted in Szeemann, *Monte Verità…*, cit., p. 117). In 1938, surprised that many women in the second half of their lives were turning to her for advice, Fröbe-Kapteyn wrote to Jung about Fellerer's marital difficulties with Frick (Olga Fröbe-Kapteyn, letter to Carl Gustav Jung, July 5, 1938 (University Archives, ETH-Bibliothek, Zurich / Eranos Foundation Archives, Ascona-Moscia). Fellerer continued to send to Jung photographs taken during the Eranos Conferences (Carl Gustav, letter to Margarethe Fellerer, October 3, 1942, in Id., *Letters…*, cit., Vol. I, pp. 320 f.). In 1944, while Jung was recovering after being hospitalized, Fellerer traveled to Zurich and took a series of photographs, which have recently been compiled and published (the images are included in Riccardo Bernardini, "Integrazioni al resoconto delle visioni connesse alla malattia di Jung del 1944," *Rivista di Psicologia Analitica*, 107 (55, 2023), pp. 127–68). See also Riccardo Bernardini, "Collezionando ricordi: Margarethe Fellerer, fotografa di Eranos, e Carl Gustav Jung," in Quaglino, Romano, and Bernardini, *Carl Gustav Jung a Eranos 1933–1952*, cit., pp. 133–41, and more recently Gianfranco Ragno, "La fotografa di Eranos: Margarethe Fellerer / Die Eranos-Fotografin: Margarethe Fellerer," *Ferien-Journal. Ascona* (March–April 2025), pp. 22–26.

[73] Fröbe-Kapteyn, "Die Eranos *Mandala*," cit.

[74] Olga Fröbe-Kapteyn, letter to Ada Hondius-Crone, February 10, 1946, quoted in Ritsema-Gris, *op. cit.*, p. 46.

Leone Ressiga Vacchini and later composer Wladimir Vogel, who conceived and promoted the Ascona Music Weeks from 1946 onwards.[75]

The arrival of music at Eranos was felt by Fröbe-Kapteyn as a synchronistic event and was also reflected in her visions of the "Eranos *Maṇḍala*," which, as we have seen, is an iconographic motif that appears in the "Meditation Plates" in 1927 *(Figure 57)* and then continues in the "Visions" since 1934 *(Figures 149–151)*. In 1947, she painted a third *maṇḍala* identified as "The fourfold breathing," which she described as follows: "The Cross of Fiery Life. The perpetual meeting and separating of the four breath-currents, as opposites, in the fivefold Center, the Rose. The Rotation of the Center, and the infolding and outfolding of the five petals are the Source of the four breathings. In time and space, the Cross is *horizontal* = of a feminine nature. That is, the mode of my realization. But in its own plane there is no horizontal or vertical, only (probably) a rhythmic emanation of radiation, possibly in all or in no direction. The event of the *entrance of music* into Eranos and into my life was synchronic with the unsealing of the center of the *fourfold breathing centre* (in the heart). Both were concerned with the heart (= feeling). A little later came the realisation of the necessity of *NON-ACTION* as the basis of a new type of 'ACTION' no longer personal, but emanating from the Self. The *horizontal* nature of the 'Cross' breathing = the feminine attitude = *das Empfangende* [the receptivity], which also makes it possible for the 'action of the Self' to function." *(Figure 199)* Jung said to her with regard to that image: "Look at Melusine and blood in *Paracelsica*. The spiritual blood. Music and alchemy. The quintessence. Five springs from four."[76] Fröbe-Kapteyn emphasized that the Rosy Cross of 1947 was evoked in the Eranos Hall just by music.[77] She also added: "From the four currents of music [there was] a fifth that transforms within them. The 'pneumatic music' of the flute! In the

[75] See Dino Invernizzi, "Sessant'anni di grande musica ad Ascona," in Vv.Aa., *Stagioni di grande musica. 1946–2005* (Ascona: Settimane Musicali di Ascona, 2005), p. 15.

[76] Fröbe-Kapteyn, "Die Eranos *Mandala*," cit.

[77] Olga Fröbe-Kapteyn, "The Cross of Milk" (unpublished manuscript and typescript, August 6, 1948; Eranos Foundation Archives, Ascona-Moscia).

Eranos *Mandala* [there manifests] their synchronistic quality of chamber music or a choir."[78]

The fourth *Maṇḍala* dates back to Pentecost 1947, about which she recalled: "During the first concert I became aware of a subtle, immaterial pink cross of rosered colour, horizontal, passing through all of the hall. During the rehearsals on Pentecost Monday, I was alone in the hall with the three musicians—together four figures. This great Cross (Rosy Cross) was now formed of flowing waves of colour, immaterial, like a mist in a movement, horizontal. During the music I saw figures coming from the garden and entering the hall, all the old alchemists I ever heard of, and many more. They have entered now, it seems, because this flowing cross, which was already in the Eranos skating *Mandala* [1934], but was there on the ice, has now become alive, and has the colour of life, of blood, and of roses. Also it is Pentecost, the hour of the descent of the Holy Ghost. Also I and the three musicians are a quaternity. In this hour, or at this point, we were linked with the alchemists of the past. They are the *Ahnen* [Ancestors] of the Eranos work. We are waiting for someone. And now Jung comes into the hall and takes his place opposite to me, not in the center, but between it and the outer ring of alchemists."[79] *(Figure 200)* Subsequently, Fröbe-

---

[78] Olga Fröbe-Kapteyn, "The 'Tönende' Breast" (unpublished manuscript and typescript, November 18, 1948 [Zurich]; Eranos Foundation Archives, Ascona-Moscia).

[79] Fröbe-Kapteyn, "Die Eranos *Mandala*," cit. Two years later, on June 22, 1949, Fröbe-Kapteyn had a dream in which she saw herself in a hotel with Paul and Mary Mellon (whose sudden death in October 1946 required Fröbe-Kapteyn to undergo a long and painful process of coming to terms with her loss). Mary Mellon invited her to have dinner with them. Retiring to her room to change her clothes, Fröbe-Kapteyn saw a large snake, a beautiful turquoise color, coming out of a hole in the middle of the room. The snake, female, had its mouth open and full of small snakes. On June 28, Fröbe-Kapteyn continued the dream with active imagination, in which she saw the same snake drawing a *maṇḍala* on the ground, inside a circle formed by the small snakes. The snake was now waiting for her. She then entered the circle and danced with the snake; this dance, which always took place with curvilinear movements, reminded her of the 1934 Eranos *Maṇḍala (Figure 151)*, in which she danced on the ice with Jung. She and the snake were in fact tracing the same lines followed with Jung. The only difference was that now the entire pattern was alive, floating, and vibrating, in constant motion. The *maṇḍala* still had the shape of a cross and, as in the 1947 depictions *(Figures 199 and 200)*, a fourfold current entered and exited the center of the figure. Intertwined with this geometric pattern was once again the shape of a large rose, whose petals, just like in the 1934 Eranos *Maṇḍala*, became four-dimensional and grew around them. The pink flower was located at the base of the green cross. At its center, she and the snake danced. Then a kind of dew began to fall, not water, but milk. Above the *maṇḍala*, like an arch, stood the faint hemispherical outline of a breast, inside which she and the snake were standing. Fröbe-Kapteyn, completely bathed in milk, heard the snake explain: "This is the Mother, inside and outside;

Kapteyn documented as a transformation of the fourfold current of "rosy breath" present in the previous image into a current of "milk" flowing from the center of the figure. Jung and Fröbe-Kapteyn are still present at the center of the configuration.[80] *(Figure 201)*

Emphasizing its intuitive, spontaneous, and creative dimension, which was also expressed in the last three *maṇḍalas* drawn in the following years, until 1949, *(Figures 202–204)* Fröbe-Kapteyn experienced Eranos in terms of a "representation" or a "game" (*Spiel*), meaning by this its "joyful and serious essence" (*heiter-ernste Wesen*). This representative or playful aspect, enacted each year on a stage (*Bühne*), was the "natural counterpart to pure intellectualism": "The wind blows wherever it pleases,[81] and how it pleases, but never in the sense of the intellect alone."[82] Although the figures in this "representation" or "game" changed, its spiritual core—its "root" (*Wurzel*)—remained unchanged, just like the "pedal" (*Orgelpunkt*) in

---

this is the flowering of the horizontal; here you are gathered, nourished, refreshed, regenerated, reborn. Now we remain together, you and I. And now I must take care of the ghost!" After saying this, the snake disappeared. Little by little, she realized that she was in her room and that she had actually been dancing on the green wooden surface of the Eranos round table. This table, placed on the floor, filled the entire room and had a rose and a cross traced on it. The snake reappeared with Mary Mellon, who approached her and said, "So, now it's a goodbye! The snake told me. My place is on another level. Remember me from time to time, or I may feel that you are forgetting me, and I will come back!" Her hand was cold. A passage then opened on one side of the *maṇḍala* and the snake slithered away, followed by Mary Mellon, heading west. She waved goodbye once more, then they both disappeared. A small flame then lit up, following them and burning the grass as they passed. Fröbe-Kapteyn felt that Mary had gone to her place and that she would never return from there. Then the snake returned and said to her, "The *maṇḍala* has been transformed. We have freed Jung. Nothing holds him here anymore, except his answer to the Womb. For the Womb and the *mandala* are one" (Olga Fröbe-Kapteyn, "Dream. 22 June 1949" (unpublished typescript, 1949; Eranos Foundation Archives, Ascona-Moscia).

[80] *Ibid.* Fröbe-Kapteyn remembered that "Jung called the Blood *Mandala* with the 4-fold breathing a woman's Mystery" (Olga Fröbe-Kapteyn, "The ancestral Blood Stream" (unpublished typescript, undated [1952?]; Eranos Foundation Archives, Ascona-Moscia). In some handwritten notes, she further commented on this vision, adding: "The 'tönende' ['resounding'] Breast, Heart + Cross + Rose. The Milk streaming rhytmically is *music.* 4 streams of music, a 5th transmuting and uniting them. The 'pneumatic Music' of the flute! In the Eranos *Mandala* … the synchronistic quality is that of a Kammer orchestra or a choir" (Fröbe-Kapteyn, "The 'Tönende' Breast," cit.). In other notes, she added: "This 4-fold milky, spiritual current is probably the healing milk, projected in the vision of Hell 9 years ago! [See the comments to *Figures 187–189*] The milky currents now 'foam'" (Fröbe-Kapteyn, "The Cross of Milk," cit.). With reference to the 4-fold breath of the *Maṇḍala* of Prāṇa, milk, and breath, she further specified that "the inbreathing comes from the subtle body, the outbreathing feeds the physical body" (*ibid.*).

[81] *John* 3:8.

[82] Olga Fröbe-Kapteyn, "Vorwort," *Eranos-Jahrbuch*, 19 (1950), pp. 6 f.

music.[83] She also wrote: "Within the group of lecturers ... scientific consonances emerge ... which interact with each other according to laws similar to those governing chamber or symphonic music. The structure of this inner harmony recalls that of a musical fugue and forms the basis for the mutual relationships between the various relationships, their impact on listeners, and the responses of the latter."[84] Fröbe-Kapteyn also referred to Eranos as a "festival" (*Fest*)[85] or a "dance of the sciences" (*Tanz der Wissenschaften*).[86] It was Rudolf Otto himself who pointed out to Fröbe-Kapteyn that the palindrome of the Green noun *eranos* was a Latin and Italian verb: *sonare* ("to sound").[87] When asked to explain Eranos, she refused in fact a rational definition: "Come with me through the garden," she wrote to her publisher Daniel Brody in 1955, "until reaching the [Eranos] Hall, look around you and, during our walk, simply don't ask me anything. We are at the heart of the Conference. Now let's go out onto the large terrace, where the Round Table is waiting for the guests. This table is the center of Eranos: this is where the most lively and fruitful discussions take place. 'Banquet' here really means 'receiving from two spheres.'"[88]

The houses and grounds of Fröbe-Kapteyn were therefore not only the setting, but also the ingredients that made possible numerous personal encounters, cultural exchanges, artistic influences, and

[83] *Ibid.*

[84] *Ibid.*; see also Olga Fröbe-Kapteyn, letter to Henry Corbin, October 18, 1953, quoted in Ritsema-Gris, *op. cit.*, p. 92.

[85] Olga Fröbe-Kapteyn, "Vorwort," *Eranos-Jahrbuch*, 22 (1953), p. 5.

[86] *Ibid.*, p. 6; see also Mircea Eliade, "Les danseurs passent, la danse reste," *Du. Schweizerische Monatsschrift*, 15 (4, 1955), pp. 60–62.

[87] Ritsema-Gris, *op. cit.*, p. 21; and Bernardini, *Jung a Eranos...*, cit., pp. 42 f. and 56.

[88] Olga Fröbe-Kapteyn, "Ein Brief der Gründerin," *Du. Schweizerische Monatsschrift*, 15 (4, 1955) ("Eranos"), p. 10. The "transcendent" dimension of the Eranos garden is also evident in some of Fröbe-Kapteyn's later visions concerning her relationship with Erich Neumann. Commenting on them, she wrote: "A dynamic hovers over the garden that cannot be described. And I understand that the garden is timeless and everlasting ... In the garden of Eranos ... many dimensions converge ... Neumann and I ... stand at the outer corner of the terrace, looking out onto the garden and the lake, and now we see a phenomenon of colors that I had already witnessed twice in the summer: the sun has just disappeared behind the mountains and pours a glow over all the trees and plants, in which the intensity of colors is multiplied a hundredfold. It is that light which I once called *Lumen Naturae*, and it truly is that. A light that pervades everything and seems to shine out from the trees and plants themselves: *The Light that never was on land or sea*" (Fröbe-Kapteyn, "Vision. Lebendige Bilder & Wandlungen," cit., p. 2).

experiences of an inner nature. From her initial contact with Monte Verità and her subsequent move to Moscia, the original property of Villa Gabriella inhabited by her since 1921—despite the subsequent construction of Casa Eranos (1928),[89] Casa Shanti (1928–1929),[90] and the Holzhütte ("Hut") (1932)[91]—has been gradually eroded over the decades in any case.

Casa Shanti was sold by Fröbe-Kapteyn in 1937 to Emma Hélène von Pelet-Narbonne (Kassel, March 13, 1892–Orselina, February 18 1967), who was joined there that same year by her friend Alwina (Alwine) von Keller (New York, June 10, 1878–Interlaken, December 31, 1965). A translator and writer, von Pelet had met von Keller at the Odenwaldschule run by Paul Geheeb (1870–1961) and Edith Geheeb-Cassirer (1885–1982), where the latter worked as an English teacher.[92]

---

[89] Cadastral mutation no. 86 of December 29, 1928. It was only in the late 1930s that the Eranos Studio was built—the apartment in Casa Eranos above the Lecture Hall, where Fröbe-Kapteyn hosted the Jung couple during the Conferences from 1940 (when the Hotel Monte Verità closed) (Hannah, *op. cit.*, pp. 306 and 382, and Cabot Reid, *op. cit.*, p. 438) and where she imagined that the Eranos Archive (which had been kept until then in Casa Gabriella, where she lived) might one day find a home. Casa Eranos thus lost its original Bauhaus appearance with its flat roof (the Eranos Studio firstly appeared in a vision (out-of-series, no. 308) of Fröbe-Kapteyn drawn in June 1937) *(Figures 185 and 186)*. Fröbe-Kaptyen's idea was that the Eranos Studio could be made available both as a studio and as a venue for group seminars and individual training, as well as accommodation for up to three scholars at a time. At least until 1941, in any case, Fröbe-Kapteyn continued to rent out the apartment during the winter months, reiterating that its main purpose was to serve as accommodation for Jung. However, as soon as it became possible to accommodate researchers for longer periods of three to six months, Casa Eranos would have fully achieved its purpose (Olga Fröbe-Kapteyn, letter to Ada Hondius-Crone, September 14, 1941, quoted in Ritsema-Gris, *op. cit.*, p. 38). The Eranos Studio was later also used by Erich Neumann for consultation of the Eranos Archive and the preparation of his *The Great Mother—An Analysis of the Archetype* (1955), which is still the only official publication of the Archive (cf. Bernardini, "Neumann at Eranos," cit.). However, due to financial difficulties, the project to make Eranos a true "Institute for Research into Symbolism" never got off the ground. The Eranos Archive remained in Casa Gabriella, the apartment in Casa Eranos was rented out, and the upper floors of Casa Gabriella were offered to students and researchers who regularly consulted the Archive during those years, while the library, also located in Casa Gabriella, gradually expanded with subsequent bequests and donations (Bernardini, *Jung a Eranos...*, cit., p. 342).

[90] Cadastral mutation no. 736 of July 27, 1932.

[91] Cadastral mutation no. 1844 of November 22, 1941.

[92] Alwine von Keller, "Abendaussprache für die Mitarbeiter der École d'Humanité, Goldern. 12.VIII.1945" (unpublished typescript, August 1945; Eranos Foundation Archives, Ascona-Moscia); Id., "Erste Eindrücke von Paul Geheeb," *Der neue Waldkauz. Zeitschrift der Odenwaldschule*, 3 (1929); rpt. in Eva Cassirer *et al.*, eds., *Erziehung zur Humanität. Paul Geheeb zum 90. Geburtstag* (Heidelberg: Lambert Schneider, 1960) pp. 21–23, and in Walter Schäfer, ed., *Paul Geheeb. Mensch und Erzieher. Eine Biographie. Aus den Deutschen Landerziehungsheimen – Heft 4* (Stuttgart: Klett, 1960), pp. 20–21; Id., "Eindrücke von Edith und Paul Geheeb [Eindrücke aus der , Ecole d'Humanité'] – Arbeit in der Schweiz 1934–45," in

A thinker, theologian, physician, educationalist, and pioneer of the "New Education" movement, Geheeb founded the Odenwaldschule in Heppenheim, between Darmstadt and Heidelberg in western Germany, in 1910, together with his wife Geheeb-Cassirer, with the aim of putting his new ideas on education into practice. Edith's father, the politician and entrepreneur Max Cassirer (1857–1943)—uncle of the philosopher Ernst Cassirer (1874–1945)—had a small village built for his daughter in the countryside, where the Odenwaldschule began. Each house in the village was named after a great philosopher or writer. The Odenwaldschule project was part of the culture of the avant-garde educational institutions of the time, also known as Waldschulen. Geheeb, in particular, believed that in order to achieve harmony in individual existence and a better understanding between people and between peoples, it was necessary to start with the proper education of children. He was also convinced that every child needed individual attention and could only be guided towards full development if their education took into account their personal strengths and weaknesses. At the school, every child was given complete freedom to act and express their thoughts without fear. A vegetarian diet, group games, long excursions into nature, and artistic and manual work also contributed to their growth. The core principles of the Odenwaldschule were co-education, the idea of education through "head, heart, and hands" according to the specific aptitudes of the child, the recognition of the pedagogical importance of music, drawing, and theater, and the acceptance of children of all nationalities, ethnies, and religions. The apprenticeship at the Odenwaldschule represented a real turning point in von Pelet's life. Paul and Edith Geheeb understood her complex nature. Their friendship lasted until their deaths. The vicissitudes of the Second World War subsequently forced the Geheebs to emigrate to Switzerland. Persecuted by the Nazis since 1933, when they were asked to expel Jewish

---

Eva Cassirer, Ewa Liesegang, and Max Weber-Schäfer, eds., *Die Idee einer Schule im Spiegel der Zeit. Festschrift für Paul Geheeb zum 80. Geburtstag und zum 40 jährigen Bestehen der Odenwaldschule* (Heidelberg: Lambert Schneider, undated [1950]), pp. 106–10; and Meike Sophia Baader, "Reformpädagogik, Religiosität und Frauenbewegung als Wege zur Selbstverwirklichung: Alwine von Keller," in Hein Retter, ed., *Reformpädagogik. Neue Zugänge – Befunde – Kontroversen* (Bad Heilbrunn, Obb.: Julius Klinkhardt, 2004), pp. 35–59.

students, the children of those who opposed the Reich's policies, and anyone who was not of the "Aryan race," they suffered the pain of seeing all the books in their library by non-German authors, including Tolstoy (acknowledged by the vegetarians of Monte Verità as "our greatest companion of all time ... a master and teacher, a patriarch and prophet") and Dostoevsky, burned in a large bonfire in the schoolyard. Having fled Germany in secret (Geheeb was a very prominent figure), they initially settled in Pont-Céard, near Versoix, ten kilometers from Geneva, where the school resumed its activities from April 1934 to December 1938 under the name Ecole d'Humanité. After various vicissitudes, the institute was transferred in January 1939 to Les Pléiades, at the Hôtel Les Sapins in Lally, where it remained in operation until April of the same year. From April to October 1939, it operated near the castle of Greng, near Morat, in the Broye Valley; from October 1939 to May 1946 at the Hôtel du Lac, near the Chalet Aurore der Naturfreunde, on Lac Noir, near Fribourg, and, from May 1946, in Goldern-Hasliberg, in the Bernese Oberland, where the Ecole d'Humanité is still active. The Odenwaldschule, on the other hand, continues its activities in Heppenheim, Germany.[93]

After her time at the Odenwaldschule, von Pelet settled in Frankfurt, where she became involved in numerous social activities. She also collaborated with various newspapers, such as *Die Tat*, for which she wrote short stories, poems, and articles on the status of women, and began her work as a translator. When Hitler came to power in 1933, von Pelet decided to leave Germany. After a stay in Florence in 1934, concerned about the pact that was taking shape between Hitler and Mussolini, she sought a "safe haven" in Switzerland. She arrived in Moscia, in the "Collinetta" area on Lake Maggiore, where she rented a house for a while. Unsatisfied with her accommodation, she continued her search for a while longer. In 1937, she saw a sign on a beautiful but simple building overlooking the lake that read "*Casa da vendere*" ("House for sale"). It was just Casa Shanti, where

[93] See Ritsema-Gris, *op. cit.*, pp. 59 ff.; Martin Näf, *Paul Geheeb. Seine Entwicklung bis zur Gründung der Odenwaldschule. Schriftenreihe des Weltbundes für Erneuerung der Erziehung. Internationale Pädagogik-Reformpädagogik. Band 4* (Weinheim: Deutscher Studien, 1998); and Dennis Shirley, *Reformpädagogik im Nationalsozialismus. Die Odenwaldschule 1910 bis 1945* (Weinheim/Munich: Juventa, 2010).

Fröbe-Kapteyn had been hosting friends and speakers at the Eranos symposia and which she had been forced to sell to cover the growing costs of her conference project.

Von Pelet consulted von Keller, a translator of Eastern spiritual texts from English into German,[94] who was living in Zurich at the time, about the purchase. Von Keller gave von Pelet her consent to purchase Casa Shanti, and the deed of sale between Fröbe-Kapteyn and von Pelet was signed on August 24, 1937.[95] Von Keller joined von Pelet at Casa Shanti shortly afterwards, and from that moment on, the two women shared it.

Initially, the two friends settled in the apartment above, while von Keller used the lower floor as a professional studio, where she received patients whom Jung himself sent to her from Zurich. However, the vicissitudes of the war had repercussions on von Pelet's financial fortunes. This led to their decision to build a second large room, a kitchen, and a bathroom on the ground floor. Von Keller also used the studio as a bedroom, while Emma's library served as a living room. This allowed them to rent out the upper floor from time to time, thus securing a small financial income. With the move of von Pelet and von Keller to Casa Shanti, their friends Paul and Edith Geheeb were also able to maintain regular and fruitful contact with them in a neutral and liberal country.

During her years at Casa Shanti, von Pelet worked on translating numerous works from English and French into German.[96] She had a brief

---

[94] Sri Aurobindo, *Gedanken und Einblicke. Studie über das Yoga des Shri Aurobindo von N.K. Gupta. Vorrede von J. Herbert, Übersetzung aus der Originalausgabe in Arya Pondichery von Alwina von Keller* (Zurich: Rascher, 1943); Id., *Die Mutter. Aus dem Englischen übertragen von Alwina v. Keller*, 2 vols. (Zurich: Rascher, 1945); and Swami Vivekananda, *Gespräche auf den tausend Inseln. Uebersetzung von Alwina von Keller* (Zurich: Rascher, 1944).

[95] Cadastral mutation no. 1253 of August 14, 1937.

[96] She is responsible, for example, for several translations (some of which she also edited) of texts by Sri Ramakrishna (1836–1886), in an edition cited by Jung himself, and by Swami Vivekananda (1863–1902). Her works also include translations of works by Eranos authors, such as Mircea Eliade, who spoke at Ascona on thirteen occasions between 1950 and 1967 and whom von Pelet certainly had the opportunity to meet during the Ascona symposia, and Daisetsu Teitarō Suzuki, who lectured at Eranos in 1963 and 1964 and whose *The Great Liberation* (1939) had already been published with an important preface by Jung. Von Pelet also translated essays by the Indologist Jean Herbert (1897–1980), the writer and philosopher Denis de Rougemont (1906–1985), the analyst Mary Esther Harding (1888–1971), the psychoanalyst and writer Marie Bonaparte (1882–1962), psychiatrist Akihisa Kondo, a scholar of the relationship between Western and Eastern psychology and psychotherapy; psychologist and

correspondence with Aline Valangin.[97] Von Pelet initially underwent analysis with Carl Alfred Meier (1905–1995) between October 11, 1940, and March 3, 1941. On February 20, 1941, she wrote to Jung for the first time and began analysis with him that same year. Their relationship, marked by more or less regular meetings in Küsnacht and at Casa Shanti in Ascona, lasted at least until 1951. Von Pelet documented the dreams she had over more than thirty years, from 1935 to 1966, in a series of notebooks and diaries. The dreams are sometimes transposed pictorially into evocative "images from the unconscious" (*Bilder aus dem Unbewußten*), according to Jung's practice of objectification.[98] The dreams are also accompanied by personal reflections, in some cases by interpretations and, above all, by the amplifications that Jung himself gave them, and by accounts of their conversations in Küsnacht and Ascona.[99]

Von Keller was in analysis first with Ernst Bernhard in Berlin and then in Rome,[100] and later with Jung in Zurich,[101] eventually becoming an analyst

theologian Howard Littleton Philp, also author of *Jung and the Problem of Evil* (1958) and *Freud and Religious Belief* (1974); Hispanic scholar Edgar Allison Peers (1891–1952), spiritualist writer Joel Solomon Goldsmith (1892–1964), and Suzanne Hausammann and Mulk Raj Anand (1905–2004). See Bernardini, "In analisi con Jung. I diari di Emma von Pelet," cit., pp. 227 f.

[97] The "Valangin Fund" at the Cantonal Library in Lugano contains two letters by Emma von Pelet from 1946: see Diana Rüesch, "Il Fondo Aline Valangin," *Cartevive. Bollettino dell'Archivio Prezzolini e degli Archivi di Cultura Contemporanea della Biblioteca Cantonale di Lugano*, 10 (2, 1998), pp. 35–52.

[98] Emma Hélène von Pelet-Narbonne, "Bilder aus dem Unbewußten" (unpublished manuscript and typescript with drawings, 1941–42; Eranos Foundation Archives, Ascona-Moscia).

[99] See Ritsema-Gris, *op. cit.*, p. 83; Riccardo Bernardini, "'Picnic' del sogno: una matrice di sogno sociale a Eranos," *Anamorphosis. Gruppi, psicologia analitica e psicodramma*, 4 (4, 2006), p. 71, fn. 4; Maurizio Gasseau and Riccardo Bernardini, "Il sogno: prospettive di Eranos," in Idd., eds., *Il sogno. Dalla psicologia analitica allo psicodramma junghiano* (Milan: FrancoAngeli, 2009), p. 21; Christa Robinson, "Eranos: A Place, an Encounter, a Story," *Spring*, 86 (2011), pp. 169 f.; Gian Piero Quaglino, Augusto Romano, and Riccardo Bernardini, "A visit paid to Jung by Alwine von Keller," *Journal of Analytical Psychology*, 56 (2, 2011), p. 237; Bernardini, *Jung a Eranos...*, cit., pp. 215 f., fn. 207; Bernardini, "The Secret of Eranos," cit., pp. 336 and 339; Bernardini, Quaglino, and Romano, "Appendix II. Alwine von Keller...," pp. 144 f; and Bernardini, "In analisi con Jung. I diari di Emma von Pelet," cit.

[100] Ernst Bernhard, letter to Carl Gustav Jung, February 26, 1947, in Giovanni Sorge, ed., *Lettere tra Ernst Bernhard e Carl Gustav Jung. 1934/1959* (Milan: La biblioteca di Vivarium, 2001), pp. 38 f.

[101] Alwine von Keller, letter to Eva Cassirer, July 4, 1943, quoted in Quaglino, Romano, and Bernardini, "A visit paid to Jung by Alwine von Keller," cit.; Id., "*In memoriam* Carl Gustav Jung" {1961}, in Quaglino, Romano, and Bernardini, *Carl Gustav Jung a Eranos 1933–1952*, cit., pp. 168 f.; Id., *Du bist eitel, sagte der Alte* (Zurich: Klusverlag, 1989), p. 41; Ritsema-Gris, *op. cit.*, p. 82; Ernst Bernhard, *Mitobiografia*, ed. Hélène Erba-Tissot (Milan: Adelphi, 1969), pp. 7 *ff.*

herself. Like von Pelet, von Keller also used to objectify her dreams in "drawings of the unconscious," which evoked, through associations and amplifications, other images in a succession of figures that helped clarify the manifest content of the dream.[102]

Alwine's patients, for the most part sent by Jung, were becoming, in the meantime, ever more numerous. She is indeed remembered as a therapist gifted with great intuition, sensitivity, and empathy.[103] Moreover, like von Pelet, she too was dedicating herself with greater and greater involvement to writing poetry. She decided, therefore, to look for a secretary, and found one in Dati Busse, who she had met in the war years at the Odenwaldschule and who now worked at the Ecole d'Humanité on the Schwarzsee.

Von Keller and von Pelet, through their relationship and work with Jung, and their connection and friendship with Fröbe-Kapteyn, played a discreet yet significant role in the development of Eranos.[104] The two women participated not only in the official conferences, but also in impromptu seminars that took place throughout the year, such as Jung's memorable lecture in the summer of 1943 on the cartographic art of the Italian priest Opicinus de Canistris.[105] Jung also used to come to Moscia not only to discuss matters concerning Eranos with Fröbe-Kapteyn, but also to spend a few hours relaxing in the company of the guests at Casa Shanti and enjoying their beautiful terrace overlooking the lake.[106]

The relationship between Fröbe-Kapteyn, who lived in Casa Gabriella, and the two guests at Casa Shanti soon developed into a normal neighborly relationship. Von Pelet's harsh character meant that she often found herself acting as a "watchdog" for von Keller, whose open and sunny nature attracted all kinds of visitors to Moscia, annoying Fröbe-Kapteyn and often

[102] Alvine von Keller, *My Story* (Madras: ADART, undated), § "Introduction."

[103] Ximena de Angulo-Roelli, personal communication, July 2, 2007; see also Rudolf Ritsema, *Alwine von Keller. * 10.6.1878, New York–† 31.12.1965, Interlaken* (privately printed, undated [1966]), p. 4; and Rudolf Ritsema and Shantena Augusto Sabbadini, "Images of the Unknown: The Eranos *I Ching* Project 1989–1997," *Eranos-Jahrbuch*, 66 (1997), p. 9.

[104] Ritsema-Gris, *op. cit.*, p. 59.

[105] Jung, *The Solar Myths and Opicinus de Canistris…*, cit.

[106] Ritsema-Gris, *op. cit.*, p. 83.

exasperating Alwine herself.[107] The relationship with Alwine von Keller, in particular, was very positive for Fröbe-Kapteyn. The open and profound nature of the former allowed Fröbe-Kapteyn to come out of her introversion, leading to the development of a genuine friendship based on mutual listening and understanding of each other's practical, psychological, and spiritual problems. There was never any real analysis between the two, but von Keller was of great help to Fröbe-Kapteyn and her work, Eranos.[108] Although von Pelet's severe, rigid, and highly methodical temperament prevented a similarly spontaneous friendship from developing between her and Fröbe-Kapteyn, von Pelet's analysis diaries nevertheless reveal a relationship of deep trust: Fröbe-Kapteyn used to help von Pelet understand her dreams, offering symbolic and iconographic parallels, according to Jung's technique of amplification. Von Pelet meticulously collected the amplifications (generally with a religious or mythological background) provided by Fröbe-Kapteyn (evidently also based on her own personal experience, previously documented in her "Visions"), together with Jung's comments and her own personal reflections.

Von Keller left Casa Shanti only in the 1960s, when her advanced age made it too difficult for her to climb the steep steps of Moscia. She accepted the invitation of her secretary, Dati Busse, to move to Interlaken, where Busse's husband ran a pharmacy. Von Keller died in Interlaken of a heart attack on December 31, 1965, at the age of 86. Emma von Pelet passed away two years later, on February 18, 1967, in Orselina, in the Canton of Ticino. Before her death, von Pelet stipulated in her last will and testament that the ownership of Casa Shanti should be transferred to a foundation, whose sole purpose would be to support Eranos, and which she named after her great friend: the Alwine von Keller Foundation.[109]

---

[107] Robinson, *op. cit.*, p. 170.

[108] Ritsema-Gris, *op. cit.*, p. 83.

[109] In 1980 the Eranos Foundation and the Alwine von Keller Foundation were joined for administrative reasons into a single body, under the name Eranos and Alwine von Keller Foundation. The name was changed again in 2008 into Eranos Foundation.

Alwine von Keller was also analyst to Rudolf Ritsema (1918–2006) and his wife, Pauline Catherine Ritsema-Gris (1917–2007).[110] *(Figures 211–214)* From 1962, Ritsema assisted the Basel zoologist and biologist Adolf Portmann, who took over from Olga Fröbe-Kapteyn as head of the Eranos Conferences when she died. *(Figure 212)* In 1982, he succeeded Portmann. Ritsema had met von Keller at the Odenwaldschule, where, since 1930, he had been attending the lessons together with Fröbe-Kapteyn's daughter, Bettina Gertrude. It was von Keller who, in 1944, acquainted him with Richard Wilhelm's translation of the *I Ching*, to the study of which he subsequently dedicated his whole life and of which, in 1970, he began to conceive a new translation that would preserve as much as possible the openness of the oracular texts, allowing the questioner direct contact with the archetypal images evoked in the texts.[111] At the Odenwaldschule Ritsema also attended the lessons held by Ellen Teichmüller (1898–1978), von Keller's daughter, who taught him History and Philosophy of Eastern Religions. In a unique twist of fate, Teichmüller and Venkatesh Narayana Sharma married in 1931: as we have seen, in 1932 Sharma baptized Casa Shanti, the house where his mother-in-law, von Keller, would live from 1937.[112] At the Ecole d'Humanité in Pont-Céard, Ritsema also met Catherine

[110] Ritsema and Sabbadini, *op. cit.*, p. 9.

[111] Shantena Augusto Sabbardini, "*I Ching* e sincronicità," *Studi junghiani*, 42 (21/2, 2015), p. 79; Id., "Rudolf Ritsema," in: *I Ching. El Libro de los Cambios*....cit., pp. 119–33; Mañas Peñalver , "El *I Ching* en Eranos," cit., p. 102.

[112] Sharma was born in Ongole, in Andhra Pradesh, on June 14, 1897. He went in touch with the Thesophical movement and worked for a period at the Theosophical School in Adyar, Madras. At the same time, he attended the training at the State University in Adyar for becoming a teacher. Travelling to Europe in order to learn the new pedagogical and educational models, he had first sojourned in London and then, at the Odenwaldschule, where, from 1930 to 1934, he was employed as a teacher. There he met von Keller's young daughter, Ellen Teichmüller, his life's companion, and married her in 1931. Sharma, who was among the listeners at the first Eranos Conference in 1933, gained his doctorate at Heidelberg in March 1935. In 1935–1936 he taught, for two semesters, Culture and Education in India at the University of Jena. In 1936 he published the results of his doctoral research, a study entitled *Pedagogy in India* (Venkatesh Narayana Sharma, *Indische Erziehung – Mit Einer Karte – Pädagogik des Auslands – Herausgegeben im Auftrag des Zentralinstituts für Erziehung und Unterricht von Prof. Dr. Peter Petersen-Jena – Vol. VIII* (Weimar: Hermann Böhlaus Nachfolger, 1936)). The Sharmas, intent on using in India those pedagogical models they had learned in Europe, arrived in Madras in 1936, after the birth of their first daughter, Gitta. The school that they founded in September of the following year in Mylapore, the central district of Madras, was named Children's Garden School, or Dvaraka "garden-colony": it was the first Indian college founded on the modern pedagogical precepts (see Ellen Sharma-Teichmüller and Venkatesh Narayana Sharma, "Unsere Odenwaldschule in Indien – The

Gris, a young piano teacher, who became his wife in 1945. When they moved to Holland, he worked as the head of the Oriental department of the prestigious E.J. Brill publishing house. Moreover, he continued to work on psychological commentaries on the *I Ching* hexagrams for von Keller's patients.[113]

The story of Eranos and the Ritsema-Gris couple would now be intertwined with that of two other houses, Casa Al Cor di Sass and Casa Aliaga, which, although not part of the Eranos property, were often rented by Fröbe-Kaptyen during the Conferences to accommodate some of the participants.[114] These houses are also linked in some way to the artistic history of Monte Verità. The building next to Casa Shanti, Casa Al Cor di Sass, was built in 1948 by Alida Sasso-Bersma and Osvaldo (Pep) Sasso. Alida Sasso-Bersma was the aunt of Enrichetta Alessandra (Hetty) Rogantini-de Beauclair (1928–2018), who was for many years the custodian of the Casa Anatta Museum and the historical witness of Monte Verità.[115] Hetty Rogantini-de Beauclair was the daughter of Nelly de Beauclair-Bersma and Alexander Wilhelm de Beauclair (1877–1962), a painter and, for a time, secretary to Oedenkoven. Alexander de Beauclair was one of the few Monteveritans—along with Karl Vester (who also lived in Villa Gabriella), Vladimir Straskraba-Czaja (1852–1934), and Paul Peter Evertz (1884–1945)—who remained in Ascona throughout their lives.[116]

Children's Garden School – Kindergarten, Middle School and Teachers Training Department, Kindergärtneerinnen-Seminar Mothers Classes," in Cassirer, Liesegang, and Weber, *op. cit.*, pp. 137 ff.), based on the models they had learned at the Odenwaldschule and on the revolutionary pedagogy of Maria Montessori (1870–1952), whose theories Sharma had had occasion to study in London (Ellen Sharma-Teichmüller and Venkatesh Narayana Sharma, *The Children's Garden. A School for the Little Ones. Mylapore, Madras* (Mylapore, Madras: The Children's Garden School Society, 1937), p. II). It remains to this day one of the most famous and esteemed educational institutions in India. See Children's Garden School Society, *Twenty-Eight Annual Report. 1964–'65* (Mylapore, Madras: The Children's Garden School Society, 1965); Id., *Golden Jubilee Year. 1937–1987. Souvenir 1987* (Mylapore, Madras: The Children's Garden School Society, 1987); Id., *Let none be like another. A History of the Children's Garden School Society* (Mylapore, Madras: Children's Garden School Society, 2007); and M. Santhanam Rajalakshmi, *Under the Banyan Tree* (Mylapore, Madras: without publishing information, undated). I would also like to thank Shanti Pappu for providing information about her great-grandmother von Keller.

[113] Ritsema and Sabbadini, *op. cit.*, p. 9.

[114] Hetty Rogantini-de Beauclair, personal communication, August 22, 2003, Ascona-Monte Verità.

[115] See Rogantini-de Beauclair, *op. cit.*, and de Paoli and Buvoli, *op. cit.*

[116] Hetty Rogantini-de Beauclair, personal communication, July 2002 and October 1, 2010, Ascona-Monte Verità.

Next to Casa Al Cor di Sass is Casa Aliaga, built in several stages in 1927, 1939, and 1961 and also owned by Alida Sasso-Bersma, who purchased the land and designed the building herself. Initially, the house was known as "Holzhüsli": it was a small, basic building where the couple lived. It was (and still is) connected to the road above by seventy-four steps. Later, a part of the house called "Studio" was added to the upper floor, which was comfortable, bright, and had a large balcony. A further part was subsequently added, where the Sasso-Bersma couple went to live.[117] Casa Aliaga was the first home of the Ritsemas. Ritsema had met Fröbe-Kapteyn in 1948 through her daughter Bettina, his schoolmate at the Odenwaldschule. From that year on, Fröbe-Kapteyn invited the Ritsemas to spend their winters in Eranos.[118] The place was ideal for Ritsema to recover from the severe polio he had suffered in his youth. Catherine was a pianist, harpsichordist, and music teacher; it was Alida Sasso-Bersma herself, a talented seamstress, who designed and made her concert dresses.[119] She was looking for an apartment with a grand piano and found it in Casa Aliaga; Osvaldo Sasso was in fact a prestigious piano maker and one of the most renowned piano tuners in Europe. Fröbe-Kapteyn, who had been invited to a private concert given by Catherine (Fröbe-Kapteyn had also been a music lover since her youth), saw the steep flight of stairs that Rudolf, who was still convalescing, had to climb every day and suggested that the couple move to Casa Eranos.[120] Another phase in the eventful life of Eranos was beginning.

The settlers of Monte Verità loved nature, preaching its purity and interpreting it symbolically as the ultimate work of art. A crucible of six hundred life experiences, each with their own personal idea of paradise, Monte Verità was one of the first and most significant attempts to re-sacralise time and space, recovering a primitive agricultural existence as a

[117] Petra Branderhorst, personal communication, October 13, 2024, Bilthoven. I would also like to thank Marco Rogantini for kindly verifying in May 2025 the information presented here.

[118] Sabbadini, *op. cit.*, p. 125.

[119] Hetty Rogantini-de Beauclair, personal communication, September 5, 2003, Ascona-Monte Verità.

[120] Rudolf Ritsema, personal communication, August 22, 2003, Ascona-Moscia; and Bernardini, *Jung a Eranos…*, cit., pp. 258 f., fn. 57.

way of expressing an anti-industrial religiosity.[121] Jung, one of the main guides at Eranos, had noted: "Our loveliest mountain, which dominates Switzerland far and wide, is called the *Jungfrau*—the 'Virgin.'[122] The Virgin Mary is the female patron saint of the Swiss. Of her Tertullian says: '*Illa terra virgo nondum pluviis rigata...*'[123], 'that virgin earth, not yet watered by the rains,' and Augustine: '*'Veritas ... de terra orta est ... : Christus ... de Virgine natus est ...*'[124] 'Truth has arisen from the earth, because Christ is born of a virgin.' These are living reminders that the virgin mother is the earth. From olden times the astrological sign for Switzerland was either Virgo or Taurus; both are earth-signs, a sure indication that the earthy character of the Swiss had not escaped the old astrologers."[125]

In the yearning for land and nature, agriculture and community life at Monte Verità, there was an intimate quest for celestial purity.[126] Jean Servier spoke of the "dream of a virgin land inhabited by an imaginary humanity without sin ... nourished by the secret desire to reverse the course of time and return to the primordial starting point, in order to be reborn into a new life."[127] Mircea Eliade lectured at Eranos in 1963 about the ideal of a "*Terre-sans-mal*,"[128] while Erich Neumann, who had inherited from Jung the role of "witness" in Analytical Psychology in the context of the Ascona conventions, saw in Mother Earth the return to the "unity of the dark and fruitful womb in the psychological sphere of humanity, the maternal Ouroborus, the *prima materia*, which represents and arouses the

---

[121] Cf. Linse, *op. cit.*; and Edith Hanke, "'L'uomo della verità'. Le idee di Leo N. Tolstoj al Monte Verità," in Schwab and Lafranchi, *op. cit.*, pp. 23–41.

[122] Meaning "Virgin," a 4158-metre peak in the Bernese Oberland.

[123] "That virgin land not yet wet with rain" (author's translation).

[124] "Truth has risen from the earth [since] Christ was born of the Virgin" (author's translation).

[125] Carl Gustav Jung, "The Swiss Line in the European Spectrum" {1928}, in *The Collected Works of C.G. Jung*, Vol. 10 (Princeton, NJ: Bollingen Series XX, Princeton University Press, 1970), par. 914.

[126] Linse, *op. cit.*, p. 32.

[127] Jean Servier, *Der Traum von der grossen Harmonie. Eine Geschichte der Utopie* (Munich: List, 1971), p. 307 (author's translation).

[128] Mircea Eliade, "Paradis et Utopie: géographie mythique et eschatologie," *Eranos-Jahrbuch*, 32 (1963), pp. 211–34.

lively chaos of a presence that devours and generates"[129] at the same time. Eliade also wondered why, between 1900 and 1920, historians of religion had taken such an interest in the theme of the mother goddesses and deities of wheat and fertility, interpreting it as the collective unconscious' nostalgia for a mythical female who was actually present in the works and ideas of many intellectuals in the early twentieth century.

The garden of Eranos itself for Fröbe-Kapteyn was a metaphor for the "garden of all schools" (*Garten aller Hochschulen*), whose "warmth" and "maternal aspect" had protected a "risky" (*riskant*), "uncertain" (*unsicher*), and "endangered" (in *Gefahr)* scientific work in the darkest years of European history.[130] After the war, Vittorino Vezzani, a lecturer involved with the International Centre for Spiritual Research and tasked with tracking down copies of some of Fröbe-Kapteyn's "Meditation Plates" from the 1930s in Turin, recalled the emotion he felt when walking through the welcoming and well-kept garden of Eranos for the first time: "In the second half of August, the northern basin of Lake Maggiore is heavenly. The air, cooled by rain and thunderstorms, is crystal clear, the sun is warm and bright, and the lake water is as blue as the sky, surrounded by a crown of green-covered mountains. Charming villages and countless villas are reflected in the water, enlivening the landscape and giving it a special cheerful tone, which only becomes melancholic in the warmer, softer colors of sunset. In this charming and restful environment, which enchants northerners and draws them in large numbers to Locarno, Ascona, and Brissago to enjoy the first splendors of the Italian sun, Eranos was founded ... named by Professor [Rudolf] Otto, who spent many of the most beautiful hours of his life there. The writer knew its uncertain beginnings and accompanied its first steps with trepidation, unable to imagine its future events and glories. At that time, it was called Casa Gabriella and its owner and *genius loci* was, as it still is today, a blonde and hospitable Dutch lady, Olga Fröbe-Kapteyn, who was in love with the

[129] Erich Neumann, "Die Bedeutung des Erdarchetypus für die Neuzeit," *Eranos-Jahrbuch*, 22 (1953), pp. 11–56 (author's translation).

[130] Olga Fröbe-Kapteyn, "Vorwort," *Eranos-Jahrbuch*, 23 (1954), p. 6 (author's translation); on the metaphysics of the Eranos garden, see James Hillman, "Nei giardini. Un ricordo psicologico" {1998}, in Id., *Politica della Bellezza* (Bergamo: Moretti&Vitali, 1999), pp. 147–55.

beauty of the lake and the flowers in her garden, a tireless reader of spiritual books, eager to do something serious to establish a center for the study of spiritual issues. When I got off the water bus in Ascona and walked down the winding road to the gate that opens onto the small shady avenues and stone steps leading to the garden and the villa, so close to the lake and hidden among the trees, a certain austerity of the place gave me the strange impression that this solitary garden and quiet house had been chosen by some hidden and great Presence for an important and fruitful work in the realms of the Spirit. This impression has never left my heart, and I still feel it when I stand at the modest gate and see the flowers in the garden, tended as if they were in a cloister reserved for the beauties of the soul."[131] *(Figures 215–220)*

Fröbe-Kapteyn spoke of Casa Gabriella as a temple of Aphrodite, also being aware that, in ancient times, on the adjacent Brissago Islands there had been a temple dedicated to the goddess.[132] She confessed to Jung of being aware that her relationship with scholars in her circle was that of a mother to her children.[133] For the 1938 symposium she organised an exhibition of images from the Eranos Archive for Research on Symbolism related to the maternal archetype.[134] These formed the basis for *The Great Mother*, the monumental work published in 1955 by Erich Neumann,[135] whose studies had revolved around female psychology for many years.[136]

The Eranos Conference of August 1938, preceded in April by a seminar given by Ernesto Buonaiuti on "The Cult of the Mother Goddess in Mediterranean Religiosity,"[137] was dedicated to the *Form and Cult of the*

---

[131] Vezzani, "Eranos (simposio)," cit., p. 301.

[132] See Hasenfratz, *op. cit.*; and Vv.Aa., *1885–1985 Cento anni dall'acquisto delle Isole di Brissago. Baroness Antoinette St. Leger. 1950–1985 Trentacinque anni d'apertura al pubblico del Parco botanico del Cantone Ticino* (Brissago: Amministrazione delle Isole di Brissago/Parco Botanico del Canton Ticino, 1985).

[133] See Bernardini, *op. cit.*, pp. 87 ff.

[134] The selection of images was reconstructed on the occasion of the exhibition *La Grande Madre: Donne, maternità e potere nell'arte e nella cultura visiva, 1900–2015*, Milan, Fondazione Nicola Trussardi/ Palazzo Reale, August 26 – November 15, 2015, curated by Massimiliano Gioni.

[135] Erich Neumann, *The Great Mother: An Analysis of the Archetype*, trans. R. Manheim (New York, NY: Pantheon Books, 1955).

[136] See Bernardini, "Neumann at Eranos," cit.

[137] See Fabio Merlini and Riccardo Bernardini, "Preface / Prefazione," in Buonaiuti, *op. cit.*, p. XLIV.

"Great Mother."[138] Fröbe-Kapteyn organized an exhibition of images from the Eranos Archive on the archetype of the "Great Mother" for the occasion; some of the works in that exhibit came from the collection of von der Heydt.[139] Jung gave a lecture titled "The Psychological Aspect of the Great Mother,"[140] which paved the way for a new female psychology. Contributing to its development were such scholars as Mary Esther Harding, Emma Jung-Rauschenbach, Antonia Anna (Toni) Wolff, Linda Fierz-David, Marie-Louise von Franz, and Rivkah Schärf Kluger, and more recently, Jean Shinoda Bolen, Marija Gimbutas, and Clarissa Pinkola Estés. Jung revised the essay in 1954, stimulated by Pope Pius XII's encyclical of November 1, 1950 on the Assumption of Mary. Through the apostolic constitution *Munificentissimus Deus*, the Christian version of the female principle was elevated to a radically new position: James Hillman, an orator at Eranos for over twenty years, recalled that for Jung it "was the symbolic content of the dogma that had the greatest importance. In it, he saw what was in the Trinity, and solely masculine, extended to a 'quaternity,' with a feminine principle, therefore a totality."[141]

A *Mater* appeared to the theorist of the "individual mythologies," Harald Szeemann. It was in 1974, before his 1978 exhibition on the history of Monte Verità, conceived as a "total work of art," which then left Ascona and the Brissago Islands to go to the places dear to the ideologies of the Monte's inhabitants, i.e., Zurich, Berlin, Wien, and Munich. He "arrived on a

[138] Cf. Hildegard Nagel, "The Eranos Conference 1938—Papers of the Analytical Psychology Club of New York" (unpublished typescript, 1939; Kristine Mann Library, New York), and Bernardini, *Jung a Eranos...*, cit., pp. 195–98.

[139] Thayer, *op. cit.*, p. 5. Hildegard Nagel, who had come to Ascona to attend the Conference, was so impressed by these images that she proposed transferring the exhibition to the Analytical Psychology Club in New York in the near future. In October 1939, following Nagel's invitation, with a gift of a thousand francs from the Mellons and accompanied by her friend Cary Baynes (1883–1977)—Jung's trusted translator—Fröbe-Kapteyn set sail for New York on the SS Conte di Savoia. The exhibition dedicated to the "Great Mother," now expanded to include three hundred images, thus marked the debut of Eranos in the United States and, in this way, Eranos made its first appearance in America "in its pictorial aspect" (see Hildegard Nagel, ed., "Eranos Archive. Images of the Great Mother Throughout the Ages. Catalogue Prepared by the Analytical Psychology Club, New York, 1938" (unpublished typescript, 1938; Warburg Institute, London); and Fröbe-Kapteyn, "Eranos—A Survey...," cit., p. 7).

[140] Carl Gustav Jung, "Die psychologischen Aspekte des Mutterarchetypus," *Eranos-Jahrbuch*, 7 (1938), pp. 403–43.

[141] James Hillman, *Il mito dell'analisi* (Milan: Adelphi, 1979 {1972}), pp. 227 (author's translation).

by now abandoned Monte Verità to begin the work of spiritual archaeology and awaken the utopias of the sleeping hill."[142] He remembered: "For nine years I have seen her before me every day. She does not appear to me in the picture postcard views that have made Ascona famous all over the world. No, I see Monte Verità from another perspective, from the North, from the Lands of Pedemonte, and from here she appears to me as a maternal hill surmounted by Balladrüm, home to a Celtic fortress now in ruins and buried by the vegetation. From dawn to dusk, the changing play of lights reveals to me the shapes, curving lines, and mysterious crevices of a feminine, mythological landscape: a meeting point between North and South, where, due to an extraordinary series of circumstances, the breasts of truth were particularly generous and fertile. I no longer know exactly when, on what night a many-breasted divinity took hold in my mind, but I remember that she imposed herself on my veneration by demanding that I offer her a sacrifice. This vision never left me. Artemis is the guiding image, the mother that inspired the research that in 1978 produced my exhibition on the utopias of Monte Verità. It is a story that deserves to be told, because in Ascona a huge prospective of utopias and new life projects was proclaimed, experienced, and endured, each very different from the other, but united by the ideals of freedom and brotherhood."[143]

These ideals were also manifested in a special way at Eranos, Fröbe-Kapteyn's existential project, rooted in a place that is unique from a geological, landscape, architectural, and cultural point of view: an initiative whose imaginary background, hitherto unknown and inscrutable, is now finally better illuminated by the fantasies that found artistic or, more neutrally, visual expression in Fröbe-Kapteyn's *Blue Book*.

---

[142] Françoise Jaunin, "Une topographie sacrée / Una topografia sacra / Eine aussergewöhnliche Topographie," *Schweizer Kunst / Art Suisse / Arte Svizzera / Art Svizzer. Zeitschrift der Gesellschaft Schweizerischer Maler, Bildhauer und Architekten (Visuelle Künstler) / Revue de la Societé des peintres, sculpteurs et architectes suisses (artistes visuels) / Rivista della Società dei pittori, scultori e architetti svizzeri (artisti visuali)*, 2 (1989) ("Monte Verità. Symposium Monte Verità 4.–7. Mai 1989"), p. 10 (author's translation).

[143] Harald Szeemann, quoted in Werner Weick's *Monte Verità. Berg der Wahrheit* [DVD] (Ascona: Fondazione Monte Verità, 2012); see also Pietro Rigolo, *La mamma. Una mostra di Harald Szeemann mai realizzata* (Milan: Johan & Levi, 2014).

Conclusion

The Eranos Foundation is currently engaged in an extensive project to recover, catalog, digitize, and organize Olga Frobe-Kaptyen's art collection. This is a fund of about 450 images, ninety percent of which are stored at the Eranos archives in Ascona. The corpus of these works is presently being restored. From 1978 to the present, the Eranos Foundation has supported the inclusion of Fröbe-Kapteyn's art materials as part of a series of exhibitions:

- Thirteen "Meditation Plates" were first included in the exhibition "Monte Verità—Le mammelle della verità," curated by Harald Szeemann (Ascona, Zurich, Berlin, Vienna, Munich, and Ascona again, 1978–1980). They are now permanently displayed at Casa Anatta, Ascona, which has functioned as the main venue for the museum exhibition on the history of Monte Verità since 1981.[1]
- Two "Meditation Plates" and some "Eranos *Maṇḍalas*" were shown during the exhibition "Eranos—Images of a Mythical Journey into Our Times," set up by the Eranos Foundation in Ascona (Aion

[1] Harald Szeemann, ed., *Monte Verità. Antropologia locale come contributo alla riscoperta di una topografia sacrale moderna* (Locarno/Milan: Armando Dadò/Electa, 1978); Germ. Ed. *Monte Verità. Berg der Wahrheit. Lokale Anthropologie als Beitrag zur Wiederentdeckung einer neuzeitlichen Topographie* (Locarno/Milan: Armando Dadò/Electa, 1978). Some images of the thirteen "Meditation Plates" originally included in Harald Szeemann's exhibition "Monte Verità—Le mammelle della verità / Monte Verità—The Breasts of Truth" (1978–1980) have been featured in the exhibition dedicated to *Harald Szeemann. Museum of Obsessions*, curated by Glen Phillips and Phillip Kaiser, in collaboration with Doris Chon and Pietro Rigolo, at the Getty Research Institute in Los Angeles from February 6 to May 6, 2018: Glen Phillips, Phillip Kaiser, Doris Chon, and Pietro Rigolo, eds., *Harald Szeemann. Museum of Obsessions* (Los Angeles, CA: The Getty Research Institute, 2018).

Art Center, Museo comunale d'arte moderna, Museo Epper, and Monte Verità) and on the Brissago Islands from June 17 to September 2, 2006, and curated by Riccardo Bernardini, Claudio Metzger, and Giovanni Sorge. After the 1978 exhibition dedicated to the history of Monte Verità, which also included the Eranos experience, the 2006 exhibition—which coincided with the relaunch of the Foundation's activities after a few years of administrative transition—was the first project to systematically present Eranos through photographs, documents, letters, books, and paintings.[2]

- Some "Eranos *Maṇḍalas*" were included in the exhibition "Carl Gustav Jung a Eranos 1933–1952," curated by Riccardo Bernardini, Gian Piero Quaglino, and Augusto Romano, on the occasion of the tenth anniversary of the Faculty of Psychology of the University of Turin, held from October 19 to November 9, 2007, at the Rectorate of the University of Turin.[3] The eighty photographs of Jung at Eranos exhibited on that occasion in Turin, most of which had never been seen before, are masterpieces by Margarita Marianne (Margarethe) Fellerer, Eranos's official photographer during the early decades of the Conferences. A monographic exhibition dedicated to her, "Margarethe Fellerer. Fotografa," curated by Diana Mirolo, was organized by the Epper Museum from March 31 to May 28, 2012.[4]
- Two "Meditation Plates" were included in the exhibition "L'energia del luogo. Jean Arp, Raffael Benazzi, Julius Bissier, Ben Nicholson,

[2] No catalog was produced for that exhibition.

[3] Gian Piero Quaglino, Augusto Romano, and Riccardo Bernardini, eds., *Carl Gustav Jung a Eranos 1933-1952* (Turin: Antigone, 2007).

[4] Diana Mirolo, ed., *Margarethe Fellerer. Fotografa* (Ascona: Museo Epper, 2012). Fellerer's photographic fund (which, in addition to the original Eranos collection, also comprises an additional bequest by Franziska Fellerer-Wistuba, on behalf of the Fellerer heirs, from 2012, thanks to the intercession of Diana Mirolo of the Epper Museum), includes a large number of images of the Eranos Conferences and the cultural life of Ascona since the 1930s. The Eranos photo collection holds works by photographers who succeeded Margarethe Fellerer, namely Tim N. Gidal (1909–1996), Luciano Soave, and Adriano Heitmann.

Hans Richter, Mark Tobey, Italo Valenti. Alla ricerca del *genius loci* Ascona–Locarno," directed by Riccardo Carazzetti and Mara Folini at the Museo comunale d'arte moderna, Ascona, Casa Serodine, Ascona, Pinacoteca Comunale Casa Rusca, Locarno, and Atelier Remo Rossi, Locarno from April 4 to July 5, 2009.[5]

- Twelve "Meditation Plates" were shown at the exhibition entitled "La Grande Madre" and organized by the Fondazione Nicola Trussardi and the City of Milan at the Royal Palace of Milan from August 25 to November 15, 2015, in conjunction with the 2015 Universal Exhibition (Expo Milano 2015) on the theme, "Feeding the Planet. Energy for Life." "The Great Mother" exhibition was directed by Massimiliano Gioni, assisted by Roberta Tenconi.[6] The curators also displayed in a slideshow the figures collected by Fröbe-Kapteyn and dedicated to the Great Mother theme, which were originally shown during exhibition "The Great Mother," set up in New York in 1939; the same slideshow was included in the exhibition "Judy Chicago: Herstory," set up at the New Museum in New York from December 10, 2023 to March 3, 2024, and curated by Massimiliano Gioni, Gary Carrion-Murayari, Margot Norton, and Madeline Weisburg.[7]
- The same twelve "Meditation Plates" shown in Milan were also included in the exhibition entitled "The Keeper," set up at the New Museum of New York from July 9 to October 2, 2016, curated by Massimiliano Gioni and Natalie Bell.[8]

---

[5] Riccardo Carazzetti and Mara Folini, eds., *L'energia del luogo. Jean Arp, Raffael Benazzi, Julius Bissier, Ben Nicholson, Hans Richter, Mark Tobey, Italo Valenti. Alla ricerca del genius loci Ascona-Locarno* (Ascona/Locarno/Milan: Museo comunale d'arte moderna/Città di Locarno, Servizi culturali/Armando Dadò, 2009).

[6] Massimiliano Gioni, ed., *La Grande Madre. Donne, maternità e potere nell'arte e nella cultura visiva, 1900–2015* (Milan: Skira, 2015); Massimiliano Gioni, ed., *The Great Mother: Women, Maternity, and Power in Art and Visual Culture, 1900-2015* (Milan: Skira, 2015).

[7] Massimiliano Gioni, Gary Carrion-Murayari, Margot Norton, and Madeline Weisburg, eds., *Judy Chicago. Herstory* (New York, NY: Phaidon, 2023).

[8] Massimiliano Gioni and Natalie Bell, eds., *The Keeper* (New York, NY: New Museum, 2016).

- Six "Meditation Plates" were shown at the exhibition entitled "Elles font l'abstraction. Une autre histoire de l'abstraction au 20e siècle," organized by the Centre Pompidou in Paris from May 19 to August 23, 2021, under the direction of Christine Macel.[9]
- The same six "Meditation Plates" were included in the exhibition reset under the title "Mujeres de la abstracción" at the Guggenheim Museum in Bilbao from October 22, 2021 to February 27, 2022, again directed by Christine Macel.[10]
- A first monographic exhibition dedicated to Fröbe-Kapteyn's art was set up, under the auspices of the Eranos Foundation, at the Kunsthalle Mainz from June 30 to October 1, 2023. The exhibition, entitled "Olga Fröbe-Kapteyn. Tiefes Wissen," was curated by Yasmin Afschar and showed forty-seven "Meditation Plates" and, for the first time, a selection of sixteen "Visions." The exhibition also included works by contemporary artists, i.e., Monia Ben Hamouda, Kerstin Brätsch, Hylozoic/Desires (Himali Singh Soin & David Soin Tappeser), Mountain River Jump!, and Sriwhana Spong.[11]
- An exhibition, titled "La scia del Monte ou les utopistes magnétiques," by Federica Chiocchetti and Nicoletta Mongini, was on view at the Musée des Beaux-Arts Le Locle (MBAL) from March 22 to September 15, 2024. Twenty-six contemporary artists dialogued with the works of artists who evoked the *genius loci* of Monte Verità in the first half of the twentieth century, such as Hans Arp, Marianne von Werefkin, and Olga Frobe-Kapteyn, with some of Fröbe-Kapteyn's "Meditation Plates." In conjunction with that exhibition, The Cool Couple artists set out to establish a dialogue between her work and

---

[9] Christine Macel and Karolina Ziebinska-Lewandowska, eds., *Women in Abstraction* (London/New York, NY: Thames & Hudson, 2021); Christine Macel and Karolina Ziebinska-Lewandowska, eds., *Elles font l'abstraction* (Paris: Centre Pompidou, 2021); Christine Macel and Laure Chauvelot, eds., *Elles font l'abstraction. Exhibition Album* (Paris: Centre Pompidou, 2021).

[10] Christine Macel and Karolina Ziebinska-Lewandowska, eds., *Mujeres de la abstracción* (Bilbao: Centre Pompidou/FMGP Guggenheim Bilbao Museoa, 2021).

[11] No catalog was produced for that exhibition.

synthetic thought: with the help of artificial intelligence, they thus combined Fröbe-Kapteyn's meditative drawings with a dataset of images of organic and inorganic elements.[12]

- A second monographic exhibition, entitled "Olga Fröbe-Kapteyn: "Artista—Ricercatrice," was set up at the Museo Casa Rusca in Locarno from August 8, 2024 to January 12, 2025. The exhibition, curated by Raphael Gygax, showed several "Meditation Plates" and "Visions" in addition to several figures from the Eranos Archives for Research in Symbolism. The exhibition also included works by contemporary artists Florian Germain, Loredana Sperini, and Lucy Stein.[13] In association with the exhibition, a display entitled "Winding and Unwinding," a project of The Cool Couple conceived for Monte Verità, was created. In a reinterpretation of Fröbe-Kapteyn's futuristic research idea, in the wake of the previous exhibition at MBAL in Le Locle, the artists moved along the ridge of the relationship between art, philosophy, psychology, and natural forms, reinterpreted by artificial intelligence.
- Three "Meditation Plates" by Fröbe-Kapteyn were on display at the Museum Catharijneconvent in Utrecht, which hosted the exhibition "Tussen hemel en oorlog. Kunst en religie in het interbellum" curated by Rozanne de Bruijne, from February 20 to June 15, 2025.[14]

---

[12] Federica Chiocchetti, ed., *les voix magnétiques—le voci magnetiche—die magnetischern stimmen—the magnetic voices* (Le Locle: MBAL Musée des Beaux-Arts Le Locle, 2024).

[13] Raphael Gygax, ed., *Olga Fröbe-Kapteyn. Artista—ricercatrice. Volume pubblicato in occasione della mostra Olga Fröbe-Kapteyn: artista–ricercatrice, Museo Casa Rusca, Locarno, 8 agosto 2024–12 gennaio 2025*, texts by Yasmin Afschar, Riccardo Bernardini, Raphael Gygax, Fabio Merlini, and Sara Petrucci (Locarno/Ascona/Bellinzona: Museo Casa Rusca/Fondazione Eranos/Casagrande, in collaboration with Kunsthalle Mainz, 2024). A contribution by Gygax dedicated to Fröbe-Kapteyn's art appeared in the recent issue of *Provence*, "Unconscious," dedicated to exploring Jung's and post-Jungian ideas as they reverberate through contemporary art, fashion, and psychoanalysis: Raphael Gygax, "Olga Fröbe-Kapteyn: Artist—Researcher," *Provence* (2025), pp. 212–20.

[14] Rozanne de Bruijne, ed., *Tussen hemel en oorlog. Kunst en religie in het interbellum*, preface by Josien Paulides, texts by Rozanne de Bruijne, Irène Lesparre, Korine Hazelzet, Lieke Wijnia, Lex van de Haterd, Tessel M. Bauduin, Katerina Sidorova, Marty Bax, Laura Stamps, and Dick Adelaar (Utrecht/Zwolle: Museum Catharijneconvent/Waanders, 2025); see also Josien Paulides, ed., *Tussen hemel en oorlog*, texts by Rozanne de Bruijne, Katjuscha Otte, Inge S. Wierda, Korine Hazelzet, Laura Stamps, Hanna

- Six "Visions" by Fröbe-Kapteyn are currently on display at the exhibition "Landscapes of the Soul: C.G. Jung and the Exploration of the Human Psyche in Switzerland," set up at the Landesmuseum (Swiss National Museum), curated by Stefan Zweifel and under the direction of Pascale Meyer, the overall management of Denise Tonella, and with the scientific collaboration of Sophie Dänzer and Valérie Lüthi, taking place from October 17, 2025, to February 15, 2026.[15]
- Another exhibition currently on display, featuring twelve "Meditation Plates" by Fröbe-Kapteyn, is entitled "Fata Morgana: Memorie dall'invisibile," curated by Massimiliano Gioni, Daniel Birnbaum, and Marta Papini; the exhibition is conceived and produced by the Fondazione Nicola Trussardi for Palazzo Morando—Costume Moda Immagine at Palazzo Morando, Milan, from October 8 to November 30, 2025.

In anticipation of a future critical edition of the *Blue Book* by the Eranos Foundation, scholarly research on Fröbe-Kapteyn's art, also based on these exhibitions, continues to this day,[16] as does interest in

---

Melse, Anouk Custers, Ingrid Henkemans, Elzemiek Aalpoel, Linda Coppens, and René de Kam, *Catharijne Museummanagize*, 43 (1, 2025).

[15] Swiss National Museum, ed., *Landscapes of the Soul. C.G. Jung and the Exploration of the Human Psyche in Switzerland* (Zurich: Scheidegger & Spiess, 2025).

[16] In addition to the already mentioned contributions, see also Eva di Stefano, "Voices and Faces of Elsewhere," *Outsider Art Observatory* 19 (2020): pp. 12–27; Marco Pasi, "The Art of Esoteric Posthumousness," in Lukas Pokorny and Franz Winter, eds., *The Occult Nineteenth Century: Roots, Developments, and Impact on the Modern World* (Camden: Palgrave Macmillan, 2021), pp. 159–76; and Sara Petrucci, "Hablamos Marciano. Los Futuros de Olga Fröbe-Kapteyn (1881–1962) y Emma Kunz (1892–1963)," *A*Desk. Critical Thinking* (September 20, 2021); Id., "Olga Fröbe-Kapteyn e il potere delle immagini: considerazioni sulle 'Tavole di meditazione'" / Olga Fröbe-Kapteyn and the Power of Images: Considerations on her 'Meditation Plates,'" in Gygax, *Olga Fröbe-Kapteyn…*, cit., pp. 166–83; Yasmin Afschar, "Olga Fröbe-Kapteyn: conoscenza profonda / Olga Fröbe-Kapteyn: Deep Knowledge," in *ibid.*, pp. 106–16; Chloë Sugden has recently completed a Ph.D. research project at the Swiss Federal Institute of Technology (ETH) in Zurich (Professur für Literatur- und Kulturwissenschaft) devoted to Fröbe-Kapteyn's occult cosmograms: see, e.g., *Newsletter of the European Society for the Study of Esotericism* 13 (2, 2022), which she edited.

her works in literature,[17] music,[18] documentary filmmaking, and cinematography.[19]

These materials are challenging to interpret solely through the lens of the Jungian technique of active imagination, as we have understood, given that Fröbe-Kapteyn's artistic activity began before her encounter with Jung and continued independently even after they met, she started collaborating with him in the context of Eranos, and had a few analytical conversations with him in Küsnacht in 1934. Furthermore, she did not produce them with a primarily aesthetic intent and indeed never recognized herself as an artist; in a letter written to Daniel Brody in 1958 at the occasion of his 75th birthday, she wrote in fact: "*Ich bin weder Künstler noch Forscher, ich habe keinen eigentlichen Beruf, sondern ich bereitete den Weg für Eranos vor*" ("I am neither an artist nor a researcher, I have no real profession, but I have paved the way for Eranos.")

It is also difficult now to write a conclusion to an initial study dedicated to an editorial project which, in the form of a hoped-for catalog raisonné, will require years of further research. If this book has succeeded in contributing at least in part to this future program, systematizing the information available to date in the most complete and organic way

[17] A painting by Fröbe-Kapteyn was used for the cover of the book by Adrian Savage, *Introduction to Chaos Magick* (New York, NY: Magickal Childe, 1989), for the cover of the book by Aleister Crowley, *Magick in Theory and Practice* (New York, NY: Magickal Childe, 1990), and more recently for the cover of Suzanne Hobson and Andrew D. Radford, eds., *The Edinburgh Companion to Modernism, Myth and Religion* (Edinburgh: Edinburgh University Press, 2023); see, though, the significance of Fröbe-Kapteyn's art in the work of Naja Marie Aidt, one of Denmark's most accomplished writers, who used a "Meditation Plate" for the cover of her *Har døden taget noget fra dig så giv det tilbage. Carls bog* (København: Gyldendal, 2017), later translated into multiple languages (on this, see also Gísli Magnússon, "Reminiscences of Eranos in Naja Marie Aidt's Novel *When Death Takes Something from You Give It Back: Carl's Book*," *Religiographies*, 4 (1, 2025), pp. 104–16); and also Jennifer Higgie's inclusion of Fröbe-Kapteyn's visionary practice in *The Other Side. A Journey into Women, Art, and the Spirit World* (London: Weidenfeld & Nicolson, 2023), pp. 231–34.

[18] A painting by Fröbe-Kapteyn was used for the cover of the vinyl by Suzanne Ciani and Jonathan Fitoussi, *Golden Apples of the Sun* (Paris: Transversales Disques, 2023), and for the forthcoming music project by Fitoussi, entitled *Delthas*.

[19] A selection of films, video testimonials, and video-documentaries—produced in particular by the Italian-language Swiss Radio and Television (RSI) over the decades—can be viewed on the Foundation's YouTube channel. The black and white video sequences included in the various films are taken from the silent movie *Eranos 1951*, directed by Ximena de Angulo-Roelli and Willy Roelli and produced by the C.G. Jung Institute of Los Angeles (1951).

possible, then its task has been accomplished. This is not, therefore, a closure, but rather an invitation to further consideration on the color that constitutes the chromatic motif, psychic quality, and metempyric instance of the *Blue Book*.

Nothing remains of Olga Fröbe-Kapteyn's reasons for using blue so frequently as the background for her "Meditation Plates": a spiritual blue, a backdrop and playground for the opposing movements of the spirit—catabatic black and anabatic gold. Nor is there any note documenting the recurring use of blue in her "Visions": a soulful blue, a tangible and sometimes uncanny sign of presence and confrontation with otherness. Finally, there is no note explaining the idea of placing or binding the impressive series of "Visions" in blue binders and albums.

To try to grasp the meaning of blue in Fröbe-Kapteyn, we should probably refer to her spiritual interests in the 1920s and thus take up the considerations of Annie Besant (1847–1933) and Charles Webster Leadbeater (1854–1934), who attributed a deeply metaphysical and devotional value to blue.[20] Alice Ann Bailey herself, with whom Fröbe-Kapteyn collaborated as we have seen in Ascona from 1930 to 1932, had composed twenty-four esoteric "Blue Books," nineteen of which were supposedly dictated to her telepathically by the "Tibetan" master, Djwhal Khul (many of which still preserved in the Eranos library). We may also recall, even earlier, Paul Cézanne's (1839–1906) conviction that "blue gives other colors their vibration."[21] Blue was also the favorite color of Wassily Kandinsky (1866–1944), author of the paradigmatic *The Spiritual in Art* (1911), which marked the artistic poetics of an entire century,[22] and of Franz Marc (1880–1916),[23] of whom Fröbe-Kapteyn kept a copy of *Antelope* (1912) at Villa Gabriella. "Cobalt—is a divine color, and there's nothing so fine as that for putting space around things," believed Vincent van Gogh

[20] Annie Besant and Charles Webster Leadbeater, *Thought–Forms: A Record of Clairvoyant Investigation* (London: Theosophical Publishing Society, 1905).

[21] Kurt Badt, *The Art of Cezanne* (Berkeley, CA: University of California Press, 1956), p. 57.

[22] Wassily Kandinsky, *Über das Geistige in der Kunst: insbesondere in der Malerei* (Munich: R. Piper & Co., 1912).

[23] James Hillman, *Psicologia alchemica* (Milan: Adelphi, 2013 {2010}), p. 390, fn. 51.

(1853–1890).[24] Even earlier, Johann Wolfgang von Goethe (1749–1832) had understood that blue and yellow are the two primary colors, from whose interaction and variation in intensity the others originate: "Yellow is a light which has been dampened by darkness; blue is a darkness weakened by the light."[25] Fröbe-Kapteyn was most likely unaware of the alchemical significance of blue: we know that when Jung asked her in 1934 to find symbolic images for his studies on the collective unconscious, she accepted the proposal even though she knew nothing about alchemy at the time.[26]

The alchemical transmutation process is marked, as is well known, by the appearance of different colors, which represent the various stages of the "Work" (*Opus*): from the initial phase of "black" (*Nigredo*) to the final stage of "red" (*Rubedo*), the work of refinement passes through the intermediate states of "white" (*Albedo*) and "yellow" (*Citrinitas*); the transition from "black" to "white," in particular, would take place under the shadowy and luminous wings of "blue": a color in which, although "black" is still present, what will become "white" already dawns on the horizon, like a "rising dawn" (*aurora consurgens*).[27] However, James Hillman points out, blue does not simply originate from the attenuation of the suffering of black. Instead, blue brings a specific quality to the incipient white, delaying

[24] Vincent van Gogh, letter to Theo van Gogh, December 28, 1885 (Van Gogh Museum, Amsterdam).

[25] Johann Wolfgang von Goethe, *Zur Farbenlehre*, Vol. I (Tubingen: J.G. Cotta'schen Buchhandlung, 1810), § 502.

[26] Fröbe-Kapteyn, "Erster Abend...," cit., p. 14; see Bernardini, *Jung a Eranos...*, cit., pp. 264 f; some of Jung's thoughts on the color blue, which didn't influence Fröbe-Kapteyn's artistic practice because she started painting at least three or four years before they met, can be found in Carl Gustav Jung, *I sogni dei bambini. Seminario tenuto nel 1936–1941*, eds. Maria Meyer-Grass and Lorenz Jung, 2 vols. (Turin: Bollati Boringhieri, 2013–2014 {2010}), p. 345. He believed that blue, in particular, was the symbol of a "spiritual vessel" and, as the color of water, a metaphor for the unconscious: just as fish can be glimpsed through the clear blue of the water, so spiritual content stands out against the darkness of the unconscious (*ibid.*, pp. 357 f.; quoted by Hoch, *op. cit.*, p. 44).

[27] Cf. *Aurora Consurgens. A Document Attributed to Thomas Aquinas on the Problem of Opposites in Alchemy. A Compation Work to C. G. Jung's Mysterium Coniunctionis*, ed. Marie-Louise von Franz, tr. Richard Francis Carrington Hull and Alan Samuel Boots Glover (New York, NY: Bollingen Series LXXVII, Pantheon Books, 1966), pp. 206 ff. The "blue" phase is sometimes preceded by the so-called "peacock tail" (*Cauda Pavonis*) and followed by the "green" work (*Viriditas*). For a comparison among the alchemical phases, which can be understood and described differently by various authors, see, e.g., Bernardini, *Simboli di rinascita nella Basilica di San Miniato al Monte a Firenze...*, cit., pp. 139–42.

its onset: that of value, thanks to the introduction of moral, intellectual, and spiritual themes. It thus gives the "whitened" mind the ability to explore, consider, and evaluate its representations: an almost "religious" devotion to images and recognition of the truth they convey. Reflective anxiety of depression, blue gives rise to deep doubts and high principles, as it wants to understand things deeply and set them right. Blue thus colors a mind that is "distanced from itself," yet mysteriously attuned to its own feelings, "darkened and illuminated, moral, immoral, and amoral all at once."[28]

A series of photographic prints of the starry sky—a dark blue, almost black firmament—were displayed in the 1920s at Villa Gabriella, perhaps to accompany "meditations on the cosmos" by the future founder of Eranos.[29] *(Figure 63)* It was indeed Rudolf Otto, the "godfather" of Eranos, who pointed to the sky as the source of the primal experience of the "numinous" (*numinosum*), the most primitive and universal feeling of the holy.[30] *(Figure 95)* According to alchemist Gerhard Dorn (1530–1584), the blue color of the sky (*caelum*) comes from an infernal experience also called "wine." The "union of the mind" (*unio mentalis*) suggested by the blue sky then takes on the meaning of a Dionysian mystery: in the Homeric hymn dedicated to Dionysus, the god is described with blue eyes and hair: "He sees with the blue eye and to see him our eye must be colored in the same way," Hillman points out, adding that "Gods live in the highs and deeps. To depict them rightly we need the expressionist's palette, not the

---

[28] Hillman, *op. cit.*, § 5, "L'azzurro alchemico e la *unio mentalis*," pp. 116 and 121. On the psychological meaning of blue, see also Claudio Widmann, *Il simbolismo dei colori* (Abano Terme: Piovan, 1988). On Hillman's involvement in Eranos, see instead Riccardo Bernardini, "Hillman a Eranos," *Anima* (2012), pp. 47–93.

[29] These prints are protected by gilded wooden frames, just as many "Meditation Plates" are framed with gold-edged passe-partouts or, for larger paintings, mounted in gilded wooden frames. It may be interesting to note that blue and gold were also Jung's heraldic colors: see Bernardini, "Integrazioni al resoconto delle visioni…," cit., pp. 133 and 135, fn. 49.

[30] Otto, *Das Heilige…*, cit.; Theodor Abt confirms that "the most common and obvious experience of blue in nature comes from the sky. Whenever there are no clouds, the sky during day time appears blue to us. That color blue gives humans the feeling of continuity. It also leads to a feeling of calmness, depth, and breadth beyond any conscious understanding and thus leads to a sense of eternity" (Theodor Abt, *Introduction to Picture Interpretation. According to C.G. Jung* (Zurich: Living Human Heritage, 2005), p. 92).

impressionist's."[31] A similar "Dionysian" quality seems to be suggested by a series of "Visions" drawn by Fröbe-Kapteyn under blue hues—from the vine plant to the bunch of grapes and the grape itself. In her art, blue seems to be the subtle thread that holds together the exterior and interior, the real and the fantastic: a holotropic condition—to use an expression from transpersonal psychology—in which thought takes on a mythical form and feeds on metaphor.[32] *(Figures 159–167)*

Almost a decade before arriving in Ascona, the twenty-year-old Kapteyn had a profound experience of deep blue, which was both disturbing and ecstatic. It did not come from a work of art she had admired in museums during her youth, nor from the cultured reading she devoted herself to with curiosity and passion alongside her formal training in drawing and art history. In August 1901, during a family vacation in the Blue Lake (Blausee) area of Kandersteg in the Canton of Bern, Kapteyn took part, together with her father Albertus and her sister May, in a series of mountaineering excursions on glaciers (one of her great passions, along

---

[31] James Hillman, "Blu alchemico e *unio mentalis*," in Id., *Anima* (Bergamo: Moretti & Vitali, 2006 {1981}), p. 28.

[32] Maria Fiorentino, "Viaggio intorno al blu," *Giornale Storico del Centro Studi di Psicologia e Letteratura*, 15 (2012), p. 146. Jung also had several encounters with the numinous blue. In 1944, during a hospital stay following a myocardial infarction, he had a series of visions, described in *Memories, Dreams, Reflections* (Carl Gustav Jung, *Memories, Dreams, Reflections* (New York, NY: Pantheon Books, 1963 {1961}), § X, "Visions") and recently supplemented by other documentary sources (Bernardini, "Integrazioni al resoconto delle visioni...," cit.). With reference to blue, in particular, he said that he had seen Earth from space, from a distance of fifty thousand miles, and that he had seen it as it must appear when viewed from the Moon: absolutely marvelous—a saturated blue, unheard of, with a magnificent azure enveloping it, intense, vast. And the sky around it (enveloping it) was itself a deep blue (Bernardini, *op. cit.*, p. 133). He found himself 15,000 km from land and saw it as an immense globe shining with an indescribably beautiful blue light. He was at a point exactly above the southern tip of India, which glowed with a bluish-silver light, with Ceylon like a sparkling opal in the deep blue sea (Carl Gustav Jung, letter to Kristine Mann, February 1, 1945, in Id., *Letters...*, cit., Vol. I, p. 358). According to Maria Michela Sassi, Jung's vision may have been modeled on Goethean reminiscences, whereby the colors of nature on earth are captured through the depth of blue, golden reflections are projected from the desert, whiteness is that of snow-capped peaks, and the prevailing effect is that of oxidized silver (Maria Michela Sassi, "La terra contemplata dall'alto (Plat., *Phaed.* 110b5–111c3): un'esperienza premorte? Da Pugliese a Jung, e oltre," *La parola del passato. Rivista di studi antichi*, 77 (1–2, 2022), p. 353; and Id., "'Come rane attorno a uno stagno...': sguardi dei filosofi antichi sugli abitanti della terra)," *Eranos-Jahrbuch*, 76 (2025) (in press)). In 1961, Jung's visionary perception was confirmed by Yuri Gagarin (1934–1968), the first man to travel into space, who reported from Sputnik that the Earth appeared blue (Fiorentino, *op. cit.*, p. 147; see also Bernardini, "Integrazioni al resoconto delle visioni connesse alla malattia di Jung del 1944," cit.).

with skiing), which made a deep impression on her. *(Figure 23)* "We slept in a shelter," she recounted to her friend Marie Stopes, "got up at 2:30 in the morning, and left at 3:10, because 'if you leave later, the snow becomes too soft.' After two hours, we were at the foot of the glacier ... and we started climbing, after tying ourselves together with ropes. How can a glacier be described? It's a mass of ice that in some places looks like frozen waves, with huge cracks and crevasses, often seemingly bottomless, of an intense blue. These waves and elevations are often raised by sharp, white peaks and folds, which are wonderful to see..."[33]

We cannot know, of course, whether the experience of glacial blue influenced his artistic practice. Nevertheless, it seems to us an evocative image with which to end this reflection, useful in reminding us, in anticipation of a future edition of the *Blue Book*, of that irreducible inseparability of body and spirit, visible and invisible, individual and universal, which makes Olga Fröbe-Kapteyn a unique and exemplary case, still to be discovered and meditated upon, in the history of our time.

[33] On the way back to Kandersteg, "they saw many avalanches, similar to tremendous waterfalls" (Olga Fröbe-Kapteyn, letter to Marie Stopes, August 1, 1901; British Library, London; transcript kindly provided by Karssenberg).

ILLUSTRATIONS

1.
Coat of arms of the Kapteyn family.
Eranos Foundation Archives, Ascona-Moscia.

2.
Coat of arms of the Muysken family.
Eranos Foundation Archives, Ascona-Moscia.

3.
Olga "Olly" Kapteyn (1881–1962) at about one year old, with her mother, Geertruida (Truus) Agneta Kapteyn-Muysken (1855–1920), in London in 1882.
Ph. Russel & Sons, Photographers to H.M. The Queen, H.R.H. The Prince of Wales, H.R.H. The Princess of Wales, H.R.H The Duke of Edinburgh, and T.H.R. The Duke & Duchess of Connaught. Eranos Foundation Archives, Ascona-Moscia.

4.
Olga Kapteyn at 2 years old in London in July 1884.
Ph. Russel & Sons, Photographers to H.M. The Queen, H.R.H. The Prince of Wales, H.R.H. The Princess of Wales, H.R.H The Duke of Edinburgh, and T.H.R. The Duke & Duchess of Connaught. Eranos Foundation Archives, Ascona-Moscia.

5.
Geertruida (Truus) Agneta Kapteyn-Muysken (1855–1920) and Albertus Philippus Kapteyn (or Kapteijn, 1848–1927), Olga Kapteyn's parents, in London in August 1888.
Ph. Thomas Charles Turner, Photographer to Their Royal Highnesses The Prince & Princess of Wales, Duke of Edinburgh and Duke of Cambridge. Eranos Foundation Archives, Ascona-Moscia. All rights reserved.

6.
Olga, Albert (1886–1964), and Marie ("May") Kapteyn (1883–1972) in London in (probably) August 1888.
Ph. Thomas Charles Turner, Photographer to Their Royal Highnesses The Prince & Princess of Wales, Duke of Edinburgh and Duke of Cambridge. Eranos Foundation Archives, Ascona-Moscia.

7.
Olga Kapteyn with her mother Geertruida (Truus) Agneta Kapteyn-Muysken around 1888 (?).
Ph. unknown. Eranos Foundation Archives, Ascona-Moscia.

8.
Albert, May, and Olga Kapteyn around 1888 (?).
Ph. unknown. Eranos Foundation Archives, Ascona-Moscia.

9.
Olga Kapteyn at 8 years old portrayed by Willem Witsen (1860–1923). Oil on canvas, completed in December 1889 (information from Gertrude Kapteyn's diaries, kindly provided by Maite Karssenberg).
Ph. Riccardo Bernardini. Eranos Foundation Archives, Ascona-Moscia.

10.
Olga Kapteyn at 8–9 years old around 1889–1890.
Ph. unknown. Eranos Foundation Archives, Ascona-Moscia.

11.
Olga Kapteyn at 12–13 years old around 1893–1894.
Ph. unknown. Eranos Foundation Archives, Ascona-Moscia.

12.
Olga Kapteyn at 13–14 years old around 1894.
Ph. unknown. Eranos Foundation Archives, Ascona-Moscia.

13.
Olga Kapteyn at 20–22 years old around 1901–1903.
Ph. unknown. Eranos Foundation Archives, Ascona-Moscia.

14.
Olga Kapteyn engaged in a circus performance training with dogs in Zurich in March 1908.
Ph. unknown. Eranos Foundation Archives, Ascona-Moscia.

15.
Olga Kapteyn at 27 years old in Zurich in December 1908.
Ph. unknown. Eranos Foundation Archives, Ascona-Moscia.

16.
Iwan Fröbe (1880–1915) around 1908–1909 (?).
Ph. unknown. Eranos Foundation Archives, Ascona-Moscia.

17.
Olga Kapteyn at 27 years old skating on ice in the Rigi area in January 1909.
Ph. unknown. Eranos Foundation Archives, Ascona-Moscia.

18.
Olga Kapteyn at 27 years old and Iwan Fröbe skating on ice in the Rigi area in January 1909 (the couple were due to marry on May 13 of that same year).
Ph. unknown. Eranos Foundation Archives, Ascona-Moscia.

19.
Olga Kapteyn at 27 years old skiing in the Rigi area in January 1909.
Ph. unknown. Eranos Foundation Archives, Ascona-Moscia.

20.
Olga Kapteyn at 27 years old, Iwan Fröbe, and friends skiing and admiring the "*Nebelmeer*" (sea of fog) in the Rigi area in January 1909.
Ph. unknown. Eranos Foundation Archives, Ascona-Moscia.

21.
Olga Kapteyn at 27 years old and Iwan Fröbe admiring the *"Nebelmeer"* (sea of fog) in the Rigi area in January 1909.
Ph. unknown. Eranos Foundation Archives, Ascona-Moscia.

22.
Olga Kapteyn at 27 years old, Iwan Fröbe, and friends admiring the "*Nebelmeer*" (sea of fog) in the Rigi area in January 1909.
Ph. unknown. Eranos Foundation Archives, Ascona-Moscia.

23.
Alpetligletscher (Kanderfirn) taken from the top of Altel, where Olga Kapteyn went on a series of glacier hikes in August 1901.
Ph. Jules Beck, c. 1880. Commissionsverlag der J. Dalp'schen Buchhandlung, Bern. ETH Library Zurich, Image Archive / Hs_1458-GK-B109-0000-0001.

24.
Piz Lucendro (2964 m) from Rotondohütte, where in 1907 Olga Kapteyn practiced ski mountaineering with Norwegian skiers.
Ph. unknown (1906).

25.
Olga Fröbe-Kapteyn at about 34–35 years in the mid-1910s (?).
Ph. unknown. Eranos Foundation Archives, Ascona-Moscia.

26.
Olga Fröbe-Kapteyn and her husband Iwan Fröbe in the mid-1910s (?).
Ph. unknown. Eranos Foundation Archives, Ascona-Moscia.

27.
Olga Fröbe-Kapteyn with her one-year-old daughter, Bettina Gertrude (born on May 3, 1915), in August 1916.
Ph. unknown. Eranos Foundation Archives, Ascona-Moscia.

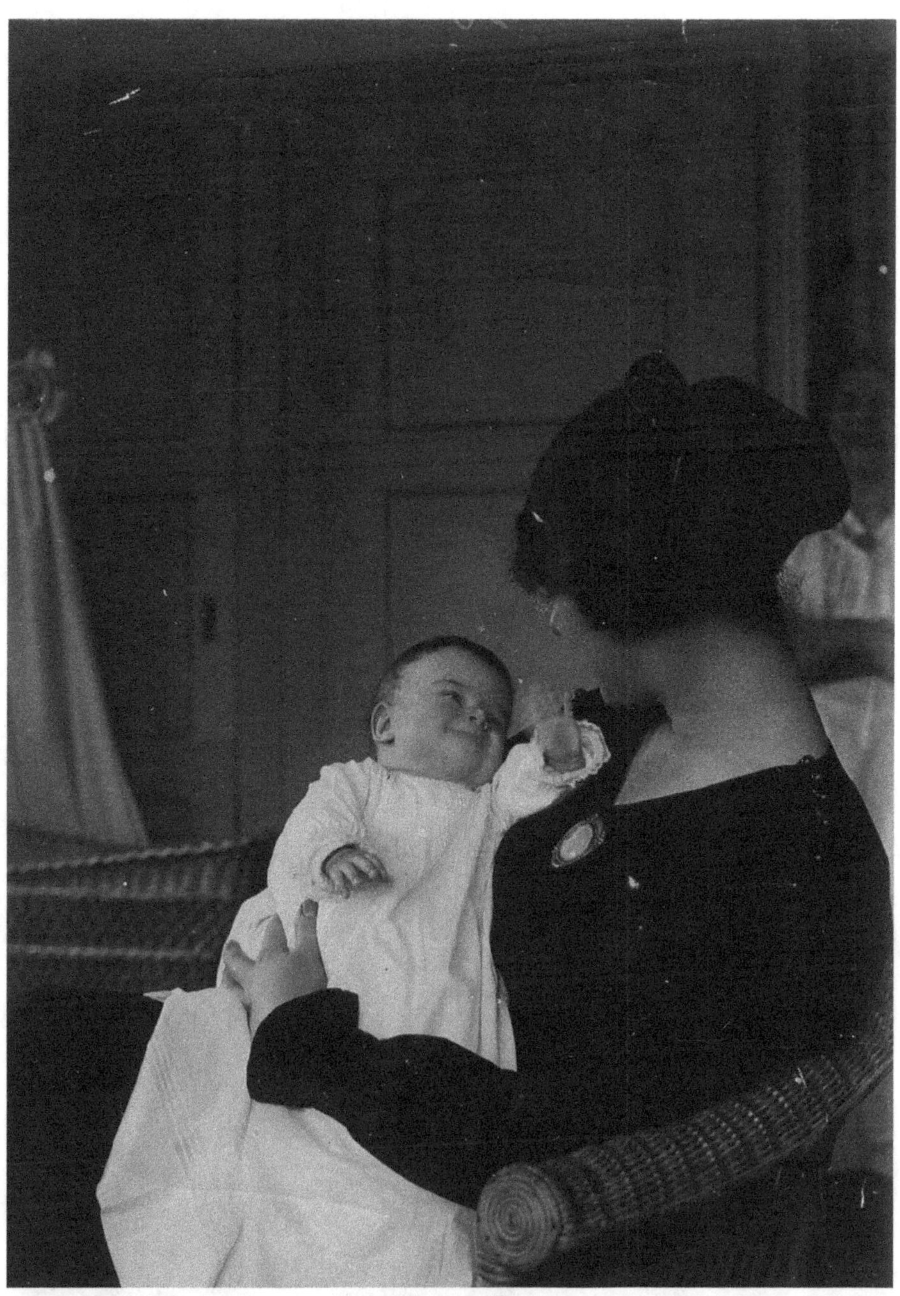

28.
Olga Fröbe-Kapteyn with her one-year-old daughter, Bettina Gertrude (born on May 3, 1915), in August 1916.
Ph. unknown. Eranos Foundation Archives, Ascona-Moscia.

29.
Olga Fröbe-Kapteyn in the mid-1910s–early 1920s.
Ph. unknown. Eranos Foundation Archives, Ascona-Moscia.

30.
Olga Fröbe-Kapteyn in the mid-1910s–early 1920s.
Ph. unknown. Eranos Foundation Archives, Ascona-Moscia.

31.
Olga Fröbe-Kapteyn in the mid-1910s–early 1920s.
Ph. unknown. Eranos Foundation Archives, Ascona-Moscia.

32.
Silk blouse with colorful embroidery created by Olga Fröbe-Kapteyn, exhibited in 1916 as part of a textile exhibition at the Museum of Applied Arts in Zurich.
Ph. from Vv.Aa., *1875–1975. 100 Jahre Kunstgewerbemuseum der Stadt Zürich*, eds. Elisabeth Grossmann, Hansjörg Budliger, and Urs Stahel (Zurich: Zürcher Hochschule der Künste, Kunstgewerbemuseum der Stadt Zürich, 1975).

33.
Girl's dress created by Olga Fröbe-Kapteyn.
Ph. Umberto Romito and Ivan Šuta. Museum für Gestaltung Zürich, Decorative Arts Collection, Zürcher Hochschule der Künste, Zurich.

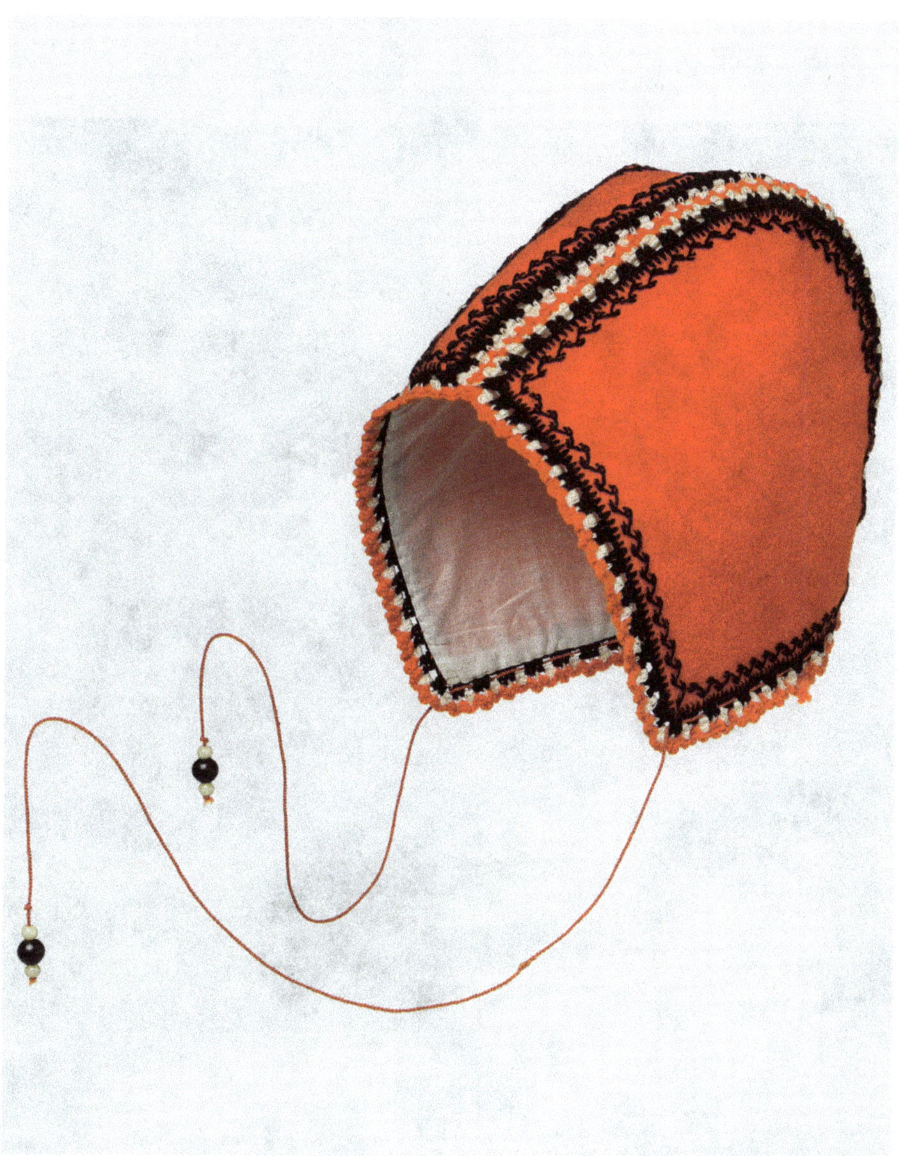

34.
Baby hat created by Olga Fröbe-Kapteyn.
Ph. Umberto Romito and Ivan Šuta. Museum für Gestaltung Zürich, Decorative Arts Collection, Zürcher Hochschule der Künste, Zurich.

35.
A view of Ronco s/Ascona in 1920s.
Ph. unknown. Eranos Foundation Archives, Ascona-Moscia.

36.
Casa Monte Tabor in Ronco s/Ascona, where Olga Fröbe-Kapteyn lived in 1920–1921. Ph. unknown (c. 1950–1960). ETH Library Zurich, Image Archive / Com_X-R045-003.

37.
Villa Gabriella, in the hamlet of Moscia or "Mosce," Ascona, in the 1910s, at that time inhabited by Karl Vester (1879–1963) and his wife Hedwig Rohde, who had purchased Villa Gabriella in 1904 from lawyer Carlo Abbondio (1859–1920). The Vesters lived there from 1904 until 1909.
Ph. unknown. Monte Verità Foundation, Harald Szeemann Collection. There is no reliable information about the rights to this photograph; any rights should be reported to the publisher.

38.
Villa Gabriella in the 1920s, purchased by Albertus Kapteyn on October 12, 1920 and where Olga Fröbe-Kapteyn and her daughter Bettina Gertrude lived since December 1921. During the years she moved to Villa Gabriella, Olga Fröbe-Kapteyn was in contact with the poet and mystic Ludwig Derleth (1870–1948), who she thus remembered: "In his youth he was one of the George Circle in Munich. But he soon separated, because he tolerated no one beside him. In him flowed together antiquity, early Christianity, the Middle Ages, and Romanticism. He did not live in the world of today, but rather led an imaginary life in those cultures, by identifying himself with the greatest men of history, the Church, and the arts. Basically, he was a medieval man. Only at that time did such figures still live. He was completely 'possessed' by the past. He surrounded himself with mystery. No one was allowed to see him eat, drink, or sleep, nor to notice when he left or entered his house. He 'appeared' or 'disappeared' always mysteriously, unapproachable, untouchable. He played the utmost authority. The highest discipline. He demanded from his friends and disciples absolute obedience. In any case, I felt him to be more than human! Around him was a circle of invisible disciples, of which none knew the other. His boundless imagination drew such into whom fantasy lay dormant. My own imagination was still asleep then, but it was ignited by Derleth's boundless imagination. What I experienced in this contact, in the sense of being assimilated by Derleth's imagination, was so fruitful for me later. Most fascinating for me were the midnight walks through old Munich. During two years, when I was in Munich, we met every night at Marienplatz, and from there began these dreamlike wanderings through the old city, through the oldest alleys, courtyards, gardens, all brought to life by his projections of the past and transformed into an eternally living, fantastic world. For me these nights were a true initiation into the times of the primordial images, the archetypes, the great symbols. It was a richness of flowing images, of fairy-tale-like stories, that Derleth 'inhabited' this world with. It was supreme magic and enchantment, and I was receptive and delighted. His tales evoked the entire historical, cultural, and symbolic world. He became its personification ..." (Olga Fröbe-Kapteyn, "Porträt von Ludwig Derleth" (unpublished typescript, undated [c. 1950-1957]; Stiftung Szondi-Institut Archives, Zurich; English translation by the author). Ph. unknown. Eranos Foundation Archives, Ascona-Moscia.

39.
Villa Gabriella in the 1920s. Olga Fröbe-Kapteyn continued her recollection of Derleth: "... By projecting onto him the image of Hermes, the guide of souls, I was identical with him and could see with his eyes. His masculinity was purely cerebral and imaginative. He could fertilize fantasy—he could give birth to entire cultures. He did not live in the present time. He was always 'lived' by one of the great historical figures. Therefore he did not create anything that would have been meaningful for our time. He invented rituals in order to bind his disciples to him. He used the 'erotic magic' of all times. He fantasized about an encounter after death. In my inexperience, I might have suffered much harm in dealing with such a personality. But the fact that I was never 'obedient' to him protected me from servitude. This also acted as a perverse asceticism. From these notes about the personality of Derleth, from the archetypal coloring of it all, it has become clear to me that here the roots of Eranos were uncovered. Only seven years later, in 1927, the idea came to me that we call Eranos. Consciously, at that time I was by no means familiar with the fields that characterize Eranos. But in the unconscious I was already, through the Derleth experience, very much at home in the archetypal world and therefore in the cultural past. For I was, just as Derleth himself was, swallowed up by the contact with him in the longing. That is, I was totally unconscious. When, at the end of 1922, I separated from him abruptly, I repressed him as well as the vast world that accompanied him. But—the archetypes had been activated. If two years are only a short span of time, in relation to Eranos, its prehistory and foundation, they are of the utmost importance ..." (Fröbe-Kapteyn, "Porträt von Ludwig Derleth," cit.; English translation by the author).
Ph. unknown. Eranos Foundation Archives, Ascona-Moscia.

40.
Villa Gabriella in the 1920s. Still reminiscent of Derleth, Olga Fröbe-Kapteyn added: "... The condensation of these experiences and the reduction to the most valuable results in a picture today of the preparation for Eranos—the archetypal inner sphere that grew out of Eranos. That is why this relationship was of inestimable value for me. The meaning of this encounter lay in the realization of the symbolic (which I did not yet possess) and in the access to the unconscious, to the world of images. Above all, the entire cultural past and its values awoke and became visible (*I Ching*). I probably learned more from Derleth than from any other human being in relation to the inner Eranos. He was the forerunner to Jung. From Jung I had to learn from his seminars and through the unconscious. For he did not concern himself with me. But about these two experiences it is written: 'I will not let you go, unless you bless me.' [*'Ich lasse dich nicht, du segnest mich denn.'* Johann Sebastian Bach, *Bach-Werke-Verzeichnis* 157, church cantata composed in Leipzig in 1726/27]. In both cases I demanded 'the blessing.' What did I want from both? Basically the 'hidden treasure'—the 'living water,' the deepest mystery, the secret knowledge. That means that treasure which lay or lies hidden in the cultural values of the past, and which I can only seek and find in myself! I projected this treasure into those two figures. What I received from both was a kind of anticipation of this goal in that I received through Derleth the first initiation into the world of images, into the collective unconscious—that is, the access to it—and through Jung the second initiation, that is, I learned the handling of the images or archetypes. Not from him personally, but through his seminars. When Jung came to Eranos for the first time in 1933, I was already at home in this inner world and 'possessed' by it! The meaning of the whole remained for me alone to find..." (Fröbe-Kapteyn, "Porträt von Ludwig Derleth," cit.; English translation by the author).
Ph. unknown. Eranos Foundation Archives, Ascona-Moscia.

41.
The terrace of Villa Gabriella in the 1920s. Still on the subject of Derleth, Olga Fröbe-Kapteyn concluded as follows: "... To what extent this time with Derleth was creative for me: I believe that my ability for visioning originates from there. I gradually learned to make my own projections visible. On the basis of Derleth, who projected his own fantastic world of images onto the outer world (e.g., Munich), and by the fact that I projected onto him, was identical with him, I saw the same as he saw! That is, I saw the archetypal world. The impression was so overwhelming that it has remained with me until today. And with it the gift of visioning. Since after the experience with Derleth I undertook and carried out a seven-year concentration training, this visioning could develop further. For in the 'empty' field of concentration the images rise up. At first I looked for years into a world of geometric symbols. These figures were colorful and always in motion. Through fixation in drawings they necessarily had to become rigid. The world itself became rigid in a certain way. The symbols—e.g., the rose, the sword, the flame, the cross, the chalice or Grail, the sun, and countless other symbols—appeared, but all stood in relation to the path of individuation. Those were the years 1926 to 1933. Then Eranos began. At the first conference Jung saw the images, made a disparaging remark about them, and they fell back into the unconscious. For a while I no longer drew them. Only later did a series of realistic mystery pictures begin in 1942. When in 1934 I was with Jung for a week and told him about the concentration training, he said: 'Since you have not gone mad, you now have it as an instrument in your hand.' To my opus, Eranos, also belongs that I make clear to myself about its origin, its roots and its place, its foundation and its continuity. The starting point lies far back in the past, in the timeless, archetypal world, in those cultural archetypes that, as patterns for the coming cultural epoch, become visible and activated in our time. I have already come to the role of the parents and ancestors. But that is not enough. The present study shows me that the impulses which stand behind Eranos lie in the distant past of history and culture altogether. For from where comes the material, the themes that are treated at Eranos? Certainly not from me. Only through the fact that I, through Derleth, found access to this past and to the unconscious in its pictorial aspects, and thereby was prepared, learned through Jung the handling of the archetypes. What I learned shows itself in Eranos ..." (Fröbe-Kapteyn, "Porträt von Ludwig Derleth" cit.; English translation by the author).
Ph. unknown. Eranos Foundation Archives, Ascona-Moscia.

42.
Bettina Gertrude Fröbe at Casa Gabriella in the early 1920s, wearing a dress probably designed and decorated by her mother.
Ph. unknown. Eranos Foundation Archives, Ascona-Moscia.

43.
Olga Fröbe-Kapteyn in the garden of Villa Gabriella in the 1920s.
Ph. unknown. Eranos Foundation Archives, Ascona-Moscia.

44.
Floral arrangement of succulents by Olga Fröbe-Kapteyn at Villa Gabriella in the 1920s.
Ph. unknown Eranos Foundation Archives, Ascona-Moscia.

45.
A view of Lake Maggiore from the garden of Villa Gabriella in the 1920s.
Ph. unknown Eranos Foundation Archives, Ascona-Moscia.

46.
A view of the sky from the garden of Villa Gabriella in the 1920s.
Ph. unknown Eranos Foundation Archives, Ascona-Moscia.

47.
A view of Lake Maggiore from inside Villa Gabriella in the 1920s; the upper floors, with the Piano Room (pictured) and the Copte Room, and the two mansard rooms, were intended to accommodate Olga Fröbe-Kapteyn's guests.
Ph. unknown Eranos Foundation Archives, Ascona-Moscia.

48.
Bettina Fröbe in the garden of Villa Gabriella in the half of the 1920s.
Ph. unknown Eranos Foundation Archives, Ascona-Moscia.

49.
Olga Fröbe-Kapteyn with Dutch naturalist painter Anton (Rudolf) Mauve Jr. (1876–1962) in the half of the 1920s.
Ph. unknown Eranos Foundation Archives, Ascona-Moscia.

50.
Olga Fröbe-Kapteyn with friend Peter Pallat on the pier of Villa Gabriella in the half of the 1920s.
Ph. unknown Eranos Foundation Archives, Ascona-Moscia.

51.
Painter and art teacher Annemarie Pallat (1875–1972), a close friend of Olga Fröbe-Kapteyn's, with writer Nettie Katzenstein-Sutro (1889–1967) at Villa Gabriella in the half of the 1920s.
Ph. unknown Eranos Foundation Archives, Ascona-Moscia.

52.
Archaeologist and educationalist Ludwig Pallat (1867–1946) at Villa Gabriella in the half of the 1920s.
Ph. unknown Eranos Foundation Archives, Ascona-Moscia.

53.
Olga Fröbe-Kapteyn with (probably) her friend Peter Pallat, son of Annemarie and sister of Marianne Pallat, bathing in a river in the Ticino valleys in the half of the 1920s.
Ph. unknown Eranos Foundation Archives, Ascona-Moscia.

54.
A view of Lake Maggiore and the Alps from the terrace of Villa Gabriella in the 1920s.
Ph. unknown Eranos Foundation Archives, Ascona-Moscia.

55.
A view of Ascona, the Locarno area, and Lake Maggiore from Villa Gabriella in the 1920s.
Ph. unknown Eranos Foundation Archives, Ascona-Moscia.

56.
A view of the Brissago Islands and Lake Maggiore from Villa Gabriella in the half of the 1920s.
Ph. unknown Eranos Foundation Archives, Ascona-Moscia.

57.
Olga Fröbe-Kapteyn, *Duality* [Eranos *Maṇḍala*, no. 1]
The image, painted in 1927, also represent the first Eranos *Maṇḍala*, which inspired the floor plan of the Lecture Hall of Casa Eranos, built in 1928.
"Meditation Plates" (c. 1927–1934). Mixed technique (tempera, India ink, and gold leaf) on cardboard.
Eranos Foundation Archives, Ascona-Moscia. All rights reserved.

58.
Casa Eranos, whose construction began in December 1928, originally with its flat Bauhaus-style roof, in 1929.
Ph. unknown. Eranos Foundation Archives, Ascona-Moscia.

59.
Olga Fröbe-Kapteyn and her daughter Bettina Gertrude at Casa Eranos in 1929. Ph. unknown. Eranos Foundation Archives, Ascona-Moscia.

60.
Olga Fröbe-Kapteyn at Casa Eranos around 1929.
Ph. unknown. Eranos Foundation Archives, Ascona-Moscia.

61.
Dutch pianist and bookseller Leo Kok (1893–1992), Olga Fröbe-Kapteyn, and friends on the small bay of Casa Eranos with its characteristic descent to the lake (still without the current staircase), in the late 1920s.
Ph. unknown. Eranos Foundation Archives, Ascona-Moscia.

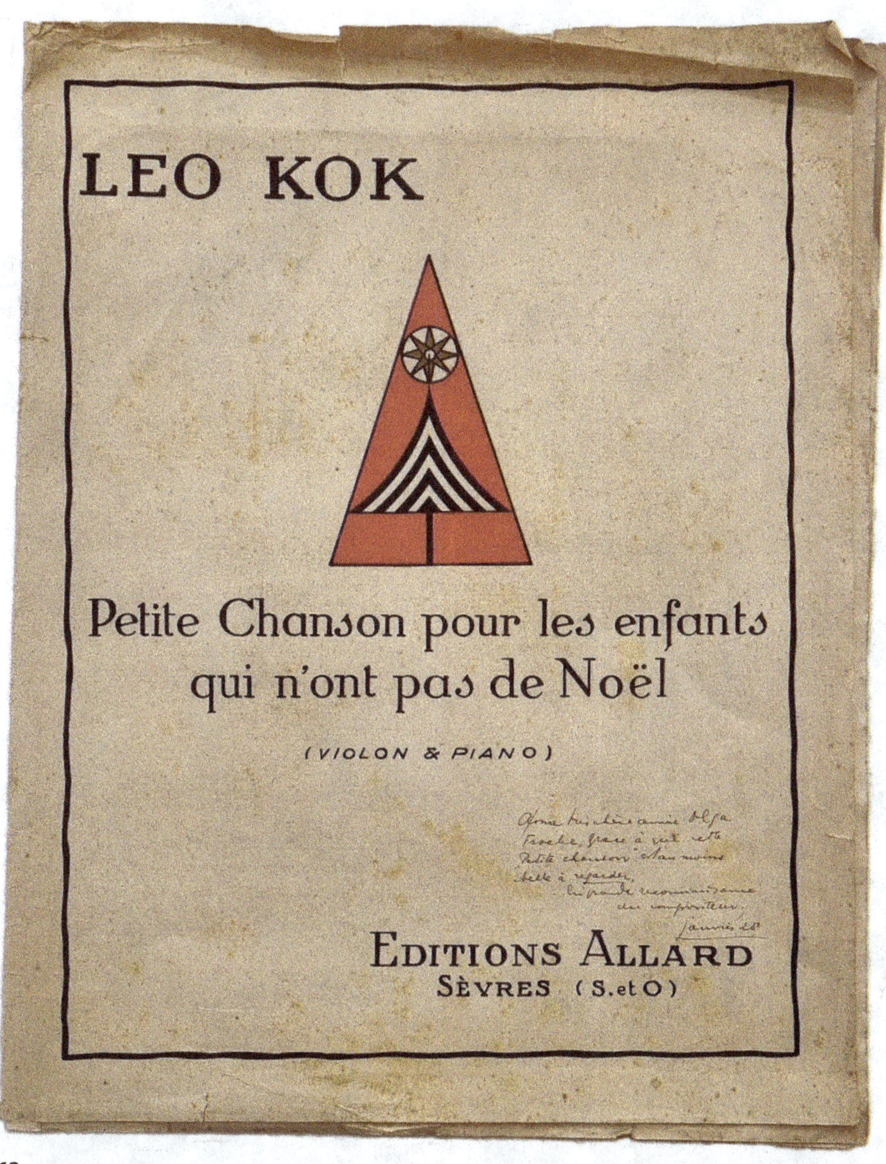

62.
Leo Kok's *Petite chanson pour les enfants qui n'ont pas de Noël* (1926), whose cover was designed in 1927 by Olga Fröbe-Kapteyn, inspired by the geometric paintings she had recently begun to produce as a form of meditative practice—the so-called "Meditation Plates." Kok had composed music for several poems written by Olga Fröbe-Kapteyn in the 1920s.
Eranos Foundation Archives, Ascona-Moscia. All rights reserved.

63.
Series of photographic prints of the starry sky—a dark blue, almost black firmament—displayed in the 1920s at Villa Gabriella, perhaps to accompany Olga Fröbe-Kapteyn's meditation.

64.
Postcard with a stylized *Om* symbol—the sacred sound (*mantra*) that refers to the Absolute, to consciousness, to Ātman, and to Brahman in various Far Eastern spiritual traditions—framed by Olga Fröbe-Kapteyn and displayed in Villa Gabriella.
Eranos Foundation Archives, Ascona-Moscia.

65.
Olga Fröbe-Kapteyn with landscape architect and garden philosopher Karl Foerster (1874–1970) in 1929; behind them, on the walls of the Lecture Hall of Casa Eranos, some "Meditation Plates" are displayed, and in particular, in the center, the larger painting entitled *Gethsemane* (*Mt* 23:36).
Ph. (probably) Eva Foerster. Archiv Haus Foerster, Marianne Foerster-Stiftung in der Deutschen Stiftung Denkmalschutz, Bonn.

66.
Olga Fröbe-Kapteyn, *Gethsemane* ["Gethsemane." *Mt* 23:36]
The painting appears in the photograph depicting the author with Karl Foerster in the Eranos Hall in 1929, so it may have been painted between c. 1926 and 1929.
"Meditation Plates," c. 1926-1934. Mixed technique (tempera, India ink, and gold leaf) on cardboard.
Eranos Foundation Archives, Ascona-Moscia.

67.
Olga Fröbe-Kapteyn, *Golgatha* ["Golgotha." *Mt* 27:33].
The painting appears in the photograph depicting the author with Karl Foerster in the Eranos Hall in 1929, so it may have been painted between c. 1926 and 1929.
"Meditation Plates," c. 1926-1934. Mixed technique (tempera, India ink, and gold leaf) on cardboard.
Eranos Foundation Archives, Ascona-Moscia.

68.
Olga Fröbe-Kapteyn, *Die Feuer der Läuterung* ["The Fires of Purification"].
The painting appears in the photograph depicting the author with Karl Foerster in the Eranos Hall in 1929, so it may have been painted between c. 1926 and 1929.
"Meditation Plates," c. 1926-1934. Mixed technique (tempera, India ink, and gold leaf) on cardboard.
Eranos Foundation Archives, Ascona-Moscia.

69.
Olga Fröbe-Kapteyn, *Begegnung mit dem Engel* ["Encounter with the Angel"].
The painting appears in the photograph depicting the author with Karl Foerster in the Eranos Hall in 1929, so it may have been painted between c. 1926 and 1929.
"Meditation Plates," c. 1926-1934. Mixed technique (tempera, India ink, and gold leaf) on cardboard.
Eranos Foundation Archives, Ascona-Moscia.

70.
Olga Fröbe-Kapteyn, *Meditation*.
The painting appears in the photograph depicting the author with Karl Foerster in the Eranos Hall in 1929, so it may have been painted between c. 1926 and 1929.
"Meditation Plates," c. 1926-1934. Mixed technique (tempera, India ink, and gold leaf) on cardboard.
Eranos Foundation Archives, Ascona-Moscia.

71.
Olga Fröbe-Kapteyn, *Die Kreuzigung* ["The Crucifixion"].
The painting appears in the photograph depicting the author with Karl Foerster in the Eranos Hall in 1929, so it may have been painted between c. 1926 and 1929.
"Meditation Plates," c. 1926-1934. Mixed technique (tempera, India ink, and gold leaf) on cardboard.
Eranos Foundation Archives, Ascona-Moscia.

72.
Olga Fröbe-Kapteyn, *The Transmutation of Pain*.
The painting appears in the photograph depicting the author with Karl Foerster in the Eranos Hall in 1929, so it may have been painted between c. 1926 and 1929.
"Meditation Plates," c. 1926-1934. Mixed technique (tempera, India ink, and gold leaf) on cardboard.
Eranos Foundation Archives, Ascona-Moscia.

73.
Olga Fröbe-Kapteyn, *Initiationen. Einweihüng. (Damaskus)* ["Initiations. Consecrations. (Damascus)." *Ac* 9:1–9; 22:6–16; 26:12–18].
The painting appears in the photograph depicting the author with Karl Foerster in the Eranos Hall in 1929, so it may have been painted between c. 1926 and 1929.
"Meditation Plates," c. 1926-1934. Mixed technique (tempera, India ink, and gold leaf) on cardboard.
Eranos Foundation Archives, Ascona-Moscia.

74.
Olga Fröbe-Kapteyn, *The Beginning of Vibration*.
The painting appears in the photograph depicting the author with Karl Foerster in the Eranos Hall in 1929, so it may have been painted between c. 1926 and 1929 (the last word of the handwritten title is barely legible).
"Meditation Plates," c. 1926-1934. Mixed technique (tempera, India ink, and gold leaf) on cardboard.
Eranos Foundation Archives, Ascona-Moscia.

75.
Olga Fröbe-Kapteyn, *Meditation*.
The "Plate" is a stylistic variation of another image, which appears in the photograph depicting the author with Karl Foerster in the Eranos Hall in 1929, so it also may have been painted between c. 1926 and 1929—see figure 70. Both Figure 70 and Figure 75 could have been "models" for the sculpture on the outer wall of Casa Eranos—see Figure 76.
"Meditation Plates," c. 1926-1934. Mixed technique (tempera, India ink, and gold leaf) on cardboard.

76.
Olga Fröbe-Kapteyn, untitled [*Meditation*].
Sculpture on the outer wall of Casa Eranos, near the entrance to the Lecture Hall, in a photo of the mid-1930s; although the title is not present, it is conceivable that it belongs to the same sub-series of the two "Meditation Plates," which are graphically very similar—see Figures 70 and 75.
"Meditation Plates," c. 1926-1934. Mural sculpture.
Ph. Margarethe Fellerer. Eranos Foundation Archives, Ascona-Moscia.

77.
(From left) Casa Eranos, Casa Gabriella, and the path leading to Casa Shanti (on the right). Ph. unknown. Eranos Foundation Archives, Ascona-Moscia.

78.
Casa Shanti, built between 1928 and 1929 and then named Casa Shanti (from Sanskrit, meaning "peace") in 1932.
Ph. unknown. Eranos Foundation Archives, Ascona-Moscia.

79.
Olga Fröbe-Kapteyn (seated, right) and theosophist and esotericist Alice Ann Bailey (1880–1949) (seated, left) on the terrace of Casa Gabriella in (probably) August 1930, at the occasion of one of the three symposa of the International Centre for Spiritual Research (1930–1932), which preceded the birth of the Eranos Conferences (1933). Standing, from left: theosophist Foster Bailey (1888–1977); Vittorino Vezzani (1885–1955), Professor of General Animal Husbandry at the Faculty of Agricultural Sciences of the University of Turin, director of the Institute of Animal Husbandry and Dairy Science for Piedmont, and metapsychic scholar; psychologist Roberto Assagioli (1888–1974), founder of Psychosynthesis; philosopher Frederick Kettner (1886–1957), founder of Biosophy; Shri Vishwanath Keskar (1880–?), author, with James Graham Phelps Stolkes (1872–1960), of *Pillars of Life* (1931); and writer and poet James H. Cousins (1873–1956).
Ph. unknown. Institute of Psychosynthesis, Assagioli Archives, Casa Assagioli, Florence.

ASCONA IST SITZ EINER INTERNATIONALE

Intellektuelle von 20 Völkern kommen hier jedes Jahr zusammen

Die Redaktion.

Internat. Zentrum für Synthese

Bei jeder Tagung waren etwa zwanzig Nationalitäten vertreten. Die Grundlage der Arbeit war international, undogmatisch, schöpferisch. Es wurde versucht, eine Verbindung herzustellen zwischen Ost und West, zwischen allen Formen des religiösen Glaubens, zwischen den Bekenntnissen der alten Mystiker und der heutigen mystischen Erfahrung einzelner. Die

Der Vortragssaal mit symbolischen Bildern von Frau Fröbe-Kapteyn

Originalaufnahme für die »Tessiner Illustrierte«

80.
"Ascona is Home to an International": an article published in the journal *Tessiner Illustrierte* concerning Olga Fröbe-Kapteyn and Alice Ann Bailey's project of the International Centre for Spiritual Research (1930–1932); among the "Meditation Plates" displayed on the walls of the Eranos Hall, *The Central Spiritual Sun* can be seen in the center; drawn in two versions, the largest one, photographed in this image, is still on display at the Hotel Tamaro in Ascona. Monte Verità Foundation, from the permanent exhibition at Casa Anatta, Ascona-Monte Verità.

81.
Olga Fröbe-Kapteyn, [Grail symbol – title not found so far].
The author donated this "Plate" to psychologist Roberto Assagioli, founder of Psychosynthesis, involved as lecturer in the International Centre for Spiritual Research (Ascona, 1930–1932).
"Meditation Plates," c. 1926-1934. Mixed technique (tempera, India ink, and gold leaf) on cardboard.
Eranos Foundation Archives, Ascona-Moscia.
Institute of Psychosynthesis, Assagioli Archives, Casa Assagioli, Florence.

82.
Olga Fröbe-Kapteyn, *Gral-Symbol* ["Grail Symbol"].
"Meditation Plates," c. 1926–1934. Mixed technique (tempera, India ink, and gold leaf) on cardboard.
Eranos Foundation Archives, Ascona-Moscia.

83.
Olga Fröbe-Kapteyn, *The Central Spiritual Sun (The Physical Sun is but a golden disc before the Spiritual Sun)*.
"Meditation Plates," c. 1926–1934. Mixed technique (tempera, India ink, and gold leaf) on cardboard.
Eranos Foundation Archives, Ascona-Moscia.

84.
Olga Fröbe-Kapteyn, [title not found so far].
"Meditation Plates," c. 1926–1934. Mixed technique (tempera, India ink, and gold leaf) on cardboard.
Eranos Foundation Archives, Ascona-Moscia.

85.
Olga Fröbe-Kapteyn, *The Light of the Soul.*
The Light of the Soul: Its Science and Effect. A Paraphrase of the Yoga Sutras of Patañjali (New York: Lucis Trust, 1927) is also the title of a volume belonging to the series of 24 "Blue Books" by Alice Ann Bailey. Of this series, composed between 1919 and 1949, 19 volumes on esoteric philosophy were dictated by the "Tibetan" (Djwhal Khul) to Bailey; she also wrote five additional tomes independently.
"Meditation Plates," c. 1926–1934. Mixed technique (tempera, India ink, and gold leaf) on cardboard.
Eranos Foundation Archives, Ascona-Moscia.

86.
Olga Fröbe-Kapteyn, [title not found so far].
"Meditation Plates," c. 1926–1934. Mixed technique (tempera, India ink, and gold leaf) on cardboard.
Eranos Foundation Archives, Ascona-Moscia.

87.
Olga Fröbe-Kapteyn, *The Grail*.
"Meditation Plates," c. 1926–1934. Mixed technique (tempera, India ink, and gold leaf) on cardboard.
Eranos Foundation Archives, Ascona-Moscia.

88.
Olga Fröbe-Kapteyn, *Sattva or Rhythm*.
In the Hindu philosophy of Sāṃkhya, *Guṇa* indicates the three ultimate components of matter (*prakṛti*): *sattva* (the component that illuminates and reveals the manifest), *rajas* (the component that sets manifestation in motion), and *tamas* (the component that tends to hinder the dynamism of manifestation): "In truth, in the beginning, there was only this darkness (*tamas*). It was in the Supreme (Brahmā). That, induced by the Supreme, moved towards diversity (*viṣama*). That formation, indeed, is *rajas*. That *rajas*, certainly, stimulated, moved towards diversity. This, indeed, is the form-nature of *sattva*" (*Maitrī Upaniṣad* V, 2). *Sattva*, *rajas*, and *tamas* "are the qualities that come out of nature; they are what bind us to the body, and through them the embodied immutable is firmly imprisoned in the body" (*Bhagavadgītā* XIV, 5). The *guṇas* are seen as responsible for the cycle of births and deaths and the transmigration of souls from one body to another (*saṃsāra*). *Rajas* is the source of attachment and passion; *tamas* is the cause of laziness and error; *sattva* is free from evil and is knowledge: by dominating *rajas* and *tamas*, *sattva* prevails, and this is the path to liberation (*mokṣa*), which will be achieved when *sattva* has also been overcome, showing equanimity towards the three influences of the *guṇa*.
"Meditation Plates," c. 1926–1934. Mixed technique (tempera, India ink, and gold leaf) on cardboard.
Eranos Foundation Archives, Ascona-Moscia.

89.
Olga Fröbe-Kapteyn, *The Grail*.
"Meditation Plates," c. 1926–1934. Mixed technique (tempera, India ink, and gold leaf) on cardboard.
Eranos Foundation Archives, Ascona-Moscia.

90.
Olga Fröbe-Kapteyn, *Reincarnation*.
"Meditation Plates," c. 1926–1934. Mixed technique (tempera, India ink, and gold leaf) on cardboard.
Eranos Foundation Archives, Ascona-Moscia.

91.
Olga Fröbe-Kapteyn, *Planes*.
"Meditation Plates," c. 1926–1934. Mixed technique (tempera, India ink, and gold leaf) on cardboard.
Eranos Foundation Archives, Ascona-Moscia.

92.
Olga Fröbe-Kapteyn, *The Breath of Creation*.
"Meditation Plates," c. 1926–1934. Mixed technique (tempera, India ink, and gold leaf) on cardboard.
Eranos Foundation Archives, Ascona-Moscia.

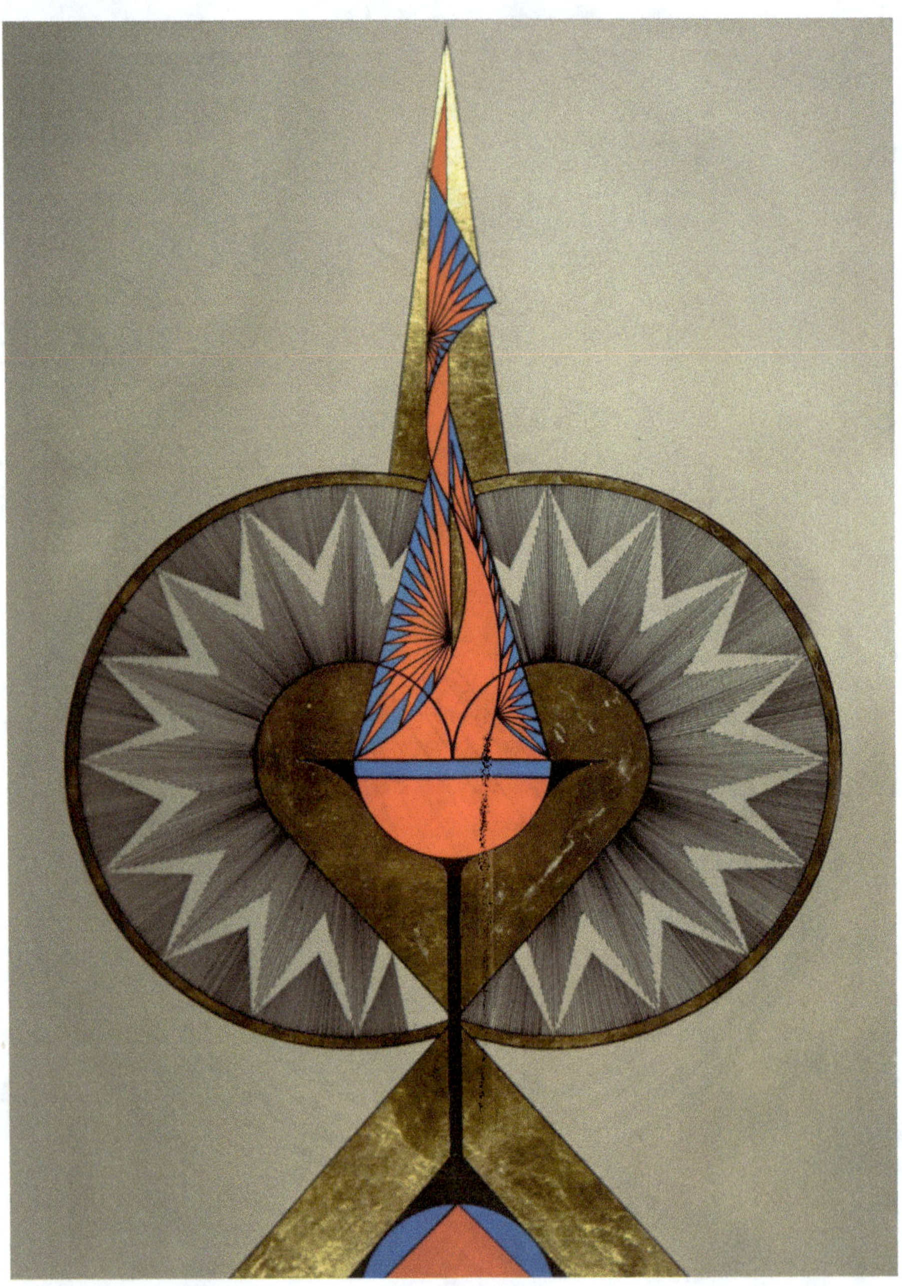

93.
Olga Fröbe-Kapteyn, *The Chalice in the Heart*.
"Meditation Plates," c. 1926–1934. Mixed technique (tempera, India ink, and gold leaf) on cardboard.
Eranos Foundation Archives, Ascona-Moscia.

94.
Olga Fröbe-Kapteyn, *The Extension of Consciousness. The Flower of the Soul.*
"Meditation Plates," c. 1926–1934. Mixed technique (tempera, India ink, and gold leaf) on cardboard.
Eranos Foundation Archives, Ascona-Moscia.

95.
Historian of religions Rudolf Otto (1869–1937), regarded by Fröbe-Kapteyn as the *Pate* ("godfather") of Eranos; behind him is the painting *The Consumation*, part of the "Meditation Plates" series.
Ph. unknown. Eranos Foundation Archives, Ascona-Moscia.

96.
Olga Fröbe-Kapteyn, *The Consumation*.
"Meditation Plates," c. 1926–1934. Mixed technique (tempera, India ink, and gold leaf) on cardboard.
Eranos Foundation Archives, Ascona-Moscia.

97.
Olga Fröbe-Kapteyn, [*Om* – title not found so far].
Olga Fröbe-Kapteyn dedicated this "Plate," dated 1933, to Rudolf Otto; a black-and-white reproduction remains, while the original has not yet been found.
"Meditation Plates," c. 1926–1934. Mixed technique (tempera, India ink, and gold leaf) on cardboard.
Eranos Foundation Archives, Ascona-Moscia.

98.
Olga Fröbe-Kapteyn, [*Om* – title not found so far].
This is the painting that Carl Gustav Jung (1875–1961) harshly criticized during his first visit to Eranos in August 1933, when he saw it on display in the Eranos Hall, together with other "Meditation Plates." Pointing to the symbol of the "black *Om*" among the eighty images, Jung is said to have exclaimed: *"Das ist der Teufel!"* ["This is the devil!"] Curiously, he pointed to the very painting with which Olga Fröbe-Kapteyn had always identified most strongly.
"Meditation Plates," c. 1926–1934. Mixed technique (tempera, India ink, and gold leaf) on cardboard.
Eranos Foundation Archives, Ascona-Moscia.

99.
Olga Fröbe-Kapteyn at the Holzhütte ("Hut"), which she built in 1932 on the original grounds of Villa Gabriella as a "refuge for herself." She painted the *Om* symbol on the façade and posted a sign saying "Private," so that no one could enter.
Ph. unknown. Eranos Foundation Archives, Ascona-Moscia.

100.
Holzhütte ("Hut").
Ph. unknown. Eranos Foundation Archives, Ascona-Moscia.

101.
Idyllic time at the Holzhütte ("Hut").
Ph. unknown. Eranos Foundation Archives, Ascona-Moscia.

102.
Idyllic time at the Holzhütte ("Hut").
Ph. unknown. Eranos Foundation Archives, Ascona-Moscia.

103.
Idyllic time at the Holzhütte ("Hut").
Ph. unknown. Eranos Foundation Archives, Ascona-Moscia.

104.
Idyllic time at the Holzhütte ("Hut").
Ph. unknown. Eranos Foundation Archives, Ascona-Moscia.

105.
Olga Fröbe-Kapteyn, *Lux in tenebris lucis. The Light shineth in the Darkness. John 1:5.* "Meditation Plates," c. 1926–1934. Mixed technique (tempera, India ink, and gold leaf) on cardboard.
Eranos Foundation Archives, Ascona-Moscia.

106.
Olga Fröbe-Kapteyn, *Radio-Activity*.
"Meditation Plates," c. 1926–1934. Mixed technique (tempera, India ink, and gold leaf) on cardboard.
Eranos Foundation Archives, Ascona-Moscia.

107.
Olga Fröbe-Kapteyn, *The Cosmic Eros. Polarity*.
On the back of the reproduction sent to Léopold Szondi (1893–1986) in the early 1950s as part of her analysis with him, the handwritten title is instead *Die Gegensätze* ("The Opposites") (Stiftung Szondi-Institut Archive, Zurich).
"Meditation Plates," c. 1926–1934. Mixed technique (tempera, India ink, and gold leaf) on cardboard.
Eranos Foundation Archives, Ascona-Moscia.

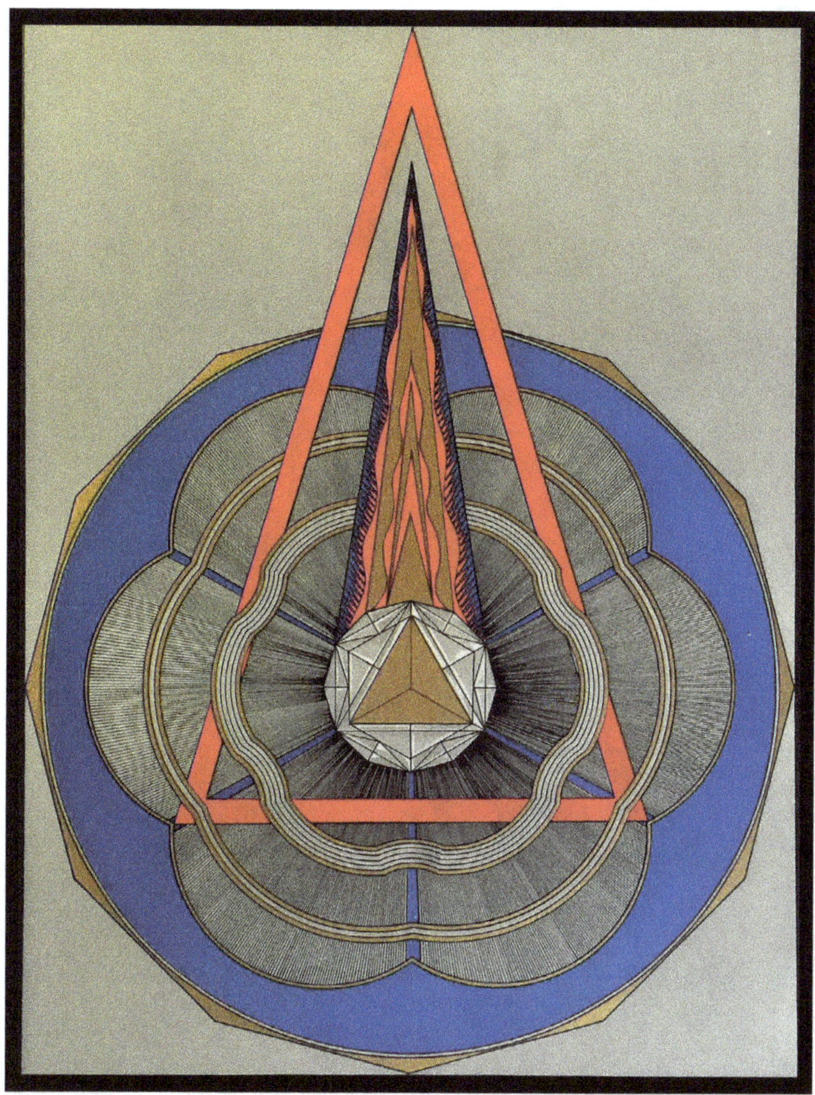

108.
Olga Fröbe-Kapteyn, *Om Mani Padme Hum*.
Oṃ Maṇi Padme Hūṃ is one of the most well-known and widespread of the numerous *mantras* that form part of the religious heritage of Mahāyāna Buddhism, particularly Tibetan Buddhism. Its literal meaning is "O Jewel of the Lotus!" referring to one of the epithets, Maṇipadma, of the bodhisattva of compassion Avalokiteśvara, to whom this mantra is explicitly addressed. On the back of the reproduction sent to Léopold Szondi in the early 1950s as part of her analysis with him, the handwritten title is instead *Das Zeichen des Feuers* ("The Sign of Fire") (Stiftung Szondi-Institut Archive, Zurich).
"Meditation Plates," c. 1926–1934. Mixed technique (tempera, India ink, and gold leaf) on cardboard.
Eranos Foundation Archives, Ascona-Moscia.

109.
Olga Fröbe-Kapteyn, *Aufstieg und Wendung* ["Rise and Reversal"].
"Meditation Plates," c. 1926–1934. Mixed technique (tempera, India ink, and gold leaf) on cardboard.
Eranos Foundation Archives, Ascona-Moscia.

110.
Olga Fröbe-Kapteyn, *Planeten-Tanz* ["Planetary Dance"].
"Meditation Plates," c. 1926–1934. Mixed technique (tempera, India ink, and gold leaf) on cardboard.
Eranos Foundation Archives, Ascona-Moscia.

111.
Olga Fröbe-Kapteyn, *The Aspirant. Now we see through a glass, darkly—but then face to face.* "Meditation Plates," c. 1926–1934. Mixed technique (tempera, India ink, and gold leaf) on cardboard.
Eranos Foundation Archives, Ascona-Moscia.

112.
Olga Fröbe-Kapteyn, *"The Universe is Burning, Vishnu, with Thy Blazing Rays"* [*Bhagavadgītā*, XI, 30, trans. Annie Besant].
"Meditation Plates," c. 1926–1934. Mixed technique (tempera, India ink, and gold leaf) on cardboard.
Eranos Foundation Archives, Ascona-Moscia.

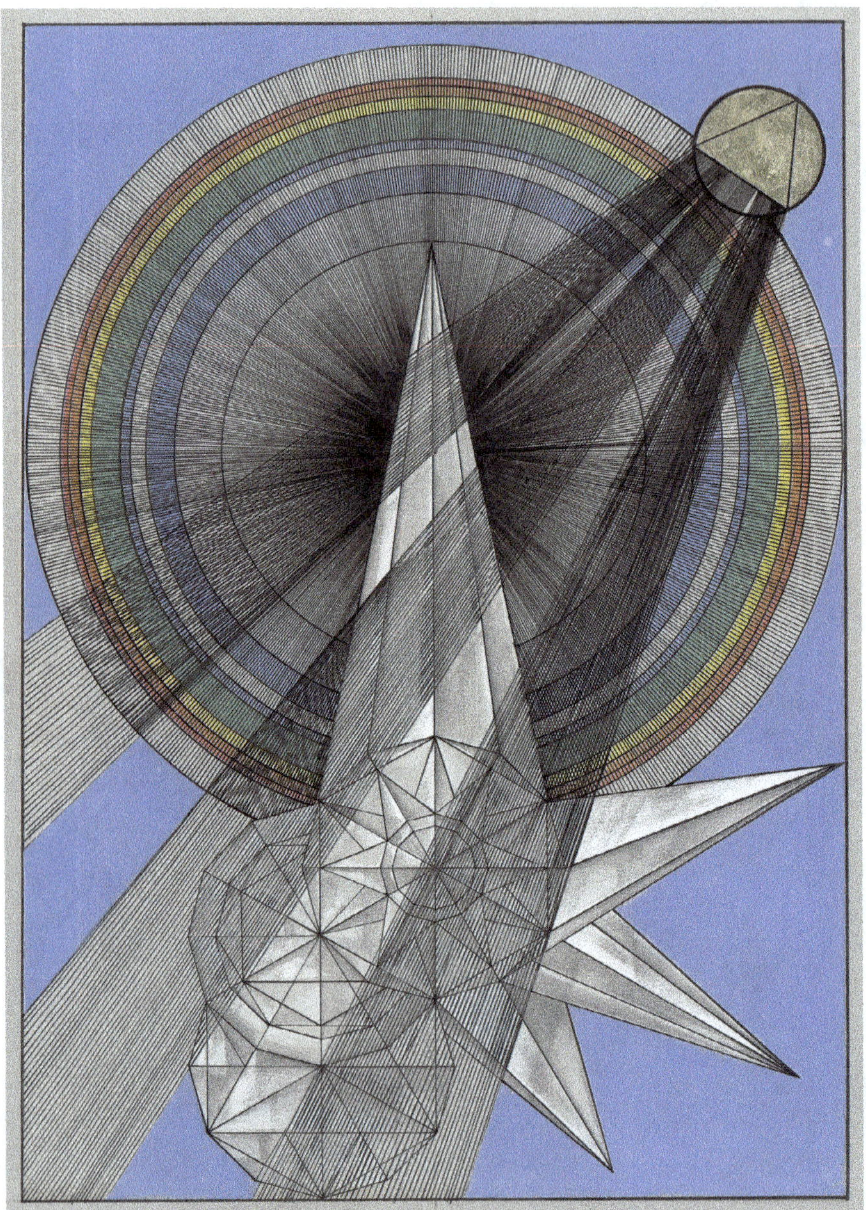

113.
Olga Fröbe-Kapteyn, [title not found so far].
In very few "Plates," such as this one and the next one—see Figure 114—the author introduces, in addition to the four basic colors (black, gold, blue, and red), further color variations (green, orange, yellow, and white-gray).
"Meditation Plates," c. 1926–1934. Mixed technique (tempera, India ink, and gold leaf) on cardboard.
Eranos Foundation Archives, Ascona-Moscia.

114.
Olga Fröbe-Kapteyn, *Agni Yoga*.
Agni Yoga or the "Living Ethics" or the "Teaching of Life" is a Neo-Theosophical religious doctrine transmitted by Helena Ivanovna Šapošnikova Roerich (1879–1955) and Nikolaj Konstantinovič (Nicholas) Roerich (1874–1947, who lectured at the International Centre for Spiritual Research in Ascona) from 1930. The term Agni Yoga means "Mergence with Divine Fire" or "Path to Mergence with Divine Fire." The followers of Agni Yoga believe that the teaching was given to the Roerich family and their associates by Master Morya, guru of the Roerichs and of Helena Petrovna Blavatsky (1831–1891). Helena Ivanovna Roerich-Šapošnikova, who was in contact with Alice Ann Bailey, was a promoter of Agni Yoga in the West and edited the first Russian translation of Blavatsky's *The Secret Doctrine*. Nicholas Roerich, an expert on Tibet, contributed to fueling the Blavatskian myth of Shambhala in the collective imagination of the West: the legendary "hidden country," surrounded by snow-capped peaks, located somewhere in the north (of India or Tibet), whose happiness is guarded by a dynasty of wise and divine kings, guardians of the Kalachakra tantra.
"Meditation Plates," c. 1926–1934. Mixed technique (tempera, India ink, and gold leaf) on cardboard.
Eranos Foundation Archives, Ascona-Moscia.

115.
Olga Fröbe-Kapteyn, [*The Portal (The Portal of Initiation)* (?) – title not found so far]. "Meditation Plates," c. 1926–1934. Mixed technique (tempera, India ink, and gold leaf) on cardboard.
Eranos Foundation Archives, Ascona-Moscia.

116.
Olga Fröbe-Kapteyn, [title not found so far].
This painting shows the beginnings of figuration, which, from the essentially geometric style of the "Meditation Plates," seems to lead to the subsequent depictions contained in the "Visions."
"Meditation Plates," c. 1926–1934. Mixed technique (tempera, India ink, and gold leaf) on cardboard.
Eranos Foundation Archives, Ascona-Moscia.

117.
Olga Fröbe-Kapteyn joins an "Indian ritual" at the occasion of the first Eranos Conference, "Yoga and Meditation in the East and West," held on August 14–26, 1933. She had also asked the historian of religions Friedrich Heiler (1892–1967) if he could organize some "spiritual exercises" for a small group of participants. Heiler accepted her proposal and replied that the exercises would be based on the mystical path to salvation in its entirety (purgative, illuminative, unitive, active paths). Sinologist Erwin Rousselle (1890–1949), director of the China Institute at the University of Frankfurt—a position he had taken over from Richard Wilhelm (1873–1930) in 1930—assisted Heiler in leading the exercises. The previous year, Rousselle had already been a lecturer at Olga Fröbe-Kapteyn and Alice Ann Bailey's International Centre for Spiritual Research, giving four lectures on "Buddhist Mysticism in China and Japan" and "Taoist Mysticism in China."
Ph. Margarethe Fellerer. Eranos Foundation Archives, Ascona-Moscia.

118.
Olga Fröbe-Kapteyn in the garden of Villa Gabriella in August 1933.
Ph. Margarethe Fellerer. Eranos Foundation Archives, Ascona-Moscia.

119.
A view of Casa Eranos at the occasion of the first Eranos Conference in August 1933. Over two hundred and ten people attended the symposium.
Ph. Margarethe Fellerer. Eranos Foundation Archives, Ascona-Moscia.

120.
A view of Casa Eranos at the occasion of the first Eranos Conference in August 1933.
Ph. Margarethe Fellerer. Eranos Foundation Archives, Ascona-Moscia.

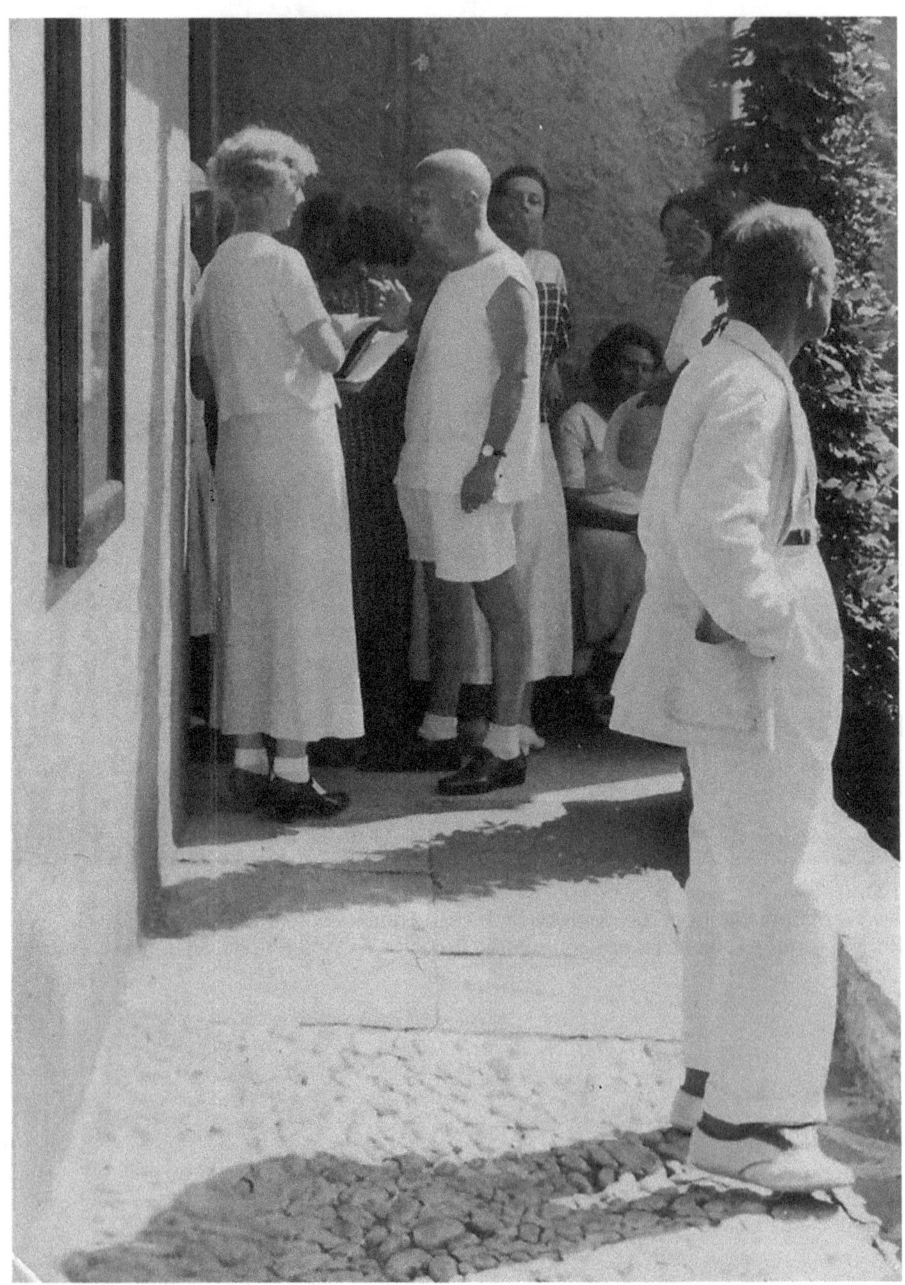

121.
Olga Fröbe-Kapteyn and Baron Eduard von der Heydt (1882–1964, owner of Monte Verità since 1926) at Casa Eranos in August 1933.
Ph. Margarethe Fellerer [?]. Eranos Foundation Archives, Ascona-Moscia.

122.
The Indian statue of Viṣṇu donated by Baron Eduard von der Heydt to Olga Fröbe-Kapteyn in the 1930s—still in the Eranos garden.
Ph. Tim Gidal (around 1955–1958). Eranos Foundation Archives, Ascona-Moscia.

123.
Olga Fröbe-Kapteyn and Carl Gustav Jung at the occasion of the first Eranos Conference in August 1933. Jung gave a mostly improvised lecture on the topic "Zur Empirie des Individuationsprozesses" ("A Study in the Process of Individuation"). His speech was included in the first *Eranos-Jahrbuch*, published the following year, before being included in his *Psychologische Abhandlungen* and then in his *Collected Works* (this was the case for all fourteen contributions presented at Eranos over a period of twenty years, from 1933 to 1951; he attended Eranos for the last time in 1952, only as a listener). In his essay, Jung outlined for the first time a systematic account of the evolution of the individuation process based on the analysis of a single clinical case. Commenting on a series of images produced by his American patient Kristine Mann (1873–1945), Jung showed how the individuation process is accompanied by the appearance of images which, in the dreams and unconscious productions of a patient on the road to recovery, can take on a characteristic "*maṇḍala*" form. Ph. Margarethe Fellerer. Eranos Foundation Archives, Ascona-Moscia.

124.
Olga Fröbe-Kapteyn and Carl Gustav Jung at the occasion of the first Eranos Conference in August 1933. From 1933 to 1939, during the Conference period, Carl Gustav Jung and Emma Jung-Rauschenbach (1882–1955) stayed at Monte Verità, on the hill of Ascona, in the elegant Bauhaus-style Hotel offering a splendid view of Lake Maggiore and the surrounding mountains; it was only in 1940 that the Jungs moved into the upper apartment of Casa Eranos, the "Eranos Studio," which had been built at the end of the 1930s and made available to them by Fröbe-Kapteyn during the Conferences.
Ph. Margarethe Fellerer. Eranos Foundation Archives, Ascona-Moscia.

125.
Olga Fröbe-Kapteyn, [untitled].
The series of Marian-themed "ritual scenes" constitutes the first of the twelve volumes of the "Visions." In this first image, Mary is depicted with her son lying on her lap and her newborn baby in her arms (from the handwritten notes by the author on the back of the black and white photograph of the drawing, sent to Carl Gustav Jung in 1934; Picture Archive, C.G. Jung-Institut, Zurich). This series of images, and this image in particular, would also be the subject of further considerations by Olga Fröbe-Kapteyn twenty years later, in relation to her identification with the "Earth Mother" (which she associated with the first Chakra, Mūlādhāra, "the root" at the base of the spine, and her relationship with her own body in general). A year earlier, he had already reflected on the connection between Mother Earth, the Mūlādhāra Chakra, the body, wisdom, the physical disorders affecting her eyesight, and her psychological need to accept a reality that had remained hidden or "invisible" until then (Olga Fröbe-Kapteyn, "The Earth Mother. Vision. Spring. 33" (unpublished typescript, 1933; Eranos Foundation Archives, Ascona-Moscia).)
"Visions," Series I, no. 1, March 1934. Pastel and pencil on onion skin paper, mounted on cardboard.
Eranos Foundation Archives, Ascona-Moscia.

126.
Olga Fröbe-Kapteyn, [untitled].
A hieroglyph in front of the entrance: the mistletoe branch, symbol of immortality and fertility (from the handwritten notes by the author on the back of the black and white photograph of the drawing, sent to Carl Gustav Jung in 1934; Picture Archive, C.G. Jung-Institut, Zurich).
"Visions," Series I, no. 2, March 1934. Pastel and pencil on onion skin paper, mounted on cardboard.
Eranos Foundation Archives, Ascona-Moscia.

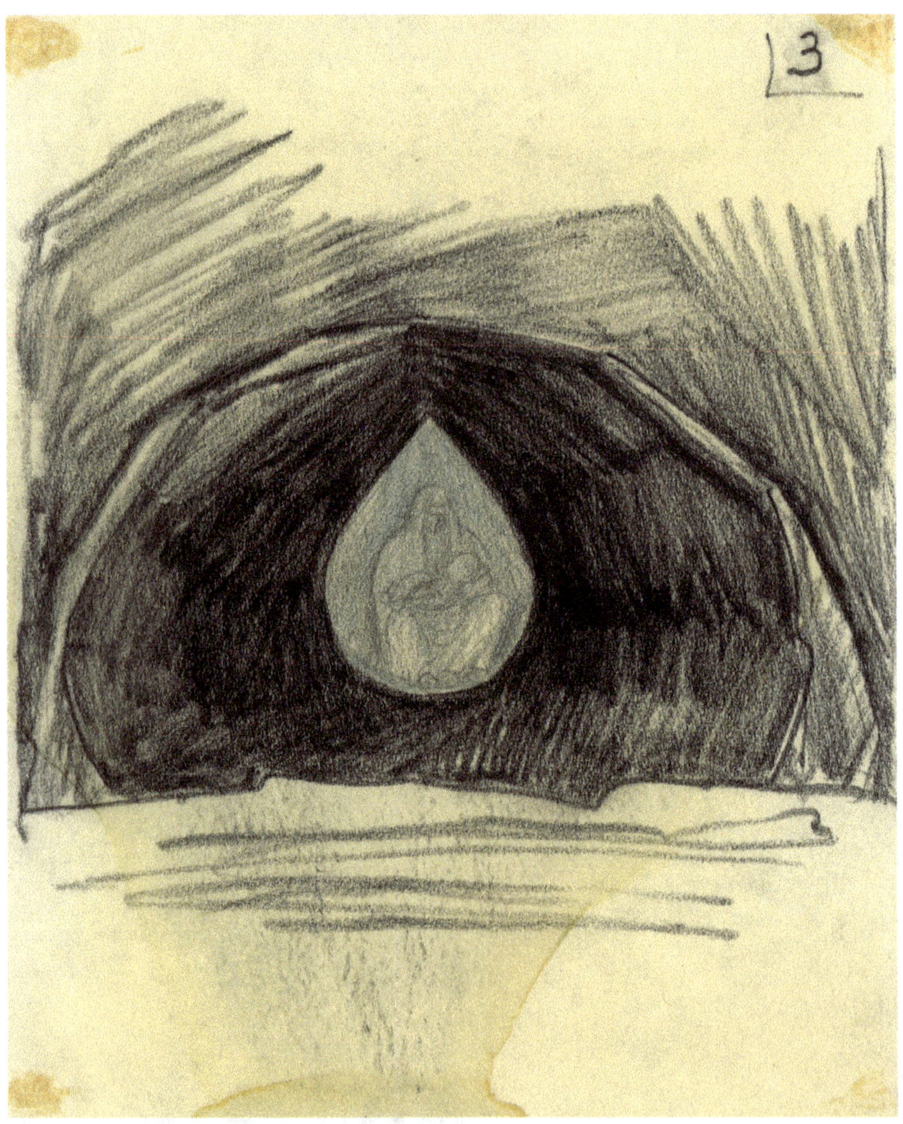

127.
Olga Fröbe-Kapteyn, [untitled].
At the bottom of the cave, Mary appears in a transparent ellipse in the church (from the handwritten notes by the author on the back of the black and white photograph of the drawing, sent to Carl Gustav Jung in 1934; Picture Archive, C.G. Jung-Institut, Zurich).
"Visions," Series I, no. 3, March 1934. Pastel and pencil on onion skin paper, mounted on cardboard.
Eranos Foundation Archives, Ascona-Moscia.

128.
Olga Fröbe-Kapteyn, [untitled].
In front of Mary, a tree trunk grows out of the ground, a snake wraps itself around it, breaks through the thick trunk, and carries an egg in its mouth (from the handwritten notes by the author on the back of the black and white photograph of the drawing, sent to Carl Gustav Jung in 1934; Picture Archive, C.G. Jung-Institut, Zurich).
"Visions," Series I, no. 4, March 1934. Pastel and pencil on onion skin paper, mounted on cardboard.
Eranos Foundation Archives, Ascona-Moscia.

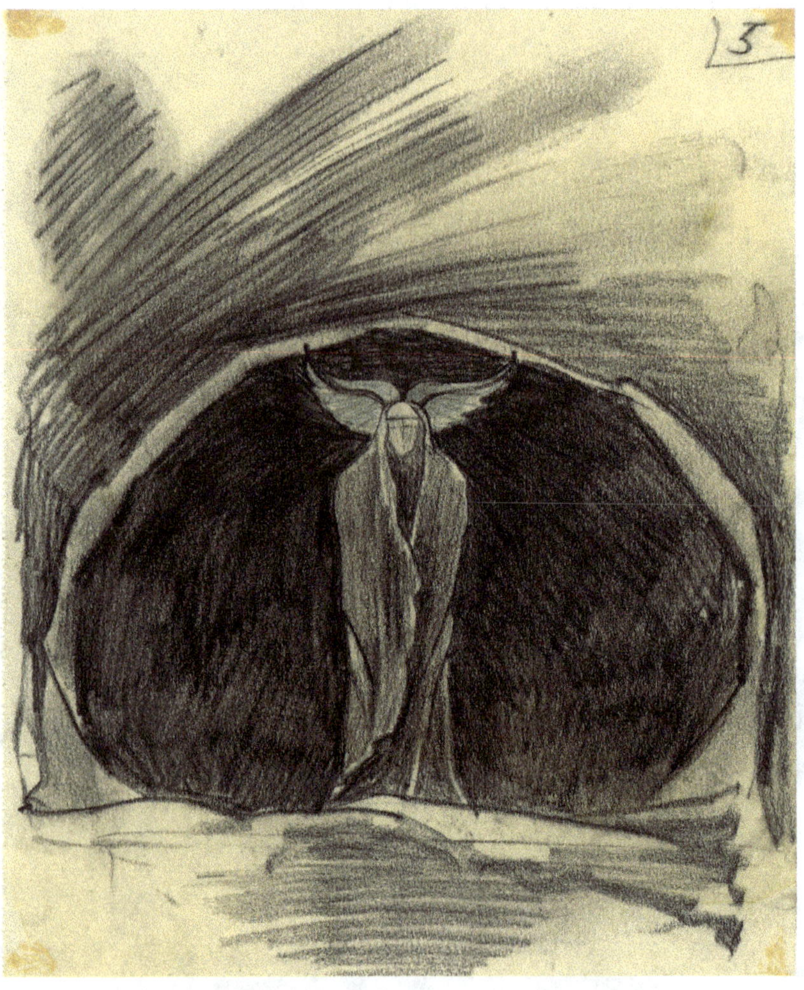

129.
Olga Fröbe-Kapteyn, [untitled].
The figure of a priest. It looks as if he is wearing the skin of a bull (from the handwritten notes by the author on the back of the black and white photograph of the drawing, sent to Carl Gustav Jung in 1934; Picture Archive, C.G. Jung-Institut, Zurich). In her commentary on this vision, Olga Fröbe-Kapteyn traces this figure back to a passage from *Wandlungen und Symbole der Libido* (1912), in which Jung refers to the Koranic figure of al-Khiḍr, known as "the Verdant One." He appears in the 18th *sūra*, "The Cave." The divine angel al-Khiḍr (Helios), in his form as Dhulqarnein (Mithra), is an emblem of the Immortal, the Wise One in divine matters; his two-horned appearance, with his head veiled, refers to his power of divine solar wisdom, born from the depths of his mother: see Carl Gustav Jung, *Rebirth—Text and Notes of the Lecture held at Eranos in 1939 / Rinascere. Testo e appunti della conferenza tenuta a Eranos nel 1939*, eds. Fabio Merlini and Riccardo Bernardini (Ascona: Eranos Classics 1, Aragno * Eranos Ascona, 2020), pp. 31–41.
"Visions," Series I, no. 5, March 1934. Pastel and pencil on onion skin paper, mounted on cardboard.
Eranos Foundation Archives, Ascona-Moscia.

130.
Olga Fröbe-Kapteyn, [untitled].
The Life-Giving Mother (from the handwritten notes by the author on the back of the black and white photograph of the drawing, sent to Carl Gustav Jung in 1934; Picture Archive, C.G. Jung-Institut, Zurich).
"Visions," Series I, no. 6, March 1934. Pastel and pencil on onion skin paper, mounted on cardboard.
Eranos Foundation Archives, Ascona-Moscia.

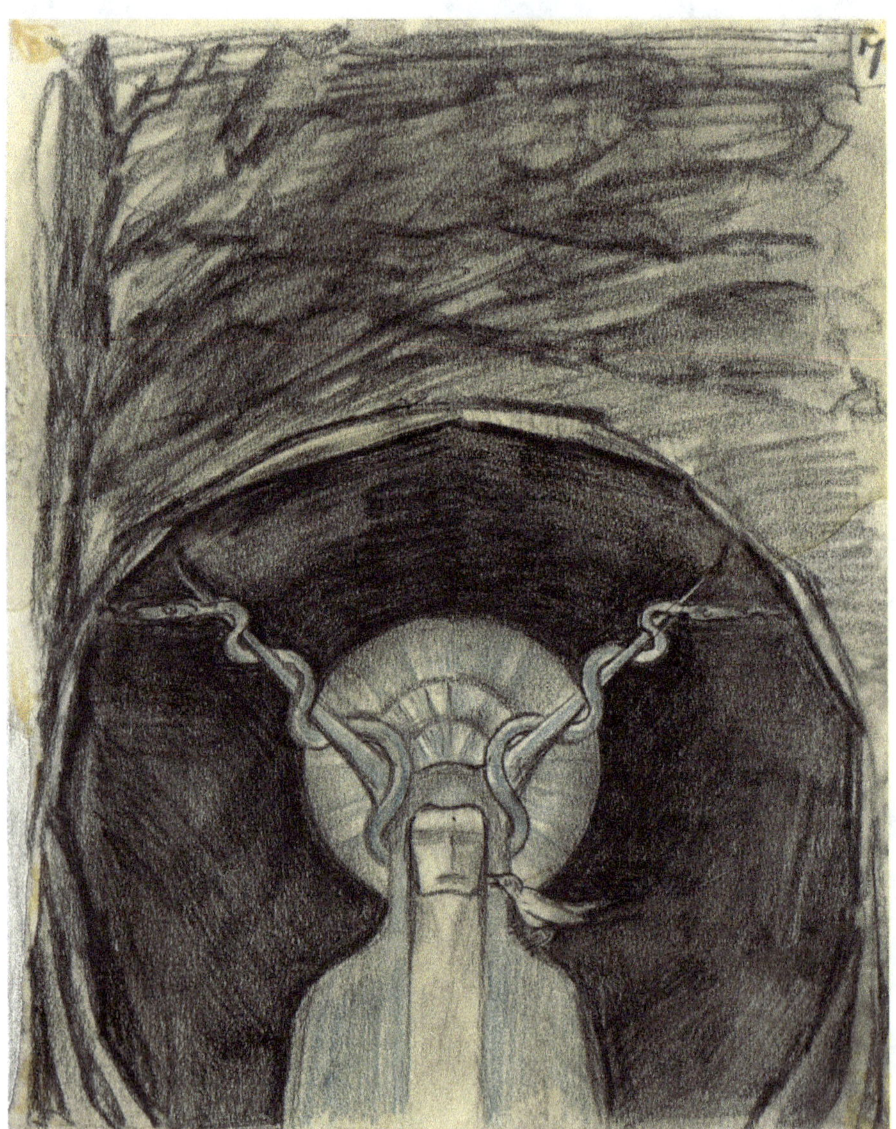

131.
Olga Fröbe-Kapteyn, [untitled].
The snakes twisted around the two horns reminded her of Kuṇḍalinī, with the bird as a symbol of the soul (from the handwritten notes by the author on the back of the black and white photograph of the drawing, sent to Carl Gustav Jung in 1934; Picture Archive, C.G. Jung-Institut, Zurich).
"Visions," Series I, no. 7, March 1934. Pastel and pencil on onion skin paper, mounted on cardboard.
Eranos Foundation Archives, Ascona-Moscia.

132.
Olga Fröbe-Kapteyn, [untitled].
"Visions," Series I, no. 8, March 1934. Pastel and pencil on onion skin paper, mounted on cardboard.
Eranos Foundation Archives, Ascona-Moscia.

133.
Olga Fröbe-Kapteyn, [untitled].
A figure drives into the cave, perhaps for an initiation; behind the figure is the Kuṇḍalinī symbol (from the handwritten notes by the author on the back of the black and white photograph of the drawing, sent to Carl Gustav Jung in 1934; Picture Archive, C.G. Jung-Institut, Zurich).
"Visions," Series I, no. 9, March 1934. Pastel and pencil on onion skin paper, mounted on cardboard.

134.
Olga Fröbe-Kapteyn, [untitled].
The entrance to the cave of a female deity is passed while holding two torches, symbols of life and death (from the handwritten notes by the author on the back of the black and white photograph of the drawing, sent to Carl Gustav Jung in 1934; Picture Archive, C.G. Jung-Institut, Zurich).
"Visions," Series I, no. 10, March 1934. Pastel and pencil on onion skin paper, mounted on cardboard.
Eranos Foundation Archives, Ascona-Moscia.

135.
Olga Fröbe-Kapteyn, [untitled].
"Visions," Series I, no. 11, March 1934. Pastel and pencil on onion skin paper, mounted on cardboard.
Eranos Foundation Archives, Ascona-Moscia.

136.
Olga Fröbe-Kapteyn, [untitled].
"Visions," Series I, no. 12, March 1934. Pastel and pencil on onion skin paper, mounted on cardboard.
Eranos Foundation Archives, Ascona-Moscia.

137.
Olga Fröbe-Kapteyn, [untitled].
"Visions," Series I, no. 13, March 1934. Pastel and pencil on onion skin paper, mounted on cardboard.
Eranos Foundation Archives, Ascona-Moscia.

138.
Olga Fröbe-Kapteyn, [untitled].
"Visions," Series I, no. 14, March 1934. Pastel and pencil on onion skin paper, mounted on cardboard.
Eranos Foundation Archives, Ascona-Moscia.

139.
Olga Fröbe-Kapteyn, [untitled].
"Visions," Series I, no. 15, March 1934. Pastel and pencil on onion skin paper, mounted on cardboard.
Eranos Foundation Archives, Ascona-Moscia.

140.
Olga Fröbe-Kapteyn, [untitled].
"Visions," Series I, no. 16, March 1934. Pastel and pencil on onion skin paper, mounted on cardboard.
Eranos Foundation Archives, Ascona-Moscia.

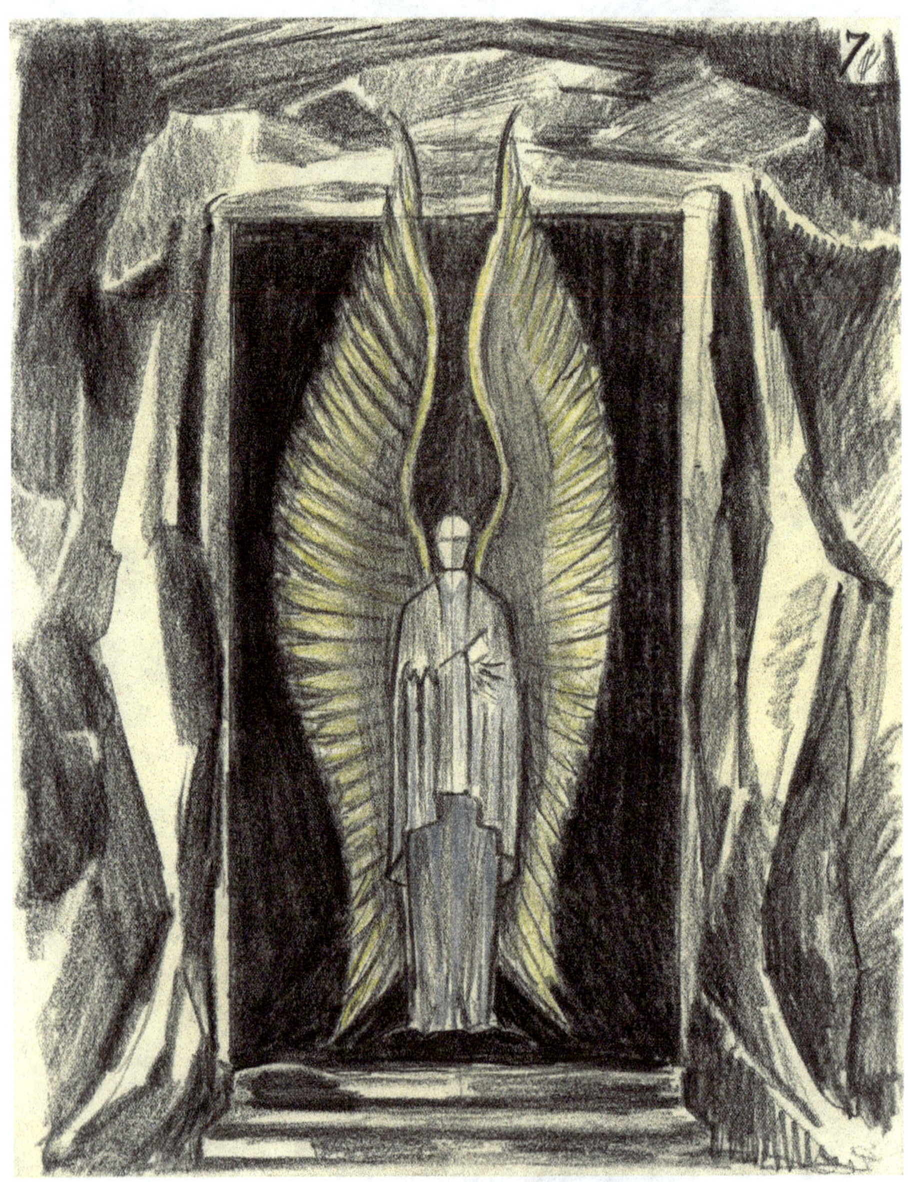

141.
Olga Fröbe-Kapteyn, [untitled].
"Visions," Series I, no. 17, March 1934. Pastel and pencil on onion skin paper, mounted on cardboard.
Eranos Foundation Archives, Ascona-Moscia.

142.
Olga Fröbe-Kapteyn, [untitled].
"Visions," Series I, no. 18, March 1934. Pastel and pencil on onion skin paper, mounted on cardboard.
Eranos Foundation Archives, Ascona-Moscia.

143.
Olga Fröbe-Kapteyn, [untitled].
"Visions," Series I, no. 19, March 1934. Pastel and pencil on onion skin paper, mounted on cardboard.
Eranos Foundation Archives, Ascona-Moscia.

144.
Olga Fröbe-Kapteyn, [untitled].
"Visions," Series I, no. 20, March 1934. Pastel and pencil on onion skin paper, mounted on cardboard.
Eranos Foundation Archives, Ascona-Moscia.

145.
Olga Fröbe-Kapteyn, [untitled].
"Visions," Series I, no. 21, March 1934. Pastel and pencil on onion skin paper, mounted on cardboard.
Eranos Foundation Archives, Ascona-Moscia.

146.
Olga Fröbe-Kapteyn, [untitled].
"Visions," Series I, no. 22, March 1934. Pastel and pencil on onion skin paper, mounted on cardboard.

147.
Olga Fröbe-Kapteyn with one of her two dogs, "Yin" and "Yang," in 1934.
Ph. Margarethe Fellerer. Eranos Foundation Archives, Ascona-Moscia.

148.
Olga Fröbe-Kapteyn with one of her two dogs, "Yin" and "Yang," in 1934.
Ph. Margarethe Fellerer. Eranos Foundation Archives, Ascona-Moscia.

149.
Olga Fröbe-Kapteyn, [untitled].
The image, drawn in October 1934 (period when Olga Fröbe-Kapteyn had had few analytical sessions with Carl Gustav Jung in Küsnacht, Zurich), also represent the first scene of the second Eranos *Maṇḍala*. Olga Fröbe-Kapteyn described this second *Maṇḍala* (the first originated in 1927, marking the start of the construction project of Casa Eranos—see Figure 57) as follows: "I am skating with Jung on the frozen surface of a lake. We perform tricks with our hands crossed and draw some figures. Then we trace the outline of a strictly architectural figure together, as can be seen in the image. All around, we trace the contours of an immense rose, which grows in three dimensions, and Jung and I find ourselves in the center of this ice flower. The petals fade away and only the basic outline remains. This too now grows and forms a small ice temple, whose roof is an inverted rose with many petals. Once again, Jung and I are standing in the center, holding hands. Jung was extremely impressed [by this account] and said, 'Who would have thought that you and I would find ourselves together in a *mandala*? (At the time, I didn't know what a *mandala* was, and I knew nothing about Jungian psychology). It was after the second Conference, and little by little I discovered that it [the *maṇḍala*] was basically a magic circle in which I had captured Jung, not on a whim, but because it had to be so. From then on, he no longer wanted to work [analytically] with me. A few years later, I told him that this circle was the Eranos *Mandala*. He admitted it, but it was impossible to get anything more out of him. All this took place in a very deep layer of the unconscious, it was all ice, frozen, still lifeless. But it was the first reflection of a still very hidden model." (Olga Fröbe-Kapteyn, "Vision Oktober 1934. Zürich (Während ich einige Mal bei Jung war). Die Eranos *Mandala*" (unpublished typescript, Zurich, October 1934; Eranos Foundation Archives, Ascona-Moscia).
"Visions," Series III ("Oktober. 1934. Arbeit bei Dr. Jung"), no. 51, October 16, 1934. Pastel and pencil on onion skin paper, mounted on cardboard.

150.
Olga Fröbe-Kapteyn, [untitled].
The image, drawn in October 1934 (period when Olga Fröbe-Kapteyn had had few analytical sessions with Carl Gustav Jung in Küsnacht, Zurich), represent the second scene of the second Eranos *Maṇḍala*. Olga Fröbe-Kapteyn wrote: "Jung and I are skating together on the ice and drawing this *mandala* on the ice. First a geometric plant, a cross with angles. Then a rose grows three-dimensionally, with the two of us standing together in the center. Then the rose disappears, and the plant remains, now rising three-dimensionally like a transparent temple, and we are once again in the center. This circle is the origin of the other circles of Eranos in this group. Twelve years passed between this first drawing and the others." (Olga Fröbe-Kapteyn, "Die Eranos *Mandala*" (unpublished typescript, 1927–49). Eranos Foundation Archives, Ascona-Moscia).
"Visions," Series III ("Oktober. 1934. Arbeit bei Dr. Jung"), no. 52, October 28, 1934. Pastel and pencil on onion skin paper, mounted on cardboard.
Eranos Foundation Archives, Ascona-Moscia.

151.
Olga Fröbe-Kapteyn, Eranos *Maṇḍala*, no. 2.
In June 1953, Olga Fröbe-Kapteyn recalled: "When I set up a shrine dedicated to Hermes in the Archive, I also set up one dedicated to Jung. For this reason, I placed not only the texts on Hermes there, but also all [Jung's] seminars! The shrine is also dedicated to the Eranos *Mandala*, in the form of a Round Table, [its] external concretization. This brings me back to the vision of Jung and me skating (dancing?) the *mandala* in 1934. And Jung said, 'Shiva and Shakti are in the middle of the *mandala*. The Dance of Creation.' So I had this projection onto him again: Shiva and Hermes!" (Olga Fröbe-Kapteyn, [untitled] (unpublished typescript, June 29, 1953; Eranos Foundation Archives, Ascona-Moscia). Referring to this "*Maṇḍala*," Jung said to her, "There are others inside too!" She noted how, in her opinion, the archetypal configuration of Eranos had already "captured" others, such as Mary Elizabeth ("Mima") Conover Mellon (1904–1946) in 1938, when, on her first visit to Eranos with her husband Paul (1907–1999), upon entering the garden of Casa Gabriella, she instantly thought: "This is my place, I belong here!" "So she took possession of Eranos, and vice versa. That is, a total and immediate identification was generated. There were then strong projections on both sides. I think I discovered that it was not her who said, 'This is my place,' but Eranos itself, which had already taken possession of her." (Olga Fröbe-Kapteyn, "Mellon Problem" (unpublished typescript, Winter 1941; Eranos Foundation Archives, Ascona-Moscia).
"Eranos Mandala," 1927–49. Pastel and pencil on paper.
Eranos Foundation Archives, Ascona-Moscia.

152.
Olga Fröbe-Kapteyn and Carl Gustav Jung at Casa Eranos in August 1935. At the Conference that August, Jung spoke about "The Meaning of Symbols in Psychic Experience." The lecture developed as a psychological commentary on a series of fifty-nine dreams by physicist Wolfgang Ernst Pauli (1900–1958), which Jung commented on, identifying the archetypal images that describe the process of centering, or the formation of a new center of personality. The essay was published the following year under the title "Individual Dream Symbolism in Relation to Alchemy—A Study of the Unconscious Process at Work in Dreams" and later became part of his book *Psychology and Alchemy* (1944).
Ph. Margarethe Fellerer. Eranos Foundation Archives, Ascona-Moscia.

153.
Olga Fröbe-Kapteyn, [untitled].
"Visions," Series V, no. 104, c. January 1935. Pastel and pencil on onion skin paper, mounted on cardboard.
Eranos Foundation Archives, Ascona-Moscia.

154.
A view of Casa Eranos from Lake Maggiore in 1935.
Ph. Margarethe Fellerer. Eranos Foundation Archives, Ascona-Moscia.

155.
Olga Fröbe-Kapteyn, [untitled].
"Visions," Series VI, no. 127, c. February–March–April 1935. Pastel and pencil on onion skin paper, mounted on cardboard.
Eranos Foundation Archives, Ascona-Moscia.

156.
A view of Casa Eranos and Lake Maggiore in 1935.
Ph. Margarethe Fellerer. Eranos Foundation Archives, Ascona-Moscia.

157.
Olga Fröbe-Kapteyn, *The Temple and the Golden Falls*.
"Visions," Series VI, no. 131, c. February–March–April 1935. Pastel and pencil on onion skin paper, mounted on cardboard.
Eranos Foundation Archives, Ascona-Moscia.

158.
A view of Casa Eranos from Lake Maggiore in the mid-1930s.
Ph. Margarethe Fellerer. Eranos Foundation Archives, Ascona-Moscia.

159.
Olga Fröbe-Kapteyn, [untitled].
This series of "Visions" immediately follows the "ritual" officiated by Carl Gustav Jung in August 1935, with him in the role of priest and Olga Fröbe-Kapteyn in that of the person who was being initiated (cf. pp. 67-69). "In front of a hut on a mountain slope sits Jung, looking down into the valley. He is waiting. I climb up the path from the valley; I carry the fruit of the lotus in my hand. Jung stands up, and we walk up the mountain together. It grows dark. Around the lotus fruit appear snow blossoms, with white petals, and they glow—they serve us as a lamp. The light shines over the snowfields; it is not snow but a slight cover of blossoms that everywhere break open and cover the violet snow blossoms—thus, it is actually a blooming meadow. The full moon rises over the peaks, and we see that we are in the midst of a silent crowd moving in a cross form, like an army moving upward. We are at the center of the cross. We walk onto a wide plateau, and the cross of the crowd spreads above us like a floor plan. It is also one. Jung and I stand opposite each other in the middle. Each is like a gate, a portal, for the other. I step into him and he into me, and we find ourselves in the middle of a temple. The entire space is filled with Templars. A gigantic vine grows from the center of the room, and its tendrils of ripe grapes form the roof of the temple. Between us stands a chalice-shaped altar, upon which is a wide, shallow bowl of wine. I still hold the lotus fruit, surrounded by the petals of the blooming flower, in my hands. I say: 'The flower is rising. Let the hour not pass unfulfilled!' Jung takes the lotus fruit from my left hand and places it in his right. I give him the lotus fruit in my right hand as well. He breaks it open crosswise, and blood-red seeds become visible. Three fall to the ground like three drops of blood. Jung says: 'The secret of the vine is now ours.' He lets the fruit fall into the chalice, it floats on the white flower petals, held by the wine, like on a pond. A sudden wind rises and carries the vines around us—We don't know where it comes from, nor where it goes. It circles us, closer and closer and more intensely, until we are fused together. Jung says: 'We stand in the living Spirit. His pinions are around us. The seed is ripe!' The Templars step into the inner circle around us, and to each one is given a red seed from the lotus fruit. The wine that was first golden has now turned red, like blood. The vine, like a world tree, bears two kinds of grapes, purple and gold, dark and light. They are broken open, and their juice drips down. It smells strongly of wine. It is as though the vine itself is bleeding. One branch hangs over us, with a large double grape, one dark and one light. Jung breaks off the grape and lays it on the fruit in the bowl..." (Olga Fröbe-Kapteyn, "10. Sept. 35" (unpublished typescript, September 26, 1935; Eranos Foundation Archives, Ascona-Moscia).
"Visions," Series VIII, no. 159, September 1935. Pastel and pencil on onion skin paper, mounted on cardboard.
Eranos Foundation Archives, Ascona-Moscia.

160.
Olga Fröbe-Kapteyn, [untitled].
The vision continues: "... The lotus fruit expands, turns into a chalice, becomes liquid, and transparent like a ruby. A red glow fills the room. The vine itself, the swaying vine of the Templars, is bathed in this red light, allowed to pass through. Jung says: 'The healing—the healing that touches nothing!' The four phases are completed!" (Fröbe-Kapteyn, "10. Sept. 35," cit.).
"Visions," Series VIII, no. 160, c. October 6–8, 1935. Pastel and pencil on onion skin paper, mounted on cardboard.
Eranos Foundation Archives, Ascona-Moscia.

161.
Olga Fröbe-Kapteyn, [untitled].
Olga Fröbe-Kapteyn continued: "I stand before the lotus flower, behind it the Hermaphrodite … On the lotus fruit lies a honeycomb full of honey. It looks like a sealed book, and seven seals are attached to it. It is also naturally 'sealed' with the wax of the comb. It appears as if the dew that covered the blossom in the earlier vision has now condensed into this amber-colored jewel in the lotus." (Olga Fröbe-Kapteyn, "13. bis 18. Okt. 35. London" (unpublished typescript, October 13–18, 1935; Eranos Foundation Archives, Ascona-Moscia).

162.
Olga Fröbe-Kapteyn, [untitled].
Olga Fröbe-Kapteyn commented: "I take the honeycomb and eat it. That is, I eat the 'book with the seals.' In doing this, I unite myself with the innermost secret of the lotus, the Hermaphrodite, the transcendent function. The sealed mystery dissolves into my substance, we are one and the same, and I recognize it." (Fröbe-Kapteyn, "13. bis 18. Okt. 35…," cit.).
"Visions," Series VIII, no. 162, c. October 13, 1935. Pastel and pencil on onion skin paper, mounted on cardboard.

163.
Olga Fröbe-Kapteyn, [untitled].
Olga Fröbe-Kapteyn commented: "Transformation: Now I sit together with Jung; we have become a single being. A golden heart lies open on the chest of this figure. On the knees rests an open golden book, which we point to. Above us is the form of the Hermaphrodite, now winged, who envelops us with his wings. He wears a kind of mitre." (Fröbe-Kapteyn, "13. bis 18. Okt. 35...," cit.).
"Visions," Series VIII, no. 163, c. October 19, 1935. Pastel and pencil on onion skin paper, mounted on cardboard.
Eranos Foundation Archives, Ascona-Moscia.

164.
Olga Fröbe-Kapteyn, [untitled].
Olga Fröbe-Kapteyn commented: "Here I sit crowned in a red-golden robe. My heart, golden in color, lies oversized and visible in the middle of my chest. Within it is an open book, from which I read. From the crown of my head rises a chalice-shaped formation of light, and two blue horns of light. I myself have become the Horned One, who had already appeared in drawings two years ago. (On Sunday, November 17, thus a month later, again near full moon, a nearly unknown man brought me a small pot of honeycomb, with two long wheat rolls and a fruit. The rolls looked like fish. The honeycomb looked like my large topaz, as if it had dissolved.)" (Fröbe-Kapteyn, "13. bis 18. Okt. 35…," cit.).
"Visions," Series VIII, no. 164, c. October 19, 1935. Pastel and pencil on onion skin paper, mounted on cardboard.
Eranos Foundation Archives, Ascona-Moscia.

165.
Olga Fröbe-Kapteyn, [untitled].
Olga Fröbe-Kapteyn commented: "The first picture is the Baptism, possibly the Baptism of Blood? The Vine grows up on both sides of me, and the grapes above my head are as if, being pressed, the juice or blood being gathered in the chalice which rises from my head. Full to the brim, the juice flows over the edge of the Cup, and I am drenched in the stream." (Olga Fröbe-Kapteyn, "From 22 October onwards. London" (unpublished typescript, from October 22 onwards, 1935; Eranos Foundation Archives, Ascona-Moscia).
"Visions," Series VIII, no. 165, c. October 22, 1935. Pastel and pencil on onion skin paper, mounted on cardboard.

166.
Olga Fröbe-Kapteyn, [untitled].
Olga Fröbe-Kapteyn commented: "With outstretched arms I form a Cross, touching the Grapes on either side. Around and within my body is the Vine, within and without are the same." (Fröbe-Kapteyn, "From 22 October onwards. London," cit.).
"Visions," Series VIII, no. 166, c. October 24, 1935. Pastel and pencil on onion skin paper, mounted on cardboard.

167.
Olga Fröbe-Kapteyn, [untitled].
Olga Fröbe-Kapteyn noted: "Within the Grape, I dance with Jung, each taking the innermost Grape of the other, an interchange of being, an answer in movement, one to the other. I remember the words of Christ in the Hymn of Jesus: 'Now answer to My dancing!' It is the opposite of the first two pictures of the Passion of the Vine, here the blissful, rhythmic creative Dance, yet happening simultaneously with the Passion." (Fröbe-Kapteyn, "From 22 October onwards. London," cit.).
"Visions," Series VIII, no. 167, c. October 26, 1935. Pastel and pencil on onion skin paper, mounted on cardboard.
Eranos Foundation Archives, Ascona-Moscia.

168.
Olga Fröbe-Kapteyn and Carl Gustav Jung among the lotus flower of the Eranos garden in August 1936. The four lectures given by Jung that August, on the theme of "Representations of Liberation in Alchemy," held the audience at Eranos spellbound for two entire mornings: it was the first time that most of those present realized how alchemy—in which Jung believed he had found a historical antecedent to his psychology—was something extremely relevant and akin to a modern process of psychological and inner transformation. The reworking of this paper was later included, as "Religious Ideas in Alchemy—An Historical Survey of Alchemical Ideas," in *Psychology and Alchemy* (1944).
Ph. Margarethe Fellerer. Eranos Foundation Archives, Ascona-Moscia.

169.
Lotus flowers in the Eranos garden in the 1930s.
Olga Fröbe-Kapteyn had a fondness for the lotus flower, which at the time grew wild on the lake in front of Casa Gabriella. In August 1930, on the occasion of Shri Vishwanath Keskar's lecture "On the Lotus," she had arranged numerous lotus flowers in the Eranos Hall.
Ph. Margarethe Fellerer. Eranos Foundation Archives, Ascona-Moscia.

170.
(From left) Anna Margarethe (Gret) Baumann-Jung (1906–1995), Barbara Hannah (1891–1986), Emma Jung-Rauschenbach (1882–1955), Carl Gustav Jung, Max Pulver (1889–1952), Jolan (Jolande) Jacobi (1890-1973), Olga Fröbe-Kapteyn, and Antonia Anna (Toni) Wolff (1888–1953), among others, attend Orientalist Paul Masson-Oursel's (1882–1961) lecture on "The Idea of Liberation in India" in the Lecture Hall of Casa Eranos in August 1936.
Ph. Margarethe Fellerer. Eranos Foundation Archives, Ascona-Moscia.

171.
A female image presented by Princess Maria Alix von Hohenzollern-Sigmaringen (1901–1990) for the Eranos Archive for Research in Symbolism, which Olga Fröbe-Kapteyn began composing in 1934 at the request of Carl Gustav Jung.

172.
Carl Gustav Jung, Princess, Princess Maria Alix von Hohenzollern-Sigmaringen, and Baroness Hertha Jay-von Seldeneck at Monte Verità in August 1936.
Ph. Margarethe Fellerer. Eranos Foundation Archives, Ascona-Moscia.

173.
Olga Fröbe-Kapteyn, [Visions of the Lohan – untitled].
In Paris, between February and June 1936, while she was engaged in iconographic research for the Eranos Archive for Research on Symbolism on Carl Gustav Jung's behalf, Olga Fröbe-Kapteyn had a vision of an entity called "Lohan." She wrote to Jung: "Regarding my work, the following: for almost a week, I have been having a visionary conversation with a personality I call 'Lohan,' because he looks like the 'Lohan' in the British Museum. You probably know this life-size figure in polychrome terracotta. I have had a reproduction of it in my room for years, but I have never had any other contact with this Chinese man. The conversation has the character of an initiation, a dialogue between guru and disciple, and at the same time between members of an alliance. The 'Lohan' sits within a *mandala*, and so even during the day he is always in front of me where I am." (Olga Fröbe-Kapteyn, letter to Carl Gustav Jung, February 15, 1936, c/o Mme de Martchenko, 39 rue de l'Arbalete, Paris 5e (University Archives, ETH-Bibliothek, Zurich / Eranos Foundation Archives, Ascona-Moscia)).
"Visions," Series IX, no. 193, February 11, 1936. Pastel and pencil on onion skin paper, mounted on cardboard.

174.
The painting depicting the Chinese statue in polychrome terracotta of the Lohan in the living room of Casa Gabriella, where Olga Fröbe-Kapteyn lived. "Lohan" (or "luohan") is the Chinese term for an arhat, i.e., a perfect being who has attained *nirvana*, according to the Buddhist tradition of the first and oldest vehicle (see its reproduction in Jessica Rawson, ed., *The British Museum Book of Chinese Art* (London: British Museum Press, 1992)).
Ph. Tim Gidal. Eranos Foundation Archives, Ascona-Moscia. All rights reserved.

175.
Olga Fröbe-Kapteyn, *Restoration of Energy*.
In one of the teachings imparted to Olga Fröbe-Kapteyn, the Lohan spoke to her as follows: "You have bathed in the Light, and have been made new. / You have entered the Palace of the King, / you have seen the White Rose beyond the Veil. / Wait in stillness that the Light may fill you. / It will go before you like a burning cloud, / dark places will be lighted, hindrances melt before It. / Lay all care aside and tend the Light. / You know the Secret: Give! And expect naught in return. / Serve and ask not for Power. / Serve and fear naught. The perfect Sphere / of Light, within and without / is invulnerable. / And again the Secrets: / Serve in perfection, / achieve each task in perfection, / move in balance on the straight and narrow Path. / You know not, your God knoweth. / Leave therefore to Him the solution of the darkness, / for you live within His Flame ..." (Olga Fröbe-Kapteyn, "Feb. 5.36. Paris" (unpublished typescript, February 5, 1936; Eranos Foundation Archives, Ascona-Moscia).
"Visions," Series IX, no. 195, February 16, 1936. Pastel and pencil on onion skin paper, mounted on cardboard.

176.
Olga Fröbe-Kapteyn, *The Opening of the Gates*.
In another teaching given to Olga Fröbe-Kapteyn, the Lohan continued to instruct her as follows: "… There is a Way—and a Way—and a Way. / Only the Middle Way leads to Me / and to Those Whose Secret I now teach you. / You have learnt to read the Signs, / learn now to read our Message in the Signs. / Open the Gates, that those who stand without / may enter in …" (Olga Fröbe-Kapteyn, "14 April 36" (unpublished typescript, April 14, 1936; Eranos Foundation Archives, Ascona-Moscia).
"Visions," Series X, no. 203, April 8, 1936. Pastel and pencil on onion skin paper, mounted on cardboard.
Eranos Foundation Archives, Ascona-Moscia.

177.
Olga Fröbe-Kapteyn, [untitled].
"Visions," Series X, no. 214, c. April 23–27, 1936. Pastel and pencil on onion skin paper, mounted on cardboard.
Eranos Foundation Archives, Ascona-Moscia.

178.
A view of Lake Maggiore and the surrounding mountains from Eranos in 1934.
Ph. Margarethe Fellerer. Eranos Foundation Archives, Ascona-Moscia.

179.
Olga Fröbe-Kapteyn, [untitled].
In a subsequent teaching, the Lohan explained further to Olga Fröbe-Kapteyn (who, as she often did, translated this dialogue into a synthetic vision, in this case also depicting Casa Eranos, the "House of Power," resting on her lap): "The Secret of the *Mandala* and of Energy are One. The Mystery of Singleness and of Relationship is contained therein. / There is a Communion Within and Without, as there is the incoming and the outgoing Tide of the Sea. / The Workers of the Middle Way are One; / they are the Ring of Fire around the Central House of Power. / This is the Order from within to the Without: / The Flower of Gold—the ball of Gold—the Ring of Gold or thus: / The Flower of Fire—the Ball of Fire—the Ring of Fire or thus again: / The Flower of Light—the Ball of Light—the Ring of Light. / Light, Fire and Gold are terms of Energy. / Its Circulation, Radiation and its Centrifugal Force are its modes. / Man is the Gateway to the Gold, and Fire and Light. / The Centre moves and leaps from each to each of those who take their place within the Game. / The inflow and the outflow of the Vital Stream, / the Rhythm of the Tide of Vital Power obeys to the Law ..." (Olga Fröbe-Kapteyn, "14 to 19 June 36" (unpublished typescript, June 14–19, 1936; Eranos Foundation Archives, Ascona-Moscia).
"Visions," Series X, no. 224, June 12, 1936. Pastel and pencil on onion skin paper, mounted on cardboard.

180.
Olga Fröbe-Kapteyn, [untitled].
The Lohan continued to teach to Olga Fröbe-Kapteyn: "Double is the Chain of the Work, / Two Steeds in one Harness, / You and C.G. [Jung] / Seven Years in darkness,— / now seven Years in the Sun. / Each Cycle runs its Term under Law. / Still pendeth the Hour of Meeting in completeness, / you between the two cycles it must strike. / Before you hold that Tryst / I teach you the Secret of the *Mandala*, the Mystery of the Centre." And again: "The Centre is One and Twofold. / Two Partners walk the Middle Way, / and meet beneath the Tent of Tryst. / The meet in Tao, / and they build the House of Power, by the consummation of their union. / The House is the Vessel of the Creator, / is the Graal, the Sphairos and the Stone, / for He alone createth, within Whom they are contained." (Olga Fröbe-Kapteyn, "June 3.36" (unpublished typescript, June 3, 1936; Eranos Foundation Archives, Ascona-Moscia); and Id., "14 to 19 June 36" (unpublished typescript, June 14–19, 1936; Eranos Foundation Archives, Ascona-Moscia).
"Visions," Series X, no. 225, June 23, 1936. Pastel and pencil on onion skin paper, mounted on cardboard.

181.
Olga Fröbe-Kapteyn, [untitled].
Towards the end of the series of teachings given by Lohan, he said to Olga Fröbe-Kapteyn: "By the Ring you were pledged unto the Isolation of Tao, / and the Communion that passeth understanding. / Once the Seal is upon you, there is no more questioning. / You were sealed by the Ring beyond all Time, / therefore the Sealed Doors have opened. / The Centre of the *Mandala* is Unleashed, / and the Middle Way passes through to That / Experience Which is Unnameable (without Name)." (Olga Fröbe-Kapteyn, "15.6 36" (unpublished typescript, June 15, 1936; Eranos Foundation Archives, Ascona-Moscia).
"Visions," Series X, no. 228, July 4, 1936. Pastel and pencil on onion skin paper, mounted on cardboard.

182.
Olga Fröbe-Kapteyn at Eranos in the mid-1930s.
Ph. Margarethe Fellerer. Eranos Foundation Archives, Ascona-Moscia.

183.
Olga Fröbe-Kapteyn, [untitled].
In September 1936, Olga Fröbe-Kapteyn had the following vision: "I am standing in the Eranos Hall. Where the lecturer's platform usually is, a curtain now falls—a veil-like fabric covered with a pattern of palms and pomegranates. In front of it stands an angel … He begins to spin—to dance. Like veils, his transformations pass over him: from female to male, from male to female, from Logos to Eros and back again, moving in a double pattern, where one thing alternates and overlaps with the other. It is like a game in a living fountain of two kinds of water, or also of two kinds of light—dark and light, silver and gold, white and red. It is also like a healing spring, the spring that is 'full' and that also 'heals,'— the vibrating, dual essence. For a long time I watch …" (Olga Fröbe-Kapteyn, "Vision. 11 Sept. 36" (unpublished typescript, September 11, 1936; Eranos Foundation Archives, Ascona-Moscia)).
"Visions," Series XI, no. 248, September 1, 1936. Pastel and pencil on onion skin paper, mounted on cardboard.
Eranos Foundation Archives, Ascona-Moscia.

184.
Olga Fröbe-Kapteyn, [untitled].
Olga Fröbe-Kapteyn's account of the vision continues: "Then I feel that the angel's transformations begin to touch me—I begin to spin and dance in the same rhythm. Now we are drawn into the center of the room, toward each other. And the contact happens. We flow into one another like wine and water, merging—and the dance continues. At times we separate again, then flow back together. Sometimes I am the female part and the angel the male, sometimes the reverse. It is a circling of two forces, two powers, two poles, which are also one and the same. Thus the union is fulfilled. In the end, we are spinning in one form of glowing red crystalline light." (Fröbe-Kapteyn, "Vision. 11 Sept. 36," cit.).
"Visions," Series XI, no. 249, September 1, 1936. Pastel and pencil on onion skin paper, mounted on cardboard.

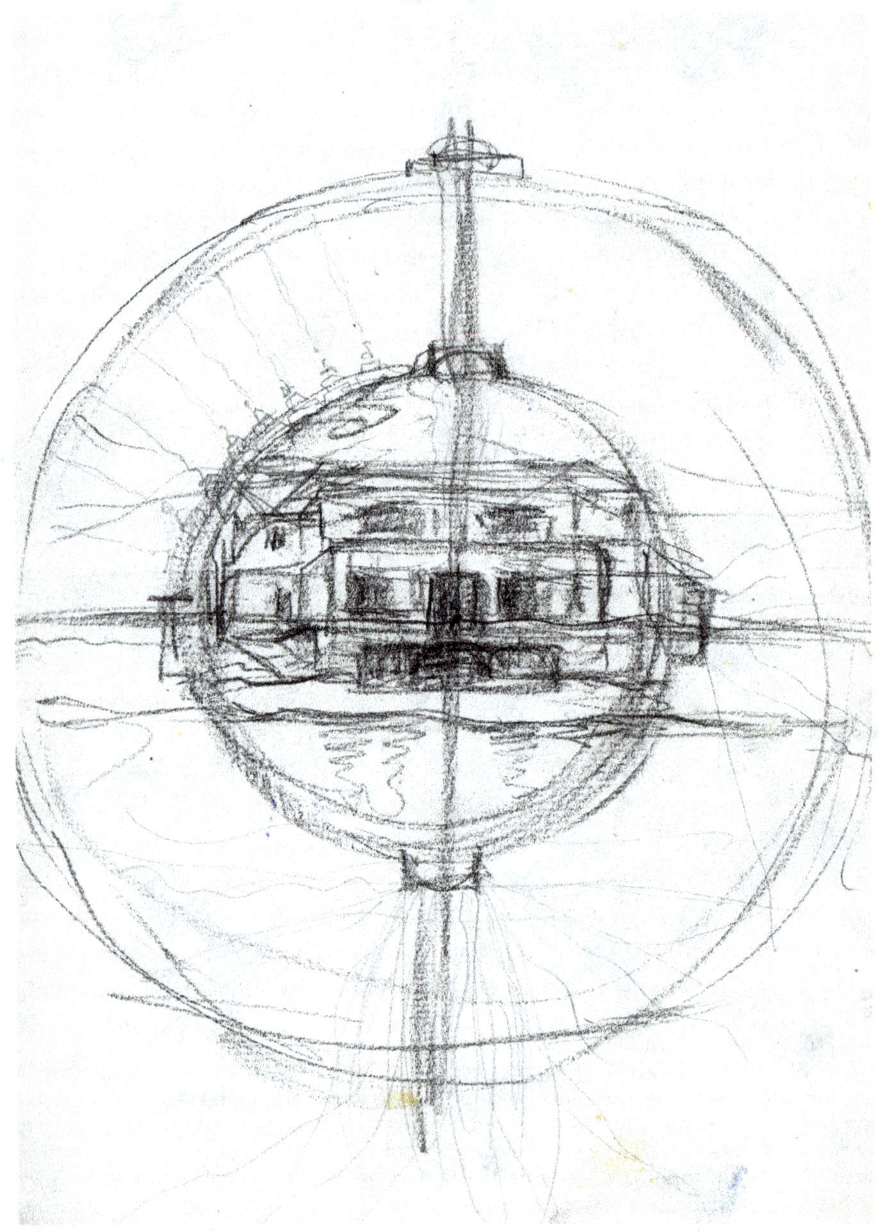

185.
Olga Fröbe-Kapteyn, [untitled].
It can be seen that, above the Lecture Hall, Casa Eranos here also houses the "Eranos Studio" on the upper floor.
"Visions," out-of-series, sketch for not numbered vision [no. 308], June 1937. Pencil on onion skin paper.
Eranos Foundation Archives, Ascona-Moscia.

186.
Olga Fröbe-Kapteyn, [untitled].
It can be seen that, above the Lecture Hall, Casa Eranos here also houses the "Eranos Studio" on the upper floor.
"Visions," out-of-series, not numbered [no. 308], June 1937. Pastel and pencil on onion skin paper, mounted on cardboard.
Eranos Foundation Archives, Ascona-Moscia.

187.
Olga Fröbe-Kapteyn, *Die Grosse Mutter* ["The Great Mother"].
A series of visions entitled "The Descent into Hell" covers a period from December 1937 to May 1941. In 1937, Olga Fröbe-Kapteyn informed Jung of her intention to collect images of the "Great Mother" for the Eranos Archive (a theme referred to in the "Vision" reproduced here). During that research, in January 1938, she experienced the "maternal aspect of hell" in the form of a cave covered with black breasts, from which milk flowed (the image reminded her of the Artemis of Ephesus (or Artemis Farnese), a sculpture dating from the second century AD of the goddess Artemis in yellow alabaster, kept at the National Archaeological Museum in Naples). Subsequently, between September and November 1938, she continued her research in Athens, Crete, and Rome. The second version of the vision, in October 1939, in Crete, took the form of the myth of the Cretan labyrinth and the encounter with the Minotaur. There she had "the greatest experience" of her life: while searching for archaeological traces of the "Great Mother," she was completely "inflated." In the Palace of Knossos in particular, where a snake god was worshipped in ancient times, she saw herself as an "island of ancient traditions." The third version, in June 1940, took place in the Catacombs of Priscilla in Rome, where the Deus Absconditus (the "Hidden God") appeared as the Great Ape. The fourth vision, in May 1941, originated from the awareness that she had suppressed the most vital details in her previous accounts, which she was then able to integrate with the help of the "White Elephant," an imaginary animal present in some of her last "Visions." This animal signaled to her that the process had to take place in the Viśuddha Chakra, the fourth, located in the throat, where the union of masculine and feminine takes place and psychic events reveal themselves as reality: a symbol of the sense of psychological reality, it does not allow deception, and therefore, if details have been withheld, it forces one to take a step back and review them (Olga Fröbe-Kapteyn, "Deus Absconditus (The Descent into Hell)" (unpublished typescript, May 1941; Eranos Foundation Archives, Ascona-Moscia).
"Visions," out-of-series, not numbered [no. 309], June 1937. Pastel and pencil on onion skin paper, mounted on cardboard.

188.
Olga Fröbe-Kapteyn, [untitled].
In this vision, part of the "Descent into Hell" series, the crucifixion is synchronized with rebirth: such visions represented for her a "liberation" of the image of her mother Geertruida, whom she imagined finding at the bottom of "hell," prey to the psychological suffering she had endured, and whom she now felt capable of freeing and "bringing back up" with her to the surface, just like a "rebirth": "The walls of Hell are of brown earth, and are covered with brown breasts, from which milk is flowing. I filled my hands with milk and let my mother drink, which she did as if in great thirst." This "reconciliation of blood" also concerned the "liberation" of her father Albert, her husband Iwan, her daughters Bettina and Ingeborg, and the entire line of her family clan. This process was for her a journey through the Chakras, first descending and then ascending, in a spiral, serpentine movement: it was also a double flow, consisting of the two blood streams of her parents and their respective ancestors, the maternal and paternal blood. At the same time, the original blood of all the generations of her ancestors flowed from her womb: "Now I am alone. My parents and all my ancestors are contained within me and are alive in my consciousness as never before." (Olga Fröbe-Kapteyn, "Die Höllenfahrt. Mitte Dezember 37 bis 6 Februar 38. London und Holland" (unpublished typescript, mid-December 1937–February 6, 1938; Eranos Foundation Archive, Ascona-Moscia); Id., "22–24 Dez 37" (unpublished typescript, December 22–24, 1937; Eranos Foundation Archive, Ascona-Moscia); Id., "11 Jan. 38" (unpublished typescript, January 11, 1938; Eranos Foundation Archive, Ascona-Moscia); these documents belong to "Die Höllenfahrt [Erste]. Dez. 37 bis März 38" (unpublished typescript, December 1937–March 1938; Eranos Foundation Archive, Ascona-Moscia)). The cross was for her the image of fear, of the "censor," which had always existed between herself and herself. Suddenly she realized that she was sweating blood: it was coming out of the pores of her skin, like the painful opening of hundreds of sealed eyes. "Sweating blood" meant fear to her, because life was finally flowing out of her (Olga Fröbe-Kapteyn, "The White Elephant" (unpublished typescript, 1940; Eranos Foundation Archive, Ascona-Moscia)).
"Visions," out-of-series, not numbered [no. 310], April 1938. Pastel and pencil on onion skin paper, mounted on cardboard.
Eranos Foundation Archives, Ascona-Moscia.

189.
Olga Fröbe-Kapteyn, [untitled].
As her vision evolved, the cross crumbled. A violent sexual encounter forced upon her by a male deity evolved into the castration of the god; his phallus, castrated by her and then expelled from her mouth, drunk with divine blood, now became a golden fish (or red, in another version): "The wound of the God takes on the form of a chalice, and I continue to drink from it. The multitude draws near and one by one they drink of the Blood and are renewed. Now they see, hear, smell, taste, touch, as I do. They are liberated from the Shadow of the Cross, they are reborn. Each approaches me, embraces me, and vanishes from my sight, as if drawn into myself. Their life is now added to mine. Light is radiating from God, he is no longer dark. He stands holding the Chalice, which is Himself and from which we have all drunk. I know now that this is the Mystery of the Grail ... The orgasm of sex has been transformed into an ecstasy of the heart. This must be the last Unsealing, after the unsealing of all the senses. And I feel that this whole experience might be called, 'the Book of Transformations.' It is also the Book with 7 Seals of the Apocalypse." (Olga Fröbe-Kapteyn, "Lisbon. Oktober 40" (unpublished typescript, October 1940; Eranos Foundation Archives, Ascona-Moscia); Id., "Ascona-Lisbon-New York-Ascona. August 1940 to May 1941" (unpublished typescript, May 4, 1941; Eranos Foundation Archives, Ascona-Moscia); and Id., "The Circle and the Point," cit.).
"Visions," out-of-series, not numbered [no. 311], undated [1938]. Pastel and pencil on onion skin paper, mounted on cardboard.

190.
Olga Fröbe-Kapteyn and Carl Gustav Jung at the Eranos Conference of August 1938, dedicated to "Form and Cult of the 'Great Mother.'" Jung gave a two-part presentation on "The Psychological Aspect of the Great Mother." Although the subject interested him, writing this lecture was a considerable sacrifice for Jung, as he wanted to return to the study of alchemy as soon as possible. His lecture inaugurated a line of research on the subject of female psychology, which would culminate in the publication of Erich Neumann's (1905–1960) *The Great Mother—An Analysis of the Archetype* (New York, NY/London: Bollingen Series XLVII, Pantheon, Routledge & Kegan Paul, 1955), which is the only publication ever produced of the Eranos Archive for Research in Symbolism.
Ph. Margarethe Fellerer. Eranos Foundation Archives, Ascona-Moscia.

191.
Carl Gustav Jung and Olga Fröbe-Kapteyn at the Round Table on the terrace of Casa Gabriella, at the occasion of the Eranos Conference of August 1940, dedicated to the theme "Sources and Beginnings of Christianity." Jung, whose name did not appear in the Conference program, was greatly impressed by the lecture given by mathematician Andreas Speiser (1885–1970), the only one actually scheduled due to the difficulties of the war, on the theme "The Platonic idea of the unknown God and the Christian Trinity." He therefore asked for a Bible and, in the afternoon, retired to the garden of Eranos, praying not to be disturbed. Although he had arrived with the intention of remaining a mere listener, the next day he improvised a lecture lasting about an hour and a half, in response to Speiser's, on the theme "On the Psychology of the Idea of the Trinity."
Ph. Margarethe Fellerer. Eranos Foundation Archives, Ascona-Moscia.

192.
Olga Fröbe-Kapteyn at Eranos at 58 years old in August 1940.
Ph. Margarethe Fellerer. Eranos Foundation Archives, Ascona-Moscia.

193.
Olga Fröbe-Kapteyn in c. 1940–1944.
Ph. Margarethe Fellerer. Eranos Foundation Archives, Ascona-Moscia.

194.
Bettina Gertrude Fröbe in the 1940s.
Ph. Margarethe Fellerer. Eranos Foundation Archives, Ascona-Moscia.

195.
Leaving their estate in Rokeby, Virginia, together with their one-year-old daughter Cathy in March 1938, Mary Elizabeth Conover Mellon and Paul Mellon stopped in London until early May, waiting to travel to Zurich to meet Jung and attend the spring session of his seminar on Nietzsche's *Zarathustra*. Here Paul Mellon hired the painter Gerald Leslie Brockhurst (1890–1978) to paint portraits of Mary and Cathy. Intent on meeting Olga Fröbe-Kapteyn after Jung's seminar, the future creators of the Bollingen Foundation then left for Ascona. Years later, Mary Mellon would write to Fröbe-Kapteyn that the first thought that crossed her mind when she set foot on the terrace of Casa Gabriella and in the garden of Eranos was: 'This is where I belong.'
Ph. unknown. Eranos Foundation Archives, Ascona-Moscia.

196.
Amethyst necklace that belonged to Mary Mellon, who died suddenly in October 1946, at the age of just 42, from a severe asthma attack. With her passing, Olga Fröbe-Kapteyn lost a source of spiritual and material support, which had been fundamental to him until that point. Her death also jeopardized the survival of the Eranos Archive for Research in Symbolism, which was in fact donated in the 1950s to the Warburg Institute in London, as well as the conference project, which Fröbe-Kapteyn imagined could continue in the United States, with the help of the Mellons, if Switzerland were invaded by Nazi Germany. In 1947, Paul Mellon sent Fröbe-Kapteyn the jewel that had belonged to his wife, who had wanted her friend to have something of hers. Coming to terms with her separation from Mary Mellon was an emotionally difficult process for Fröbe-Kapteyn. Several years earlier, Jung had written to Fröbe-Kapteyn that the great disappointment she felt following the breakdown of relations with the Bollingen Foundation, which had been severed by the US side for reasons related to the war, could be traced back to her more or less unconscious "adoption" of Mary Mellon as her daughter, that is, her belief that Mary would continue Eranos. Once again, he warned her against identifying herself with her work: "Your heart should not be tied to anything, because it belongs only to the Self. Everything else is transient." (Carl Gustav Jung, letter to Olga Fröbe-Kapteyn, January 17, 1943 (University Archives, ETH-Bibliothek, Zurich / Eranos Foundation Archives, Ascona-Moscia; © 2007 Foundation of the Works of C.G. Jung, Zurich)).
Ph. Riccardo Bernardini. Eranos Foundation Archives, Ascona-Moscia.

197.
Olga Fröbe-Kapteyn, *De Profundis Mihi Nunciatum Est* [the Eranos Totem].
The Eranos Totem, with which Olga Fröbe-Kapteyn describes her psychic functioning in terms of permanent ecstasy (in both its creative and problematic aspects), includes the heraldic element common to the Kapteyn and Muysken coats of arms, i.e., the fish—see *Figures 1 and 2*. The name "Olga" itself means "fish" in the language of the Chaldeans. But, she also writes, "The Totem might almost be a symbol of Eranos: and of the times: the synthesis of the values of the Past, in a cultural and religious sense, into the Host; or the New Sun, the New Dawn of an Age. Eranos is taking its place in that happening, a small place, yet a creative one." (Olga Fröbe-Kapteyn, "The Totem-Lingam. Vision and drawing Pfingsten 1942" (unpublished typescript, Pentecost 1942). Eranos Foundation Archives, Ascona-Moscia).)
1942. Mixed techniques on wood.
Eranos Foundation Archives, Ascona-Moscia.

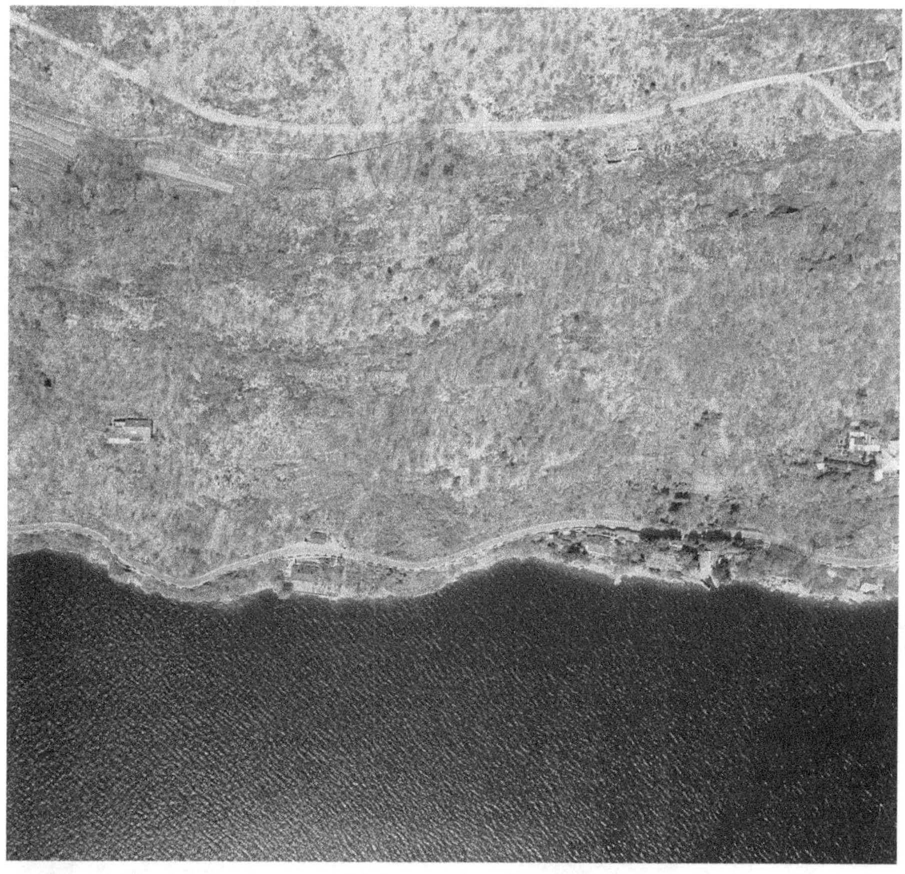

198.
Aerial photograph of the Moscia area of Ascona, with Casa Eranos, Casa Gabriella, Casa Shanti, and the "Hut," in 1943.
Federal Office of Topography Swisstopo.

199.
Olga Fröbe-Kapteyn, Eranos *Maṇḍala*, no. 3.
The third Eranos *Maṇḍala*, titled "The fourfold breathing," drawn by Olga Fröbe-Kapteyn in 1947.
"Eranos Mandala," 1927–49. Pastel and pencil on paper.
Eranos Foundation Archives, Ascona-Moscia.

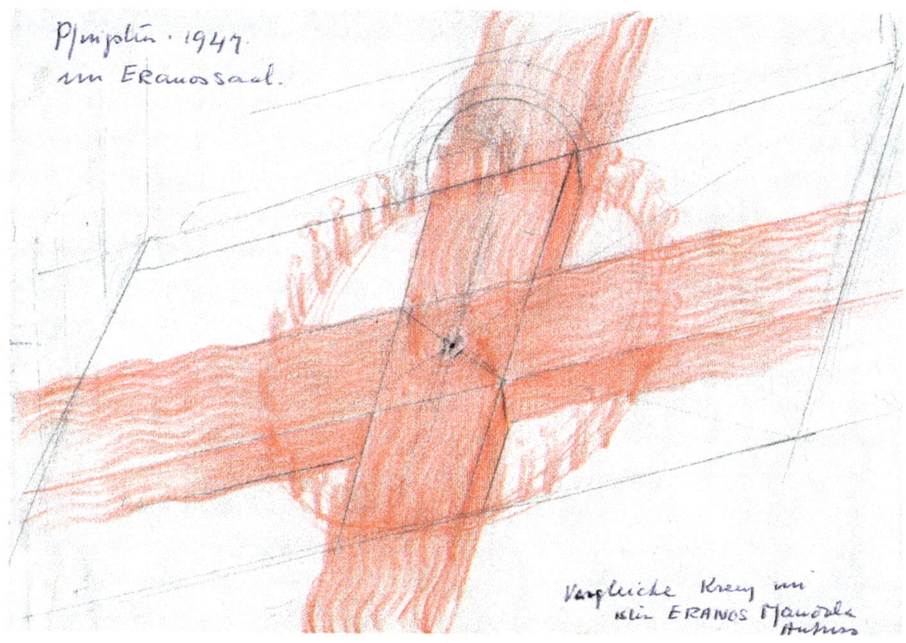

200.
Olga Fröbe-Kapteyn, Eranos *Maṇḍala*, no. 4.
The fourth Eranos *Maṇḍala*, drawn at Pentecost 1947. During a concert, Olga Fröbe-Kapteyn saw a thin, immaterial Rosy Cross, horizontal in shape, crossing the entire Eranos Hall, formed by flowing waves of color, immaterial, like a moving mist. During the music, she also saw ancient alchemists coming from the garden and entering the hall: they were the "ancestors" of Eranos. This flowing cross, which was already present in the first Eranos *maṇḍala* in 1927, but was there on the ice, had now become alive and had the color of life, blood, and roses. Carl Gustav Jung then entered the hall and took his place between her and the outer circle of alchemists.
"Eranos Mandala," 1927–49. Pastel and pencil on paper.

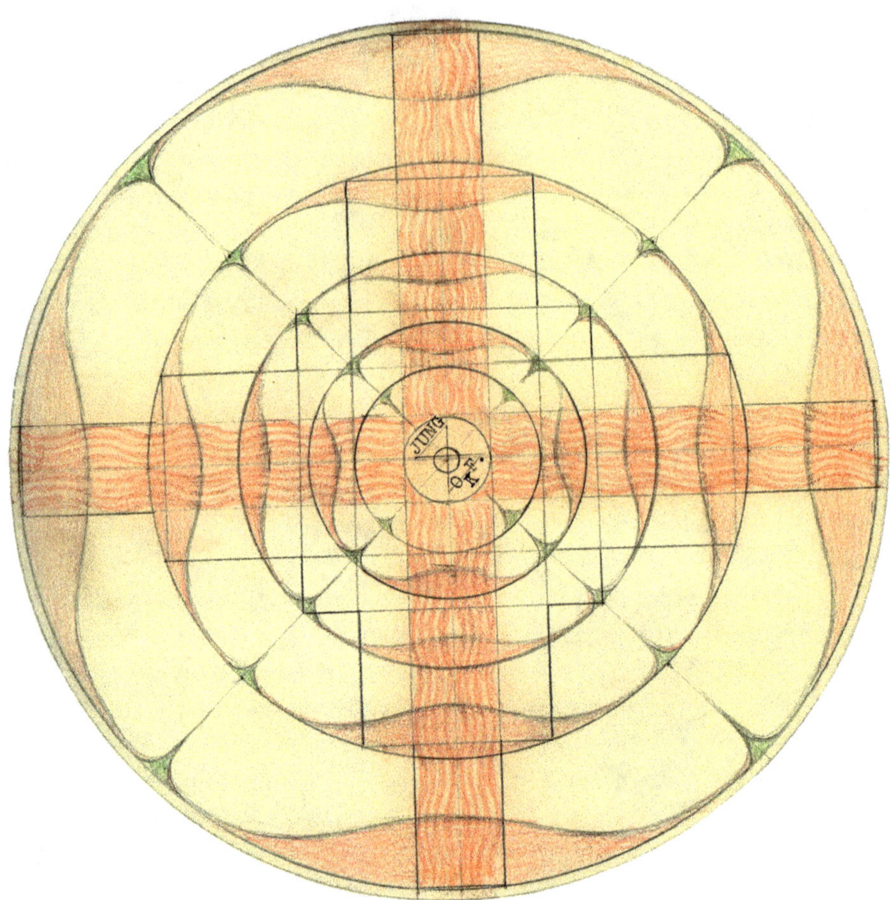

201.
Olga Fröbe-Kapteyn, Eranos *Maṇḍala*, no. 5.
The fifth Eranos *Maṇḍala* also dates back to Pentecost 1947, which Olga Fröbe-Kapteyn intuitively experienced as a transformation of the fourfold current of "rosy breath" present in the previous image into a current of "milk," flowing from the center of the figure. The figures of Carl Gustav Jung and Olga Fröbe-Kapteyn are still present at the center of the configuration, this time identified by their names.
"Eranos *Mandala*," 1927–49. Pastel and pencil on paper.
Eranos Foundation Archives, Ascona-Moscia.

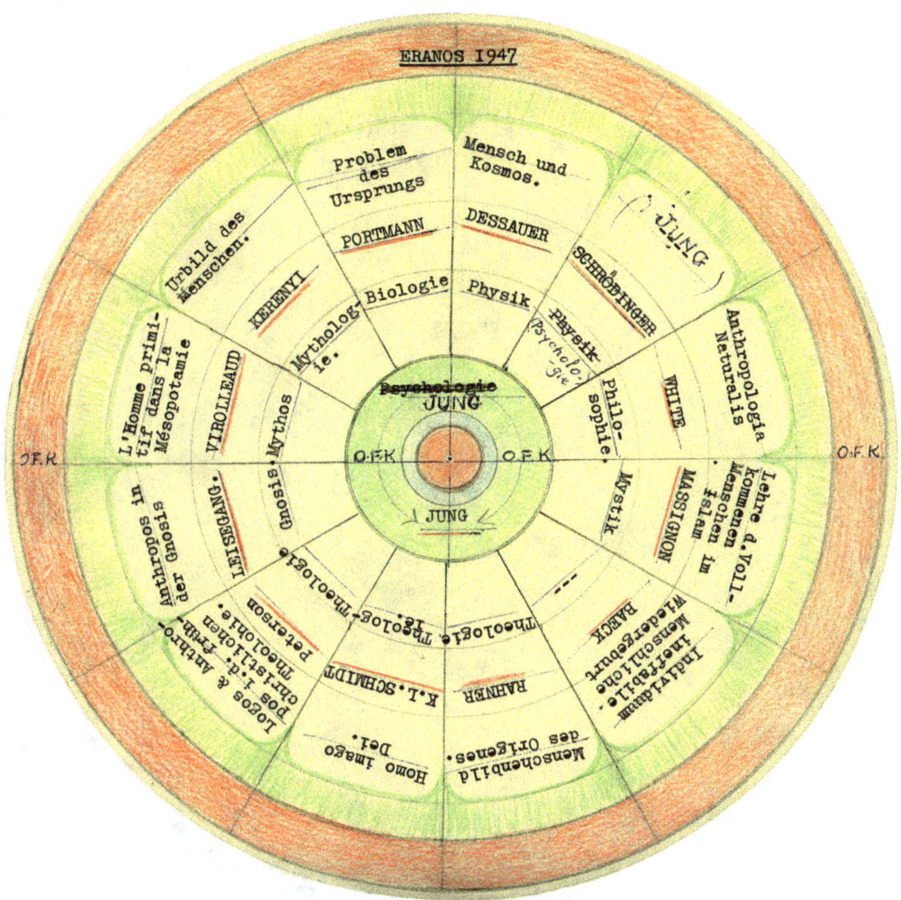

202.
Olga Fröbe-Kapteyn, Eranos *Maṇḍala*, no. 6.
In the sixth Eranos *Maṇḍala*, painted in 1947, the disciplines represented at that year's Conference, on the theme "The Human Being," are arranged in a circle; their center is identified by a circular motion that unites the names of Carl Gustav Jung and Olga Fröbe-Kapteyn. She described this image as "the true *mandala*, or Circle, of Eranos." The *Maṇḍala*, from its original frozen configuration, was now revitalized and made even more dynamic by means of the dance of mother and father—a spiritual dance or game performed at every Conference. The center of the *Maṇḍala* is empty: there is the idea we call "Eranos." The lecturers revolve around this center. Each represents an idea for the duration of their lecture. The circle closest to the center is that of Psychology, represented by Jung. The twelve sections of the circle, comparable to the petals of the lotus flower, are all connected to the center and the psychological circle. Yet none of the fields of research is more important than another; in their connection to the center, in fact, they are equivalent. Each Eranos program stages a similar circle. Behind this circle are all the previous circles or programs. They are always present. All the lecturers from previous Conferences stand invisibly but effectively behind the speakers of the 1947 program.
"Eranos *Mandala*," 1927–49. Pastel and pencil on paper.
Eranos Foundation Archives, Ascona-Moscia.

203.
Olga Fröbe-Kapteyn, Eranos *Maṇḍala*, no. 7.
In the seventh Eranos *Maṇḍala*, painted in 1948, Olga Fröbe-Kapteyn illustrated the themes of the Conferences from 1933 to 1948, explaining that at the heart of each symposium is a circular image, in which all the gatherings are synchronistic. No Conference has priority, none is first or last; all previous lecturers are invisibly behind each speaker. In front of today's speakers are all those yet to come, whom we do not yet know. Anyone who has spoken at least once at the Conference is forever in the *Maṇḍala*, that is, connected to Eranos. Psychology has this function of connection and cohesion. For this reason, the psychological zone is closest to the center in the *Maṇḍala*.
"Eranos *Mandala*," 1927–49. Pastel and pencil on paper.
Eranos Foundation Archives, Ascona-Moscia.

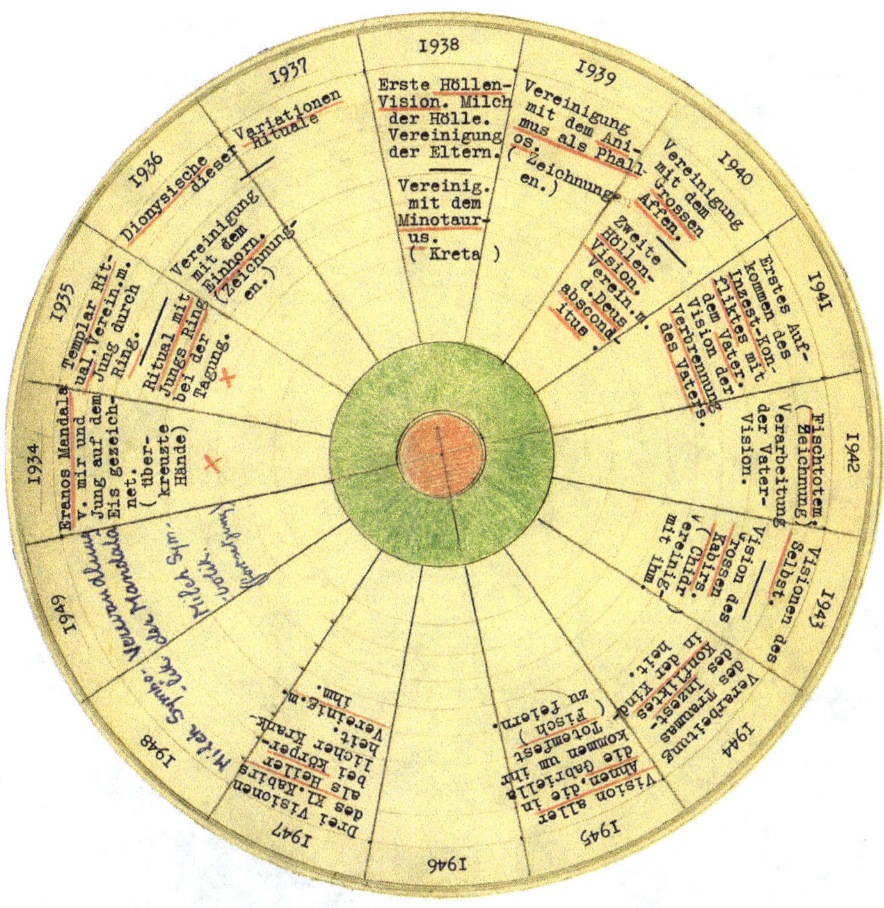

204.
Olga Fröbe-Kapteyn, Eranos *Maṇḍala*, no. 8.
In the eighth and final Eranos *Maṇḍala*, created in 1949, the visions and drawings of the fourteen years are arranged in a circle around a center. Brought back to a single common denominator, they all represent the *coniunctio*. And, precisely, with the spirit of the earth (*Erdgeist*), i.e., the Nature. On the outer edge of the circle, the years are represented, yet the visions are synchronistic, bursting into time only one at a time. In a document probably written that same year, Olga Fröbe-Kapteyn added: "This process can only be communicated in Images, in the same way that it can be only experiences in Images. The various stages are therefore expressed as separate images or patterns in TIME. There are however essentially and in the TIMELESS synchronistic and form together or can be reduced to One Single Image, the CIRCLE and the POINT. All is contained in this simple figure, and with it I return to the first hour I had with Jung in 1934, when he spoke for an hour on the Circle and the Point." (Olga Fröbe-Kapteyn, "The Circle and the Point" (unpublished typescript, 1949; Eranos Foundation Archives, Ascona-Moscia)).
"Eranos *Mandala*," 1927–49. Pastel and pencil on paper.
Eranos Foundation Archives, Ascona-Moscia.

205.
The Eranos Round Table in 1947. Olga Fröbe-Kapteyn gave to this photograph the title "*Die Tafelrunde wartet*" ("The Round Table is waiting.") When Carl Gustav Jung saw this picture, he said: "The image is perfect: they are all there." As expressed by Fröbe-Kapteyn particularly in the sixth Eranos *Maṇḍala* of 1947, each Eranos Conference, organized around an invisible circular model, would make possible the simultaneity and coexistence of themes and lecturers from the past, present, and future. Yet, when she once told Jung that a speaker who had given a lecture at Eranos even once was there forever, even if he never spoke at Eranos again, he replied, "Never say that to a professor."
Ph. Margarethe Fellerer. Eranos Foundation Archives, Ascona-Moscia.

206.
Olga Fröbe-Kapteyn and Dutch historian of religions Gerardus van der Leeuw (1890–1950) at the Eranos Round Table in c. 1948–1949.
Ph. Margarethe Fellerer. Eranos Foundation Archives, Ascona-Moscia. All rights reserved.

207.
(From left) Emma Jung-Rauschenbach, Erich Neumann, Aniela Jaffé (1903–1991), John David ("Jack") Barrett, Jr. (1903–1981) of the Bollingen Foundation, Carl Gustav Jung, philosopher, theoretical physicist, historian of science, and financier Lancelot Law Whyte (1896–1972), Olga Fröbe-Kapteyn, and scholar of Gnosis Gilles Quispel (1916–2006), among others, at the Eranos Round Table, on the terrace of Casa Gabriella, in August 1952.
(Ph. Margarethe Fellerer. Eranos Foundation Archives)

208.
(From left) Pauline Catherine Ritsema-Gris (1917–2007), Olga Fröbe-Kapteyn, psychologist Erich Neumann, and his wife Julie Neumann-Blumenfeld (1905–1985) at the Eranos Round Table, on the terrace of Casa Gabriella, in the late 1950s. Behind Fröbe-Kapteyn, the monument dedicated "to the unknown spirit of the place" (*genio loci ignoto*) sculpted by Paul Speck (1896–1966), from an idea that Carl Gustav Jung and Gerardus van der Leeuw shared in August 1949.
Ph. Tim Gidal. Eranos Foundation Archives, Ascona-Moscia.

209.
Olga Fröbe-Kapteyn at Casa Gabriella in the late 1950s.
In September 1946, Olga Fröbe-Kapteyn had a vision that emblematically documents her profound relationship with Casa Gabriella and the Eranos Archive for Research into Symbolism, which he would soon donate to the Warburg Institute in London following a long and laborious process of inner separation: "I am crouching on the 'Hearthstone' of the living room in the Gabriella, 'keening' like a Celtic woman in the old legends (lamenting) over the separation from the Gabriella, which in the vision is called 'the HOUSE of IMAGES.' Before me on the hearthstone, in the dying embers of a fire lies a large, heart-shaped red, transparent stone, the colour of blood, flecked with gold. This seems to be the 'HEART-STONE,' a stone—yet not a stone, for it is pulsing with my own pulse and is alive. As if it had been cut out of my body and laid upon the fire. From it, veinlike red cords go out to all things in the house, and to every picture in the Archive. These veins are filled with my blood and the Heart is mine. Through it I am bound to the Gabriella and to the Archive, that is—to the House of Images. From the Heart come Sounds, a song without words, Words of Power circling the room in the strong wind which is blowing through it. I wonder whether I can get through this circling Wind, and put my hand into it. But it is almost flattened back against my arm, and I realise that I cannot stand against it. It is a more effectual barrier to my escape than a circle of fire could be ..." (Olga Fröbe-Kapteyn, "Vision. 5 Sept. 46" (unpublished typescript, September 5, 1946; Eranos Foundation Archives, Ascona-Moscia)).
Ph. Tim Gidal. Eranos Foundation Archives, Ascona-Moscia.

210.
Olga Fröbe-Kapteyn at Casa Gabriella in 1958.
The "Heart-Stone" vision continues: "I see a candle lying on the hearth, and I take it and light it at the dying embers of the fire. Getting up, I know that my hour has come (*Es ist in der Zeit*). As I arise with the burning candle in my hand (it burns quietly, for here on the hearth is no wind)—the veinlike cords issuing from the heart snap where they enter the heart and blood pours forth, but only for a moment. Then the breaks are sealed, and the cords lie lifeless and withered. No more blood passes from the Heart to the Images. The Heart-Stone seems to become more and more transparent and its pulse becomes stronger within myself. Finally even its outline disappears, and I realise that my heart has come back to me. Life is added to me in the form of warmth and energy and a new vibration. Candle in hand, I step into the circle of wind and find that the flame does not waver. Its radius seems to stretch beyond the house, and I am free to pass out into the garden. I am no more bound to the HOUSE OF IMAGES by my blood. The bond is broken and I am free of the tyranny and the power of the Images. A golden haze is spread over all nature, it is early morning and the sun is about to rise. The garden too is free of the Images which had lain so heavily upon it for many years. The garden and the mountain, the lake and the two houses are once more just themselves and not of the enormous dimensions caused by the timeless nature of the Images. All my sorrow drops away like a huge load, which I had been carrying. My exhaustion vanishes because my strength is no more flowing to the Images. The ROUND TABLE on the terrace is solitary, and I sit down there alone. I place the burning candle in the exact middle of the table, and I know that between that CANDLE and myself is a relationship, a new thing, never experienced before." (Fröbe-Kapteyn, "Vision. 5 Sept. 46," cit.). With the decision to give up the Archive, she realized: "I have lived an archetypal or mythological life. Now I am becoming human, having freed myself—I suppose—from the world of archetypes. This is a kind of rebirth." (Olga Fröbe-Kapteyn, [untitled] (unpublished typescript, October 17, 1950; Eranos Foundation Archives, Ascona-Moscia), p. 3).
Ph. Tim Gidal. Eranos Foundation Archives, Ascona-Moscia.

211.
Olga Fröbe-Kapteyn with Pauline Catherine Ritsema-Gris and graphologist Anita Forrer (1901–1996) in the alleys of Casa Eranos in the late 1950s.
Ph. Tim Gidal. Eranos Foundation Archives, Ascona-Moscia.

212.
(From left) Pauline Catherine Ritsema-Gris, biologist and zoologist Adolf Portmann (1897–1982), Sister Margrit Guhl, Olga Fröbe-Kapteyn at 79–80 years old, Rudolf Ritsema, and John David (Jack) Barrett, Jr. (1903–1981) of the Bollingen Foundation in 1961.
Ph. unknown. Eranos Foundation Archives, Ascona-Moscia.

213.
Olga Fröbe-Kapteyn at 79–80 years old with Rudolf Ritsema in 1961.
Ph. unknown. Eranos Foundation Archives, Ascona-Moscia.

214.
Olga Fröbe-Kapteyn at 79–80 years old with Rudolf Ritsema in 1961.
Ph. unknown. Eranos Foundation Archives, Ascona-Moscia.

215.
Casa Gabriella and the Eranos garden in 1962, year of Olga Fröbe-Kapteyn's passing at 80 years old.
Ph. Rudolf Ritsema or Pauline Catherine Ritsema-Gris (?). Eranos Foundation Archives, Ascona-Moscia.

216.
The Eranos garden in 1962, year of Olga Fröbe-Kapteyn's passing at 80 years old.
Ph. Rudolf Ritsema or Pauline Catherine Ritsema-Gris (?). Eranos Foundation Archives, Ascona-Moscia.

217.
The Eranos garden and Casa Eranos in 1962, year of Olga Fröbe-Kapteyn's passing at 80 years old.
Ph. Rudolf Ritsema or Pauline Catherine Ritsema-Gris (?). Eranos Foundation Archives, Ascona-Moscia.

218.
The Eranos garden from Casa Eranos in 1962, year of Olga Fröbe-Kapteyn's passing at 80 years old.
Ph. Rudolf Ritsema or Pauline Catherine Ritsema-Gris (?). Eranos Foundation Archives, Ascona-Moscia.

219.
The Eranos garden in 1962, year of Olga Fröbe-Kapteyn's passing at 80 years old.
Ph. Rudolf Ritsema or Pauline Catherine Ritsema-Gris (?). Eranos Foundation Archives, Ascona-Moscia.

220.
The Eranos garden and Lake Maggiore in 1962: after Olga Fröbe-Kapteyn's passing, a new phase began for Eranos, whose work continues to this day.
Ph. Rudolf Ritsema or Pauline Catherine Ritsema-Gris (?). Eranos Foundation Archives, Ascona-Moscia.

Afterword

The harmonious interconnectedness of all of Earth's lifeforms is so beautifully perfect that it catches my breath once I see, feel, listen, and open up to being part of this oneness.

Unfortunately, our understanding of the symphony of life has drastically changed in the history of human thinking, placing ourselves above and beyond. This has been a terrible misunderstanding, which has resulted in a grave misbalance of life itself and in ourselves. We humans need to become whole again, harmonizing our analytical brain with our feelings, emotions, and intuitions; as is the goal of Eranos in Switzerland, where science and experience still go hand in hand. Science can teach us the how; experience the feelings of. Becoming whole, part of, in contact with our true inner nature can lead us to the interconnection of life on Earth, opening to the true magic of nature. Since all different forms of life on Earth and humanity are actually one, every individual healing, yours and mine, can heal the whole. We can see ourselves as a droplet of water in the ocean of life; each and every human soul's healing and clarity may bring greater clarity to the ocean of life.

At this point in history, it is the ancient cultures around the world that still retain the energy of oneness. We can learn from them by understanding their way of life, starting from ourselves as the starting point for all thoughts, decisions, and actions, rather than from the ego, the individual we have been educated to become. Darwin understood that the most interconnected life forms would survive longer in the evolutionary process. These truths were understood by Mrs. Olga Fröbe-Kapteyn in the twentieth century. She was inspired by Eastern and Western cultures, and now we can observe her interconnection with nature through her art. As Riccardo Bernardini mentions, in her *Blue Book* she seems to suggest that the "secret" of Eranos lies precisely in its roots in nature. The garden of Eranos itself was for Mrs. Fröbe-Kapteyn a metaphor for a "garden of all schools" (*Garten aller Hochschulen*), whose "warmth" and "motherly aspect" had protected a "risky" (*riskant*), "uncertain" (*unsicher*), and "endangered" (*in Gefahr*) scientific work.[1]

Mrs. Fröbe-Kapteyn lived in an era when it was mainly women who were open to mystical experiences felt deep within their souls, connecting them with nature and beyond, with the cosmos itself. I understand why my mother, Queen Juliana, recognized the value of Mrs. Fröbe-Kapteyn's research. When Queen Juliana, who was interested in the phenomenology of religions, invited Mrs. Fröbe-Kapteyn to her residence for tea on October 19, 1951, to hear about Eranos, all the *Eranos-Jahrbücher* published up to that point were prominently displayed on a shelf in her library. That meeting took place on the very day of Mrs. Fröbe-Kaptetyn's seventieth birthday. She recalled my mother's simplicity, her lack of any formality, and her interest in everything that was going on at Eranos; these elements made the two hours of conversation particularly light.[2] Moreover, on the occasion of the August 1951 Eranos Conference dedicated to the theme "Man and Time," a short silent documentary was shot, with the aim of

[1] Olga Fröbe-Kapteyn, "Vorwort," *Eranos-Jahrbuch*, 23 (1954), p. 6.

[2] Olga Fröbe-Kapteyn, letter to Henry Corbin, November 1, 1951 (Eranos Foundation Archives, Ascona-Moscia); also quoted in Catherine Ritsema-Gris, "L'Œuvre d'Eranos et Vie d'Olga Froebe-Kapteyn" (unpublished typescript, undated; Eranos Foundation Archives, Ascona-Moscia), p. 90 and in Riccardo Bernardini, *Jung a Eranos. Il progetto della psicologia complessa* (Milan: FrancoAngeli, 2011), pp. 52 f.; and Emma Hélène von Pelet-Narbonne, letter to Olga Fröbe-Kapteyn, October 19, 1951 (Eranos Foundation Archives, Ascona-Moscia), quoted in Ritsema-Gris, *op. cit.*, pp. 85 f. and in Riccardo Bernardini, "In analisi con Jung. I diari di Emma von Pelet," *Rivista di Psicologia Analitica*, 91 (39, 2015), pp. 228 f.; cf. also William McGuire, *Bollingen—An Adventure in Collecting the Past* (Princeton, NJ: Bollingen Series, Princeton University Press, 1982), p. 144. Fröbe-Kapteyn wrote about her "connection to the spiritual blood of my ancestors also [as] a connection to the collective Dutch psyche and its 'mother' Juliana. In psychological terms: to the Self" (Olga Fröbe-Kapteyn, "Anschluss an den Blutstrom der Ahnen" (unpublished typescript, May 22, 1952; Eranos Foundation Archives, Ascona-Moscia); and Id., "The Blood Consciousness and the Feeling function" (unpublished typescript, undated [1952?]; Eranos Foundation Archives, Ascona-Moscia). A reference to their meeting also appears in a late handwritten untitled note by Olga Fröbe-Kapteyn (Eranos Foundation Archives, Ascona-Moscia). [Editorial note by Riccardo Bernardini].

showing Queen Juliana a glimpse of the "Eranos life." I wonder if my mother and Mrs. Fröbe-Kapteyn watched it together when they met.[1]

Unfortunately, I never spoke to my mother about her meeting with Mrs. Fröbe-Kapteyn and her spiritual interest in the topics discussed at Eranos, because back then, even more so than today, people were shy about sharing these inner mystical experiences. This is sad, because sharing these feelings, even if words are often insufficient to describe what one has seen, heard, or understood, can help others to be less shy about talking about their most intimate truths.

Focusing on ourselves has taken us as far as it can; conflicts and killings leave nothing but fear and anger; our anthropocentric lifestyle is no longer fulfilling, because it can only bring more emptiness. Now we need to embark on a long journey to lose ourselves and discover that we are more than we know when we are in harmony with the Earth. In other words, to become, to recognize what it means to be truly human. Whole. And to know: I am because nature is.

This book will unite the world of science and inner experience for you. While awaiting a future complete edition of Mrs. Fröbe-Kapteyn's wonderful *Blue Book*, I wish you an exciting and inspiring read.

Her Royal Highness Princess Irene of the Netherlands
Champéry, June 2, 2025

[1] Ximena de Angulo-Roelli and Willy Roelli, *Eranos 1951* (Los Angeles, CA: C.G. Jung Institute of Los Angeles, 1951).

Bibliography

Abt, Theodor, *Introduction to Picture Interpretation. According to C.G. Jung* (Zurich: Living Human Heritage, 2005).

Abtei Thelema, ed., *Oriflamme*, 95 (September 23, 1969).

Afschar, Yasmin, "Olga Fröbe-Kapteyn: conoscenza profonda / Olga Fröbe-Kapteyn: Deep Knowledge," in Raphael Gygax, ed., *Olga Fröbe-Kapteyn. Artista—ricercatrice. Volume pubblicato in occasione della mostra Olga Fröbe-Kapteyn: artista-ricercatrice, Museo Casa Rusca, Locarno, 8 agosto 2024–12 gennaio 2025* (Locarno/Ascona/Bellinzona: Museo Casa Rusca/Fondazione Eranos/Casagrande, in collaboration with Kunsthalle Mainz, 2024), pp. 106–16.

Aidt, Naja Marie, *Har døden taget noget fra dig så giv det tilbage. Carls bog* (København: Gyldendal, 2017).

Amman, Jean-Cristophe, and Suter, Margrit, ed., *Elisàr von Kupffer. Kunsthalle, Basilea 1979* (Basel/Muttenz: Schwabe & Co. AG, 1979).

Ammann, Ruth, Kast, Verena, and Riedel, Ingrid, eds., *Das Buch der Bilder. Schätze aus dem Archiv des C.G. Jung-Instituts Zürich*, (Ostfildern: Patmos, 2018).

Andrigo Moreira de Ulhoa Coelho, Mônica, *Imagens de Almas: Um encontro entre Hilma af Klint e Carl G. Jung* (São Paulo: privately printed, 2010).

Anthony, Maggy, *The Valkyries—The Women Around Jung* (Shaftesbury, Dorset: Element Books Limited, 1990).

Assagioli, Roberto, *Educare l'uomo domani. Appunti e note di lavoro* (Florence: Istituto di Psicosintesi, 1988).

Aurobindo, Sri, *Gedanken und Einblicke. Studie über das Yoga des Shri Aurobindo von N.K. Gupta. Vorrede von J. Herbert, Übersetzung aus der*

Originalausgabe in Arya Pondichery von Alwina von Keller (Zurich: Rascher, 1943).
— *Die Mutter. Aus dem Englischen übertragen von Alwina v. Keller*, 2 vols. (Zurich: Rascher, 1945).
Baader, Meike Sophia, "Reformpädagogik, Religiosität und Frauenbewegung als Wege zur Selbstverwirklichung: Alwine von Keller," in Hein Retter, ed., *Reformpädagogik. Neue Zugänge – Befunde – Kontroversen* (Bad Heilbrunn, Obb.: Julius Klinkhardt, 2004), pp. 35–59.
Badt, Kurt, *The Art of Cezanne* (Berkeley, CA: University of California Press, 1956).
Bailey, Alice Ann, "August 1930," 1930 (unpublished typescript, 1930; Eranos Foundation Archives, Ascona-Moscia).
— and Fröbe-Kapteyn, Olga, "International Centre for Spiritual Research. First Session. August 1930" (unpublished typescript, 1930; Eranos Foundation Archives, Ascona-Moscia).
— and Fröbe-Kapteyn, Olga, "International Centre for Spiritual Research. Program of Lectures. Second session. August 2nd to 22nd, 1931" (unpublished typescript, 1931; Eranos Foundation Archives, Ascona-Moscia).
— *The Unfinished Autobiography of Alice A. Bailey* (New York, NY: Lucis Publishing Co., 1951).
Baillet, Philippe, "Monte Verità (1900–1920) ou la complexité du 'romanticisme anticapitaliste.' Une première approche historique et bio-bibliographique," *Politica Hermetica*, 14 (2000), pp. 199–218.
— "Monte Verità: Une 'communité alternative' entre mouvance völkisch et avant-garde artistique," *Nouvelle Ecole*, 52 (2001), pp. 109–35.
Bair, Deirdre, *Jung—A Biography* (New York, NY: Little, Brown and Company, 2003).
Bancroft, Mary, *Autobiography of a Spy* (New York, NY: William Morrow, 1983).
Barassi, Sebastiano, "Arte e anti-arte: due dadaisti in Ticino / Art and anti-art: two dadaists in the Ticino," in Riccardo Carazzetti and Mara Folini, eds., *L'energia del luogo. Jean Arp, Raffael Benazzi, Julius Bissier, Ben Nicholson, Hans Richter, Mark Tobey, Italo Valenti. Alla ricerca del genius*

loci Ascona-Locarno (Ascona/Locarno/Milan: Museo comunale d'arte moderna/Città di Locarno, Servizi culturali/Armando Dadò, 2009), pp. 95–101.

Barone, Elisabetta, Fabris, Adriano, and Monceri, Flavia, eds., *Eranos. Monte Verità. Ascona* (Pisa: ETS, 2003).

— Riedl, Matthias, and Tischel, Alexandra, eds., *Pioniere, Poeten, Professoren. Eranos und der Monte Verità in der Zivilisationsgeschichte des 20. Jahrhunderts* (Würzburg: Eranos Neue Folge XI, Königshausen & Neumann, 2004).

Beraldo, Michele, "Krishnamurti nell'occhio della polizia politica," in Gianfranco De Turris, ed., *Esoterismo e fascismo* (Rome: Mediterranee, 2006), pp. 67–73.

Berk, Tjeu van den, *In de ban van Jung. Nederlanders ontdekken de analytische psychologie* (Alblasserdam: Meinema, 2014).

Besant, Annie, and Leadbeater, Charles Webster, *Thought-Forms: A Record of Clairvoyant Investigation* (London: Theosophical Publishing Society, 1905).

Bernardini, Riccardo, "Da Monte Verità a Eranos. Elementi di una rete culturale per lo studio della psiche e della complessità umana," M.A. Dissertation, Facoltà di Psicologia, Università degli Studi di Torino, Turin, 2003.

— "'Picnic' del sogno: una matrice di sogno sociale a Eranos," *Anamorphosis. Gruppi, psicologia analitica e psicodramma*, 4 (4, 2006), pp. 67–72.

— "Collezionando ricordi: Margarethe Fellerer, fotografa di Eranos, e Carl Gustav Jung," in Gian Piero Quaglino, Augusto Romano, and Riccardo Bernardini, eds., *Carl Gustav Jung a Eranos 1933–1952* (Turin: Antigone, 2007), pp. 133–41.

— "Carl Gustav Jung a Eranos. Il contributo junghiano al Circolo di Eranos: ideazione, contributi e iniziative dal 1933 al 1952," Ph.D. Dissertation, Dottorato di Ricerca in Studi religiosi: Scienze sociali e studi storici delle religioni, Alma Mater Studiorum—Università di Bologna, Bologna, 2009.

— *Jung a Eranos. Il progetto della psicologia complessa*, forewords by Fabio Merlini, Gian Piero Quaglino, Maurizio Gasseau, and Hans Thomas

Hakl, afterword by Her Royal Highness Princess Irene of the Netherlands, Princess of Lippe-Biesterfeld and Oranje-Nassau (Milan: FrancoAngeli, 2011).

— "Jung nel giardino di Eranos: il paesaggio dell'analisi," *Eranos Yearbook*, 70 (2009–2010–2011), pp. 731–38.

— "The Secret of Eranos," *Spring: A Journal of Archetype and Culture*, 88 (2012), pp. 331–39.

— "Hillman a Eranos," *Anima* (2012), pp. 47–93.

— "La corrispondenza Carl Gustav Jung-Henry Corbin," *Historia religionum*, 5 (2013). pp. 93–108.

— "Jung nel giardino di Eranos: il paesaggio dell'analisi," in Ferruccio Vigna, ed., *L'Ombra del Flâneur. Scritti in onore di Augusto Romano* (Bergamo: Moretti&Vitali, 2014), pp. 35–46.

— "Guest Editor's Introduction," *Spring: A Journal of Archetype and Culture*, 92 (2015) ("Eranos: Its Magical Past and Alluring Future: The Spirit of a Wondrous Place"), pp. 1–26.

— Quaglino, Gian Piero, and Romano, Augusto, "Appendix II. Alwine von Keller (1878–1965). A Biographical Memoir," in Carl Gustav Jung, *The Solar Myths and Opicinus de Canistris. Notes of the Seminar Given at Eranos in 1943*, eds. Riccardo Bernardini, Gian Piero Quaglino, and Augusto Romano (Einsiedeln: Daimon, 2015), pp. 124–39; It. Ed. "Appendice II. Alwine von Keller (1878–1965). Un ricordo biografico," in Carl Gustav Jung, *I miti solari e Opicino de Canistris. Appunti del Seminario tenuto a Eranos nel 1943*, eds. Riccardo Bernardini, Gian Piero Quaglino, and Augusto Romano (Bergamo: Moretti&Vitali, 2014), pp. 139–54.

— "In analisi con Jung. I diari di Emma von Pelet," *Rivista di Psicologia Analitica*, 91 (39, 2015), pp. 219–36.

— "The Historiography of Eranos. An Homage to Hans Thomas Hakl," in Hans Thomas Hakl, ed., *Octagon—The Quest for Wholeness Mirrored in a Library Dedicated to Religious Studies, Philosophy, and Esotericism in Particular*, Vol. II (Gaggenau: scientia nova, 2016), pp. 207–23.

— "Neumann at Eranos," in Murray Stein and Erel Shalit, eds., *Turbulent Times, Creative Minds: Erich Neumann and C. G. Jung in Relationship* (Wilmette, IL: Chiron, 2016), pp. 199–236.

— "Jung nelle Nuove Edizioni Ivrea (NEI). Con la corrispondenza inedita C.G. Jung-Cesare Musatti/NEI," *L'Ombra. Tracce e percorsi a partire da C.G. Jung*, 9 (1, 2018) ("Jung e Ivrea"), pp. 167–200.

— "Nota introduttiva a: Alwine von Keller: Appunti sul Cristianesimo," *L'Ombra. Tracce e percorsi a partire da C.G. Jung*, 9 (1, 2018) ("Jung e Ivrea"), pp. 333–35.

— "Nota introduttiva a: Ernst Bernhard e Alwine von Keller (?): Tema natale di Emma von Pelet e sinastria Emma von Pelet-C.G. Jung," *L'Ombra. Tracce e percorsi a partire da C.G. Jung*, 9 (1, 2018) ("Jung e Ivrea"), pp. 317–19.

— "L'ultimo Jung nella stanza di analisi," *Elephant & Castle*, 18 (2018) ("Postludi. Lo stile tardo"), pp. 4–34.

— "Donne terrene, divine e demoniache. Le iniziazioni femminili: materiali antropologici per la psicologia del profondo," in Marina Barioglio, ed., *La danza delle streghe. Energie femminili per una pedagogia spregiudicata* (Milan: FrancoAngeli, 2018), pp. 176–90.

— and Merlini, Fabio, "Olga Fröbe-Kapteyn (1881–1962): A Woman's Individuation Process through Images at the Origins of the Eranos Conferences," *ARAS Connections: Image and Archetype*, 4 (2020), pp. 1–18.

— *Simboli di rinascita nella Basilica di San Miniato al Monte a Firenze. Da Gioacchino da Fiore a C.G. Jung / Rebirth Symbols in the Basilica of San Miniato al Monte in Florence. From Joachim of Fiore to C.G. Jung*, preface by Abbot Bernardo Francesco Gianni, O.S.B., photographs by Mariangela Montanari (Bergamo: Moretti & Vitali, 2022).

— "Itineraries of the Feminine from Monte Verità to Eranos," in Nicoletta Mongini, Chiara Gatti, and Sergio Risaliti, eds., *Monte Verità. Back to Nature* (Turin: Lindau, 2022), pp. 25–43.

— and Merlini, Fabio, "L'arte di Olga Fröbe-Kapteyn, fondatrice di Eranos," *Rivista di Psicologia Analitica*, 108 (56, 2024), pp. 281–303.

— and Merlini, Fabio, "L'arte di Olga Fröbe-Kapteyn, fondatrice di Eranos," in Veronica Caciolli, ed., *Atti del convegno Arte, Mistica, Comunità, Seconda edizione. MUSEC—Museo delle Culture, Lugano, 11 e 12 febbraio 2022* (Milan: Postmedia Srl, 2024), pp. 34–44.

— and Merlini, Fabio, "Il *Libro blu* di Olga Fröbe-Kapteyn, fondatrice di Eranos / The *Blue Book* of Olga Fröbe-Kapteyn, Founder of Eranos," in Raphael Gygax, ed., *Olga Fröbe-Kapteyn. Artista—ricercatrice. Volume pubblicato in occasione della mostra Olga Fröbe-Kapteyn: artista-ricercatrice, Museo Casa Rusca, Locarno, 8 agosto 2024–12 gennaio 2025* (Locarno/Ascona/Bellinzona: Museo Casa Rusca/Fondazione Eranos/ Casagrande, in collaboration with Kunsthalle Mainz, 2024), pp. 34–51.

— "Jung in the Garden of Eranos: The Landscape of Analysis," in Henry Abramovitch and Murray Stein, eds., *Eranos. A Play* (Asheville, NC: Chiron, 2025), pp. 127–40.

— and Merlini, Fabio, "The *Blue Book* of Olga Fröbe-Kapteyn, Founder of Eranos," *Religiographies*, 4 (1, 2025), pp. 7–39.

— "Notas sobre la historiografía de Eranos," *Interpretatio. Revista de Hermenéutica*, 10 (2, 2025) (in press).

Bernhard, Ernst, *Mitobiografia*, ed. Hélène Erba-Tissot (Milan: Adelphi, 1969).

Bernoulli, Rudolf, *Okkultismus und bildende Kunst* (Pfullingen: Baum, 1920).

— "Prof. E. Bleuler und der Okkultismus," *Zeitschrift für Parapsychologie*, 2 (1927), pp. 234–36.

— and Müller, E.K., "Experimentelles. Eine neue Untersuchung der Eigenschaften des Teleplasma," *Zeitschrift für Parapsychologie*, 6 (1931), pp. 313–21.

— "Zur Symbolik geometrischer Figuren und Zahlen: I. Allgemeines, II. Die Zahlensymbolik des Tarotsystems," *Eranos Jahrbuch*, 2 (1934), pp. 369–415.

— "Seelische Entwicklung im Spiegel der Alchemie und verwandter Disziplinen," *Eranos Jahrbuch*, 3 (1935), pp. 231–87.

Berti, Alessandro, *Roberto Assagioli 1888–1988* (Florence: Centro Studi di Psicosintesi "R. Assagioli," 1988).

Bertschinger-Joos, Esther and Butz, Richard, *Ernst Frick 1881–1956. Anarchist in Zürich, Künstler und Forscher in Ascona, Monte Verità* (Zurich: Limmat, 2014).

Besant, Annie, ed., *The Bhagavadgītā or the Lord's Song* (London: The Theosophical Publishing House Limited, 1904).

Biasca-Caroni, Andrea, *Luigi Pericle: il maestro ritrovato* (Turin: Nino Aragno, 2022).

Bignardi, Irene, *Le piccole utopie* (Milan: Feltrinelli, 2003).

Biondi, Massimo, "Orizzonti spiritici di Jung," *Luce e Ombra*, 103 (1, 2003), pp. 33–42.

Birkner, Nicoletta, and Birkner, Othmar "L'arte come espressione di una nuova vita," in Harald Szeemann, ed., *Monte Verità. Antropologia locale come contributo alla riscoperta di una topografia sacrale moderna* (Locarno/Milano: Armando Dadò/Electa, 1978), pp. 123–27.

Bishop, Paul, "The Members of Jung's Seminar on Zarathustra," *Spring* (1994), pp. 92–122.

Blavatsky, Helena Petrovna, *The Secret Doctrine* (London, Theosophical Publishing Company, 1888).

Bochsler, Regina, "Esodo dall'Egitto—Margarethe Hardegger e i coloni pionieri del *Sozialistischer Bund* nel Canton Ticino," in Andreas Schwab and Claudia Lafranchi, eds., *Senso della vita e bagni di sole. Esperimenti di vita e arte al Monte Verità* (Ascona: Fondazione Monte Verità, 2001), pp. 170–87.

Bock, Hans Manfred, and Tennstedt, Florian, "Raphael Friedeberg: medico e anarchico ad Ascona," in Harald Szeemann, ed., *Monte Verità. Antropologia locale come contributo alla riscoperta di una topografia sacrale moderna* (Locarno/Milano: Armando Dadò/Electa, 1978), pp. 38–53.

Bodmer, Hans-Caspar, Lioba, Paul, and Holdenrieder, Ottmar, "Shaping the Mountain of Truth: An Introduction to the Monte Verità," in Frank A. Klötzli and Gian-Reto Walther, eds., *Conference on Recent Shifts in Vegetation Boundaries of Deciduous Forests, Especially Due to the General Global Warming* (Basel: Birkhäuser, 1999), pp. 1–13.

— Holdenrieder, Ottmar, and Seeland, Klaus, *Monte Verità: Landschaft Kunst Geschichte* (Frauenfeld/Stuttgart/Wien: Huber, 2000).

Boesch, Ina, *Gegenleben. Die Sozialistin Margarethe Hardegger und ihre politischen Bühnen* (Zurich: Chronos, 2003).

Bollmann, Stefan, *Monte Verità: 1900. Il primo sogno di una vita alternativa* (Turin: EDT, 2019 {2017}).

Bölt, Yvonne, and Checchi, Maurizio, *Guida storico artistica di Ascona* (Ascona: Serodine, 1993).

— and Milani, Gian Piero, eds., *Ascona caleidoscopio. Storie e testimonianze del passato / Geschichten und Zeugnisse aus der Vergangenheit* (Ascona, Unicorno, 2024).

Boni, Gastone de, "Una visita a Carl Gustav Jung," *Luce e Ombra*, 49 (4, 1949), pp. 212–19.

Bottiglieri, Adele, "Eranos tra i tempi e i luoghi della storia: la metafora dell'esilio," in Elisabetta Barone, Adriano Fabris, and Flavia Monceri, eds., *Eranos. Monte Verità. Ascona* (Pisa: ETS, 2003), pp. 49–70; rpt. in Elisabetta Barone, Matthias Riedl, and Alexandra Tischel, eds., *Pioniere, Poeten, Professoren. Eranos und der Monte Verità in der Zivilisationsgeschichte des 20. Jahrhunderts* (Würzburg: Eranos Neue Folge XI, Königshausen & Neumann, 2004), pp. 127–141.

Broggini, Romano, "Anarchia e libertarismo nel locarnese dal 1870," in Harald Szeemann, ed., *Monte Verità. Antropologia locale come contributo alla riscoperta di una topografia sacrale moderna* (Locarno/Milano: Armando Dadò/Electa, 1978), pp. 15–25.

Bruijne, Rozanne de, ed., *Tussen hemel en oorlog. Kunst en religie in het interbellum*, preface by Josien Paulides, texts by Rozanne de Bruijne, Irène Lesparre, Korine Hazelzet, Lieke Wijnia, Lex van de Haterd, Tessel M. Bauduin, Katerina Sidorova, Marty Bax, Laura Stamps, and Dick Adelaar (Utrecht/Zwolle: Museum Catharijneconvent/Waanders, 2025).

— Otte, Katjuscha, Wierda, Inge S., Hazelzet, Korine, Stamps, Laura, Melse, Hanna, Custers, Anouk, Henkemans, Ingrid, Aalpoel, Elzemiek, Coppens, Linda, and Kam, René de, *Catharijne Museummanagize*, 43 (1, 2025) ("Tussen hemel en oorlog"), ed. Josien Paulides.

Butz, Richard, "Die Okkultisten von Stein AR. Mächtig geheim: Iris Blums Buch über die Psychosophische Gesellschaft und ihre ‚Collectio Magica et Occulta'," *Saiten* (November 3, 2016).

Cabot Reid, Jane, ed., *Jung, My Mother and I—The Analytic Diaries of Catharine Rush Cabot* (Einsiedeln: Daimon, 2000).

Carazzetti, Riccardo, and Folini, Mara, eds., *L'energia del luogo. Jean Arp, Raffael Benazzi, Julius Bissier, Ben Nicholson, Hans Richter, Mark Tobey, Italo Valenti. Alla ricerca del genius loci Ascona-Locarno* (Ascona/Locarno/Milan: Museo comunale d'arte moderna/Città di Locarno, Servizi culturali/Armando Dadò, 2009).

Cassirer, Eva, Liesegang, Ewa, and Weber-Schäfer, Max, eds., *Die Idee einer Schule im Spiegel der Zeit. Festschrift für Paul Geheeb zum 80. Geburtstag und zum 40jährigen Bestehen der Odenwaldschule* (Heidelberg: Lambert Schneider, undated [1950]).

Ceccarelli, Luisa, "Ellen Key e la rete delle scuole nuove in Europa (1899–1914)," Ph.D. Dissertation, Dottorato di Ricerca in Scienze Pedagogiche, Alma Mater Studiorum—Università di Bologna, Bologna, 2020.

Charet, F.X., *Spiritualism and the Foundations of C. G. Jung's Psychology* (Albany, NY: State University of New York, 1993).

Chiappini, Rudy, ed., *Arte in Ticino 1803–2003*, 4 vols., Vol. I: "La ricerca di un'appartenenza. 1803–1870"; Vol. II: "L'affermazione di un'identità. 1870–1914"; Vol. III: "Il confronto con la modernità. 1914–1953"; Vol. IV: "Il superamento delle avanguardie. 1953–2003" (Bellinzona: Salvioni, 2003).

Children's Garden School Society, *Twenty-Eight Annual Report. 1964–'65* (Mylapore, Madras: The Children's Garden School Society, 1965).

— *Golden Jubilee Year. 1937–1987. Souvenir 1987* (Mylapore, Madras: The Children's Garden School Society, 1987).

— *Let none be like another. A History of the Children's Garden School Society* (Mylapore, Madras: Children's Garden School Society, 2007).

Chiocchetti, Federica, ed., *les voix magnétiques—le voci magnetiche—die magnetischern stimmen—the magnetic voices* (Le Locle: MBAL Musée des Beaux-Arts Le Locle, 2024).

Christol, Guilherme Zacharias, *Um lugar ao sol: ensaio sobre as idéias naturistas da experiência de Monte-Veritá, Suíça, e seu desdobramento brasileiro na década de 1920*, M.A. Dissertation, Universidade Estadual de Campinas, Instituto De Filosofia E Ciências Humana, Campinas, 2015.

Corbin, Henry, "A Olga Fröbe Kapteyn" {1951}, in Chistian Jambet, ed., *Henry Corbin. L'Herne* (Paris: L'Herne, 1981), pp. 264–65.

— "I. Eranos: à la mémoire de C.G. Jung et Olga Fröbe – II. Eranos: Freiheit und Spontaneität," *Eranos-Jahrbuch*, 31 (1962), pp. 9–15.

— "De l'Iran à Eranos," *Du. Schweizerische Monatsschrift*, 15 (4, 1955) ("Eranos"), p. 29; rpt. in Chistian Jambet, ed., *Henry Corbin. L'Herne*, L'Herne, Paris 1981, pp. 261–63.

Corti, Walter Robert, "Die Eranos – Begegnungsstätte für Ost und West in Moscia-Ascona," *Schweizer Annalen*, 1 (1935), pp. 52–59.

— "Zwanzig Jahre Eranostagungen in Moscia-Ascona (Schweiz)," *Psyche*, 4 (1952–53), pp. 155–60.

— "Die Platonische Akademie im Wandel der Geschichte und als Aufgabe unserer Zeit," *Eranos Jahrbuch*, 36 (1957), pp. 387–413.

— "Nachrichten vom Plan der Akademie," *Du. Schweizerische Monatsschrift*, 15 (4, 1955) ("Eranos"), pp. 66–74.

Crimaldi, Paolo, "L'insegnamento di Eranos," *Luce e Ombra. Rivista trimestrale informativa dedicata alla ricerca psichica e ai problemi connessi*, 121 (1, 2021), pp. 29–35.

— "Il grande Insegnamento Spirituale ed Archetipico della Fondazione Eranos: un'Analisi Astrologica," *Linguaggio Astrale Plus. Trimestrale di cultura astrologica del Centro Italiano di Astrologia*, 51 (204/4, 2021), pp. 127–44.

— *Iniziazione all'Astrologia dei cicli di vita* (Rome: Mediterranee, 2023), § 5: "Due esistenze profondamente individuate: analisi psico-astrologica di Olga Fröbe-Kapteyn e di Hermann Hesse," pp. 131–48.

Crowley, Aleister, *The Confessions* (London: Mandrake, 1929).

— *Magick in Theory and Practice* (New York, NY: Magickal Childe, 1990).

Derleth, Christine, *Das Fleischlich-Geistige. Meine Erinnerungen an Ludwig Derleth* (Hessen: Hinder + Deelmann, Bellnhausen über Gladenbach, 1973).

Derleth, Ludwig, *Gedenkbuch*, texts by Lothar Helbing, Stefan George, Dominik Jost, Christine Derleth, and Anna Maria Derleth (Amsterdam: Castrum Peregrini, 1958).

Dörr, Georg, "Archetipo e storia ovvero Monaco-Ascona: prossimità tipologica e umana (con lettere di Olga Fröbe a Ludwig Derleth)," in Elisabetta Barone, Adriano Fabris, and Flavia Monceri, eds., *Eranos. Monte Verità. Ascona* (Pisa: ETS, 2003), pp. 105–21; Germ. Ed. "Archetyp und Geschichte oder München-Ascona: Typologische und menschliche Nähe (Mit einigen Briefen Olfa Fröbes an Ludwig Derleth)," in Elisabetta Barone, Matthias Riedl, and Alexandra Tischel, eds., *Pioniere, Poeten, Professoren. Eranos und der Monte Verità in der Zivilisationsgeschichte des 20. Jahrhunderts* (Würzburg: Eranos Neue Folge XI, Königshausen & Neumann, 2004), pp. 155–69.

Druvins, Ute, "Alternative Projekte um 1900. Utopie und Realität auf dem ‚Monte Verità' und in der ‚Neuen Gemeinschaft'," in Hiltrud Gnüg, ed., *Literarische Utopie-Entwürfe* (Frankfurt am Main: Suhrkamp, 1982), pp. 236–49.

Eerden, Enno van der, *Ascona: Bezield paradijs* (Amsterdam: Uitgeverij bas Lubberhuizen, 2011).

Eliade, Mircea, "Les danseurs passent, la danse reste," *Du. Schweizerische Monatsschrift*, 15 (4, 1955) ("Eranos"), pp. 60–62.

— "Paradis et Utopie: géographie mythique et eschatologie," *Eranos-Jahrbuch*, 32 (1963), pp. 211–34.

— *Fragments d'un journal I–III, 1945–1985* (Paris: Gallimard, 1973–91); It. Ed. *Giornale* (Turin: Boringhieri, 1976).

Ellenberger, Henri F., *The Discovery of the Unconscious—The History and Evolution of Dynamic Psychiatry* (New York, NY: Basic Books, 1970); It. Ed. *La scoperta dell'inconscio. Storia della psichiatria dinamica*, 2 vols. (Turin: Bollati Boringhieri, 1976).

Epting, Karl, "Der Sinn als wirkende Kraft. Über Olga Fröbe-Kapteyn, Gründerin und Leiterin der Eranos-Tagungen," *Christ und Welt*, 10 (39, September 26, 1957), p. 14.

Eschmann, Ersnt Wilhelm, "Olga Fröbe-Kapteyn. Ein Porträt" (unpublished typescript, 1958; Eranos Foundation Archives, Ascona-Moscia).

Faber, Richard, "Der Schwabinger Imperatorenstreit, (k)ein Sturm im Wasserglas. Über die Münchener Bohème im allgemeinen und die ‚Kosmiker Runde' insbesondere," in Richard Faber and Christine Holste, eds., *Kreise, Gruppen, Bünde. Zur Soziologie moderner Intellektuellenassoziation* (Würzburg: Könighausen + Neumann, 2000), pp. 37–64.

Faesi, Robert, *Erlebnisse, Ergebnisse, Erinnerungen* (Zurich: Atlantis, 1963).

Fährte, W.G., "Die Brötchen Vom Nachbartisch. Ein Brief zu O.R. Schlag von W.G. Fährte," in Peter-Robert König, ed., *Das OTO–Phänomen. 100 Jahre Magische Geheimbünde und ihre Protagonisten von 1895–1994* (Munich: Arbeitsgemeinschaft für Religions- und Weltanschauungsfragen, 1994), pp. 220–22.

Falkenberg Brown, Peter, *Waking Up Dead and Confused is a Terrible Thing—Stories of Love, Life, Death & Redemption* (Gray, ME: World Community, 2020).

Feitknecht, Thomas, eds., *„Die dunkle und wilde Seite der Seele". Briefwechsel von Hermann Hesse mit seinem Psychoanalytiker Josef Bernhard Lang. 1916–1944* (Frankfurt am Main: Suhrkamp, 2006).

Ferrara, Marianna, "Olga Fröbe-Kapteyn's *Ashram*: The Great Mother and the Personal History of Eastern Religions," *ASDIWAL. Revue genevoise d'anthropologie et d'histoire des religions*, 16 (2021), pp. 79–94.

Filoramo, Giovanni, *Il risveglio della gnosi ovvero diventare dio* (Rome-Bari: Laterza, 1990), p. 26.

— "Pic-nic ad Ascona. Eranos e i suoi autori," *Leggere*, 17 (1989–1990), pp. 24–27.

— "Fantasmi ritrovati. Il ritorno della gnosi," *Immediati dintorni* (1990), pp. 168–77.

Fiorentino, Maria, "Viaggio intorno al blu," *Giornale Storico del Centro Studi di Psicologia e Letteratura*, 15 (2012), pp. 139–50.

Fischer, Thomas, and Kaufmann, Bettina, "C.G. Jung e l'arte moderna," in Foundation of the Works of C.G. Jung, Ulrich Hoerni, Thomas Fischer, and Bettina Kaufmann, *L'arte di C.G. Jung* (Turin: Bollati Boringhieri, 2019 {2018}).

Flach, Jakob, *Ascona: Gestern und Heute* (Zurich/Stuttgart: Wernen Classen, 1960).

Fodor, Nandor, *Freud, Jung and Occultism* (New York, NY: University Books, 1971).

Folini, Mara, and Zaza Sciolli, Lidia, "La collezione del Barone Eduard von der Heydt al Monte Verità," in Manuela Khan-Rossi, ed., *Dal Seicento olandese alle avanguardie del primo Novecento. La collezione Eduard von der Heydt al Monte Verità. Sguardi sulla Collezione dello Stato del Cantone Ticino. Museo Cantonale d'Arte, 30 marzo–5 maggio 1996* (Lugano/Zurich: Museo Cantonale d'Arte/Pro Litteris, 1996), pp. 9–27.

— *Il Monte Verità di Ascona: Guide di monumenti svizzeri SSAS* (Bern: Società di Storia dell'Arte in Svizzera SSAS, 1998).

— "Percorso architettonico. Dalle capanne 'aria-luce' all'albergo del Monte Verità," in Andreas Schwab and Claudia Lafranchi, eds., *Senso della vita e bagni di sole. Esperimenti di vita e arte al Monte Verità* (Ascona: Fondazione Monte Verità, 2001), pp. 77–89.

Fortune, Dion, *Psychic Self-Defense* (London: Rider & Co., 1930).

— *The Magical Battle of Britain* [Cheltenham: Skylight, 2012 {1939}).

— "Lettera mensile n° 18, per il maggio 1944 – 'Introduzione alla Psicologia Esoterica,'" in Id., *La battaglia magica d'Inghilterra* (Rome: Tre Editori, 2000), pp. 185–89.

Foundation of the Works of C.G. Jung, Ulrich Hoerni, Thomas Fischer, and Bettina Kaufmann, eds., *The Art of C.G. Jung* (New York, NY: W.W. Norton & Company, Inc., 2018); It. Ed. *L'arte di C.G. Jung* (Turin: Bollati Boringhieri, 2019).

Franzosini, Edgardo, *Sul Monte Verità. Romanzo* (Milan: Il Saggiatore, 2014).

Frecot, Janos, Geist, Johann Friedrich, and Kerbs, Diethart, *Fidus 1868–1948: Zur ästhetischen Praxis bürgerlicher Fluchtbewegungen* (Munich: Rogner & Bernhard, 1972).

— "Die Lebensreform bewegung," in Klaus Vondung, eds., *Das wilhelminische Bildungsbürgertum. Zur Sozialgeschichte seiner Ideen* (Göttingen: Vandenhoeck & Ruprecht, 1976), pp. 138–52.

— "Corona agreste sull'Europa: Monte Verità quale campo centrale di esperimenti per modi di vita alternativi fra l'inizio del secolo e la prima Guerra Mondiale," in Harald Szeemann, ed., *Monte Verità. Antropologia locale come contributo alla riscoperta di una topografia sacrale moderna* (Locarno/Milano: Armando Dadò/Electa, 1978), pp. 54–64.

Frick, Wolfgang, ed., *Ernst Frick 1881–1956. Zum 50. Todestag* (privately printed, 2006).

Fröbe-Kapteyn, Olga, "Die Eranos *Mandala*" (unpublished typescript, 1927–49; Eranos Foundation Archives, Ascona-Moscia).

— "Im Anfang war das Wort. Geschrieben für Bettina. Ostern. 1928" (unpublished typescript; 1928; Eranos Foundation Archives, Ascona-Moscia).

— "Zwei Erzählungen. Der Ewige Gefährte. Der Turm. Geschrieben für Bettina. Zu Weihnachten. 1929" (unpublished typescript; 1929; Eranos Foundation Archives, Ascona-Moscia).

— "Know Thy Self," *The Beacon. A Periodical devoted to Occultism*, 8 (May 2, 1929), pp. 31–35.

— "Lecture Program. August. 1930" (unpublished typescript, 1930; Eranos Foundation Archives, Ascona-Moscia).

— "Erzählungen. Geschrieben für Bettina. Ostern. 1931" (unpublished typescript; 1931; Eranos Foundation Archives, Ascona-Moscia).

— "Vorwort," *Eranos-Jahrbuch*, 1 (1933), pp. 5–6.

— "Gleichnisse" (unpublished typescript, October 1933; Eranos Foundation Archives, Ascona-Moscia).

— "The Earth Mother. Vision. Spring. 33" (unpublished typescript, 1933; Eranos Foundation Archives, Ascona-Moscia).

— "Vorwort," *Eranos-Jahrbuch*, 2 (1934), pp. 5–8.

— "Drei Zeichnungen" (unpublished typescript and drawings, March 23, 1934; Eranos Foundation Archives, Ascona-Moscia).

— "Visionen. Juni–Juli. 1934" (unpublished typescript; Eranos Foundation Archives, Ascona-Moscia).

— "Vision Oktober 1934. Zürich (Während ich einige Mal bei Jung war). Die Eranos *Mandala*" (unpublished typescript, Zurich, October 1934; Eranos Foundation Archives, Ascona-Moscia).
— "10. Sept. 35" (unpublished typescript, September 26, 1935; Eranos Foundation Archives, Ascona-Moscia).
— "13. bis 18. Okt. 35. London" (unpublished typescript, October 13-18, 1935; Eranos Foundation Archives, Ascona-Moscia).
— "From 22 October onwards. London" (unpublished typescript, from October 22 onwards, 1935; Eranos Foundation Archives, Ascona-Moscia).
— "Vorwort," *Eranos-Jahrbuch*, 3 (1935), pp. 3–7.
— "Vorwort," *Eranos-Jahrbuch*, 4 (1936), pp. 5–9.
— "Feb. 5.36. Paris" (unpublished typescript, February 5, 1936; Eranos Foundation Archives, Ascona-Moscia).
— "14 April 36" (unpublished typescript, April 14, 1936; Eranos Foundation Archives, Ascona-Moscia).
— "June 3.36" (unpublished typescript, June 3, 1936; Eranos Foundation Archives, Ascona-Moscia).
— "14 to 19 June 36" (unpublished typescript, June 14–19, 1936; Eranos Foundation Archives, Ascona-Moscia).
— "15.6 36" (unpublished typescript, June 15, 1936; Eranos Foundation Archives, Ascona-Moscia).
— "22 June 36" (unpublished typescript, June 22, 1936; Eranos Foundation Archives, Ascona-Moscia).
— "Vision. 11 Sept. 36" (unpublished typescript, September 11, 1936; Eranos Foundation Archives, Ascona-Moscia).
— "Die Höllenfahrt [Erste]. Dez. 37 bis März 38" (unpublished typescript, December 1937–March 1938; Eranos Foundation Archive, Ascona-Moscia).
— "Die Höllenfahrt. Mitte Dezember 37 bis 6 Februar 38. London und Holland" (unpublished typescript, mid-December 1937-February 6, 1938; Eranos Foundation Archive, Ascona-Moscia).
— "22-24 Dez 37" (unpublished typescript, December 22–24, 1937; Eranos Foundation Archive, Ascona-Moscia).

— "11 Jan. 38" (unpublished typescript, January 11, 1938; Eranos Foundation Archive, Ascona-Moscia).
— "Vorwort," *Eranos-Jahrbuch*, 5 (1937), pp. 5–8.
— "Vorwort," *Eranos-Jahrbuch*, 6 (1938), pp. 5–7.
— "Vorwort," *Eranos-Jahrbuch*, 7 (1939), pp. 5–7.
— "The Psychological Background of Eranos" (typescript, 1939; Eranos Foundation Archives, Ascona-Moscia), rpt. in *Spring: A Journal of Archetype and Culture*, 92 (2015) ("Eranos: Its Magical Past and Alluring Future: The Spirit of a Wondrous Place"), pp. 29–38 [lecture given on October 27, 1939 at the Analytical Psychology Club, New York, NY].
— "Eranos Vortrag" (unpublished typescript, 1939; Eranos Foundation Archives, Ascona-Moscia) [lecture given at the Psychology Club, Zurich, and at Ada Hondius's home, Amsterdam, in 1939].
— "The White Elephant" (unpublished typescript, 1940; Eranos Foundation Archive, Ascona-Moscia).
— "Lisbon. Oktober 40" (unpublished typescript, October 1940; Eranos Foundation Archives, Ascona-Moscia).
— "Ascona-Lisbon-New York-Ascona. August 1940 to May 1941" (unpublished typescript, May 4, 1941; Eranos Foundation Archives, Ascona-Moscia).
— "Vorwort," *Eranos-Jahrbuch*, 8 (1940 –41), pp. 5–7.
— "Deus Absconditus (The Descent into Hell)" (unpublished typescript, May 1941; Eranos Foundation Archives, Ascona-Moscia).
— "Mellon Problem" (unpublished typescript, Winter 1941; Eranos Foundation Archives, Ascona-Moscia).
— "Vorwort," *Eranos-Jahrbuch*, 9 (1942), pp. 5–6.
— "Eranos—A Survey of its history since 1933, of the facts connected with it, a. the *Tagungen*, b. the Eranos Archive. The conclusions I have arrived at, my psychological realisations concerning it, its differences from other congress centres, and its chief problem" (unpublished typescript, 1942; Eranos Foundation Archives, Ascona-Moscia).
— "The Totem-Lingam. Vision and drawing Pfingsten 1942" (unpublished typescript, Pentecost 1942). Eranos Foundation Archives, Ascona-Moscia).

— "Mary and Eranos" (unpublished typescript, November 23, 1942; Eranos Foundation Archives, Ascona-Moscia).
— "Vorwort," *Eranos-Jahrbuch*, 10 (1943), pp. 5–6.
— "The veil of ectoplasm" [belonging to a series of visions beginning on April 9, 1943] (unpublished manuscript, April 9, 1943; Eranos Foundation Archive, Ascona-Moscia).
— "Vorwort," *Eranos-Jahrbuch*, 11 (1944), pp. 5–8.
— "The 4th Function and the Tibetan" (unpublished typescript, 1944; Eranos Foundation Archives, Ascona-Moscia).
— "Erklärung über Eranos für die Amerikanischen Gesandtschaft, Bern" (unpublished typescript, 1944; Eranos Foundation Archives, Ascona-Moscia).
— "12 Mai 44" (unpublished typescript, May 12, 1944; Eranos Foundation Archives, Ascona-Moscia).
— "19 Mai 44" (unpublished typescript, May 19, 1944; Eranos Foundation Archives, Ascona-Moscia).
— "11 June 44" (unpublished typescript, June 11, 1944; Eranos Foundation Archives, Ascona-Moscia).
— "The Curse" (unpublished typescript, undated [1944?]; Eranos Foundation Archives, Ascona-Moscia).
— "Thinking Function" (unpublished typescript, undated [1944?]; Eranos Foundation Archives, Ascona-Moscia).
— "Feeling Function" (unpublished typescript, undated [1944?]; Eranos Foundation Archives, Ascona-Moscia).
— "Der Durchbruch" (unpublished typescript, undated [1944?]; Eranos Foundation Archives, Ascona-Moscia).
— "Paul Zillmann. 1926–1935" (unpublished typescript, undated [1944?]; Eranos Foundation Archives, Ascona-Moscia).
— "Tibet" (unpublished typescript, undated [1944?]; Eranos Foundation Archives, Ascona-Moscia).
— "The new situation of Eranos, caused by Jung's absence" (unpublished typescript, undated [1944?]; Eranos Foundation Archives, Ascona-Moscia).
— "Vorwort," *Eranos-Jahrbuch*, 12 (1945), pp. 5–7.

— "Vorwort," *Eranos-Jahrbuch*, 13 (1945), pp. 5–7.
— "The Hut and the Sacred Word" (unpublished typescript, Easter Monday 1945; Eranos Foundation Archives, Ascona-Moscia).
— "My marriage" (unpublished typescript, undated [1945?]; Eranos Foundation Archives, Ascona-Moscia).
— "The Mandala" (unpublished typescript, undated [1945?]; Eranos Foundation Archives, Ascona-Moscia).
— "Vision. 5 August 1946" (unpublished typescript, August 5, 1946; Eranos Foundation Archives, Ascona-Moscia).
— "Vision. 5 Sept. 46" (unpublished typescript, September 5, 1946; Eranos Foundation Archives, Ascona-Moscia).
— "Vorwort," *Eranos-Jahrbuch*, 14 (1946), pp. 5–7.
— "Arcane School. Positive Values. Negative Values" (unpublished typescript, undated [second half of the 1940s?]; Eranos Foundation Archives, Ascona-Moscia).
— "Vorwort," *Eranos-Jahrbuch*, 15 (1947), pp. 5–7.
— "The Eranos Archive" (unpublished typescript, undated [1947?]; Eranos Foundation Archives, Ascona-Moscia).
— "Eranos Archive for Research in Symbolism" (unpublished typescript, undated [1947?]; Eranos Foundation Archives, Ascona-Moscia).
— "Eranos Institute for Research into Religious Symbolism (Archetypal Images)" (unpublished typescript, 1947; Eranos Foundation Archives, Ascona-Moscia).
— "Vision. 3 Juli 1947" (unpublished typescript, July 3, 1947; Eranos Foundation Archives, Ascona-Moscia).
— "Eranos Institut für Symbolforschung" (unpublished typescript, September 28, 1947; Eranos Foundation Archives, Ascona-Moscia).
— "Vorwort," *Eranos-Jahrbuch*, 16 (1948), pp. 5–7.
— "The Cross of Milk" (unpublished manuscript and typescript, August 6, 1948; Eranos Foundation Archives, Ascona-Moscia).
— "The 'Tönende' Breast" (unpublished manuscript and typescript, November 18, 1948 [Zurich]; Eranos Foundation Archives, Ascona-Moscia).

— "Dream. 22 June 1949" (unpublished typescript, 1949; Eranos Foundation Archives, Ascona-Moscia).
— "Vorwort," *Eranos-Jahrbuch*, 17 (1949), pp. 5–7.
— "The Circle and the Point" (unpublished typescript, 1949; Eranos Foundation Archives, Ascona-Moscia).
— "History of a Symptom. Rhinitis vasomotoris" (unpublished typescript, 1949; Eranos Foundation Archives, Ascona-Moscia).
— [untitled] (unpublished typescript, October 17, 1950; Eranos Foundation Archives, Ascona-Moscia).
— "Vorwort," *Eranos-Jahrbuch*, 18 (1950), pp. 5–8.
— "Vorwort," *Eranos-Jahrbuch*, 19 (1950), pp. 5–8.
— "*In memoriam* Gerardus van der Leuuw, " *Eranos-Jahrbuch*, 19 (1950), pp. 9–11.
— "7 November 1950" [belonging to the "Arbeit mit Dr. Szondi"] (unpublished typescript, November 7, 1950; Eranos Foundation Archives, Ascona-Moscia).
— "Winter 1938. London.Vorläufer der jetzigen, 12 Jahre späteren Visionen in der Arbeit mit Dr. Szondi" [belonging to the "Arbeit mit Dr. Szondi"] (unpublished typescript, undated [1950]; Eranos Foundation Archives, Ascona-Moscia).
— "Porträt von Ludwig Derleth" (unpublished typescript, undated [c. 1950-1957]; Stiftung Szondi-Institut Archives, Zurich).
— "[The Mysteries of the Nether'Lands] 11 Mai 1951" (unpublished typescript, May 11, 1951; Eranos Foundation Archives, Ascona-Moscia).
— "Vorwort," *Eranos-Jahrbuch*, 20 (1951), pp. 5–7.
— "Vorwort," *Eranos-Jahrbuch*, 21 (1952), pp. 5–8.
— "Eranos. Fortsetzung" (unpublished typescript, 1952; Eranos Foundation Archives, Ascona-Moscia).
— "The Lapis Exilis and the Grail MSS" (unpublished typescript, February 20, 1952; Eranos Foundation Archives, Ascona-Moscia).
— "Anschluss an den Blutstrom der Ahnen. 22 Mai 1952" (unpublished typescript, May 22, 1952; Eranos Foundation Archives, Ascona-Moscia).

— "28 Mai 1952" (unpublished typescript, May 28, 1952; Eranos Foundation Archives, Ascona-Moscia).

— "The Blood Consciousness and the Feeling function" (unpublished typescript, undated [1952?]; Eranos Foundation Archives, Ascona-Moscia).

— "The ancestral Blood Stream" (unpublished typescript, undated [1952?]; Eranos Foundation Archives, Ascona-Moscia).

— "Die Geschichte von Eranos" (unpublished typescript, 1952–58; Eranos Foundation Archives, Ascona-Moscia).

— "Die sich überlagernde Visionen" (unpublished typescript, undated [1953?]; Eranos Foundation Archives, Ascona-Moscia).

— "Vorwort," *Eranos-Jahrbuch*, 22 (1953), pp. 5–7.

— "An Attempt at Definition and Description of Eranos and of the *Eranos-Jahrbücher*" (unpublished typescript, 1953; Eranos Foundation Archives, Ascona-Moscia).

— [untitled] (unpublished typescript, June 29, 1953; Eranos Foundation Archives, Ascona-Moscia).

— "Vorwort," *Eranos-Jahrbuch*, 23 (1954), pp. 5–6.

— "Shadow of my Dedication to Eranos" (unpublished typescript, February 11, 1954; Eranos Foundation Archives, Ascona-Moscia).

— "Preface," in Joseph Campbell, ed., *Spirit and Nature—Papers from the Eranos Yearbooks—Selected and translated from the Eranos-Jahrbücher, ed. Olga Fröbe-Kapteyn* (Princeton, NJ: Bollingen Series XXX/1, Princeton University Press, 1954), pp. xv–xvi.

— "Vorwort," *Eranos-Jahrbuch*, 24 (1955), pp. 5–7.

— "A Note on Eranos," in: *The Mysteries—Papers from the Eranos Yearbooks—Selected and translated from the Eranos-Jahrbücher, ed. Olga Fröbe-Kapteyn* (Princeton, NJ: Bollingen Series XXX/2, Princeton University Press, 1955), pp. xv–xvi.

— "Ein Brief der Gründerin," *Du. Schweizerische Monatsschrift*, 15 (4, 1955) ("Eranos"), p. 10.

— "Vorwort," *Eranos-Jahrbuch*, 25 (1958), pp. 5–8.

— "Vision. Lebendige Bilder & Wandlungen" [belonging to "Neumann und ich"] (unpublished typescript, January 3–20, 1957; Eranos Foundation Archives, Ascona-Moscia).

— "Vorwort," *Eranos-Jahrbuch*, 26 (1957), pp. 5–6.

— "*In memoriam* Karl Reinhardt," 26 (1957), p. 7.

— ed., *25 Jahre Eranos. 1933–1957* (Zurich: Rhein-Verlag, 1957).

— "Notes for the Story of Eranos" (unpublished typescript, undated [1957?]; Eranos Foundation Archives, Ascona-Moscia).

— "Der unbekannte Genius" (unpublished typescript, 1957; Eranos Foundation Archives, Ascona-Moscia).

— "Mein Vater. Albertus Philippus Kapteyn. Vision" (unpublished typescript, February 1 and 5, 1957; Eranos Foundation Archives, Ascona-Moscia),

— "Vision meiner Mutter" (unpublished typescript, February 15–27, 1957; Eranos Foundation Archives, Ascona-Moscia).

— "Der Schatten" (unpublished typescript, May 17–August 1, 1957; Eranos Foundation Archives, Ascona-Moscia).

— "Erster Abend…" (unpublished typescript, undated [prob. around 1957–58]; Eranos Foundation Archives, Ascona-Moscia).

— "Im Schatten von Eranos…" (unpublished typescript, undated [prob. 1958]; Eranos Foundation Archives, Ascona-Moscia).

— "Visionen Olga F.-K. Mai–Juni 1960. Kilnik Bellinzona nach der Staroperation aus einem Brief vom 24.6.60 an C.G. Jung" (unpublished typescript, June 24, 1960; Eranos Foundation Archives, Ascona-Moscia).

— "*In memoriam* Erich Neumann," 29 (1960), pp. 7–8.

Gasseau, Maurizio, and Bernardini, Riccardo, "Il sogno: prospettive di Eranos," in Idd., eds., *Il sogno. Dalla psicologia analitica allo psicodramma junghiano* (Milan: FrancoAngeli, 2009), pp. 15–55.

Germain, André, *Florence et Ascona* (Paris: Sun, 1952).

Gerrish Fine Art, *The "Meditation Plates"—Olga Fröbe-Kapteyn. 17/07/2025–17/10/2025, Gerrish Fine Art, London* (London: Gerrish Fine Art, 2025).

Gilardoni, Virgilio, "Lettere di Alfredo Pioda a Emilia Franzoni. Appunti per la storia di un grande pittore lombardo: Filippo Franzoni," *Archivio Storico Ticinese*, 3 (5, 1960–61).

— *Filippo Franzoni 1857–1911* (Bellinzona: La Vesconta, 1968).

— "Un terreno predisposto," in Harald Szeemann, ed., *Monte Verità. Antropologia locale come contributo alla riscoperta di una topografia sacrale moderna* (Locarno/Milano: Armando Dadò/Electa, 1978), pp. 10–11.

— *Fonti per la storia di un borgo del Verbano: Ascona* (Bellinzona: Archivio Storico Ticinese, 1980).

Gioni, Massimiliano, and Bell, Natalie, eds., *The Encyclopedic Palace. 55th International Art Exhibition: La Biennale di Venezia*, 2 vols. (Venice: Marsilio, 2013).

— ed., *La Grande Madre. Donne, maternità e potere nell'arte e nella cultura visiva, 1900–2015* (Milan: Skira, 2015); Eng. Ed. *The Great Mother: Women, Maternity, and Power in Art and Visual Culture, 1900-2015* (Milan: Skira, 2015).

— and Bell, Natalie, eds., *The Keeper* (New York, NY: New Museum, 2016).

— Carrion-Murayari, Gary, Norton, Margot, and Weisburg, Madeline, eds., *Judy Chicago. Herstory* (New York, NY: Phaidon, 2023).

Giovanettina, Martino and Giovanettina, Niccolò, *Ascona. Un reportage* (Foroglio: Agenzia Kay, 2012).

Giovetti, Paola, *Roberto Assagioli. La vita e l'opera del fondatore della Psicosintesi* (Rome: Mediterranee, 1995).

— *I luoghi di forza. Guida alle località che emanano energia, pace e armonia* (Rome: Mediterranee, 2002), § "Monte Verità e i convegni di Eranos (Ascona, Canton Ticino)," pp. 129–31.

Girgis, Samir, *Jakob und der Berg der Wahrheit: Historischer Roman über die Geschichte Asconas und des Monte Verità* (Oldenburg: Schardt, 2005).

Glauser, Friedrich, *DADA, Ascona e altri ricordi* (Palermo: Sellerio, 1991 {1976}).

Goethe, Johann Wolfgang von, *Zur Farbenlehre*, Vol. I (Tubingen: J.G. Cotta'schen Buchhandlung, 1810).

Goodrick-Clark, Nicholas, *Le radici occulte del nazismo* (Carnago: SugarCo, 1993 {1985}).

Graevenitz, Antje von, "Capanna e tempio: verso l'autocoscienza," in Harald Szeemann, ed., *Monte Verità. Antropologia locale come contributo alla riscoperta di una topografia sacrale moderna* (Locarno/Milano: Armando Dadò/Electa, 1978), pp. 85–100.

Graur, Patrick, "(Er-)Schöpfungstendenzen um 1900. Ida Hofmann und der Monte Verità im feministischen Kontext," in Denise Dumschat-Rehfeldt, Julia Ingold, Simone Ketterl, Jonas Meurer, Magdalena Sperber, and Anna Lena Westphal, eds., *Literatur am Ende. Putting *Schöpfung* in *Erschöpfung** (Marburg: Büchner, 2024), pp. 131–42.

Green, Martin, *The von Richthofen Sisters: The Triumphant and the Tragic Mode of Love. Else and Frieda von Richthofen, Otto Gross, Max Weber, and D. H. Lawrence, in the Years 1870–1970* (New York, NY: Basic Books, 1974).

— *Mountain of Truth: The Counterculture begins. Ascona 1900–1920* (Hanover, NH/London, University Press of New England, 1986).

— *Prophets of a New Age: The Politics of Hope from the Eighteenth through the Twenty-first Centuries* (New York, NY: Charles Scribner's Sons, 1992).

— "Una Nuova Era. New Age e nuovi 'Centri di vita' dal 1890 al 1920," in Andreas Schwab and Claudia Lafranchi, eds., *Senso della vita e bagni di sole. Esperimenti di vita e arte al Monte Verità* (Ascona: Fondazione Monte Verità, 2001), pp. 207–22.

— *Otto Gross, Freudian Psychoanalyst, 1877–1920: Literature and Ideas* (Lewiston, NY: The Edwin Mellen Press, 1999).

Grohmann, Adolf, *Die Vegetarier-Ansiedlung in Ascona und die sogenannten Naturmenschen im Tessin* (Halle a.S.: Verlag von Carl Marhold, 1904; rpt. Ascona: Edizioni della Rondine, 1997).

Gross, Otto, *Senza freni* (Florence: Gratis, [undated]).

Guénon, René, *Le Théosophisme. Histoire d'une Pseudo-Religion* (Paris: Ed. Traditionelles, 1975).

Guerra, Gabriele, ed., *Tra ribellione e conservazione. Monte verità e la cultura tedesca* (Rome: Istituto Italiano di Studi Germanici, 2019).

Guidi, Manuel, "Olga Fröbe-Kapteyn: la 'grande madre' di Eranos / Olga Fröbe-Kapteyn: die ‚Grosse Mutter' von Eranos," *Ferien Journal. Ascona*, 67 (489/5, 2021–22), pp. 88–96.

Gygax, Raphal, ed., *Olga Fröbe-Kapteyn. Artista—ricercatrice. Volume pubblicato in occasione della mostra Olga Fröbe-Kapteyn: artista-ricercatrice, Museo Casa Rusca, Locarno, 8 agosto 2024–12 gennaio 2025*, texts by Yasmin Afschar, Riccardo Bernardini, Raphael Gygax, Fabio Merlini, and Sara Petrucci (Locarno/Ascona/Bellinzona: Museo Casa Rusca/Fondazione Eranos/Casagrande, in collaboration with Kunsthalle Mainz, 2024).

— "La ricerca artistica di Olga Fröbe-Kapteyn: l'Archivio di Eranos per la Ricerca sul Simbolismo / Olga Fröbe-Kapteyn's Artistic Research: The Eranos Archive for Research in Symbolism," in Id., ed., *Olga Fröbe-Kapteyn. Artista—ricercatrice. Volume pubblicato in occasione della mostra Olga Fröbe-Kapteyn: artista–ricercatrice, Museo Casa Rusca, Locarno, 8 agosto 2024–12 gennaio 2025*, texts by Yasmin Afschar, Riccardo Bernardini, Raphael Gygax, Fabio Merlini, and Sara Petrucci (Locarno/Ascona/Bellinzona: Museo Casa Rusca/Fondazione Eranos/Casagrande, in collaboration with Kunsthalle Mainz, 2024), pp. 74–87.

— "Olga Fröbe-Kapteyn: Artist—Researcher," Provence (2025), pp. 212–20.

Haag, Hans Jakob, "Sammlung Oskar R. Schlag der Zentralbibliothek Zürich," in Oskar Rudolf Schlag, *Von alten und neuen Mysterien. Die Lehren des A.* (Stäfa: Rothenhäusler, 1995), p. 563.

Hakl, Hans Thomas, *Der verborgene Geist von Eranos. Unbekannte Begegnungen von Wissenschaft und Esoterik. Eine alternative Geistesgeschichte des 20. Jahrhunderts* (Bretten: Scientia nova-Neue Wissenschaft, 2001).

— "Der verborgene Geist von Eranos. Unbekannte Begegnungen von Wissenschaft und Esoterik. Beitrag zu einer alternativen Geistesgeschichte des 20. Jahrhunderts," *Gnostika. Zeitschrift für Wissenschaft & Esoterik*, 5 (17, 2001), pp. 21–42.

— "Anmerkungen des Autors Dr. H.T. Hakl [zur Rezension von Friedrich Niewöhner]," *Gnostika. Zeitschrift für Wissenschaft & Esoterik*, 6 (20, 2002), pp. 62–63.

— "Plauderei über C.G. Jung und die Eranos-Tagungen," in Psychologischer Club, *Jahresbericht* (2002–2003), pp. 19–20.

— "Eranos im Spiegel der Geistesgeschichte des 20. Jahrhunderts," *Archævs. Études d'Histoire des Religions/Studies in the History of Religions* 6 (1–2, 2002), pp. 183–200; rpt. in *Zeitschrift für Ganzheitsforschung*, 1 (2004), pp. 31–47.

— [Review to] "Riccardo Bernardini, 'Da Monte Verità a Eranos. Elementi per lo studio della psiche e della complessità umana' [M.A. diss., Turin University, 2003]," *Gnostika. Zeitschrift für Wissenschaft & Esoterik*, 8 (26, 2004), pp. 4–22.

— [Review to] "Elisabetta Barone / Matthias Riedl / Alexandra Tischel (Hg.), *Pioniere, Poeten, Professoren*," *Aries*, 5 (2, 2005), pp. 284–87.

— "*„Die wahre Magie ist ein Akt der Liebe." 3 Aufsätze und Bibliographie von Hans Thomas Hakl zum 60. Geburtstag* (Sinzheim: AAGW, 2007).

— [Review to] "Riccardo Bernardini, 'Carl Gustav Jung a Eranos. Il contributo junghiano al Circolo di Eranos. Ideazione, contributi e iniziative dal 1933 al 1952' [Ph.D. diss., University of Bologna, 2010]," *Gnostika. Wissenschaft. Esoterikforschung. Lebenswelt* 14 (44, 2010), pp. 10–11.

— "Prefazione," in Riccardo Bernardini, *Jung a Eranos. Il progetto della psicologia complessa* (Milan: FrancoAngeli, 2011), pp. 19–20.

— *Eranos. An Alternative Intellectual History of the Twentieth Century* (Montreal & Kingston: McGill-Queen's University Press, 2013).

— *Eranos: Nabel der Welt. Glied der goldenen Kette. Die alternative Geistesgeschichte* (Bretten: Scientia nova-Neue Wissenschaft, 2015).

Hanegraaff, Wouter Jacobus, "Generous Hermeneutics: Hans Thomas Hakl and Eranos," *Religiographies*, 2 (1, 2023) ("Hans Thomas Hakl and His Library"), ed. Marco Pasi, pp. 59–75.

— "Eranos and the Arts," *Religiographies*, 4 (1, 2025), pp. 1–6.

Hanke, Edith, "'L'uomo della verità.' Le idee di Leo N. Tolstoj al Monte Verità," in Andreas Schwab and Claudia Lafranchi, eds., *Senso della vita e bagni di sole. Esperimenti di vita e arte al Monte Verità* (Ascona: Fondazione Monte Verità, 2001), pp. 23–41.

Hannah, Barbara, *Vita e opere di C.G. Jung* (Milan: Rusconi, 1980 {1976}).

Hartmann, Franz, *Die weiße und schwarze Magie oder Das Gesetz des Geistes in der Natur* (Leipzig: Lotus, undated; Collection Karl Vester, Ascona).

— *An Adventure among the Rosicrucians* (Boston, MA: Occult Publishing, 1887).

— "Ein Abenteuer unter den Rosenkreuzern," *Neue Metaphysische Rundschau*, 1 (1898), pp. 156–67, 232–43, 333–41, 386–89, 429–34.

— "Ein Abenteuer unter den Rosenkreuzern," *Neue Metaphysische Rundschau*, 2 (1899), pp. 18–22, 46–51, 93–105, 241–54, 273–81, 305–14, 337–46.

— ed., *Die Bhagavad Gita. Das Lied von der Gottheit oder die Lehre vom Göttlichen Sein* (Leipzig: Max Altmann, 1929).

Hasenfratz, Doris, "Il destino delle Isole di Brissago: dal tempio di Venere all'albero di eucalipto / Das Schicksal der Brissago-Inseln. Vom Venustempel zum Eukalyptusbaum" *Ferien-Journal. Ascona* (1994).

Hesse, Hermann, *In den Felsen. Notizen eines Naturmenschen* (1908); It. Ed. "Tra le rocce," in Id., *Racconti* (Milan: Adelphi, 1987).

— *Monte Verità* (Carnago: SugarCo, 1988 {1911}).

Heuer, Gottfried, ed., *2. Internationaler Otto Gross Kongress. Burghölzli, Zürich 2000* (Marburg an der Lahn: LiteraturWissenschaft.de, 2002).

— "Otto Gross between Freud and Jung: The Secret Story of Jung's Twin Brother," in Mary Ann Mattoon, ed., *Cambridge 2001: Proceedings of the Fifteenth International Congress for Analytical Psychology* (Daimon: Einsiedeln, 2003), pp. 118–29.

Heydt, Eduard von der, and Rheinbaben, Werner von, *Auf dem Monte Verità. Erinnerungen und Gedanken über Menschen, Kunst und Politik* (Zurich: Atlantis, 1958).

— et al., *Ascona und sein Berg Monte Verità* (Zurich: Arche, 1979).

Heydt, Vera von, "Jung and Religion," *Journal of Analytical Psychology*, 22 (2, 1977), pp. 175–83.

Heyer-Grote, Lucy, ed., "Gratulationen zum 70. Geburtstag Olga Froebe-Kapteyn am 19 Oktober 1951" (unpublished manuscripts and typescripts, 1951; Eranos Foundation Archives, Ascona-Moscia).

Higgie, Jennifer, *The Other Side. A Journey into Women, Art, and the Spirit World* (London: Weidenfeld & Nicolson, 2023).

Hillman, James, *Il mito dell'analisi*, (Milan: Adelphi, 1979 {1972}).

— "Blu alchemico e *unio mentalis*," in Id., *Anima* (Bergamo: Moretti & Vitali, 2006 {1981}), pp. 11–30.

— "Nei giardini. Un ricordo psicologico" {1998}, in Id., *Politica della Bellezza* (Bergamo: Moretti&Vitali, 1999), pp. 147–55.

— *Psicologia alchemica* (Milan: Adelphi, 2013 {2010}).

Hobson, Suzanne, and Radford, Andrew D., eds., *The Edinburgh Companion to Modernism, Myth and Religion* (Edinburgh: Edinburgh University Press, 2023).

Hoch, Medea, "La concezione junghiana del colore nel contesto dell'arte moderna," in Foundation of the Works of C.G. Jung, Ulrich Hoerni, Thomas Fischer, and Bettina Kaufmann, *L'arte di C.G. Jung* (Turin: Bollati Boringhieri, 2019 {2018}), pp. 33–49.

Höfer, Josef, and Rahner, Karl, eds., *Lexikon für Theologie und Kirche* (Freiburg im Breisgau: Herder, 1959).

Hoffman, William S., *Paul Mellon—Portrait of an Oil Baron* (Chicago, IL: Follett, 1974).

Hofmann-Oedenkoven, Ida, *Wie gelangen wir Frauen zu harmonischen und gesunden Daseinbedingungen? – Offener Brief an die Verfasserin von "Eine Mutter für Viele"* (Ascona: Selbstverlag, Carlo Vester, 1902).

— *Vegetabilismus! Vegetarismus! Blätter zur Verbreitung vegetarischer Lebensweise* (Monte Verità/Ascona: Selbstverlag von Ida Hofmann-Oedenkoven, 1905).

— *Beiträge zur Frauenfrage* (Winnenden/Württemberg: Zentralstelle zur Werbreitung guter deutscher Literatur, 1915).

— *Monte Verità. Verità senza poesia*, foreword by Edgardo Franzosini, afterword by Nicoletta Mongini (Bellinzona: Casagrande, 2023).

Holz, Hans Heinz, "Eranos – eine moderne Pseudo-Gnosis," in Jacob Taubes, ed., *Gnosis und Politik. Religionstheorie und Politische Theologie* (München: Wilhelm Fink/Ferdinand Schöningh, 1984), Vol. II, pp. 249–63.

Hurwitz, Emanuel, "Otto Gross – Dalla psicanalisi al Paradiso," in Harald Szeemann, ed., *Monte Verità. Antropologia locale come contributo alla riscoperta di una topografia sacrale moderna* (Locarno/Milano: Armando Dadò/Electa, 1978), pp. 109–18.

— *Otto Gross, „Paradies"-Sucher zwischen Freud und Jung – Leben und Werk* (Zurich: Suhrkamp, 1979).

— "Conflitto e verità. La dimensione politica della psicanalisi per Otto Gross," in Andreas Schwab and Claudia Lafranchi, eds., *Senso della vita e bagni di sole. Esperimenti di vita e arte al Monte Verità* (Ascona: Fondazione Monte Verità, 2001), pp. 143–55.

Idel, Moshe, "The Eranos myth of integration: Olga Fröbe-Kapteyn, Mircea Eliade, and Gershom Scholem," *Studi e Materiali di Storia delle Religioni*, 89 (2, 2023) ("Conflicts, Tensions, and Mythmaking at Eranos Before and After World War II"), pp. 517–38.

Illerhaus, Florian, *Gegenseitige Beeinflussungen von Theosophie und Monte Verità* (Munich: Grin, 2009).

Illner, Eberhard, ed., *Eduard von der Heydt. Kunstsammler, Bankier, Mäzen*, (Munich/London/New York, NY: Prestel, 2013).

Introvigne, Massimo, *Il cappello del mago. I nuovi movimenti magici, dallo spiritismo al satanismo* (Carnago: SugarCo, 1990).

Invernizzi, Dino, "Sessant'anni di grande musica ad Ascona," in Vv.Aa., *Stagioni di grande musica. 1946–2005* (Ascona: Settimane Musicali di Ascona, 2005), pp. 15–32.

Jaffé, Aniela, "C.G. Jung und die Eranostagungen (Zum 100. Geburtstag von C.G. Jung)," *Eranos-Jahrbuch*, 44 (1975), pp. 1–14; Engl. Ed. "C.G. Jung and the Eranos Conferences," *Spring* (1977), pp. 201–12; It. Ed. "Carlo Gustav Jung e i convegni di Eranos," in Id., *Saggi sulla psicologia di Carl Gustav Jung* (Rome: Paoline, 1984), pp. 103–17.

— *From the Life and Work of C.G. Jung* (Einsiedeln: Daimon, 1989).

Jaunin, Françoise, "La constellation de l'imaginaire sur la Montagne de la Vérité / Die Konstellation des Imaginären auf dem Berg der Wahrheit / La costellazione dell'immaginario sulla Montagna della Verità," *Schweizer Kunst / Art Suisse / Arte Svizzera / Art Svizzer. Zeitschrift der Gesellschaft Schweizerischer Maler, Bildhauer und Architekten (Visuelle Künstler) / Revue de la Societé des peintres, sculpteurs et architectes suisses (artistes visuels) / Rivista della Società dei pittori, scultori e *architetti svizzeri (artisti visuali)*, 2 (1989) ("Monte Verità. Symposium Monte Verità 4. -7. Mai 1989"), pp. 4–12.

— "Une topographie sacrée / Una topografia sacra / Eine aussergewöhnliche Topographie," *Schweizer Kunst / Art Suisse / Arte Svizzera / Art Svizzer. Zeitschrift der Gesellschaft Schweizerischer Maler, Bildhauer und Architekten (Visuelle Künstler) / Revue de la Societé des peintres, sculpteurs et architectes suisses (artistes visuels) / Rivista della Società dei pittori, scultori e architetti svizzeri (artisti visuali)*, 2 (1989) ("Monte Verità. Symposium Monte Verità 4. -7. Mai 1989"), pp. 4–12.

Jost, Dominik, *Ludwig Derleth. Gestalt und Leistung* (Stuttgart: W. Kohlhammer GmbH, 1965).

Jung, Carl Gustav, *Septem Sermones ad Mortuos. Die sieben Belehrungen der Toten. Geschrieben von Basilides in Alexandria, der Stadt, wo der Osten den Westen berührt* ([without publishing information] 1916); It. Ed. "I sette sermoni ai morti. Scritti da Basilide in Alessandria, la città in cui l'Oriente tocca l'Occidente," in Id., *Ricordi, sogni, riflessioni*, ed. Aniela Jaffé (Milan: Biblioteca Universale Rizzoli, 1992), pp. 449–63.

— *Psychological Types* {1921}, in *The Collected Works of C.G. Jung*, Vol. 6 (Princeton, NJ: Bollingen Series XX, Princeton University Press, 1971).

— "The Swiss Line in the European Spectrum" {1928}, in *The Collected Works of C.G. Jung*, Vol. 10 (Princeton, NJ: Bollingen Series XX, Princeton University Press, 1970), pp. 479–88.

— "Zur Empirie des Individuationsprozesses (Hiezu fünf Bildtafeln)," *Eranos-Jahrbuch*, 1 (1933), pp. 201–14; Engl. Ed. "A Study in the Process of Individuation" {1934/1950}, in *The Collected Works of C.G. Jung*, Vol. 9i (Princeton, NJ: Bollingen Series XX, Princeton University Press, 1969[2]), pp. 290–354.

— "Über die Archetypen des kollektiven Unbewußten," *Eranos-Jahrbuch*, 2 (1934), pp. 179–229; Engl. Ed. "Archetypes of the Collective Unconscious" {1934/1954}, in *The Collected Works of C.G. Jung*, Vol. 9i (Princeton, NJ: Bollingen Series XX, Princeton University Press, 1969[2]), pp. 3–41.

— "Psychological Commentary on the *Tibetan Book of the Dead*" (1935/1953), in *The Collected Works of C.G. Jung*, Vol. 11 (Princeton, NJ: Bollingen Series XX, Princeton University Press, 1970), pp. 509–26.

— "Die psychologischen Aspekte des Mutterarchetypus," *Eranos-Jahrbuch*, 7 (1938), pp. 403–43; Engl. Ed. "Psychological Aspects of the Mother Archetype," in *The Collected Works of C.G. Jung*, Vol. 9i (Princeton, NJ: Bollingen Series XX, Princeton University Press, 1969[2]), pp. 75–110.

— "Dank an Frau Froebe," August 1951 (unpublished typescript; Eranos Foundation Archives, Ascona-Moscia).

— *Aion: Researches into the Phenomenology of the Self* (1951), in *The Collected Works of C.G. Jung*, Vol. 10ii (Princeton, NJ: Bollingen Series XX, Princeton University Press, 1969).

— *Memories, Dreams, Reflections* (New York, NY: Pantheon Books, 1963 {1961}).

— *Letters: 1906–1961*, ed. Aniela Jaffé and Gerhard Adler, 2 vols. (Princeton, NJ: Bollingen Series XCV/1–2, Princeton University Press, 1973–75).

— *C.G. Jung Speaking—Interviews and Encounters*, eds. William McGuire and Richard Francis Carrington Hull (Princeton, NJ: Bollingen Series XCVII, Princeton University Press, 1977); It. Ed. *Jung parla. Interviste e incontri* (Milan: Adelphi, 1995).

— *Visions. Notes from the Seminar Given in 1930–1934*, ed. Claire Douglas (London/New York, NY: Routledge, 1998).

— *Children's Dreams: Notes from the Seminar Given in 1936–40*, eds. Maria Meyer-Grass and Lorenz Jung (Princeton, NJ: Princeton University Press, 2010); It. Ed. *I sogni dei bambini. Seminario tenuto nel 1936–1941*, 2 vols. (Turin: Bollati Boringhieri, 2013–2014).

— *The Solar Myths and Opicinus de Canistris. Notes of the Seminar Given at Eranos in 1943*, eds. Riccardo Bernardini, Gian Piero Quaglino, and Augusto Romano (Einsiedeln: Daimon, 2015); It. Ed. *I miti solari e Opicino de Canistris. Appunti del Seminario tenuto a Eranos nel 1943*, eds. Riccardo Bernardini, Gian Piero Quaglino, and Augusto Romano (Bergamo: Moretti&Vitali, 2014).

— *The Red Book. Liber Novus*, ed. Sonu Shamdasani (New York, NY: W.W Norton & Company, Inc., 2009).

— *The Black Books: 1913–1932, Notebooks of Transformation*, ed. Sonu Shamdasani, 7 vols. (New York, NY: W.W. Norton & Company, Inc., 2020).

— *Rebirth. Text and Notes of the Lecture held at Eranos in 1939 / Rinascere. Testo e appunti della conferenza tenuta a Eranos nel 1939*, eds. Fabio Merlini and Riccardo Bernardini (Ascona: Eranos Classics 1, Aragno * Eranos Ascona, 2020).

Kamber, Peter, *Storia di due vite. Wladimir Rosenbaum e Aline Valangin* (Armando Dadò, Locarno, 2010 {1990}).

Kandinsky, Vasilij Vasil'evič, *Über das Geistige in der Kunst: insbesondere in der Malerei* (Munich: R. Piper & Co., 1912).

Karssenberg, Maite, "Muysken, Geertruida Agneta," in *Digitaal Vrouwenlexicon van Nederland*: https://resources.huygens.knaw.nl/vrouwenlexicon/lemmata/data/Muysken).

— *Dubbelleven. Geertruida Kapteyn-Muysken 1855–1920* (Amsterdam: De Arbeiderspers, 2026 {in press}).

Keller, Alwine von, "Abendaussprache für die Mitarbeiter der École d'Humanité, Goldern. 12.VIII.1945" (unpublished typescript, August 1945; Eranos Foundation Archives, Ascona-Moscia).

— "Erste Eindrücke von Paul Geheeb," *Der neue Waldkauz. Zeitschrift der Odenwaldschule*, 3 (1929); rpt. in Eva Cassirer *et al.*, eds., *Erziehung zur Humanität. Paul Geheeb zum 90. Geburtstag* (Heidelberg: Lambert Schneider, 1960) pp. 21–23; rpt. in Walter Schäfer, ed., *Paul Geheeb. Mensch und Erzieher. Eine Biographie. Aus den Deutschen Landerziehungsheimen – Heft 4* (Stuttgart: Klett, 1960), pp. 20–21.

— "Eindrücke von Edith und Paul Geheeb [Eindrücke aus der ‚Ecole d'Humanité'] – Arbeit in der Schweiz 1934–45," in Eva Cassirer, Ewa Liesegang, and Max Weber-Schäfer, eds., *Die Idee einer Schule im Spiegel der Zeit. Festschrift für Paul Geheeb zum 80. Geburtstag und zum 40jährigen Bestehen der Odenwaldschule* (Heidelberg: Lambert Schneider, undated [1950]), pp. 106–10.

— *My Story* (Madras: ADART, undated).

— *Du bist eitel, sagte der Alte* (Zurich: Klusverlag, 1989).

— "Appunti sul Cristianesimo" {1943}, *L'Ombra. Tracce e percorsi a partire da C.G. Jung*, 9 (1, 2018) ("Jung e Ivrea"), pp. 333–41.

— "*In memoriam* Carl Gustav Jung" {1961}, in Gian Piero Quaglino, Augusto Romano, and Riccardo Bernardini, eds., *Carl Gustav Jung a Eranos 1933–1952* (Turin: Antigone, 2007), pp. 168–69.

Kerényi, Magda, "Psychologie, mythologie. Les rapports entre C.G. Jung et Karl Kerényi," in Michel Cazenave, ed., *Carl G. Jung. L'Herne* (Paris: L'Herne, 1984, pp. 218–26; It. Ed. "Psicologia e mitologia. I rapporti tra C.G. Jung e Karl Kerényi," *L'immaginale. Rassegna di psicologia immaginale*, 4, (6, 1986), pp. 53–62.

Khan-Rossi, Manuela, ed., *Dal Seicento olandese alle avanguardie del primo Novecento. La collezione Eduard von der Heydt al Monte Verità. Sguardi sulla Collezione dello Stato del Cantone Ticino. Museo Cantonale d'Arte, 30 marzo–5 maggio 1996* (Lugano/Zurich: Museo Cantonale d'Arte/Pro Litteris, 1996).

Kingsley, Peter, *Catafalque: Carl Jung and the End of Humanity*, 2 vols. (London: Catafalque, 2018).

Kneubühler, Theo, "Gli artisti, gli scrittori e il Canton Ticino (dal 1900 ad oggi)," in Harald Szeemann, ed., *Monte Verità. Antropologia locale come contributo alla riscoperta di una topografia sacrale moderna* (Locarno/Milano: Armando Dadò/Electa, 1978), pp. 138–83.

Knight, Gareth, *Dion Fortune and the Inner Light* (Loughborough: Toth, 2000).

Kok, Leo, *Petit Chanson pour les enfants qui n'ont pas de Noël (Dessin de la couverture de Olga Froebe-Kapteyn). Violon & piano* (Sèvres: Allard, 1927).

König, Peter-Rober ed., "Thelema and suppressed homosexuality," *Abraxas* (1990).

— *Der Kleine Theodor-Reuss-Reader* (Munich: Arbeitsgemeinschaft für Religions- und Weltanschauungsfragen, 1993).

— ed., *Das OTO-Phänomen. 100 Jahre Magische Geheimbünde und ihre Protagonisten von 1895–1994* (Munich: Arbeitsgemeinschaft für Religions- und Weltanschauungsfragen, 1994).

— ed., *Materialien zum OTO* (Munich: Arbeitsgemeinschaft für Religions- und Weltanschauungsfragen, 1994).

— ed., *Der Grosse Theodor-Reuss-Reader* (Munich: Arbeitsgemeinschaft für Religions- und Weltanschauungsfragen, 1997).

— ed., *Ecclesia Gnostica Catholica* (Munich: Arbeitsgemeinschaft für Religions- und Weltanschauungsfragen, 1998).

— ed., *Noch Mehr Materialien zum OTO* (Munich: Arbeitsgemeinschaft für Religions- und Weltanschauungsfragen, 2000).

— ed., *Der O.T.O. Phänomen Remix* (Munich: Arbeitsgemeinschaft für Religions- und Weltanschauungsfragen, 2001).

Kropp, Heinrich, *Monte Verità: Schauspiel in 3 Akten aus dem Naturleben zu Ascona* (Ascona: [without publishing information], 1914).

Kugler, Paul, "Eranos and Jungian Psychology: A History in Images," in Lyn Cowan, ed., Barcelona 2004—Edges of Experience: Memory and Emergence—Proceedings of the Sixteenth International Congress for Analytical Psychology (Einsiedeln: Daimon, 2006), pp. 99–114; rpt. as "Eranos and Jungian Psychology: A Photographic History," in Christine Downing, ed., *Disturbances in the Field—Essays in Honor of David L. Miller* (New Orleans, LO: Spring Journal, Inc., 2006, pp. 69–112.

Kuiper, Yme, "On Monte Verità: Myth and Modernity in the *Lebensreform* Movement," in Jitse Dijkstra, Justin Kroesen, and Yme Kuiper, eds., *Myths, Martyrs, and Modernity—Studies in the History of Religions in Honour of Jan N. Bremmer* (Leiden/Boston, MA: Numen Book Series 127, Brill, 2010), pp. 629–50.

Kunz, Stephan, Müller, Lars, and Wismer, Beat, eds., *Sophie Taeuber-Arp, zum 100. Geburtstag* (Aarau: Aargauer Kunsthaus, 1989).

Kurzmeyer, Roman, *Viereck und Kosmos. Künstler, Lebensreformer, Okkultisten, Spiritisten in Amden 1901–1912. Max Nopper, Josua Klein, Fidus, Otto Meyer-Amden* (Wien: Voldemeer, 1999).

Laban, Rudolf von, *Ein Leben für den Tanz* (Dresden: Carl Reissner, 1935).

Lafranchi, Claudia, and Schwab, Andreas, eds., *Dalla visione al chiodo. Dal chiodo alla visione. Il Fondo Harald Szeemann dell'Archivio Fondazione Monte Verità*, "Quaderni del Bollettino Storico della Svizzera Italiana," Vol. 12 (Bellinzona: Salvioni, 2013).

Landmann, Robert, *Ascona—Monte Verità. Auf der Suche nach dem Paradies* (Berlin: Albert Schultz, 1930; rpt. Frauenfeld/Stuttgart/Wien: Huber, 2000).

— *Monte Verità—Ascona. Die Geschichte eines Berges* (Ascona: Pancaldi, *Ascona 1934).*

Lincoln, Bruce, *Emerging from the Chrysalis. Studies in Rituals of Women's Initiation* (Cambridge, MA/London: Harvard University Press, 1981).

Linse, Ulrich, "Il ribelle e la 'Madre terra': il monte sacro di Ascona nell'interpretazione dell'anarchico bohémien Erich Mühsam," in Harald Szeemann, ed., *Monte Verità. Antropologia locale come contributo alla riscoperta di una topografia sacrale moderna* (Locarno/Milano: Armando Dadò/Electa, 1978), pp. 26–37.

— "Il Monte Verità e la valle di Hunza – Alla riscoperta di una moderna "topografia sacrale" in Ticino e in Pakistan," in Andreas Schwab and Claudia Lafranchi, eds., *Senso della vita e bagni di sole. Esperimenti di vita e arte al Monte Verità* (Ascona: Fondazione Monte Verità, 2001), pp. 238–59.

Lo Russo, Michelantonio, *Otto Gross. Psiche, Eros, Utopia* (Rome: Editori Riuniti, 2011).

Lowy, Michael, *Redemption and Utopia: Jewish Libertarian Thought in Central Europe—A Study in Elective Affinity* (Stanford, NJ: Stanford University Press, 1992).

Luban-Plozza, Boris, "Lernen am Monte Verità," *Forum. Galenus Mannheim*, 17 (1988), pp. 1–4.

— "Creatività e Monte Verità: verso il centenario," *Schweizerisch Ärzte-zeitung/Bollettino dei medici svizzeri*, 53 (20, 1999), p. 1253.

— "Creatività al Monte Verità," in Hans-Caspar Bodmer, Ottmar Holden-rieder, and Klaus Seeland, eds., *Monte Verità: Landschaft Kunst Geschichte* (Frauenfeld/Stuttgart/Wien: Huber, 2000), pp. 21–22.

Lucet, Anatole, "Natures féminines et radicalités féministes : l'émancipation des femmes sur le Monte Verità," *Cahiers d'histoire culturelle*, 29 (2018) ("Monte Verità : communautés d'expériences du corps et de retours à la nature"), pp. 53–66.

Lunghi, Nancy, and Peter, Sébastien, "Prefazione / Foreword," in Raphael Gygax, ed., *Olga Fröbe-Kapteyn. Artista—ricercatrice. Volume pubblicato in occasione della mostra Olga Fröbe-Kapteyn: artista–ricercatrice, Museo Casa Rusca, Locarno, 8 agosto 2024–12 gennaio 2025* (Locarno/Ascona/Bellinzona: Museo Casa Rusca/Fondazione Eranos/ Casagrande, in collaboration with Kunsthalle Mainz, 2024), pp. 6–11.

Luscher, Ingeborg, *Dokumentation über Armand Schulthess. „Der grösste Vogel kann nicht fliegen,"* 2 vols. (Luzern/Poschiavo, 2021).

Macel, Christine, and Ziebinska-Lewandowska, Karolina, eds., *Women in Abstraction* (London/New York, NY: Thames & Hudson, 2021).

— and Ziebinska-Lewandowska, Karolina, eds., *Elles font l'abstraction* (Paris: Centre Pompidou, 2021).

— and Laure Chauvelot, eds., *Elles font l'abstraction. Exhibition Album* (Paris: Centre Pompidou, 2021).

— and Ziebinska-Lewandowska, Karolina, eds., *Mujeres de la abstracción* (Bilbao: Centre Pompidou/FMGP Guggenheim Bilbao Museoa, 2021).

Magnússon, Gísli, "Reminiscences of Eranos in Naja Marie Aidt's Novel When Death Takes Something from You Give It Back: Carl's Book," *Religiographies*, 4 (1, 2025), pp. 104–16.

Maffioli, Alessandra, "Abbondio," in *Dizionario Storico della Svizzera DSS*, version of May 7, 2020.

Mañas Peñalver, Maria Cruz, "El Oráculo del *I Ching*: Un Capitulo de la Historia de la Psicología Profunda," Ph.D. Dissertation, Escuela Internacional de Doctorado, Universidad Nacional de Educación a Distancia (UNED), Madrid, 2021.

— "El *I Ching* en Eranos," in *I Ching. El Libro de los Cambios. El proyecto del I Ching de Eranos*, eds. Rudolf Ritsema, Shantena Augusto Sabbadini, and María Cruz Mañas Peñalver (Córdoba: Editorial Cántico, 2022), pp. 93–118.

Mander, Micaela, "Monte Verità, Ascona: il lascito di un esperimento comunitario," in Bertrando Bonfantini, ed., *Attivare risorse latenti. Metodi sperimentali per l'analisi, la mappatura e la gestione informativa integrata delle trasformazioni di territori e manufatti del patrimonio culturale diffuso* (Planum, 2017), pp. 249–63.

Mandozzi, Graziano, *Elisarion. Un Santuario per il Clarismo* (Minusio: Comune di Minusio, 1996).

Manz, Hanspeter, "Vom Buchhandel im Locarnese. Fremdenverkehr und Lesevergnügen," *Ferien-Journal. Ascona*, 326 (1996), pp. 5–7.

— "Der Mann im Bild: zu einem Foto von O.R. Schlag," *Ferien-Journal. Ascona*, 326 (1996), p. 49.

Margolin, Ron, "Tre approcci allo studio della religione a Eranos: Martin Buber, C.G. Jung e Mircea Eliade," in Elisabetta Barone, Adriano Fabris, and Flavia Monceri, eds., *Eranos. Monte Verità. Ascona* (Pisa: ETS, 2003), pp. 189–200; Eng. Ed. "Three Approaches to the Study of Religion at Eranos: Martin Buber, C.G. Jung and Mircea Eliade," in Elisabetta Barone, Matthias Riedl, and Alexandra Tischel, eds., *Pioniere, Poeten, Professoren. Eranos und der Monte Verità in der Zivilisationsgeschichte des 20. Jahrhunderts* (Würzburg: Eranos Neue Folge XI, Königshausen & Neumann, 2004), pp. 97–104.

Martinoni, Renato, *La cultura nel Locarnese fra Otto e Novecento* (Bellinzona: Salvioni, 2014).

— *Il ritorno dello gnosticismo* (Carnago: SugarCo, 1993).

Mauer, Bruno, "Carl Weidemeyer und ‚die Rationalisten von Ascona‘," in Letizia Tedeschi, ed., *Carl Weidemeyer 1882–1976. Künstler und Anarchist zwischen Worpswede und Ascona* (Mendrisio/Ascona/Milano: Accademia di architettura, Università della Svizzera italiana/Museo comunale d'arte moderna/Skira, 2001), pp. 135–57.

Mazzotta, Martina, "Heterography: Luigi Pericle and Herbert Read: Encounters in Ascona through the Eranos Circle," *Religiographies* 4 (1, 2025), pp. 131–39.

McGuire, William, "The Arcane Summer School," *Spring* (1980), pp. 146–56.

— *Bollingen—An Adventure in Collecting the Past* (Princeton, NJ: Bollingen Series, Princeton University Press, 1982).

— "Jung and Eranos in America," *Spring* (1984), pp. 51–59.

— "Firm Affinities: Jung's Relations with Britain and the United States," *Journal of Analytical Psychology* 40 (3, 1995), pp. 301–26.

Mellick, Jill, *The Red Book Hours. Discovering C.G. Jung's Art Mediums and Creative Process* (Zurich: Scheidegger and Spiess, 2018).

Menapace, Luigi, *Sole d'Ascona* (Lugano: Edizioni del Cantonetto, 1970 {1957}).

Merlini, Fabio, and Bernardini, Riccardo, eds., *Eranos 85 Years. 85 anni di Eranos. 1933–2018* (Savigliano: Nino Aragno, 2018).

— and Bernardini, Riccardo, eds., *Eranos in the Mirror: Views on a Moving Heritage. Eranos allo specchio: sguardi su una eredità in movimento* (Ascona: Aragno*Eranos Ascona, 2019).

— and Bernardini, Riccardo, "Olga Fröbe-Kapteyn. 1881, Londres (Royaume-Uni)–1962, Ascona (Suisse)," in Christine Macel and Laure Chauvelot, eds., *Elles font l'abstraction. Exhibition Album* (Paris: Centre Pompidou, 2021), p. 54 ; rpt. in *AWARE: Archives of Women Artists, Research and Exhibitions a pour objet la création, l'indexation et la diffusion de l'information sur les artistes femmes du XIXe et XXe siècle*, https://awarewomenartists.com/en/artiste/olga-frobe-kapteyn/.

— and Bernardini, Riccardo, "Preface / Prefazione," in Carl Gustav Jung, *Rebirth. Text and Notes of the Lecture held at Eranos in 1939 / Rinascere. Testo e appunti della conferenza tenuta a Eranos nel 1939*, eds Fabio Merlini and Riccardo Bernardini (Ascona: Eranos Classics 1, Aragno * Eranos Ascona, 2020), pp. XI–LV.

— and Bernardini, Riccardo, "Preface / Prefazione," in Ernesto Buonaiuti, *Palingenesis, Resurrection, and Immortality in Primitive Christianity / Palingenesi, resurrezione e immortalità nel Cristianesimo primitivo*, ed. Adriano Fabris (Ascona: Eranos Classics 2, Aragno * Eranos Ascona, 2020), pp. VII–LII.

Michaels, Jennifer E., *Anarchy and Eros: Otto Gross' Impact on German Expressionist Writers. Leonhard Frank, Franz Jung, Johannes R. Becher, Karl Otten, Curt Corrinth, Walter Hasenclever, Oskar Maria Graf, Franz Kafka, Franz Werfel, Max Brod, Raoul Hausmann and Berlin Dada* (New York, NY: Peter Lang, 1983).

— "Otto Gross und das Konzept des Matriarchats," in Gottfried Heuer, ed., *2. Internationaler Otto Gross Kongress. Burghölzli, Zürich 2000* (Marburg an der Lahn: LiteraturWissenschaft.de, 2002), pp. 105–15.

Michalzik, Peter, *1900. Vegetarier, Künstler und Visionäre suchen nach dem neuen Paradies* (Köln: Dumont, 2018).

Minazzi, Fabio, "Vivere secondo natura? L'esperienza del Monte Verità nel contesto del dibattito filosofico," in Andreas Schwab and Claudia Lafranchi, eds., *Senso della vita e bagni di sole. Esperimenti di vita e arte al Monte Verità* (Ascona: Fondazione Monte Verità, 2001), pp. 59–73.

Mirolo, Diana, ed., *Maggy Reichstein e Mischa Epper. Ricami in seta e disegni dell'inconscio. Catalogo della mostra* (Ascona: Museo Epper, 2009).

— ed., *Margarethe Fellerer. Fotografa* (Ascona: Museo Epper, 2012).

Möller, Helmut, and Howe, Ellic, *Jahrhundertfeier. Vom Untergrund des Abendlandes* (Göttingen: Buchdruckerel R. Walter, 1975).

— and Howe, Ellic, "Theodor Reuss—Irregular Freemasonry in Germany, 1900–23," *Ars Quatuor Coronatorum*, 91 (1978), pp. 28–47.

— and Howe, Ellic, *Merlin Peregrinus. Vom Untergrund des Abendlandes* (Würzburg: Könighausen + Neumann, 1986), pp. 206–23.

Mondada, Giuseppe, *Le isole di Brissago nel passato e oggi* (Isole di Brissago/Locarno: Amministrazione delle Isole di Brissago/Tipografia Stazione S.A., 1975).

Mongini, Nicoletta, Gatti, Chiara, and Risaliti, Sergio, eds., *Monte Verità. Back to Nature* (Turin: Lindau, 2022).

Montabord, Karine, "Zurich et le Monte Verità, un binôme favorable aux échanges entre Dada et la danse," *Transversales*, 18 (2021) ("Corps, Lieux et Appartenances").

Moser, Fanny, *Der Okkultismus. Täuschungen und Tatsachen*, 2 vols. (Zurich: Orell Füssli, 1935).

Moura, Vicente de, *Two Cases from Jung's Clinical Practice. The Story of Two Sisters and the Evolution of Jungian Analysis* (London/New York, NY: Routledge, 2019).

Mros, Eberhard, *Phänomen Monte Verità*, 8 vols. (Ascona: Selbstverlag des Verfassers, 2007–2008).

Mühsam, Erich *Ascona: Eine Broschüre* (Locarno/Berlin: Birger Carlson/Klaus Guhl, 1905).

— *Ascona: Vereinigte texte. Aus den jahren 1905, 1930 und 1931* (Zurich: Sanssouci, 1979).

— *Ascona, Monte Verità e Schegge* (Salorino: L'Affranchi, 1989).

Mulacz, Peter, "Oscar R. Schlag," *Journal of the Society for Psychical Research*, 60 (1995), pp. 263–66.

Müller, Hermann, "Monte Gioia. Il Monte Verità di Gusto Gräser," in Andreas Schwab and Claudia Lafranchi, eds., *Senso della vita e bagni di sole. Esperimenti di vita e arte al Monte Verità* (Ascona: Fondazione Monte Verità, 2001), pp. 188–203.

— ed., *Meister Diefenbachs Alpenwanderung: Ein Künstler und Kulturrebell im Karwendel* (Recklinghausen: Umbruch, 2003).

— ed., *Der Himmelhof. Künstlerfamilie und Landkommune* (Recklinghausen: Umbruch, 2003).

Näf, Martin, *Paul Geheeb. Seine Entwicklung bis zur Gründung der Odenwaldschule. Schriftenreihe des Weltbundes für Erneuerung der Erziehung. Internationale Pädagogik-Reformpädagogik. Band 4* (Weinheim: Deutscher Studien, 1998).

Nagel, Hildegard, ed., "Eranos Archive—Images of the Great Mother Throughout the Ages—Catalogue Prepared by the Analytical Psychology Club, Analytical Psychology Club, New York, NY 1938" (unpublished typescript, 1938; Warburg Institute, London).

— "The Eranos Conference 1938—Papers of the Analytical Psychology Club of New York" (unpublished typescript, 1939; Kristine Mann Library, New York).

Neri, Nadia, *Oltre l'Ombra. Donne intorno a Jung* (Rome: Borla, 1995).

Nespolo, Ugo, "Quando l'arte si fa numinosa. Oltre il visibile. Nella straordinaria mostra al Museo Casa Rusca di Locarno, le opere di Olga Fröbe-Kapteyn restituiscono un raro connubio di spiritualità e agire artistico, tra simboli e aperture," *Il Sole 24 Ore. Domenica*, 290 (October 20, 2024), p. XI.

Nessi, Angelo, *Scrittori ticinesi*, eds. Renato Martinoni and Clara Cavezzano Tanzi (Locarno: Armando Dadò, 1997).

Nessi, Alberto, "La via delle comete," in Andreas Schwab and Claudia Lafranchi, eds., *Senso della vita e bagni di sole. Esperimenti di vita e arte al Monte Verità* (Ascona: Fondazione Monte Verità, 2001), pp. 263–75.

Neumann, Erich, "Die Bedeutung des Erdarchetypus für die Neuzeit," in *Eranos-Jahrbuch*, 22 (1953), pp. 11–56.

— *The Great Mother—An Analysis of the Archetype* (New York, NY: Bollingen Series XLVII, Pantheon Books, 1955); It. Ed. *La Grande Madre. Fenomenologia delle configurazioni femminili dell'inconscio* (Rom: Astrolabio, 1981).

Noschis, Kaj, *Monte Verità. Ascona e il genio del luogo* (Bellinzona: Casagrande, 2013 {2011}).

Oppenheimer, Wolfgang, *Das Refugium: Erinnerungen an Ascona* (Munich: Universitas, 1998).

Otto, Rudolf, *Das Heilige. Über das Irrationale in der Idee zum Göttlichen und sein Verhältnis zum Rationalen* (Breslau: Trewendt & Granier, 1922).

— *West-Östliche Mystik. Vergleich und Unterscheidung zur Wesensdeutung* (Gotha: Leopold Klotz, 1926).

Pallat, Annemarie, "Olga Fröbe" (unpublished typescript, April 29, 1962; Eranos Foundation Archives, Ascona-Moscia).

Paoli, Alfio de and Buvoli, Teo, [DVD] *Il monte di Hetty. L'ultima guardiana del Monte Verità* (Lugano: Ethiva Video/PGV communications/RSI, 2009).

Pasi, Marco, "The Art of Esoteric Posthumousness," in Lukas Pokorny and Franz Winter, eds., *The Occult Nineteenth Century: Roots, Developments, and Impact on the Modern World* (Camden: Palgrave Macmillan, 2021), pp. 159–76.

Pedrotta, Fausto, *Alfredo Pioda nella vita e nelle opere* (Bellinzona: [without publishing information], undated [1935]).

Pelet-Narbonne, Emma Hélène von, "Bilder aus dem Unbewußten" (unpublished manuscript and typescript with drawings, 1941–42; Eranos Foundation Archives, Ascona-Moscia).

Perrottet, Claude, "Rudolf Laban. Il rinnovatore della danza nel nostro secolo," in Harald Szeemann, ed., *Dalla danza libera, all'arte pura. Catalogo della mostra, 15 aprile–10 giugno 1990* (Ascona: Museo Comunale di Arte Moderna di Ascona, 1990).

Petrucci, Sara, "Hablamos Marciano. Los Futuros de Olga Fröbe-Kapteyn (1881–1962) y Emma Kunz (1892–1963)," *A*Desk. Critical Thinking* (September 20, 2021).

— "Olga Fröbe-Kapteyn e il potere delle immagini: considerazioni sulle 'Tavole di meditazione'" / Olga Fröbe-Kapteyn and the Power of Images: Considerations on her 'Meditation Plates,'" in Raphael Gygax, ed., *Olga Fröbe-Kapteyn. Artista—ricercatrice. Volume pubblicato in occasione della mostra Olga Fröbe-Kapteyn: artista–ricercatrice, Museo Casa Rusca, Locarno, 8 agosto 2024–12 gennaio 2025* (Locarno/Ascona/Bellinzona: Museo Casa Rusca/Fondazione Eranos/Casagrande, in collaboration with Kunsthalle Mainz, 2024), pp. 166–83.

Petzold, Ernst R., "Balint-Arbeit und Monte Verità-Gruppen als Teil das Ascona-Modells," *Klinikarzt*, 11 (22, 1993), pp. 485–89.

— and Pöldinger, Walter, eds., *Beziehungsmedizin auf dem Monte Verità. 30 Jahre Psychosomatik in Ascona* (Wien: Springer, 1998).

Phillips, Glen, Kaiser, Phillip, Chon, Doris, and Rigolo, Pietro, eds., *Harald Szeemann. Museum of Obsessions* (Los Angeles, CA: The Getty Research Institute, 2018).

Piccardi, Carlo, "Wladimir Vogel e l'accoglienza dei musicisti nella Svizzera Italiana tra le due guerre," *Schweizer Jahrbuch für Musikwissenschaft*, 39 (2022), pp. 85–95.

Pioda, Alfredo, *Statuti, Norme e Schema del Convento Laico da fondarsi sulle rive del Lago nella Svizzera* (Bellinzona: Stamperia Colombi, 1889).

Pöldinger, Walter, "Monte Verità-Gruppen," in Ernst Petzold and Volker Beck, eds., *Der alternde Mensch und sein Umfeld* (Jena: Universitätsverlag, 1993).

Portmann, Adolf, "Vom Sinn und Auftrag der Eranos-Tagungen (zum 80. Geburtstag von Olga Fröbe-Kapteyn)," *Eranos-Jahrbuch*, 30 (1961), pp. 7–28.

— "Zur Erinnerung an Olga Fröbe," *Eranos-Jahrbuch*, 31 (1962), pp. 6–8.

Prange, Oliver, *Das Sonnenfest* (Berlin: Edition D, 2016).

Preston-Dunlop, Valerie, *Rudolf Laban: An Extraordinary Life* (Alton: Dance Books, 2008).

Prinz, Alois, *Vita di Hermann Hesse* (Rome: Donzelli, 2003 {2001}).

Provenzale, Veronica, "L'energia del luogo. Il Locarnese come crocevia di spiriti erranti / The Energy of a place. The Locarnese as the crossroad of wondering spirits," in Riccardo Carazzetti and Mara Folini, eds.,

L'energia del luogo. Jean Arp, Raffael Benazzi, Julius Bissier, Ben Nicholson, Hans Richter, Mark Tobey, Italo Valenti. Alla ricerca del genius loci Ascona-Locarno (Ascona/Locarno/Milan: Museo comunale d'arte moderna/Città di Locarno, Servizi culturali/Armando Dadò, 2009), pp. 21–83.

Quaglino, Gian Piero, Romano, Augusto, and Bernardini, Riccardo, eds., *Carl Gustav Jung a Eranos 1933–1952* (Turin: Antigone, 2007).

— Romano, Augusto, and Bernardini, Riccardo, "A visit paid to Jung by Alwine von Keller," *Journal of Analytical Psychology*, 56 (2, 2011), pp. 232–54.

Radermacher, Martin, "Hermann Hesse—Monte Verità. Wahrheitssuche abseits des Mainstreams zu Beginn des 20. Jahrhunderts," *Zeitschrift für junge Religionswissenschaft*, 6 (2011), pp. 1–20.

Ragno, Gianfranco, "La fotografa di Eranos: Margarethe Fellerer / Die Eranos-Fotografin: Margarethe Fellerer," *Ferien-Journal. Ascona* (March–April 2025), pp. 22–26.

Rajalakshmi, M. Santhanam, *Under the Banyan Tree* (Mylapore, Madras: hout publishing information, undated).

Reibnitz, Barbara von, "Der Eranos-Kreis. Religionswissenschaft und Weltanschauung oder der Gelehrte als Laien-Priester," in Richard Faber and Christine Holste, eds., *Kreise, Gruppen, Bünde. Zur Soziologie moderner Intellektuellenassoziation* (Würzburg: Könighausen + Neumann, 2000), pp. 425–40; rpt. in Renate Schleiser and Roberto Sanchiño Martinez, eds., *Neuhumanismus und Anthropologie des griechischen Mythos. Karl Kerényi im europäischen Kontext des 20. Jahrhunderts* (Locarno: Rezzonico, 2006), pp. 107–23.

Reventlow, Franziska zu, *Herrn Dames Aufzeichnungen- oder Begebenheiten aus einem merkwürdigen Stadtteil* (Munich: Albert Langen, 1913).

— *Der Geldkomplex* (Munich: Albert Langen, 1916).

Rezzonico, Giò, ed., *Antologia di cronaca del Monte Verità* (Locarno: I quaderni dell'Eco di Locarno, 1992).

Rieger, Jonny, *Ein Balkon über dem Lago Maggiore. Tessiner Reiseverführbuch* (Zurich: Sanssouci, 1981).

Ries, Elisabeth, "Monte Verità, Ascona: superficie e correnti sotterranee", in Elisabetta Barone, Adriano Fabris, and Flavia Monceri, eds., *Eranos. Monte Verità. Ascona* (Pisa: ETS, 2003), pp. 219–36; Germ. Ed. "Monte Verità, Ascona. Oberfläche und Unterströmungen am Berg der Wahrheit", in Elisabetta Barone, Matthias Riedl, and Alexandra Tischel, eds., *Pioniere, Poeten, Professoren. Eranos und der Monte Verità in der Zivilisationsgeschichte des 20. Jahrhunderts* (Würzburg: Eranos Neue Folge XI, Königshausen & Neumann, 2004), pp. 21–32.

Riess, Curt, *Ascona, Die Geschichte des seltsamsten Dorfes der Welt* (Zurich: Buchclub Ex Libris, 1964).

Rigolo, Pietro, *La mamma. Una mostra di Harald Szeemann mai realizzata* (Milan: Johan & Levi, 2014).

Ritsema, Rudolf, "Eranos: Selbstdarstellung einer Idee in der Zeit. Olga Fröbe-Kapteyn zum 80. Geburtstag, 19. Oktober 1961" (unpublished typescript, 1961; Eranos Foundation Archives, Ascona-Moscia).

— *Alwine von Keller. * 10.6.1878, New York–† 31.12.1965, Interlaken* (privately printed, undated [1966]).

— "The Origins and Opus of Eranos: Reflections at the 55th Conference – Eranos: Ursprünge und Werk. Eine Betrachtung anläßlich der 55th Tagung – L'œuvre d'Eranos et ses origines: Réflexions à l'occasion de la 55me session," *Eranos-Jahrbuch*, 56 (1987), pp. VII–XLVII.

— "Encompassing Versatility: Keystone of the Eranos Project / Allumfassende Wendigkeit: Schlußstein des Eranos-Projekts / Versatilité englobante: Clef de voûte du projet Eranos," *Eranos-Jahrbuch*, 57 (1988), pp. VII–LVII.

— and Shantena Augusto Sabbadini, "Images of the Unknown: The Eranos *I Ching* Project 1989–1997," *Eranos-Jahrbuch*, 66 (1997), pp. 7–43.

— "The Periplus of the Eranos Archetype" (unpublished typescript, 2002; Eranos Foundation Archives, Ascona-Moscia).

Ritsema-Gris, Catherine, "L'Œuvre d'Eranos et Vie d'Olga Froebe-Kapteyn" (unpublished typescript, undated; Eranos Foundation Archives, Ascona-Moscia).

Robinson, Christa, "Eranos: A Place, an Encounter, a Story," *Spring*, 86 (2011), pp. 165–82.

Rogantini-de Beauclair, Hetty, *Dal Monte Verità di Ascona... a Berzona in Onsernone. Hetty De Beauclair racconta il meraviglioso mondo della sua infanzia*, eds. Yvonne Bölt and Gian Pietro Milani (Losone: Serodine, 2004).

Rosenbaum-Kroeber, Sybille, "Eranos e Olga Fröbe-Kapteyn," in Harald Szeemann, ed., *Monte Verità. Antropologia locale come contributo alla riscoperta di una topografia sacrale moderna* (Locarno/Milano: Armando Dadò/Electa, 1978), pp. 119–21; Germ. Ed. "Was ist Eranos und wer war Olga Fröbe-Kapteyn?," in Harald Szeemann, ed., *Monte Verità. Berg der Wahrheit. Lokale Anthropologie als Beitrag zur Wiederentdeckung einer neuzeitlichen Topographie* (Locarno/Milan: Armando Dadò/Electa, 1978), pp. 117–19.

Rosenberg, Alfons, "Eranos oder Der Geist am Wasser," *Flugblätter für Freunde* 80 (1977), pp. 7–8.

— *Die Welt im Feuer. Wandlungen meines Lebens* (Freiburg im Breisgau/Basel/Wien: Herder 1983).

Rotzler, Willy, "Il barone a Monte Verità. Breve profilo biografico di Eduard von der Heydt," in Harald Szeemann, ed., *Monte Verità. Antropologia locale come contributo alla riscoperta di una topografia sacrale moderna* (Locarno/Milano: Armando Dadò/Electa, 1978), pp. 101–07.

— "Der Baron auf dem Monte Verità. Kleines Lebensbild von Eduard von der Heydt," in Harald Szeemann, ed., *Von Marées bis Picasso. Meisterwerke aus dem Von der Heydt-Museum Wuppertal. Ascona, 7. Juni bis 17. August 1986–Bern, 4. September bis 2. November 1986. Albergo Monte Verità, Museo Comunale di Arte Moderna, Centro Culturale Beato Pietro Berno, Ascona, Kunstmuseum Bern, Bern* (Ascona: Museo Von der Heydt - Monte Verità S.A., 1986), pp. 21–32.

Rüesch, Diana, "Il Fondo Aline Valangin," *Cartevive. Bollettino dell'Archivio Prezzolini e degli Archivi di Cultura Contemporanea della Biblioteca Cantonale di Lugano*, 10 (2, 1998), pp. 35–52.

Sabbadini, Shantena Augusto, "*In memoriam*: Rudolf Ritsema (1918–2006)," *Harvest* (2010), pp. 140–43.

— "Una breve biografia di Rudolf Ritsema," in Wilma Scategni and Franco Livorsi, eds., *Il mistero di Eranos tra passato e presente. Civiltà e spiritualità tra Oriente e Occidente dal punto di vista della Psicologia Analitica (e dintorni)* (Alessandria: Falsopiano, 2011), pp. 59–63.

— "*I Ching* e sincronicità," *Studi junghiani*, 42 (21/2, 2015), pp. 85–83.

— "Rudolf Ritsema," in *I Ching. El Libro de los Cambios. El proyecto del I Ching de Eranos*, eds. Rudolf Ritsema, Shantena Augusto Sabbadini, and María Cruz Mañas Peñalver (Córdoba: Editorial Cántico, 2022), pp. 119–33.

Sassi, Maria Michela, "La terra contemplata dall'alto (Plat., *Phaed.* 110b5–111c3): un'esperienza premorte? Da Pugliese a Jung, e oltre," in *La parola del passato. Rivista di studi antichi*, 77 (1–2, 2022), pp. 339–57.

Savage, Adrian, *Introduction to Chaos Magick* (New York, NY: Magickal Childe, 1989).

Scategni, Wilma, "Introduzione. Olga Fröbe e lo sguardo sul gruppo: l'individuazione, la ricerca, l'incontro," in Wilma Scategni and Franco Livorsi, eds., *Il mistero di Eranos tra passato e presente. Civiltà e spiritualità tra Oriente e Occidente dal punto di vista della Psicologia Analitica (e dintorni)* (Alessandria: Falsopiano, 2011), pp. 13–35.

Schiavoni, Giulio, "Figure della bohème in Ascona. Hugo Ball e Erich Mühsam lettori di Bakunin," *Studi germanici*, 15/16 (2019), pp. 31–44.

Schlag, Oskar Rudolf, "Max Pulvers Lebenswerk," *Beiheft zur Schweizer. Zeitschrift für Parapsychologie und ihre Anwendungen*, 20 (1953), pp. 5–16.

— "Zum 100. Geburtstag von Max Pulver," *Zeitschrift für Menschenkunde*" (April 1989), pp. 194–211.

— *Von alten und neuen Mysterien. Die Lehren des A.* (Stäfa: Rothenhäusler, 1995).

Schlienger, Alfred, "Die Frau zwischen allen Welten. Kann man alles mit allem verbinden? Kunst mit Wissenschaft und Spiritualität? Antike mit Moderne? Olga Fröbe-Kapteyn (1881–1962) hat es versucht. Das Museo Casa Rusca (Locarno) zeigt eine Ausstellung über ihr Schaffen," *Cültür* (November 14, 2024).

Schönenberger, Walter, "Monte Verità e le idee teosofiche," in Harald Szeemann, ed., *Monte Verità. Antropologia locale come contributo alla riscoperta di una topografia sacrale moderna* (Locarno/Milano: Armando Dadò/Electa, 1978), pp. 65–79.

Schwab, Andreas and Lafranchi, Claudia, eds., *Senso della vita e bagni di sole. Esperimenti di vita e arte al Monte Verità* (Ascona: Fondazione Monte Verità, 2001).

— *Sinnsuche und Sonnenbad. Experimente in Kunst und Leben auf dem Monte Verità* (Zurich: Limmat, 2001).

— and Lafranchi, Claudia, "Cento anni di verità?," in Id. and Claudia Lafranchi, eds., *Senso della vita e bagni di sole. Esperimenti di vita e arte al Monte Verità* (Ascona: Fondazione Monte Verità, 2001), pp. 9–21.

— "'Frattanto gridava in me la nostalgia…' – Vedute d'esterno del Monte Verità," in Id. and Claudia Lafranchi, eds., *Senso della vita e bagni di sole. Esperimenti di vita e arte al Monte Verità* (Ascona: Fondazione Monte Verità, 2001), pp. 105–18.

— *Monte Verità – Sanatorium der Sehnsucht* (Zurich: Orell Füssli, 2003).

— *Zeit der Aussteiger. Eine Reise zu den Künstlerkolonien von Barbizon bis Monte Verità* (Munich: C.H.Beck, 2021).

Serrano, Miguel, *C.G. Jung and Hermann Hesse: A Record of Two Friendships* (New York, NY: Schocken Books, 1966).

Servier, Jean, *Der Traum von der grossen Harmonie. Eine Geschichte der Utopie* (Munich: List, 1971).

Sgorbati, Matteo, *L'I Ching a Eranos. Wilhelm, Jung e la ricezione del classico dei mutamenti* (Naples, Orientexpress, 2021).

Shamdasani, Sonu, "Jung's Journey to the East," in Carl Gustav Jung, *The Psychology of Kundalini Yoga—Notes on the Seminar given in 1932*, ed. Sonu Shamdasani (Princeton, NJ: Princeton University Press, 1996), pp. xvii–xlvi; It. Ed. "Il viaggio di Jung verso l'Oriente," in Carl Gustav Jung, *La psicologia del Kundalini-Yoga. Seminario tenuto nel 1932* (Turin: Bollati Boringhieri, 2004), pp. 23–49.

— *Jung and the Making of Modern Psychology—The Dream of a Science* (Cambridge: Press Syndicate of the University of Cambridge, 2003).

— "*Liber Novus*: The 'Red Book' of C.G. Jung," in Carl Gustav Jung, *The Red Book. Liber Novus*, ed. Sonu Shamdasani (New York, NY: W.W Norton & Company, Inc., 2009), pp. 193–221.

Sharma, Venkatesh Narayana, *Indische Erziehung – Mit Einer Karte – Pädagogik des Auslands – Herausgegeben im Auftrag des Zentralinstituts für Erziehung und Unterricht von Prof. Dr. Peter Petersen-Jena – Vol. VIII* (Weimar: Hermann Böhlaus Nachfolger, 1936).

Sharma-Teichmüller, Ellen, and Sharma, Venkatesh Narayana, "Unsere Odenwaldschule in Indien – The Children's Garden School – Kindergarten, Middle School and Teachers Training Department, Kindergärtneerinnen-Seminar Mothers Classes," in Eva Cassirer, Ewa Liesegang, and Max Weber-Schäfer, eds., *Die Idee einer Schule im Spiegel der Zeit. Festschrift für Paul Geheeb zum 80. Geburtstag und zum 40jährigen Bestehen der Odenwaldschule* (Heidelberg: Lambert Schneider, undated [1950]), pp. 132–35.

— and Sharma, Venkatesh Narayana, *The Children's Garden. A School for the Little Ones. Mylapore, Madras* (Mylapore, Madras: Children's Garden School Society, 1937).

Shirley, Dennis, *Reformpädagogik im Nationalsozialismus. Die Odenwaldschule 1910 bis 1945* (Weinheim/Munich: Juventa, 2010).

Sirost, Olivier, "The recosmologisation of the world. From Monte Verità to naturism,"), in Bernard Andrieu, Jim Parry, Alessandro Porrovecchio, and Olivier Sirost, eds., *Body Ecology and Emersive Leisure* (London/New York, NY: Routledge, 2018), pp. 150–63.

Sorge, Giovanni, ed., *Lettere tra Ernst Bernhard e Carl Gustav Jung. 1934/1959* (Milan: La biblioteca di Vivarium, 2001).

— "Love as Devotion: Olga Fröbe-Kapteyn's Relationship with Eranos and Jungian Psychology," *Eranos-Jahrbuch*, 70 (2009–2010–2011), pp. 388–434.

Stadler, Edmund, "Teatro e danza ad Ascona," in Harald Szeemann, ed., *Monte Verità. Antropologia locale come contributo alla riscoperta di una topografia sacrale moderna* (Locarno/Milano: Armando Dadò/Electa, 1978), pp. 128–37.

Stefano, Eva di, "Voices and Faces of Elsewhere," *Outsider Art Observatory* 19 (2020), pp. 12–27.

Stein, Murray, ed., *Jung's Red Book for our Time: Searching for Soul in the 21st Century. An Eranos Symposium* (Asheville, NC: Jung's Red Book for our Time V, Chiron Publications, 2022).

— and Abramovitch, Henry, eds., *Eranos. A Play* (Asheville, NC: Chiron, 2025).

Steiner, George, *Nostalgia for the Absolute* (Toronto: CBC, 1974).

Steiner, Rudolf, *Die esoterische Christentum und die geistige Führung der Menschheit* (Dornach: Verlag der Rudolf Steiner-Nachlassverwaltung, 1962).

Swift Furlotti, Nancy, *Eternal Echoes—Erich Neumann's Timeless Relevance to Consciousness, Creativity, and Evil* (Asheville, NC: Zurich Lecture Series X, Chiron, 2023), § "Erich Neumann's Watercolor Paintings," pp. 8–24.

Swiss National Museum, ed., *Landscapes of the Soul. C.G. Jung and the Exploration of the Human Psyche in Switzerland* (Zurich: Scheidegger & Spiess, 2025).

Szeemann, Harald, ed., *Monte Verità. Antropologia locale come contributo alla riscoperta di una topografia sacrale moderna* (Locarno/Milano: Armando Dadò/Electa, 1978).

— *Monte Verità. Berg der Wahrheit. Lokale Anthropologie als Beitrag zur Wiederentdeckung einer neuzeitlichen Topographie* (Locarno/Milan: Armando Dadò/Electa, 1978).

— "Monte Verità. La montagna della verità," in Id., ed., *Monte Verità. Antropologia locale come contributo alla riscoperta di una topografia sacrale moderna* (Locarno/Milano: Armando Dadò/Electa, 1978), pp. 5–9.

— "Monte Verità, Ascona. Eine Chronologie [Mit Beiträgen von Theo Kneubühler und Willy Rotzler]," in *Du. Europäische Kunstzeitschrift*, 10 (1978), pp. 32–78.

— ed., *Dalla danza libera, all'arte pura. Catalogo della mostra, 15 aprile–10 giugno 1990* (Ascona: Museo Comunale di Arte Moderna di Ascona, 1990).

— ed., *Visionäre Schweiz. Zur Ausstellung im Kunsthaus Zürich, 1. November bis 26. Januar 1992, und im Städtische Kunsthalle und Kunstverein für die Rheinlande und Westfalen, Düsseldorf, 26. Juni bis 30. August 1992* (Aarau/Frankfurt am Main/Salzburg: Sauerländer, 1991).

Szittya, Emil, *Das Kuriositäten-Kabinett* (Konstanz: See, 1923).

Tedeschi, Letizia, "Un teatro per la danza. L'incontro tra Charlotte Bara e Carl Weidemeyer," in Andreas Schwab and Claudia Lafranchi, eds., *Senso della vita e bagni di sole. Esperimenti di vita e arte al Monte Verità* (Ascona: Fondazione Monte Verità, 2001), pp. 156–69.

— ed., *Carl Weidemeyer 1882–1976. Künstler und Anarchist zwischen Worpswede und Ascona* (Mendrisio/Ascona/Milano: Accademia di architettura, Università della Svizzera italiana/Museo comunale d'arte moderna/Skira, 2001).

Tevebring, Frederika, "Images from the Collective Unconscious. Olga Fröbe-Kapteyn and the Eranos Archive," *The Public Domain Review* (February 22, 2023).

Thayer, Ellen, *Eranos and Ascona* (unpublished typescript, 1938; Kristine Mann Library, New York, NY).

Tischel, Alexandra, "Tra i profeti. I romanzi di Franziska zu Reventlow e le 'tensioni' di fine secolo," in Elisabetta Barone, Adriano Fabris, and Flavia Monceri, eds., *Eranos. Monte Verità. Ascona* (Pisa: ETS, 2003), pp. 253–67.

Tosatti, Bianca and Brüdelin, Friedrich Reinhard, *Armand Schulthess. Il giardino della conoscenza* (Bellinzona: Sottoscala, 2013).

Tuchman, Maurice, and Freeman, Judi, eds., *The Spiritual in Art. Abstract Painting 1890–1985* (Los Angeles, CA / New York, NY: Los Angeles County Museum of Art / Abbeville, 1986).

Thys, Walter, ed., *André Jolles (1874–1946), „Gebildeter Vagant."Brieven en documenten* (Amsterdam/Leipzig: Amsterdam University Press/ Leipziger Universität GmbH, 2000).

Vacchini, Giorgio [*alias* Vacchino d'Ascona], "Febbricità storica," in Harald Szeemann, ed., *Monte Verità. Antropologia locale come contributo alla riscoperta di una topografia sacrale moderna* (Locarno/Milano: Armando Dadò/Electa, 1978), pp. 12–13.

— "Monte Verità," Harald Szeemann, ed., *Monte Verità. Antropologia locale come contributo alla riscoperta di una topografia sacrale moderna* (Locarno/Milano: Armando Dadò/Electa, 1978), pp. 80–84.

— ed., *Ascona. Verdetti popolari e documenti* (Ascona: Comune di Ascona, 1996).

Veenendaal, Augustus J., Jr., "Kapteijn, Albertus Philippus (1848–1927)," in *Biografisch Woordenboek van Nederland*, http://resources.huygens.knaw.nl/bwn1880-2000/lemmata/bwn2/kapteijnap).

Vegt, Jan van der, *A. Roland Holst. Biografie* (Baarn: de Prom, 2000).

Verne, Jules, *Vingt Mille Lieues sous les Mers* (Paris: J. Hetzel et Cie, 1889).

— *Le tour du monde en quatre-vingts jours* (Paris: J. Hetzel et Cie, undated).

— *Les enfants du Capitaine Grant. Voyage autour du monde* (Paris: Librairie Hachette, undated).

— *L'Île mystérieuse* (Paris: Librairie Hachette, undated).

— *Cinq Semaines en Ballon. Voyage de découverte en Afrique* (Paris: J. Hetzel et Cie, undated).

— *Les Indes-Noires* (Paris: J. Hetzel et Cie, undated).

Vester, Karl [Carl, Carlo], "Tagebuecher. 16. Juni 1902 – 31. Dezember 1919" (unpublished typescript, 1902–1919; The Getty Research Institute, Los Angeles / 2011.M.30 Harald Szeemann papers, 1800–2011, bulk 1949–2005 / Topical files, 1806–2005, bulk 1967–2005 / Places, 1851–2004, undated / Switzerland, 1851–2004, undated / Ticino (Tessin), 1851–1855, 1863, 1874–1876, 1886–2005, undated / A to Z, 1855, 1900–2005, undated / Box 3399, Vacchini–Vester, 1919, 1946–1968, 1975–1998, undated / Folder 25, Vester, Carl (Carlo), 1919).

— "[Tagebuecher] Ascona. 1. Januar 1920 bis 31. Dezember 1922 (unpublished typescript, 1920–1922; The Getty Research Institute, Los Angeles / 2011.M.30 Harald Szeemann papers, 1800–2011, bulk 1949–2005 / Topical files, 1806–2005, bulk 1967–2005 / Places, 1851–2004, undated / Switzerland, 1851–2004, undated / Ticino (Tessin), 1851–1855, 1863, 1874–1876, 1886–2005, undated / A to Z, 1855, 1900–2005, undated / Box 3400, Vester–Werefkin, 1922–1923, 1932, 1945, 1965–1972, 1988–1996, undated / Folder 1, Vester, Carl (Carlo), 1922).

— "[Tagebuecher]. Askona. 1. Januar 1923 bis 31. Juli 1925 (unpublished typescript, 1923–1925; The Getty Research Institute, Los Angeles / 2011.M.30 Harald Szeemann papers, 1800–2011, bulk 1949–2005 / Project files, 1836–2007, bulk 1949-2005 / Monte Verità: The breasts of truth (Monte Verità/Berg der Wahrheit) (1978 July 7 to August 30) / Papers / Box 349 / Folder 3).

Vezzani, Vittorino, *Il misticismo cristiano e indiano* (Milan: Fratelli Bocca, 1951).

— *Il fine dell'Uomo e altri saggi spirituali* (Milan: Fratelli Bocca, 1952).

— "Eranos (simposio)," *Luce e Ombra*, 52 (5, 1952), pp. 301–04.

— *Le mysticisme dans le monde* (Paris: Payot, 1955).

Virz, Claudia, "Aline Valangin (1889–1986). Fidèle à la liberté," in Tibère Adler, Verena Parzer Epp, and Claudia Wirz, eds., *Pionnières de la Suisse moderne : des femmes qui ont vécu la liberté* (Geneve: Slatkine, 2014), pp. 205–08.

Vitolo, Antonio, "Le conferenze di Eranos," in Aldo Carotenuto, ed., *Trattato di Psicologia Analitica* (Turin: UTET, 1992), Vol. I, pp. 641–67.

— [Review to] "Riccardo Bernardini, *Jung a Eranos. Il progetto della psicologia complessa*, FrancoAngeli, Milano 2012," *Rivista di Psicologia Analitica*, 84 (32, 2011), pp. 268–70.

Vivekananda, Swami, *Gespräche auf den tausend Inseln. Uebersetzung von Alwina von Keller* (Zurich: Rascher, 1944).

Von Franz, Marie-Louise, ed., *Aurora Consurgens. A Document Attributed to Thomas Aquinas on the Problem of Opposites in Alchemy. A Compation Work to C. G. Jung's Mysterium Coniunctionis*, tr. Richard Francis Carrington Hull and Alan Samuel Boots Glover (New York, NY: Bollingen Series LXXVII, Pantheon Books, 1966).

Voswinckel, Ulrike, *Freie Liebe und Anarchie: Schwabing-Monte Verità. Entwürfe gegen das etablierte Leben* (Munich: Allitera, 2009).

Vv.Aa., *1875–1975. 100 Jahre Kunstgewerbemuseum der Stadt Zürich*, eds. Elisabeth Grossmann, Hansjörg Budliger, and Urs Stahel, texts by O. Birkner, K. Akeret, E. Grossmann, E. Billeter, and P. Obermüller (Zurich: Zürcher Hochschule der Künste, Kunstgewerbemuseum der Stadt Zürich, 1975).

Vv.Aa., *1885–1985 Cento anni dall'acquisto delle Isole di Brissago. Baroness Antoinette St. Leger. 1950–1985 Trentacinque anni d'apertura al pubblico del Parco botanico del Cantone Ticino* (Brissago: Amministrazione delle Isole di Brissago/Parco Botanico del Canton Ticino, 1985).

Vv.Aa., *Anthropos. Boletín de información y documentación*, 153 (1994) ("El Círculo de Eranos: una hermenéutica simbólica del sentido"), ed. Andrés Ortiz-Osés.

Vv.Aa., *Anthropos. Suplementos. Materiales de trabajo intellectual*, 42 (1994) ("Una interpretación evaluativa de nuestra cultura. Análisis y lectura del almacén simbólico de Eranos. Antología y estudios"), ed. Dónoan.

Vv.Aa., *Arte e storia*, 16 (74, 2017) ("Storia architettonica e restauro del Monte Verità. Volume realizzato in occasione della riapertura del Museo di Casa Anatta").

Vv.Aa., *ASDIWAL. Revue genevoise d'anthropologie et d'histoire des religions*, 16 (2021) (§ "Spiritual Scholarship and the Study of Religion as Self-Improvement: The Search for a Personalized History of Religion at the Eranos Meetings," pp. 73–145, ed. Marianna Ferrara and Eduard Iricinschi).

Vv.Aa., *Baj/Bakunin. Atti del Convegno. Monte Verità, Ascona, 5 ottobre 1996* (Lugano: La Baronata, 1996).

Vv.Aa., *Cahiers d'histoire culturelle*, 29 (2018) ("Monte Verità : communautés d'expériences du corps et de retours à la nature"), ed. Marc Cluet and Olivier Sirost.

Vv.Aa., *Du. Schweizerische Monatsschrift*, 15 (4, 1955) ("Eranos").

Vv.Aa., *Enkelados* 4 (7, 2017) ("Viaggio a Eranos"), eds. Pasqualino Ancona, Riccardo Mondo, and Caterina Vezzoli.

Vv.Aa., *Eranos-Jahrbuch*, 32 (1963) ("Vom Sinn der Utopie – Vorträge gehalten auf der Eranos-Tagung in Ascona 28. August bis 5. September 1963"), ed. Adolf Portmann.

Vv.Aa., *Initiales*, 4 (2014) ("MV").

Vv.Aa., *Interpretatio. Revista de Hermenéutica* 10 (1–2, 2025) ("Dossier: Eranos: Imaginación simbólica y hermenéutica / Eranos: Symbolic Imagination and Hermeneutics"), ed. Blanca Solares.

Vv.Aa., *Klaros. Quaderni di Psicologia Analitica*, 16 (1–2, 2003) ("Jung Eranos"), ed. Ira Regina Zoccoli-Francescini.

Vv.Aa., *Le labyrinthe poétique de Armand Schulthess* (Bellinzona: Sottoscala, 2014).

Vv.Aa., *L'Elisarion e le sue origini* (Tenero: Edizioni del Comune di Minusio, 2011).

Vv.Aa., *L'Ombra. Tracce e percorsi a partire da C.G. Jung*, 9 (1, 2018) ("Jung e Ivrea"), ed. Riccardo Bernardini.

Vv.Aa., *Quarto. Zeitschrift des Schweizerischen Literaturarchivs*, 45 (2018) ("Lago Maggiore. Literarische Topografie eines Sees / Lago Maggiore. Topografia letteraria di un lago"), eds. Corinna Jäger-Trees and Christa Baumberger.

Vv.Aa., *Religiographies*, 4 (1, 2025) ("The Eranos Experience: Spirituality and the Arts in a Comparative Perspective"), ed. Wouter Jacobus Hanegraaff.

Vv.Aa., *Schweizer Kunst / Art Suisse / Arte Svizzera / Art Svizzer. Zeitschrift der Gesellschaft Schweizerischer Maler, Bildhauer und Architekten (Visuelle Künstler) / Revue de la Societé des peintres, sculpteurs et architectes suisses (artistes visuels) / Rivista della Società dei pittori, scultori e architetti svizzeri (artisti visuali)*, 2 (1989) ("Monte Verità. Symposium Monte Verità 4.–7. Mai 1989"), ed. Françoise Jaunin.

Vv.Aa., *Spring: A Journal of Archetype and Culture*, 92 (2015) ("Eranos: Its Magical Past and Alluring Future: The Spirit of a Wondrous Place"), eds. Nancy Cater and Riccardo Bernardini.

Vv.Aa., *Stagioni di grande musica. 1946–2005* (Ascona: Settimane Musicali di Ascona, 2005).

Vv.Aa., *Studi e Materiali di Storia delle Religioni*, 89 (2, 2023) ("Conflicts, Tensions, and Mythmaking at Eranos Before and After World War II"), ed. Marianna Ferrara and Eduard Iricinschi.

Vv.Aa., *Turicum. Schweizer Kultur und Wirtschaft*, 23 (June–July 1993) ("Ascona-Monte Verità").

Vv.Aa., *Wissende, Eingeweihte und Verschwiegene. Esoterik im Abendland. Katalog der Ausstellung vom 23. Sept. bis 22. Nov. in der Zentralbibliothek Zürich* (Zurich: Zentralbibliothek Zürich, 1986).

Wasserstrom, Steven M., *Religion after Religion—Gershom Scholem, Mircea Eliade, and Henry Corbin at Eranos* (Princeton, NJ: Princeton University Press, 1999).

Webb, James, *Il sistema occulto: La fuga dalla ragione nella politica e nella società del XX secolo* (Milan: SugarCo, 1989 {1976}).

Wehr, Gerhard, "Eranos in seiner Geschichte" (unpublished typescript, 1995–96; Eranos Foundation Archives, Ascona-Moscia).

— *Jean Gebser. Individuelle Transformation vor dem Horizont eines neuen Bewußtseins* (Petersberg: Via Nova, 1996).

Weick, Werner, *La lunga estate di Hermann Hesse* [VHS] (Montagnola: RTSI/Fondazione Hermann Hesse, 1987).

— *Monte Verità. Berg der Wahrheit* (Ascona: Fondazione Monte Verità, 2012).

Welti, Francesco, *Der Baron, die Kunst und das Nazigold* (Frauenfeld/ Stuttgart/Wien: Huber, 2008).

Whimster, Sam, and Heuer, Gottfried, "Otto Gross and Else Jaffé and Max Weber," *Theory, Culture & Society*, 15 (3–4, 1998), pp. 129–60.

— "Conversazioni con gli anarchici. Max Weber ad Ascona," in Andreas Schwab and Claudia Lafranchi, eds., *Senso della vita e bagni di sole. Esperimenti di vita e arte al Monte Verità* (Ascona: Fondazione Monte Verità, 2001), pp. 42–58.

Widmann, Claudio, *Il simbolismo dei colori* (Abano Terme: Piovan, 1988).

Wiegers, Gerard, "Henry Corbin and the *Gospel of Barnabas*," in: Mohammad Ali Amir-Moezzi, Christian Jambet, and Pierre Lory, eds., *Henry Corbin. Philosophies et sagesses des Religions du Livre. Actes du Colloque « Henry Corbin ». Sorbonne, November 6–8, 2003. Colloquium organized by the École Pratique des Hautes Études and the Centre d'Études des Religions du Livre* (Turnhout: Brepols, 2005), pp. 177–94.

Wilhelm, Richard, ed., *Das Geheimnis der Goldenen Blüte. Ein Chinesisches Lebensbuch* (Munich: Dornverlag, 1929).

ed., *I Ging. Das Buch der Wandlungen*, (Jena: Eugen Diederichs, 1924).

Wimmer, Clemens Alexander, *Gärtner der Nation. Die vier Leben des Karl Foerster* (Weimar: Verlag und Datenbank für Geisteswissenschaften, 2024).

Wirz, Albert, "Sanitarium, non sanatorio! Spazi per la salute," in Andreas Schwab and Claudia Lafranchi, eds., *Senso della vita e bagni di sole. Esperimenti di vita e arte al Monte Verità* (Ascona: Fondazione Monte Verità, 2001), pp. 119–38.

Zanda, Carlo, *Un bel posticino. La Spoon River di Hermann Hesse* (Milan: Marcos y Marcos, 2012).

Zimmer, Henrich, *The Art of Indian Asia—Its Mythology and Transformations* (New York, NY: Bollingen Series XXXIV, Pantheon Books, 1955).

Index of names